DĀNA

Giving and Getting in Pali Buddhism

BUDDHIST TRADITION SERIES

Edited by

ALEX WAYMAN

VOLUME 52

DĀNA

Giving and Getting in Pali Buddhism

ELLISON BANKS FINDLY

MOTILAL BANARSIDASS PUBLISHERS
PRIVATE LIMITED • DELHI

First Edition: Delhi, 2003

COVER DESIGN: Los Angeles County Museum of Art, from the Nasli and Alice Heeramaneck Collection, Museum Associate Purchase

ISBN: 81-208-1956-x

Also available at:

MOTILAL BANARSIDASS

41 U.A. Bungalow Road, Jawahar Nagar, Delhi 110 007
8 Mahalaxmi Chamber, 22 Bhulabhai Desai Road, Mumbai 400 026
236, 9th Main III Block, Jayanagar, Bangalore 560 011
120 Royapettah High Road, Mylapore, Chennai 600 004
Sanas Plaza, 1302 Baji Rao Road, Pune 411 002
8 Camac Street, Kolkata 700 017
Ashok Rajpath, Patna 800 004
Chowk, Varanasi 221 001

Printed in India

BY JAINENDRA PRAKASH JAIN AT SHRI JAINENDRA PRESS,
A-45 NARAINA, PHASE-I, NEW DELHI 110 028
AND PUBLISHED BY NARENDRA PRAKASH JAIN FOR
MOTILAL BANARSIDASS PUBLISHERS PRIVATE LIMITED,
BUNGALOW ROAD, DELHI 110 007

For
Fred and Tendol la
two generous
beings

Contents

Foreword

This book takes up an extremely important topic—*dāna* ('giving'). The Buddha started this giving by giving scriptures. Then there were the 'alms' or more material gifts, which the followers gave to monks, etc. May I congratulate this author, Prof. Ellison Banks Findly, for taking up and giving us this topic. She shows how wealthy persons helped out the Buddhist Sangha, and enabled it to adapt to changing circumstances, and thus to survive difficult situations. By this exposition of Buddhist donation, the author demonstrates an ability to expose and develop properly this remarkable topic.

ALEX WAYMAN

Acknowledgements

Many people have made contributions to this book. My greatest thanks go to Gay Weidlich who gave monumental effort to the preparation of the manuscript. I also thank my colleagues in the field and at Trinity College for their thoughtful good words, my students who have discussed these issues round and again, and many friends who have sustained me over the years. I thank as well the venerables Lobsang Samten, Tenzin Yignyen, Ngawang Tendol, Tenzin Sherab, Dolma, Yangchen Dolkar, Ngawang Dolma, Tenzin Lhamo, and Dickie who have taught me much about the elaborate renunciant etiquette surrounding the practice of *dāna*.

For many years, Craig has been a kind facilitator for my projects, and I thank him immensely for all he has done for me. As always, I live on the strong foundation of my children's affection, for their greatest gift is the intimacy of our shared lives. I thank my parents as well who have been exemplars of the householder life. My mother has given me a belief in the goodness of all people and my father a belief in the strength of family ties. His title for this book was always "Bringing in the Dough."

Finally, I dedicate this book to two generous beings. A friend in the dharma, Fred readily shares his possessions with those in need and is unfailingly generous with his time and presence. A wonderful listener, he hears on many levels and returns in kind. In trouble, he stays the course; in joy, he has great wit and humor; and in all he offers up his attention with full goodwill.

Like Fred, the ANI Ngawang Tendol dedicates herself to the lives of others. A mainstay of her nunnery and her refugee community in Kathmandu, she has been chief liaison for Trinity's exchange of students and Buddhist renunciants. Tendol is unflappable in all she does, generous with her time and energy, and mindful of all demands. I thank them both for their gifts to me and others, and for being good friends and teachers.

ELLISON BANKS FINDLY

Preface

Our experience of the world is of interdependence. In that we are mindful of things in our experience, we notice that they appear in our field of knowing through the five senses and as various components of the five aggregates. Investigation of these things brings us to see that they are not isolated elements but related to one another in manifold reverberations of cause and condition. A tree depends on soil, soil depends on organic matter, organic matter depends on carbon, and so forth, in waves of infinite regress. Coming to see experience as the result of causes and conditions is part of vipassanā or insight.

Those who are interested in the Buddhist pathway, but who are still some distance from awakened being, often need the guidance of the teaching, of Dhamma, to turn them toward greater insight. Dhamma provides structure through which trustworthy views of experience can be developed. Dānadhamma, or the teaching on dāna, donation, is one such guide; through it the practitioner is provided a structure by which she or he comes, daily, to the moment of contact between those staying at home and those who have chosen to go forth, and sees that they are mutually dependent one on the other. This very elementary teaching which is the teaching on giving has the power to bring laypeople and renunciants alike to the realization that interdependence is not just a mark of nature or of the body, but of human social life. Renunciants are said to live upanissāya 'depending on' the resources given to them by householders in villages, towns, and cities; likewise, laypeople progress in the Dhamma depending on renunciants whose presence at the household door models the equanimity, anonymity, and humility of a life without possession, and whose teachings give guidance for following the path. The dāna system, then, is a formalized code much like a contract which, if followed in confidence, can give rise to authentic experience of, and insight into, interdependence.

The teachings on dāna also provide evidence that one of the central postures of the early Buddhist community toward being in the world is one of accommodation. In that the survival of the community depends on having enough food, clothing, lodging, and medicine, the practice of dāna allows the interaction which provides these resources to be flexible and adaptable, and suited in every case to the particular needs and circumstances of the individual lay-renunciant transaction. The charge to give teachings, for example, only in the local language and not in chandas or meter, that is, in Vedic dialect, is indicative of a desire to meet potential followers at their own starting point. And the teaching which lets donors wish the "blessings" of a long life on a monk who sneezes and who then must respond in kind, not only appeases donor sensibilities, but also helps to break renunciant attachment to monastic custom and habit.

The experience of interdependence and the practice of accommodation are rich benefits of dāna practice, a doctrine set up, in part, as an exchange: householders give according to the teachings on donation called dānadhamma, and renunciants return householders' offerings with a gift of teaching called dhammadāna. While the benefits of giving and getting dāna and Dhamma are immense, it is the ritual form of this exchange itself which continues to have its own power to teach and to transform.

November 26, 2002 ELLISON BANKS FINDLY
Hartford, Connecticut

Abbreviations

A	Aṅguttara Nikāya
AB	Aitareya Brāhmaṇa
ĀpDS	Āpastamba Dharma Sūtra
ĀpŚS	Āpastamba Śrauta Sūtra
Artha	Artha Śāstra
ĀrU	Āruṇi Upaniṣad
ĀS	Ācārāṅga Sūtra
ĀśGS	Āśvalāyana Gṛhya Sūtra
ĀśŚS	Āśvalāyana Śrauta Sūtra
ĀśU	Āśrama Upaniṣad
AU	Aitareya Upaniṣad
AV	Atharva Veda
BAU	Bṛhadavadhūta Upaniṣad
BĀU	Bṛhatāraṇyaka Upaniṣad
BDS	Baudhāyana Dharma Sūtra
BhU	Bhikṣuka Upaniṣad
BSU	Bṛhatsaṃnyāsa Upaniṣad
BU	Brahma Upaniṣad
Cp	Cariyā Piṭaka
CU	Chāndogya Upaniṣad
D	Dīgha Nikāya
GDS	Gautama Dharma Sūtra
GGS	Gobila Gṛhya Sūtra
HGS	Hiraṇyakeśin Gṛhya Sūtra
Iti	Itivuttaka
J	Jātaka
JU	Jābāla Upaniṣad
KB	Kauṣītaki Brāhmaṇa
KBU	Kauṣītaki Brāhmaṇa Upaniṣad
Kh	Khuddaka Pāṭha
KhGS	Khādira Gṛhya Sūtra

KS	Kāṭhaka Saṃhitā
KŚS	Kātyāyana Śrauta Sūtra
KśU	Kaṭhaśruti Upaniṣad
KV	Kathāvatthu
LŚS	Lāṭāyana Śrauta Sūtra
LSU	Laghusaṃnyāsa Upaniṣad
M	Majjhima Nikāya
Manu	Manusmṛti
MP	Milindapañha
MS	Maitrāyaṇī Saṃhitā
MU	Maitrī Upaniṣad
Nd²	Cullaniddesa
NpU	Nāradaparivrājaka Upaniṣad
P.	Pali
PGS	Pāraskara Gṛhya Sūtra
PhU	Paramahaṃsa Upaniṣad
PpU	Paramahaṃsaparivrājaka Upaniṣad
Ps	Paṭisambhidāmagga
Pv	Petavatthu
RV	Ṛg Veda
S	Saṃyutta Nikāya
ŚB	Śatapatha Brāhmaṇa
ŚGS	Śāṅkhāyana Gṛhya Sūtra
Skt.	Sanskrit
ŚU	Śāṭyānīya Upaniṣad
TaU	Turīyātītāvadhūta Upaniṣad
TB	Taittirīya Brāhmaṇa
Thera	Theragāthā
Therī	Therīgāthā
TS	Taittirīya Saṃhitā
TU	Taittirīya Upaniṣad
Ud	Udāna
VDS	Vasiṣṭha Dharma Sūtra
Vin	Vinaya
VS	Vājasaneyi Saṃhitā
Vv	Vimānavatthu

Introduction

When a person goes forth from home into the homeless life, a momentous transition occurs. Moving from a stable, settled life centered around the domestic fires, the renunciant is now a wandering mendicant, free from domestic responsibilities but dependent upon the same culture for the maintenance of life needs. In the Pali Buddhist context, as in those of other early heterodox Indian traditions, the domestic agent or householder and the renunciant become the two primary poles of religious choice, but they are not, however, independent of one another. While the renunciant depends on the householder for food, clothing, and resting place, the householder depends on the renunciant for exemplifying the fullness of the spiritual quest and for providing the opportunity for making merit. This interdependence is expressed in the practice of *dāna* or donation, present in a number of early South Asian traditions but developed with great complexity and nuances in early Buddhism. The relationship between Buddhist donors and renunciants is a dynamic one, with each responding fully and flexibly to the other. As negotiations unfold, clear and precise *dāna* relationships emerge and, as these relationships become formalized and institutionalized, something like a "contract" emerges. Through the process of negotiating this *dāna* contract, the genesis of a genuinely cooperative society is in evidence that is marked by a spectrum of reciprocity between householders and renunciants.

The rise of Buddhism in the sixth and fifth centuries BCE coincides with the appearance of the *gahapati* or householder as the mark of a newly influential social grouping. The occupational range of the *gahapati*, a functional alternate to the *vessa* (Skt. *vaiśya)* in the Pali Vinaya and Nikāyas, is wide and he (together with the *gahapatānī,* his wife) is often described as a figure of substantial wealth. The reciprocal relationship that develops between this emerging householder sector and the young Saṅgha meets the Buddhist community's needs for material support as well as the householders' needs for clear religious involvement and demarcation not available to them at the time. In return for their giving gifts, householders receive appropriate merit normally reflected in better rebirths in the future. In return for their receiving gifts, Saṅgha members have to make sure that their public behavior and appearance conform to householders' expectations, for householders are not shy about complaining of breach in what they perceive to be monastic etiquette. With the accumulation of property as a more broadly significant phenomenon, then, wealth is not discredited in the new religion but rather given serious spiritual cachet.

The evolution of *dāna* relationships and their codification in a "*dānic* system" is one that incorporates at least two processes. The first is the adaptation of ideas and practices already known to the young tradition from its religious environment, in particular those with origins in Brāhmaṇism and Jainism. Followers of Gotama Buddha have substantial contact with followers of these traditions, and many aspects of what comes to be the full Pali practice of *dāna* are drawn from contemporary and antecedent Vedic culture: e.g., the *dakkhiṇeyya* or 'gift-worthiness' of a donee, the constructs of causality that describe the production of future fruit resulting from present action, and the paradigm of creating bodies for ancestors by offering *piṇḍa* or rice cakes. The second is the new configuration of ideas of relationship, of values that inform them, and of structures that ritualize them, in ways that respond more directly to changes that are taking place in north Indian culture. Central here are the ethics of acquiring and using wealth, the precise posture of the person inclined to give (e.g., her or his confidence), and donees as fields of merit, with implications for how merit can get transferred. This reconfiguration of ideas of relationship, then, is accompanied by the forthright acknowledgement that the worldly-otherworldly division of personnel must be mediated with clear attention to the particular parties' mutual benefit. Thus, Pali Buddhism's practice of *dāna* arises out of both the enduring ties it has to extant religious traditions and the new, often radical, proposals it offers about religious life; that is, the power of the new *dāna* practices derives from its descent—and divergence—from older established religious patterns.

As with so much else in the history of Buddhism, *dāna* practice is based in a Buddhist posture of accommodation. In *dāna,* this accommodation is both behavioral and doctrinal, and takes place between householders and the Saṅgha as the dynamic of their reciprocity is an often shifting balance of needs and responses. It is clear from the Vinaya texts that the relationship of Saṅgha to benefactor has to be managed carefully, and that there is a proper threshold of dependency that has to be maintained with self-conscious delicacy. The institution of the Saṅgha needs the wealth of an affluent society for its survival and growth, and because the emergent householders find themselves as a group without clear religious placement in a cultural matrix where status within ritualized hierarchy is essential, the relationship between the two becomes carefully guarded and nurtured.

This emergent contract between donors and renunciants is a prime example of the Buddhist posture of accommodation because the transactions of giving and receiving are honed continually for precision and efficacy. Especially intricate is the balance between the elements of straight-forward exchange, e.g. gifts of food for gifts of teaching (and vice versa), and elements of patronage or grant-making that involve more complicated ties and obligations. Moreover, the *dāna* contract's use of ideas of credit and debit, currencied transactions, and savings and surplus tie early Buddhism to rising mercantile and financial interests of the time. Such connections make the young religion an especially competitive one among its sectarian rivals as it, unlike most of them, takes seriously the need for material support and the complexity of guaranteeing its physical continuation over time. The accommodational bent of early Buddhism is seen as well in the community's self-conscious willingness to adapt and compromise, especially in response to local and what might be called minority issues. One of the great beneficiary groups of this openness is women, who carve new places for themselves as charitable donors in their own right and who, because of the depth of their material support of the Saṅgha, exert significant influence on the development, especially, of disciplinary practice. This accommodational approach in the tradition is also responsible for the soteriological elevation of the lay householder. Instead of rejecting the salvific role of ordinary folk as is done in earlier Vedic contexts, Buddhism redefines the householder life in the light of its essential interconnections with the renunciant life, thereby making the householder life itself of prodigious salvific value. Arising as part of substantial cultural change, early Buddhism thus adapts to it by making ongoing and fairly rapid response to change a foundational posture.

A part of Buddhism's reconfiguration of "relationships" is its focus on the idea of "being in relation" itself. Donors appear in Pali narratives not as isolated figures with histories separable from their Buddhist actions but as people who are defined precisely because they are "in relation to." But rather than being in relation to their gifts or in relation to the persons they are giving to, they are portrayed as being in relation to the act of giving itself. Likewise, the prescriptions for receiving place Buddhist renunciants in relation not to the donors themselves, or to the gifts they are given, but, instead in relation to the act of receiving itself. Buddhist *dāna*, then, is not about the separable parts of the giving relationship but about the fluid dynamic of individuals within the increasingly complex network of conditioned interdependencies of the time, with the interdependency of the donative process being mediated in particular by wealth.

THE MEDIATIONAL VALUE OF WEALTH

In that the *dāna* contract places a premium on the interpersonal nature of conventional identity in Buddhism, this means that, in renunciant practice, there can be a shift away from the normative "be a refuge unto yourself" view, a tendency in early Buddhism with affinity to the *kaivalya,* or isolationist, theme of classical Hinduism, and an acknowledgement that, at least on the ordinary level of experience, relations with others have some degree of salvific value. Moreover, for lay practice, most discussions of ethics touch at some point on the teachings of the Dīgha Nikāya's Siṅgālovāda Sutta, a discourse the Buddha gives to a young householder on friendship, and on the proper understanding of six specific relationships that are thought to be central to the householder's life.[1]

The general tenor of the *sutta's* teaching is the personal posture of being *anukampaka* or compassionate, literally, being 'one who vibrates because of.'[2] The Buddha's teaching here describes the mental posture and behavior of the lay follower and charts two fields of discourse: a foundational field based on friendship and empathic association, and six specific types of relationships that draw on friendship as their paradigm. Friendship here is "the model for social harmony in the mundane sphere and the model for spiritual encouragement of the laity by the monks in the transmundane sphere,"[3] and the Buddha, in placing friendship so centrally, emphasizes loyalty, acceptance, protection, empathy, and good counsel as the hallmarks of every sound householder relationship.[4] The six specific relationships, as associated with the six directions of Siṅgāla's ritual morning ministrations, are as follows:

1. parents—east;
2. teachers—south;
3. wife and children—west;
4. friends and companions—north;
5. servants and workmen—nadir and
6. recluses and brahmins—zenith.[5]

For each of these, the Buddha makes clear that responsibility for the soundness of the relationship rests upon the shoulders of both parties equally, not any more on one than on another, and that infusing both parties' commitments to the relationship should be *anukampā,* compassion or empathy for the other.

This teaching, then, reflects the canonical thrust of householder ethics as being thoroughly relational or other-oriented. Contrary to what is perceived as the separatist emphasis of the renunciant posture, the non-renunciant posture involves the householder fully in a personal network of human interdependencies.[6] While the Siṅgālovāda Sutta, for example, presents these relationships as an idealized vision, it is clear that, contrary to the *pre*scriptive quality of these materials, other materials are in fact quite *de*scriptive of what relationships in early Buddhist times are actually like. In actual practice, relationships reflected in Pali texts are often tension-filled, and a number of stories are overtly illustrative of the disquiet and even anxiety that color the ties between people belonging to the very groups under discussion in this *sutta*. The tension in these relationships are charged with a kind of "liminality," for the newness of the social and economic contexts, and of the resulting religious possibilities, cast the players into arenas where traditional expectations are undermined, old rules of decorum are questioned, and customary commitments are no longer so customary.

The new tension in relationships that thrusts ordinary linkages into betwixt and betweenness—and the reason why such a *sutta* is necessary—is accommodated by experimentation. Narratives of the Vinaya and four Nikāyas reflect a tendency to test out, to inquire by trial and error, and to make tentative forays in the hopes that such experimentation will help establish parameters for the new institution. A central feature of this way of defusing tension is negotiation, a process of informal, creative, and yet very serious-minded arbitration between concerned parties that plunges them into the tricky web of affiliation and produces a variety of agreements that govern the relationships with seemingly binding authority. Thus, the early Buddhist landscape can be seen as a milieu conducive to the jostling and jockeying of the market-place, where the Buddha and influential members of his Saṅgha succeed in mediating transactions between people and groups of people such as to ensure the survival and growth of the young institution.

Central to the negotiation of these contracts is wealth, whose successful management mediates the liminal areas between parties. Not only is lay poverty not encouraged but great wealth is celebrated; what is taught is proper accumulation and proper use, rather than hoarding, of wealth as well as the instrumental value of wealth for social and soteriological good.[7] Most significant is the way in which wealth plays a role in the tensions between parties to a relationship, and the way in which wealth becomes an element in the resolution of these tensions. In the Siṅgālovāda Sutta, there is the householder who is once supported by his parents and must now support them; the pupil who is enjoined to wait upon and serve his teacher, and the teacher who is enjoined to provide for the pupil's safety and welfare; the husband who is to provide for his wife and the wife who is to guard and protect the household goods; the friends and associates who are to guard each other's property and offer constant material refuge for the other; the employer who is to ensure food, wages, and medicine to employees and the employees who are to be content with what is given; and the donor who is to keep an open door for recluses and brahmins, always serving their temporal needs.[8] In these ways the canon recognizes that wealth and material goods underlie many ethical contracts and that not only do the possessions of this world exacerbate the choices one has to make, but that they also, if understood and handled properly, can provide a working solution to each dilemma as well.

Four areas stand out as particularly pivotal places of relational irresolution, places of contractual discussion and maneuvering, places where persuasion has to take place, often hinging on the uses and abuses of wealth:

1. between a child and his family as he or she decides to renounce.
2. between a renunciant and the Saṅgha as he or she gives up the household life and decides, finally, to commit to the Saṅgha,
3. between a donor and the Saṅgha as he or she negotiates what to give, how to give, and to whom to give, and
4. between a donor and society as his or her acts of donation and support for the Saṅgha "buy" places of religious reputation and status.

1. A Child and the Family

The relationship between a child and his family, and especially between a child and his parents, is in the most normal circumstances fraught with tensions of growth, independence, and divided loyalties and responsibilities. If a society is to add to this the possibility of renunciation, the possibility of wholesale, lifelong abandonment of the family for a quest that may or may not ever again touch the family, normal parental frustrations may be multiplied. It is no wonder, then, that the reluctant parents of the Pali texts try to use whatever leverage they have to prevent a child's going forth or when, at whatever stage they see the wisdom (or inevitability) of the decision, they try to demonstrate their wholehearted support for their child in his or her new life. The leverage most often used in these discussions, not surprisingly, is wealth: the pleasures and good deeds of wealth glorified to entice the candidate to stay at (or return) home, or the benefits of donated wealth held up as a way to continue to reach a child now gone forth. Wealth, then, as either an inhibitor or a facilitator of the non-renunciant/renunciant decision, becomes an important negotiating tool as this contract comes, often with difficulty, to closure.

The fear of a parent that a child might renounce is brought to the forefront in the story of the sage Asita's prophecy to Siddhattha's father, Suddhodana, that the young boy will either be a great king or an enlightened being. Suddhodana's response, of course, is to safeguard the child and to supply him all bodily gratifications in order to prevent the most horrific possibility, at least to Suddhodana, that the son will forsake the family by leaving home.[9] The contrast between the life of the home and the homeless life is discussed in many passages. In the Dīgha Nikāya, for example, the benefits of both are made clear but it is also made clear that the householder life ultimately precedes and is inferior to the homeless life, and that the greatest achievement is the religious life after full renunciation.[10] The ocher-robes and shaved head are thus an external sign that some momentous, and ordinarily irreversible, transformation has taken place.

A number of passages also illustrate not only the parental fear of losing a child to the Saṅgha, but the possibility that the Saṅgha might lose a renunciant back to the householder life. This eventuality is known as *hīnāya āvattati* 'he returns to the low life' and it involves renouncing one's training up to that time. Several reasons are given for this when it happens: the renunciant has failed to guard his senses, has overeaten, and has not been watchful over the righteous life;[11] he or she is without confidence, conscientiousness, fear of blame, energy, and insight into the wholesome teaching;[12] he or she delights in business, gossip, sleeping, and keeping company; and he or she does not reflect on the mind as freed.[13] Another list gives the following reasons for the decline of the in-training monk or nun:

1. he takes on too much and tries to be clever at it;
2. he fritters away the day doing trifling things;
3. he associates with unrighteous company;
4. he goes into the village too early, and leaves too late; and
5. he does not engage in spiritually conducive talk.[14]

Finally, a set of water images describes the four great perils that plague a renunciant and to which a renunciant might succumb, sending him back to the 'low life': the peril of 'waves' or being filled with anger, the peril of 'crocodiles' or overfilling the stomach, the peril of 'whirlpools' or the five strands of sense pleasures, and the peril of 'fierce fish' or women.[15]

How fluid non-renunciant/renunciant ties really are is illustrated in stories of two different monks, Sudinna and Raṭṭhapāla. While the stories begin in the same way with the same dilemma, they have different conclusions: the "bad" Sudinna is expelled from the Saṅgha while the "good" Raṭṭhapāla, knowing the proper place of wealth acts wisely. Sudinna is the son of a great merchant who, hearing the Dhamma one day, decides to go forth. When he asks his parents, however, they refuse on the grounds, first, that he's their only child and, second, that he can't possibly want to leave behind all the comforts they've provided him. Sudinna persists and, in the face of continued opposition, lies down on the ground to fast unto death. When neither his parents nor his friends can dissuade him from the fast, his parents give in and agree to his ordination. As an almsman, Sudinna eventually encounters a shortage of alms food and decides to go back to his relatives. A woman slave of the family recognizes him as he petitions for scraps and tells his parents. Hoping to entice him back into the householder's life, his parents invite him to a meal in their home now heaped with gold coins (including his mother's treasure) and housing Sudinna's former wife dressed in all her ornaments. When presented with the family's wealth and with his father's argument that as a layman he can still enjoy riches and perform good actions, Suddina consistently declines. His mother then asks the former wife to go to the monk and, successfully seducing Sudinna, she in due time bears a son, Bījaka. The remorseful Sudinna, rebuked by his fellow renunciants and by the Buddha, is charged with a *pārājika* offense (sexual misconduct) and is expelled from the Saṅgha.[16]

Raṭṭhapāla's story proceeds in much the same way: the hearing of the Dhamma, the decision to go forth, the need for parental consent, the refusal of consent by the parents three times on the grounds that Raṭṭhapāla is the only child, Raṭṭhapāla's fast unto death, the parents' and friends' inability to dissuade him, the parents' eventual consent to ordination, and Raṭṭhapāla's going forth.[17] The story at this point, however, diverges from Sudinna's: now a monk, Raṭṭhapāla returns home, not because there is a shortage of food, but because he wants to see his parents. The Buddha gives him permission because he knows that it's impossible for Raṭṭhapāla to abandon his training and to return to the 'low life' because, unlike Sudinna, he has become an *arahant.*[18] Raṭṭhapāla returns but, when his father sees him, he is heaped with abuse. Eventually, Raṭṭhapāla is invited to eat a meal and, as for Sudinna, the family house is prepared, heaps of coins are amassed,[19] and the daughters-in-law are finely adorned. Before eating, the family asks him to return home, to abandon his training and take up the secular life, and to enjoy riches and do meritorious things. Raṭṭhapāla not only refuses, however, but tells his family to throw all the piles of wealth into the river Gaṅgā because it causes nothing but grief and distress.[20] Then, fending off his former wives, Raṭṭhapāla eats his meal, gives a Dhamma talk on the foolishness of bodily adornment, and leaves.

A comparison of these two stories suggests the following: 1) that one still in training is more likely to succumb to worldly pleasures than one already an *arahant*; 2) that, of the two enticements to stay in or return to the householder life (wealth and sex), the greater one is sex; but 3) that, of the two enticements, the one that is most successful in negotiating the disjunction between a child and his family is wealth. While women and sex can be a part of the problem, wealth can be not only a part of the problem but also a part of the solution. The candor of the stories thus helps to illustrate the frustrations of families of renunciants as they attempt desperately to recover their filial losses.

2. A Renunciant and the Saṅgha

Discussions about wealth and property also play a pivotal role in the negotiations between the renunciant and the Saṅgha. While parents of prospective renunciants may glorify the social and religious uses of wealth in performing meritorious deeds as a way to persuade a child that he or she can live a good Buddhist life and yet remain a householder, the opposite of this argument is rarely used. For example, there are few, if any, wholesale malignments of wealth designed to wrest a would-be-renunciant from his family; rather, the normal focus is on his progress on the spiritual path. Whether a householder comes from the most impoverished of circumstances or from those of great wealth, it is the strength of his or her mental bonds to that material life that helps or hinders the break from the householder's life and allows a vow of homelessness. Although it's one's wealth and property that are central at the moment of decision, wealth in and of itself isn't the issue; it's the clinging to or casting off of it that makes the difference.[21]

Three examples show this negotiation. Each assesses the problem of the renunciant-to-be's ties to the pleasures of wealth and the material world, and each demonstrates the kind of mental posture necessary to bring about the life-style transformation. The first case involves a brahmin who, seeing the good meals and sheltered bedding the Buddhist renunciants are afforded, decides to renounce. At some point, the luxurious invitational meals dry up and his fellow renunciants ask him to accompany them on an alms tour. The former brahmin is stunned and says: 'Your reverences, I didn't go forth in order to do this, that I should walk around for alms food. If you'll give to me, I'll eat; but if you'll not give to me, I'll leave the Saṅgha.'[22] The other monks then ask him if he's gone forth solely for his 'belly's sake,' to which he replies 'yes, indeed.'[23] In their shame of him, the group of monks look away and tell the Buddha, who rebukes the former brahmin for receiving alms from donors under false pretenses. The Buddha reminds his audience of the four resources *(nissaya)*, but doesn't suggest a clear conclusion to the case of the offending brahmin[24]—though the story does illustrate how ties to pleasurable items can interfere with the successful relations between a renunciant and the institution.

The second case describes the eventual going forth of Anuruddha and other Sakyans after disposing of their property. Mahānāma the Sakyan decides one day that since no one from his immediate Sakyan family has gone forth yet, he or his brother Anuruddha should be the first. Anuruddha declines because 'I am too delicate.'[25] Mahānāma responds by describing at length the endlessness of householder life and the endurance needed to do the great work of sowing and harvesting the fields year after year: 'The workings do not stop,'[26] you'll always be bound, he argues. Eventually, Anuruddha is convinced and asks his mother for her consent, but three times she refuses. To put an end to Anuruddha's monastic aspirations, she decides to involve the Sakyan chieftain, Bhaddiya, and says to Anuruddha that she'll let him renounce if Bhaddiya does—thinking, of course, that Bhaddiya can't possibly renounce with all of his responsibilities. Overjoyed, Anuruddha goes to Bhaddiya who agrees but asks him to wait for seven years while he puts his affairs in order. Anuruddha, convinced by now that going forth is possible for him, negotiates with Bhaddiya to lessen the waiting time from seven years to seven days. After the seven-day wait, Bhaddiya and Anuruddha as well as Ānanda, Bhagu, Kimbila, Devadatta, and Upāli the barber all go forth into the homeless life.[27] This story shows not only the parental reluctance to let a child go forth as illustrated in the previous section, but also the role of peers both in making the decision (Mahānāma) and in carrying it out (Bhaddiya). Finally, it shows that entering the Saṅgha involves attention to the disposition of properties and responsibilities, a considerable source of attachment for any renunciant-to-be.

The third case involves a response to a query from King Ajātasattu of Magadha. Once, Ajātasattu enumerates a long list of occupations that are followed by people in his realm and notes that the fruits of these crafts and services are visible when they're enjoyed by the people who live off them.[28] Could you tell me, then, he asks the Buddha, whether there are similar visible fruits for the life of a recluse?[29] After hearing what Ajātasattu has learned from the teachers of other sects when asked this very same question, the Buddha then answers affirmatively as follows. A man, once an anxious slave, is treated with great reverence and respect upon going forth.[30] A free man, once a taxpayer beholden to the king, gives up those worldly concerns and becomes visibly unburdened by them upon his going forth.[31] A householder, in renouncing, gives up all the hindrances, the dusty path, and all the difficulties of his domestic life in exchange for the freedom of the renunciant life on the road.[32] Thus, the renunciant life is visibly full of moral habit and guarding of the sense doors, and its follower is mindful, self-possessed, and content.[33]

Woven through this description of the visible fruits of the life of the recluse is a consistent theme about wealth and material property: the recluse is no longer bound by his worldly treasures. His freedom and "at ease-ness" are evident in his self-possession and in his lack of enslavement to the opulence of the lay life. Although the *sutta's* description of the results of the life of the Buddhist renunciant is concise, it serves as a marketing tool—an advertisement to those not yet gone forth—about what the experience after ordination can be. In this way, the *sutta* is an important vehicle in the negotiation process of bringing renunciants into the Saṅgha, demonstrating that beyond the rich foil of the material world are the even richer fruits of a new life.

3. A Donor and the Saṅgha

Negotiations between donors and the Saṅgha touch on many elements of their lives—social, economic, and soteriological—and, in this complexity, are indeed precarious. This uncertainty finds resolution in a reciprocity of behaviors and attitudes that stem from the vulnerability of each side and that accommodate their shifting parameters of activities. And, once again, the equilibrium for both donor self-consciousness in the face of the new renunciant movement, and for monastic susceptibility in the face of ongoing survival needs, is provided by material property and its disposition. Wealth grounds the discussion between the two parties and provides a talking point around which new constructs can be built.

From the donor's vantage point the vulnerability is that there are, from the start, no rules. Aside from *suttas* like the Siṅgālovāda, there is no real Vinaya for the lay,[34] much less for the general householder who can be called upon at a moment's notice to give to renunciants at her or his door, and who are thus "never absent, never far distant"[35] from the renunciant lives depicted in the Vinaya. It is clear, however, that aside from all the canonical teachings on *dāna*, there are some kinds of established codes that govern donor-renunciant relations, for the Cullavagga refers specifically to renunciant rules of training *(sikkhāpada)* that have an effect on householders *(gihigata)* and that 'householders know concerning us' *(gihī pi no jānanti).*[36] When, after the Buddha's death, Saṅgha members entertain Ānanda's remark that the Buddha encouraged the abolition of the lesser and minor rules of training *(khuddānukhuddakāni sikkhāpadāni)*, it is determined that Ānanda has forgotten to ask what those lesser and minor rules of training might be. In the absence of such knowledge, the senior monk Kassapa makes the motion to leave things as they are: not to lay down rules not already laid down and not to abolish what has already been laid down before.[37] While the householder rules are amongst those determined to be kept "on the books," the content of those rules is never explicitly made clear. Another text, however, gives a hint. Although the Aṅguttara Nikāya gives no details when it speaks of *gihidhamma* or 'a householder's duties,'[38] the term occurs in a section on donation. Here, not straying from the *gihidhamma* is considered to be one of the five advantages or benefits of *dāna,* suggesting that *gihidhamma* has some close association with *dāna* teachings.

In terms of the negotiation between donor and Saṅgha, then, a householder is identified in one of two ways: either he or she is a hearer of the Dhamma who might someday be an *upāsaka-upāsikā* or layperson and thereby a fellow journeyer on the same spiritual quest, or he or she is a potential donor, someone to give one or more of the four requisites to members of the community. These two options meet when there is an exchange of gift and Dhamma at the time of *dāna.* The preeminence of wealth here needs no restating. Making what is already understood into the cornerstone of the new relationship, then, brings householders as donors into the precarious liminal space inventively and resourcefully; what keeps them there is ongoing and careful cultivation of householder sensibility.

From the Saṅgha's vantage point, the vulnerability of the relationship is multiplied manifoldly by the fact of *upanissaya* or 'being dependent upon.' 'The *bhikkhu* lives depending upon the village or the market-town;'[39] 'my life,' says the *bhikkhu* 'is dependent on others;'[40] and donors to the Saṅgha, luckily, are many for, say the monks, 'if you do not give to us, then who is there who will give to us?'[41] The renunciant is certainly in a bind, for he or she is one of many of a considerable number of people across northern India who are no longer in the work force but for whom material provisions have to be made. Thus, as Gombrich notes, total dependency on lay support is ensured:

> *...a monk may not live as a solitary hermit in the forest; ...[and] he may not grow his own food... [so he must follow] the general precept not to take what is not given.*[42]

The *bhikkhu*—literally, 'he who seeks to share'—then, has to live out a paradox. He has renounced the world to pursue more otherworldly ends, yet he still needs to live in the world to do so; and to live in the world he has to live off the world, thus taking the provisions of donors. The catch is that if donors perceive the intensity of the need, or especially of the desire for provisions, they will be affronted and turn away.

The canon has several examples of dishonest renunciants who are more interested in their hungers than they are in their spiritual states. There is a mendicant brahmin who thinks himself to be mendicant just because he seeks alms;[43] there is a teacher who claims moral goodness only in order to continue receiving gifts from householders;[44] and there is, of course, the brahmin turned *bhikkhu* who decides to go forth only for his 'belly's sake.'[45] Significant in these examples is that the concern in the narratives is less with the renunciant himself, that he has proved to be ill-suited to the renunciant posture, and more with the donors, that they will be displeased to discover that there are counterfeits among the recipients of their gifts and will, in consequence, stop giving. The burden then falls on the *bhikkhu* to be honest for, as Gombrich notes, among renunciants only real indifference "to comforts thus cause[s]...them to be provided."[46] The *bhikkhu* has really not to need the world in order for the world really to be there for him. As Horner states:

> *Those who had gone forth into homelessness are to withstand all temptation and ambition offered by life "in the world," they are to be beyond the reach of its quarrels, loves and hatreds. For, if they continued to behave as those who had not gone forth, their supporters would fall away, the non-believers would think but little of them, and the believers would not increase in number.*[47]

Much, then, hangs in the balance as donors and Sangha members work to effect a serviceable agreement. While both come to the relationship initially through uncharted territories, and despite the great responsibility that the donor has in acquiring and using his wealth appropriate to Buddhist *dāna,* the greater responsibility falls on each member of the Saṅgha who, by vow, 'wanders forth out of the home into the homeless state' and is not to touch on worldly matters at all, but whose paradoxical position on these matters makes being 'in' but not 'of' the world a difficult task.

4. A Donor and Society

Gombrich calls early Buddhist lay ethics "an ethic for the socially mobile."[48] The new social and economic circumstances that are present at the time of early Buddhism, and that are reflected in the expanding role of the householder, necessitate a new ethic that will appeal to the increasing numbers of small businessmen and traveling merchants[49] who are available in towns and the countryside as well as to wealthy urban groups. The old Brāhmaṇical system has serviced only the conservative elite, and in the process has left many others to fend for themselves, being largely unaccounted for in the early textual traditions. There is no clear place within the established range of religious possibilities for those in the middle and lower levels of society who are outside the range of Vedic rites and who are thus in need of more substantial religious affiliation. Thus, it will be for religions like Buddhism and Jainism to provide opportunities that are not only easily accessible to extra-Vedic practitioners but that, through their patronage of these new religions, allow recognized and respected placement in the religious spectrum. Concerning this, Thapar has identified some of the reasons for the appeal of these religions to non-elite groups: their anti-caste implications, their urban settings, their lack of expenses in worship, and their use of local languages over Sanskrit.[50]

While Buddhism may not rise because these groups need clear religious placement, the conjunction of Buddhism and the newly emergent and more broadly designated householder category is certainly fortuitous. This conjunction, for example, allows the patrons of the religion to prosper socially in terms of their status and reputation, for *dāna* teachings tell potential donors that the more one gives the greater will be the report that will go abroad about them and the greater their reputations. Moreover, jockeying among donors over the issue of giving meals often occurs, as competition develops in providing for the Buddha's followers. Broad religious appeal, then, means not only that the good man *(sappurisa)* to whom the Dhamma is addressed can now come from any social ranking—his worth being based on merit not on birth[51]—but also that renunciants of any background will now be the objects of attention by donors of any background. In understanding the 'report and reputation' advantage of *dāna* to be the central element in the contract between donor and society, the full force of the cultural changes of this period becomes clear: donors of all social origins can enhance their reputation among all sectors of society by giving donations to renunciants who are themselves of all social origins.

The match between Buddhist donor and a society that allows the negotiation over status and reputation to take place is not coincidental. Rather, it is carefully crafted to best facilitate the interests, abilities, and habits of the donor. It is not just happenstance that the elements of the contract with the Saṅgha that appeal to donors—e.g., the focus on individual effort, on earned rather than assigned value, on initial investments and postponed rewards, and on the acceptability of any size "store" upon which to draw—are exactly those same elements that in this period appear to have characterized the success of householder efforts in society. What donors admire in the renunciants they support —prudence, diligence, and thrift, for example—are those very same things that they are encouraged to express in their own accumulation and use of wealth and are the very same things that are probably operative in the continued expansion and development of the middle class at large. Just as in the case of the renunciant, where the less he desires the more he gets, so it is also in the case of the donor: the more he gives up of one sign of social status (e.g., material possessions), the more he gets of another (e.g., report and reputation as a great benefactor). So, although the grantor, by granting, reflects his status within a hierarchy and, by increasing the grant, increases his status as well, there is also a clear *quid pro quo:* giving in exchange for reputation. And just as the merit system operates in a manner parallel to the cash economy that is so well-known now to donors—earn cash/merit through hard work and then use it to purchase an appropriate and desirable reward—so the social contract follows suit: you invest in the Saṅgha, and society will invest in you.

Through material support of the Saṅgha, then, the householder earns a clear place in the new religious landscape. While the great merchant of Rājagaha can hear the Buddha spell out the traditional agreement of giving donations and getting Dhamma in return,[52] he also knows that, additionally, with his gifts to the Saṅgha, he will be buying religious respectability and social status. Although there is no way to tell why each individual is motivated to give—reputation and status, a good rebirth, or personal spiritual development—the Buddhist teaching on *dāna* pays tribute to all of these as worthy reasons. The Buddhist tradition is successful because, above all others, it is open to broad human eccentricity in the deciding what gets done with material property.

ENDNOTES

1.. Rājavaramuni (p. 35) has called this *sutta* "a typical example of the Buddhist code of social ethics," while C. A. F. Rhys Davids notes the unique role this *sutta* has in early Buddhist literature as the Vinaya of the householder *(gihin)*. She argues that, in a religious canon "compiled by members of a religious order and largely concerned with the mental experiences and ideals of recluses...it is of great interest to find in it a Sutta entirely devoted to the outlook and relations of the layman on and to his surroundings" (T. W. and C. A. F. Rhys Davids, *Dialogues* 3:168-69).

2. This, C. A. F. Rhys Davids argues, is a "doctrine of love and goodwill between man and man...set forth in a domestic and social ethic...with more comprehensive detail than elsewhere" (T. W. and C. A. F. Rhys Davids, *Dialogues* 3:179n, 186).

3. Rājavaramuni, p. 36.

4. D 3.181-88.

5. D 3.188-191.

6. Rājavaramuni (pp. 37-38) tries to reconcile these two extremes.

7. Rājavaramuni, pp. 43, 52.

8. D 3.188-191.

9. Jātakas; Sn pp. 131-136; Thomas, pp. 38ff.

10. D 3.142-179.

11. S 4.103-104.

12. A 3.3-9.

13. A 3.116.

14. A 3.116-118.

15. M 1.459-462; A 2.123-26.

16. Vin 3.11-21.

17. M 2.54-60.

18. M 2.61.

19. M 2.63.

20. M 2.64.

21. M 1.449-454.

22. *nāhaṃ āvuso etaṃ kāraṇā pabbajito piṇḍāya carissāmīti, sace me dassatha bhuñjissāmi, no ce me dassatha vibbhamissāmīti.* Vin 1.57.

23. Vin 1.57-58.

24. Vin 1.58-59.

25. Vin 2.180.

26. Vin 2.181.

27. Vin 2.180-84.

28. D 1.51.
29. D 1.51.
30. D 1.60-61.
31. D 1.61-62.
32. D 1.62-63.
33. D 1.63-71.
34. Horner, *Discipline* 1:xvii.
35. Horner, *Discipline* 1:xvi.
36. Vin 2.288.
37. Vin 2.287-89.
38. A 3.41.
39. M 1.369. *idha jīvaka bhikkhu aññataraṃ gāmaṃ vā nigamaṃ vā upanissāya viharati.*
40. A 5.87. *parapaṭibaddhā me jīvikā.*
41. Vin 3.265. *tumhe ce amhākaṃ na dassatha atha ko carahi amhākaṃ dassati.*
42. Gombrich, *Theravada Buddhism*, p. 101.
43. S 1.182.
44. Vin 2.186.
45. Vin 1.57-59.
46. Gombrich, *Theravada Buddhism*, p. 95.
47. Horner, *Discipline* 1:xxiii.
48. Gombrich, *Theravada Buddhism*, p. 78; Olivelle, *Saṃnyāsa Upaniṣads*, p. 36.
49. Note that monks are allowed to spend the rainy season with a traveling caravan (Vin 1.151). See also Wagle, pp. 147-48; Misra, pp. 263-65.
50. Thapar, pp. 63-69.
51. M 3.37-45.
52. Vin 2.147-48.

CHAPTER 1

Buddhist Donation: A Religious Response to a Changing World

The contract that is Buddhist *dāna* emerges as the young religion accommodates to changes taking place in the Gaṅgā Valley. In the period just prior to Buddhism, amidst signs of a new civic vitality,[1] settlement patterns develop over a wide area, with the most dramatic increases taking place along the river, "showing an eastward shift of power that continued up to the time of the Mauryas."[2] This culture is marked by expanded grain cultivation and domestication of animals, use of a variety of ornaments and tools including those made of iron,[3] lack of sanitation facilities,[4] and a relatively low population density. [5] Textually, this period corresponds to the compilation of the late Saṁhitās and Brāhmaṇas, when the center of the Vedic tradition is shifting away from the Ṛg Veda's *sapta sindhu* 'seven river' area[6] to the *madhya deśa* 'middle country' of subsequent texts.[7] As this period develops, greater attention is given to the drawing of stable political boundaries and, by the time of the early Upaniṣads and Śrauta Sūtras, beginning in the sixth century BCE onwards, a clear association between political organization and territory comes to be made.[8] The firm establishing of Vedic orthodoxy continues throughout this period, and texts increasingly refine ideas about kingship and its relation to religious sanction, and to stratified group affiliation, through a complex and often cumbersome ritual system. The culture of the late Vedic age, however, will not be sufficient to meet the challenge of the changes taking place in the eastwardly expanding *madhya deśa*.[9]

A NEW URBANISM IN THE MIDDLE COUNTRY

Buddhism emerges in the second period of urbanization in

northern India.[10] Work in archaeology[11] and textual analysis [12] identify this period, ca. 550-250 BCE, as characterized by significant change: dramatic population growth and clustering, new clearing and building in forested areas away from waterways (facilitated by the increased use of iron implements in agriculture), and the reappearance of long-distance trade, an economy based on cash currency, and written communication.[13] Alliances marked by lineage give way to states marked by territorial boundaries and, as territorial expansion intensifies, hostilities increase until the ascendance of a single focus of rule, the Mauryas, around 325 BCE.[14] The process of state formation, then, replaces a centering in lineage and ritual performance with a political organization overseeing administrative and economic functions, and these structures are in turn reflected in hierarchically differentiated settlement patterns.[15]

Material evidence suggests the increased use of iron from about 550 BCE on, the use of a coinage system alongside or in place of barter from about 400 BCE on, substantial increase in wealth from the third century BCE on, extensive construction with baked bricks (instead of mud), and an expanded and interconnecting system of arterial roads.[16] The shape of the culture attending these new elements is marked by "a quickening commercial sense"[17] that is made possible by developments in agriculture. The tillage of greater stretches of land, the intensified use of the plough, the preference for the cultivation of rice (whose higher yield supports more people than wheat), and the increased use of irrigation and concern for water control make an economic surplus possible, thus providing support for a larger population.[18] This surplus, and the accompanying administrative structures, encourage trade and, in time, an economic infrastructure emerges that includes continued development of road networks and distribution centers, merchant groups of various backgrounds and affiliations who are able to travel, and a coin-based medium of exchange reaching across social boundaries.[19] The manufacture of transportable goods, the development of consumer markets, and an increasing state purview over agriculture, trade, and industry become features of a burgeoning urbanization where cities come to function as administrative and trade centers.[20]

In the process, Vedic values and structures prove "ill-suited [to] an expanding national economy and the mercantile nature of cities."[21] The earlier stratified, lineage-based tradition, that is oriented toward a rural, static, village-bound society, cannot respond as well as more egalitarian religions to the developments of the time. The Buddhist Saṅgha with its commitment to transcend family, village, and caste[22] parallels the evolving state system with "an ideological framework for integrating diverse groups."[23] Moreover, the increased economic surplus and resulting availability of leisure time, the network of improved roadways kept open and free for travel by an adherence to *ahiṃsā*, and a detailed ethic of householder donation all allow for the development of wandering renunciant traditions.

Settlement Hierarchies: Where the Dāna Contract Accommodates

One of the features of the early Buddhist period is an expanded range of settlement hierarchies.[24] Within these new broader patterns, Erdosy has delineated four increasingly large and complex categories: the nucleated village, focusing primarily on pastoral and agricultural activities; the minor center, evidencing ceramic and iron-smelting activities and associated with marketing, policing, and tax-collection; the town, incorporating manufacture and distribution of commercial items, including luxury pieces using semi-precious stones, shell, and copper; and the capital city, containing all of the above activities under a centralized political power.[25] From about 400 BCE on, a fifth category emerges, that of the secondary center set in a rural area and participating in long-distance trade.[26]

Pali texts give striking confirmation that Buddhist life in the eastwardly-expanding middle country takes place in a range of locales from jungle to city. Sixteen *mahājanapadas* or 'great realms' are listed in the Aṅguttara Nikāya as fairly unified socio-cultural regions containing various sub-units.[27] In time, four of these *mahājanapadas* survive the political rivalries of their particular settings (Avanti, Vaṃsa/Vatsa, Kosala, and Magadha) and eventually a single power, that of Magadha, emerges.[28] Pali sources describe the strong and unwavering support given the

Buddha and the early Saṅgha by Magadha's King Bimbisāra, and the Dīgha Nikāya's eulogy of him upon his death is testimony not only of the confidence of this one layman in the teachings of the new religious leader, but of the commitment of his realm, and of his people, to supporting the new religious movement.[29] An early Buddhist sense of "own place," in which Buddhist life prevails and from which Buddhist renunciants go out to teach, underlies many of the early texts and is reflected in the Pali distinction between the *majjhima janapada* 'middle realm' and *paccantima janapada* 'border or outlying realm'—where the *majjhima janapada* represents a "more or less culturally homogeneous region vis-à-vis the others."[30] In fact, the development of monastic law in the Pali Vinaya reflects this division, for there is a relaxation of disciplinary rules as the Saṅgha expands into outlying regions from the middle country.[31] The next level below the *janapada* is the *nagara* or 'city.' Traditionally, the *nagara* is the highest ranked member of a sequence of smaller settlement hierarchies listed in ascending size, *gāma* 'village,' *nigama* 'town, market town,' and *nagara*;[32] although six great cities *(mahānagara)* are enumerated in the Dīgha as possible worthy places where the Buddha might choose to die.[33] Other lists sometimes expand this sequence to include *janapada* as its highest member, ranking beyond *nagara*.[34]

In the day-to-day practice of the Buddhist life, however, the two most important categories of settlement are the two smallest, the *gāma* 'village' and the *nigama* 'town.' These two terms, the village and the town, are regularly listed together to indicate those places where Buddhist renunciants and lay most often interact with one another. Distinguished in the texts by clearly defined features, the village and the town are the two smallest collective units tied to geographic settings that separate human culture from the wild surrounds of forest and jungle.[35] By choice of life-style, Buddhist renunciants routinely traverse the divide between jungle and village in their daily wanderings and evening lodgings.[36] Taught to stray not too far from nor too near to a village,[37] the renunciant lives at the threshold of organized culture for which the *gāma* is the first order of human settlement with which he or she interacts.

As village, the *gāma* is small and vulnerable enough to be easily plundered,[38] though often distinguished by recognizable boundaries.[39] Roadways connect villages to other areas of settlement, allowing for travel between and preventing isolation, but these roads often cross through areas of danger and insecurity making policing sometimes critical for anyone wishing to enter or re-enter village areas.[40] A *gāma* can be as small as a single *kuṭi* or 'hut,' which Wagle interprets as "a hamlet of one large house perhaps surrounded by a few smaller buildings in which the dependants and servants of the family dwelt."[41] Small *gāmas* of about four *kuṭis* may constitute scattered habitations "in the forests, outlying woodlands, hilly tracks and mountainous areas that surrounded the rich plains of the Gaṅgā valley."[42] Though small, these settlements are not insignificant for emergent Buddhism, as they host not only organized renunciant communities, but forest dwellers and wanderers of all seniority as well. *Gāmas* can be permanent habitations or temporary encampments, as when the term refers to the extended stops of merchant caravans[43] or of migrant peoples.[44] Some *gāmas* are homogeneous groups representing one occupation or profession, such as park attendants,[45] reedmakers,[46] or saltmakers.[47] Others represent a single extended kin group,[48] or a group defined by *vaṇṇa* or caste such as the *brāhmaṇa* settlements liberally mentioned in the texts, some of which are situated on land given by a king specifically to *brāhmaṇas* in exchange for ritual services.[49] *Gāma* can even refer to a village of renunciants who have stopped and stayed in a place to wait out the rainy season.[50]

As characterized by Pali narratives, villages are places where everyone knows each other and each other's business, where gossip flourishes and social and occupational bonds are strong, and where ties to place are critical markers of who one is. Moreover, villages are settlements from which new renunciants go forth into the homeless life, breaking vital ties of family, work, and place and stepping out of accepted rules and rituals into the new ones of the Saṅgha. As the world left behind, the village is also the world reentered by the renunciant every day for alms, a reentry governed by a strict etiquette of proper dress and comportment and by the anonymous distance of silence. Not only does the renunciant hope for hospitality and respect from villagers newly his donors, but because the village is now a world so "other"—with its normal life oriented to the pleasurable habits of householders—that the etiquette also provides a shield against renunciant waywardness. It is the tight smallness and familiarity of the village, then—that the renunciant is now perhaps more fully engaged with in his new life than with other types of settlement—that tests both the strength of the original renunciation as well as the confidence of its continued cultivation.

Tied conceptually to the village, the *nigama* 'town or market town' is the next level of settlement. Although many of the features characterizing the village are applied equally to the town,[51] including the renunciant's need for ritualized structures of interaction when entering it, the *nigama* is distinguished both in size and in function from the *gāma*. Bigger than a village and smaller than a city, the town is more than just a 'great village;' rather, a *nigama* is a meeting place or point of coming together.[52] That *nigama* is probably a small-scale collecting place for trade and commerce, a market town as it is so often rendered, does not override the fact that it is also a place of permanent residence. Here might live those specializing in particular crafts or occupations, those involved in commercial connections with other centers or with rural areas, or those whose profession comes to be organizing general market activity.[53]

The single feature that sets the *nigama* apart from the *gāma* in Pali texts is the consistency with which *nigamas* are given names. Although there are a few villages with individual names—e.g., Ambatittha[54] and Beluva[55]—naming is not a regular feature of this smallest settlement level. Naming does appear regularly, however, with towns,[56] due to the larger size of a town over a village and to a town's greater diversity of population, among whom there is common commerce. Because the mix of peoples in a town is more heterogeneous than in a village, where homogeneous groupings of family, occupation, or *vaṇṇa* prevail, and because travel to and from a town in the regular course of market activities is the norm, providing a name for a town allows distinction from other sites, recognition by all those served, and specific singling out of no one member group of the population.

One other phrase is important in describing the spatial and social arena in which Buddhist renunciants live out their tradition, *negamajānapada* or 'town-folk and country folk.' This term is used to cover those who might live in rural as well as in small to mid-range settlement areas, for it distinguishes those town and country people who are "unmarked" and differentiates them from the specialized categories of royalty, military, and religion,[57] as well as from those whose professions place them in the denser, more diverse setting of urban centers: e.g., government ministers, treasury officials, city wardens, bodyguards, and courtiers.[58] Being unmarked by occupational or social distinction does not mean that 'town and country-folk' live in different places from their more distinctive fellows, however. Rather, it signifies those who might otherwise go unmentioned, and reaffirms that it is from the whole continuum of peoples that Buddhism gathers material and religious momentum. The context of the term thus demonstrates the wide range of commitment to the new religion, and the inclusion of persons distinct for no other reason than their presence and support. Not all from this wide continuum are counted as supporters, however, for the continued differentiation of Buddhist followers (as those who adhere to *ariya* doctrine) from the untaught or ignorant many-folk *(assutavant puthujjana)*[59] indicate the presence, in town and countryside, of large numbers of those not yet converted to the new tradition.

The Renunciant Alternative

Many factors contribute to the complex culture of the Gaṅgā Valley that emerges around the sixth and fifth centuries BCE. The invention of iron smelting, for example, allows for the clearing and cultivation of land leading to a surplus that has to be managed by a layered administration; the evolution of society from lineage to state is a response to the pressures of population growth; and political competition and warfare create an underclass of captives and necessitate a structure for the dispersal of booty.[60] Whatever the primary causes of the evolution, however, conditions are now conducive to widespread renunciant life:[61] sufficient surplus to provide for numbers of non-workers, safe and accessible roadways connecting centers where support is available, a shift from the lineage household defined along ritual lines to a nuclear household defined along economic lines, and increasing state compatibility with other institutions endorsing egalitarian treatment of diverse peoples.

Text materials point to other processes related to Vedic religion. J.C. Heesterman, for example, argues for "the orthogenetic, internal development of Vedic thought" into the renunciant tradition, in which *śrauta* ritual practice provides a context for the emerging self-conscious agency of the single worshipper and, in time, for the individualization and interiorization of the sacrifice as it puts aside the need for external religious officiants.[62] Steven Collins' argument for the cultural hegemony of Brāhmaṇical thought over Buddhist philosophy and psychology—e.g., that "Brahmanical thought and practice...has the decisive intellectual influence on Buddhism"—would support the importance of Heesterman's theory in understanding the development of Buddhism. But he does, however, see extra-Brāhmaṇical roots to ideas—for example, of *saṃsāra* and rebirth as well as of world renunciation.[63] Patrick Olivelle postulates a "'new' element that at least initially challenged and contradicted many of the central premises of sacrificial theology." In particular, he and Louis Dumont argue that the concept of the individual that is present in renunciant traditions like Buddhism is, on the whole, absent in Vedic views on religious life,[64] suggesting its development as a distinctive alternative rather than as a traditional option.

Factors relating to the emergence of the concept of the individual and of the renunciant ideal fit with those already noted by historians and archaeologists. In the evolution from lineage to state society, a relatively closed and community-oriented structure is opened up, providing the opportunity for individual choice. The breakdown and realignment of traditional family and kin networks allow greater freedom for independent initiatives and challenges, especially among traders, merchants, and bankers. In this spirit, voluntary religious organizations can freshly affiliate and attract patronage from varied sources out of surpluses widely available. Population growth takes pressure off the need for ubiquitous child-bearing and allows for the possibility of voluntary celibacy. Safe and efficient roads and waterways afford easier travel for the dissemination of new ideas and practices. And consonant with these developments are cultural revaluations of "wilderness over village, celibacy over marriage, economic inactivity over economic productivity, ritual inactivity over ritual performance, [and] instability over stable residence."[65] Buddhism is not alone in participating in these developments, for a religious pluralism sustains not only established family traditions of Vedic lineage and renunciant lifestyles of groups like early Sāṃkhya followers,[66] but ascetic and wandering groups of more diverse persuasions.[67]

Voluntarily committed to lives of simplicity in poverty and of equality in "communitas,"[68] renunciants, nevertheless, compete with each other for the commitments of lay followers and for the sustaining resources of an increasingly wealthy Gaṅgā Valley population. As ascetic institutions proliferate, Buddhism needs to offer a reasonable, persuasive, and appealing option for potential donors in order to guarantee continued maintenance of its chosen path. The adoption of a policy of accommodation and flexibility serves the early tradition well and the middle way, the *majjhimā paṭipadā*,[69] emerges not only as a philosophy of non-extremism but as an ethic of balance, adjustment, and harmony. Fully cognizant of the distinctive role of greed and desire for human well-being, early Buddhist mental cultivation focuses on the achievement of *sati*, a mindfulness that transcends possession and aversion. In an environment of greater abundance, Buddhism responds with moderation and, while curbing the temptation to explore all the possibilities, it does not fully reject the benefits of the new urban order. Rather, Buddhism provides its renunciants adaptive ways to negotiate the maze of new Gaṅgā Valley culture while preserving the integrity of their admission and ordination vows. This it does by developing an etiquette that can be used in all situations of interaction with non-renunciants no matter what the complexity of settlement activity.

THE BUDDHIST RENUNCIANT

The Buddhist commitment to the renunciant life is fully evident in texts like the Sāmaññaphala Sutta[70] in which the many benefits of the homeless life, personal and communal, as against the householder life, are detailed. That going forth from the home comes to be seen as a major life-altering change for the individual is reflected in the development of a precise ritual for becoming a renunciant.[71] The act of going forth is attended by several changes of both practical and symbolic value: cutting off the hair and beard, clothing the body in ocher-colored robes, using a clay or iron bowl for receiving alms food, and committing oneself to a life without fixed dwelling.[72] These external, visible changes foster, and mark, the freeing of the renunciant from attachment to the former life and personality, and the identification of the renunciant with a group espousing communal equality for the purpose of internal development. Within this new community, renunciants live a life characterized by democratic governance, harmonious development, social concord, and respect for the seniority of elders of long-standing, and where spiritual training and mental cultivation is found both in solitude and in the company of others.[73]

Renunciant Etiquette in Village and Town

Awareness of the habits and practices of other, non-Buddhist, groups of ascetics helps shape the young Buddhist community as well. In addition to the followers of the six heretical teachers,[74] other ascetics, including Brāhmaṇical renunciants eventually known as *saṃnyāsins*[75] and 'bovine and canine ascetics,' distinguished by habits and behaviors of cattle and dogs,[76] appear prominently—particularly because their behavior is an example of how not to live. Injury to living things, the hoarding of material goods, addiction to worldly pleasures and recreations, excessive adornment and care of the body, gossiping and telling tales, fortune-telling and divination, and fixing astrological dates and giving charms all count as marks of conduct unbecoming to the Buddhist renunciant.[77] Moreover, such practices as wearing bark, hide, or hair clothing, sleeping on spikes, planks or the bare ground, and eating leather parings, roots from the woods, or cow-dung[78] are all cited as examples of excessive behavior unnecessary and ultimately unhelpful to the full spiritual life. Perhaps most problematic is behavior that offends potential donors, as when ascetics are openly noisy and prattling in their talk,[79] appear naked in public and loose in behavior, lick their hands after eating, and refuse food offered by householders in any number of settings. These unconventional habits are at odds with the results of Dhammic mental cultivation[80] and, eschewing such external attention-getters, Buddhist followers choose a different way.

Knowing that they are branded as 'recluses' *(samaṇa)* by the people, Buddhist renunciants accept the obligation that such an attribution means undertaking a clear and precise training. Such training invests them with a practice that, publicly, is proper to the place they now occupy.

> *We will follow those practices*
> *which are fitting for recluses; thus*
> *will this designation of ours become*
> *true and the vocation real.*[81]

That a *samaṇa* be someone who not only looks like one but properly acts like one is critical—primarily, for the pleasing of donors. As the Majjhima passage continues, the Buddha notes that once the *behavior* of the renunciant perfectly suits the *visible form* of the renunciant then the gifts of needful things, such as robes, food, lodging, and medicine, will appear for the full advantage of the renunciant community. It is the appearance of these gifts, the passage artfully concludes, that then makes the going forth into the homeless life fruitful *(saphala)* and prosperous *(sa-udraya).*[82]

As petitioners of alms, Buddhist renunciants are continually exposed to abusive terms, like *piṇḍola* 'scrap gatherer,' from the householders among whom they move.[83] Buddhist teaching responds by asking renunciants to cultivate a mental posture that sees only the good in these housefolk and that, by its continued stable reflection in proper behavior, will eventually work to distinguish the Buddhist alms petitioner from others in the minds of the public. Overcoming such terms of abuse, is a function, then, not only of convincing potential donors of the authenticity and rightness of the Buddhist's internal transformation, but of keeping clearly in mind that the original impetus to renounce is to find an end to suffering.

The need to distinguish Dhamma followers from other renunciants and ascetics is matched even more strongly by the need to distinguish true renunciant life from householder life. Whether householder life is followed by a Buddhist lay or by a person of some other affiliation, it is marked by its general orientation toward pleasure. Most often, criticism of renegade monks and nuns is based on thought, speech, or action that belies an addiction to sensual enjoyment. Donors and potential donors are quick to pick this up and their criticism of renunciant behavior for looking too much like householder pursuit of desires, in turn, helps shape disciplinary rule. Thus, the Dīgha describes the moral conduct of Gotama as providing a model for the whole community: his own curb on pleasure-oriented activities and material luxuries is quite distinct from those practices followed on the 'village way' *(gāma-dhamma)*.[84]

Renunciant etiquette develops primarily in village and town, where according to Pali narratives, there are complex situations that have to be met by mental and behavioral cultivation. Movement between settlements is basic to the renunciant life-style and the spreading systems of paths and roadways[85] make renunciants increasingly vulnerable to the vagaries of highway robbers[86] as well as the dangers of exposure to uncleared jungle and forest areas.[87] Moreover, the new urban settings bring risk of pleasurable distractions, especially in the form of women and wily connivers. But because renunciants have to meet their daily needs and have to spread the doctrine among all types of people, they are obliged to travel everywhere, especially where there might be 'untaught many-folk' available for conversion. Travel through dangerous places for material support and missionary activity has an advantage, however: the chance, given fear and concern for safety, to develop even-mindedness in the face of unpleasant things.[88] Likewise, travel through rich fields and intimate village and town life,[89] gives a renunciant the chance to develop even-mindedness in the face of pleasurable things.[90]

Thus, liminal life-style on the skirts of village and town is conducive to meeting daily material needs, to proselytizing the Dhamma, but most importantly, to advancing spiritual life.

The Buddhist renunciant's basic relationship to village and town involves, in this way, a structured ambivalence. On the one hand, the renunciant is enjoined to have no ties to village and town-folk, no ties to those he once had ties to: not to share their joys or sorrows, not to be happy or sad with them, not to involve himself in any of their business or affairs.[91] He is enjoined, in fact, to be an island unto himself, a refuge unto himself, with no one other than himself for support. On the other hand, however, he does need others: because of his vows of renunciation he cannot produce or buy his own food and clothing, and so has to live in dependence on *(upanissāya)* villages, towns, and cities for the requisites *(parikkhāra)* of robes, food, lodging, and medicine.[92] Unlike other ascetic groups who scrabble off the abundances of nature for a livelihood, Buddhist renunciants eat cooked food and wear woven cloth, both the products of human culture. Surplus product, then, is essential for the continuation of the Saṅgha and, by necessity, this is to be found in association with centers of human activity.

To attract this surplus their way, beating out some of their rivals who also seek it, Buddhist renunciants develop an ethic founded on principles of balance and moderation, an ethic called the 'middle way' *(majjhimā paṭipadā)*.[93] Not only is this a practice midway between hedonistic sensuality and extreme self-torture,[94] but it is a life-style that in all things, in all attitudes, and in all practices, calls for moderation.[95] Moderate use of robes means use only for warding off cold and heat, wind and sun, and insects and creeping things, and to cover nakedness. Moderate use of food means use not for savory indulgence or personal beauty but use just enough for sustaining a healthy body. Moderate use of lodgings means use only for warding off cold, heat, insects, inclement weather and seasons, and for providing seclusion when necessary. And moderate use of medicine means use only for overcoming injury and maintaining health.[96]

Practice of the middle way involves a mental cultivation that places individuals beyond competition with members of other religious groups and beyond competition with fellow Buddhist renunciants, either for gifts to the Saṅgha or for respect and honor in the religious community.[97] Practice of the middle way means overcoming injurious emotions like anger that can deflect and distract one from balance in the training of the self.[98] Practice of the middle way, ultimately, means adapting to the new urbanized environment in two ways. First, it means taking advantage of the new setting and opportunities by celebrating, and even encouraging, benefit from the social and economic openness that continues to be available to the Saṅgha. Second, however, in teaching against the excesses of the new environment, it means continually having to work against adopting the negative aspects of an increasingly competitive and wealth-oriented milieu. The middle way, then, charts a course that avoids the pitfalls but allows some of the advantages of a life in but not of the village, town, and city.

The ethic of moderation develops in tandem with an ethic of egalitarianism that, likewise, is a natural desideratum of life in an urban setting. Emerging as a worldview "solvent to the caste system,"[99] Buddhism appears increasingly tolerant of social and economic diversity and generates within its own Saṅgha walls a sense of "communitas" in which "accidents of birth" mean little.[100] As a hallmark of the Buddhist ethical posture, moreover, egalitarianism, like moderation, shapes a public etiquette conducive to donor expectations and helps cement a reciprocal ritual relationship operating at the boundaries of the two communities that pays no mind to social and personal background.

Buddhist rules of discipline develop to provide behavioral structure for the renunciant "who wishes his life to be externally blameless, so far as his relations with his fellow monks, with the Order as a whole, and with the laity are concerned."[101] Although many of the rules are attributed to Gotama, it is unlikely that they originate as a single unit of teaching but rather "that the majority of the rules grow up gradually, as need arose, and are the outcome of historical developments that went on within the Order."[102] Many disciplinary rules grow up at the point of interface between lay and renunciant where accommodation is necessary, and come to govern, in particular, the proper posture for the renunciant as he or she comes in contact with the lay person. Most of these admonitions cover two specific areas, proper dress and proper comportment on the alms tour, and become critical markers of the particularly Buddhist qualities of these renunciants now on view in public.

The etiquette of proper dress is the result of Saṅgha negotiation among its members in consultation with vocally opinionated householders.[103] What evolves as positive practice for Buddhists requires that each renunciant dress fully in the morning, before going out on alms tour by putting on the inner robe *(santara)*, the upper robe *(uttara)*, and the outer robe *(saṅghāṭī)*.[104] The inner robe is to cover the 'three circles' of the abdomen and is to be tied with a waistband, while feet must be bare—sandals are not allowed to be worn when entering the village except during sickness. Full dress for nuns includes the addition of a vest or bodice *(saṅkacchā)*, a covering that goes from below the collarbone to above the navel.[105] Careful attention to dress is important in village and town and full covering by all three robes becomes a public sign of modesty and humility. While the discipline allows for varying degrees of liberality in private undress, movement into the public spheres of village, town, and city means adopting a full dress code sufficient for marketing a young religion to its patrons.[106]

Like etiquette for clothing, etiquette for proper behavior is at once an authentication and modeling in external form of the internal transformation at work, and a way of drawing donor attention to the worthiness of potential recipients. While on public alms tour, renunciants are to enter the village at the proper time (well before noon) and to go in silence among houses, properly clad and with bowl, with eyes down and in full control over mind and body. There is to be full care and consideration, going not too fast and not too slow, entering only appropriate urban and domestic spaces, and interacting with donors with full moderation and appreciation of the hardships of householder life. When petitioning for and receiving gifts on alms tour, renunciant silence is to be observed as well as the proper procedure for receiving and handling of food and water. Eating the meal, whether at an invited occasion hosted by a donor at his or her home or in the Saṅgha refectory with other renunciants, is to be done in moderation as well—with full attention to low noise, to not playing with food, to eating in reasonable bites, and to cleaning oneself and the bowl inconspicuously afterward.[107] The practiced silence of the alms tour is to be broken only if, at an appropriate point, a renunciant is to give a talk on Dhamma.

While walking on the alms tour, proper practice is to be observed among the group as well, with the formation of the renunciants into a line,[108] the designation of certain ones to be at the head,[109] and the putting aside of all quarrels that might exist between individuals[110]—that is, the creation of an orderly, quiet, and harmonious procession. Perhaps, the most important is the development of a mental culture that allows this public etiquette to be carried out. The Piṇḍapātapārisuddhi Sutta, or discourse on the development of complete purity for the alms tour, describes at length the mindfulness training needed by a renunciant in moving from a quiet, reflective setting into the hustle and bustle of village and town. In walking along the roadways, in entering the village, in doing business there, and in returning along the roadways, the renunciant needs to be continuously aware of his or her attentiveness to an ever-changing experience of sensory data and to any mental and emotional responses to it.[111] The distractions and disturbances that can occur for the renunciant on the tour into, and back out of, the village and town are substantial and the practice of an etiquette can be tremendously beneficial. Such a posture of guarded openness to stimuli makes advantageous interaction with donors possible and ultimately ensures continued provisions for a liminal life-style.[112]

Rules also develop for conduct on return from an alms tour. While they pertain primarily to the development of harmony and moderation among renunciants themselves, their larger implications are public. It can be easily observed and reported among householders if private practice is inconsistent with public behavior.[113] Thus, disciplinary rules make it clear that consistent mental posture and practice, in public and in private, are the Buddhist life, and that movement through forest, jungle, village, town, and city is a continuum, at each point of which is an opportunity for developing mindfulness leading to calm and insight.

Dāna: A Religious Response

Because the support and maintenance of the Saṅgha is ensured only by renunciants engaging each day with the folk of village and town, an ethic underlying not only the renunciants' involvement but also the donors' as well becomes essential. The ethic of *dāna* grows over time into a complex understanding of behavior at this interface that guides the giving and receiving implicit as settlement hierarchies expand and differentiate throughout the Gaṅgā Valley. If Buddhism is a new doctrine well suited to the new urban culture, *dāna* is a doctrine critical to Buddhism's survival as it negotiates the urban-to-rural network. In this way, Buddhist *dāna* is an important response to the increased wealth and to the recharting of social and economic schema in the middle country.

Within the emerging doctrinal structure of Dhamma, Buddhist *dāna* develops in tandem with values of the larger culture. The pattern of settlement hierarchies, first, reflects the distributional function many of the centers have with respect to goods.[114] Similarly, *dāna* becomes a doctrine that governs the redistribution of goods from, often, the increasingly wealthy to the voluntarily impoverished. As *dāna* rules come to focus on issues of proper acquisition and use of wealth, they support the new surge in market activities at the same time as they curb excessive self-interest. The redistribution of goods under *dāna* guidance then becomes not only the acceptable but also the religiously advantageous practice.

Secondly, in the increasing differentiation of settlement hierarchies, Buddhist *dāna* is a doctrine adaptable to all kinds of settings. Confident giving to a Buddhist renunciant can take place on a jungle road, in a downtown market,[115] or in a palace chamber. No matter what the changes in settlement hierarchies, *dāna* guidelines suit the one-on-one patronage of an obscure by-way as easily as they do the large hosting of a meal or the extravagant gifting of five hundred robes by a major urban merchant. Because *dāna* focuses on the personal qualities of the giver and receiver, and on the rewards ensured by a proper and successful transaction, it is an eminently flexible doctrine.

The emergent culture, thirdly, is an increasingly mobile one, not only as commercial professionals travel to and from centers of trade, but also as birth and geographical ties become weaker in the presence of new opportunities. With mobility comes a new focus—the worthiness of a participant in a transaction—that has less to do with his or her forebears and much more to do with the quality of an individual's work. Buddhist *dāna*, likewise, focuses on the internal qualities of both givers and receivers, and graded worthiness on each side is reflected both in current tangibles and in future spiritual rewards.[116]

Fourthly, the market-oriented culture, in which Buddhism emerges, reflects a shift away from the valuation of traditional duty and obligation and a greater celebration of individual choice. This shift is based in the increased freedom brought about by social and economic changes, and allows for individual initiative and creativity. It also means, however, in the case of renunciant petitioners, that householders are not obligated by preset affiliation to support them, as they are in Vedic settings. Just as a householder's economic fate now rests in his own hands, so also for the renunciant: goods come his or her way as the result of personal action, and this means the necessity of cultivating donor goodwill. Because householders can choose not to give, as they can increasingly choose the path and direction of their own economic careers, Buddhist renunciants become especially wary of overly exuberant begging and of outright harassment of donors.[117] Putting donors and potential donors off is not conducive to a renunciant's continued life on the middle way, and recognition of donor choice in where his or her wealth is allocated helps shape a large portion of Saṅgha rules.

> *What is important, is that the monks should neither abuse their dependence on...[lay-people], nor alienate...[non-Buddhists], but should so regulate their lives as to give no cause for complaint.*[118]

Dāna is not a term or concept new with Buddhism but belongs instead to some of the oldest strata of the Ṛg Veda. In its early use, *dāna* involves gifts[119] given to priestly functionaries in return for ritual services that are designed to bring blessings of long life, victory, prosperity, and sons to the paying patron. As the tradition develops, noble patrons become increasingly linked to family schools of priestly lineage, and obligations of *dāna* become central to the interaction of these socially and ritually distinct, but interdependent, groups. *Dāna* evolves along with the formalized sets of obligations mediating the relationships of kings and priests, students and teachers, and hosts and guests—all the while remaining tightly bound to the perpetuation of family lineage and of the social order idealized by the Vedas. When the lineage system falters as a system of affiliation in the face of changes in the middle country,[120] teachings on *dāna* are revised to suit the conditions of greater wealth for distribution, greater mixing of social groups, and greater personal anonymity as travel becomes a norm. Family and lineage obligations give way to a more universally applicable moral sensibility and, as "a national polity worked against the accumulation of wealth and power in the hands of traditional status groups"[121] and as groups like the *vaiśyas* who are ordinarily disenfranchised from dominant religious options find their religious possibilities expanding significantly, new wealth in new hands goes to fund new religious alternatives.

In the increasingly differentiated settlement patterns, two new figures emerge who are not explicitly associated with lineage patterns: that of the householder *(gahapati)* and the housemistress *(gahapatānī)*. Although occasionally marked by caste, family, or occupational place, the householder and housemistress are heads of households and "persons whose growing wealth and influence mark....them out as separate from their extended kin groups."[122] Unlike in the Vedic tradition, however, where giving in bound by strict lines of lineage affiliation, giving by Buddhist householders includes kin but expands well beyond kin to friends, colleagues, and acquaintances of varied social place.[123] As unaffiliated giving comes to be a hallmark of *gahapati* presence in villages, towns, and cities, then, *dāna* shifts from being an obligation to being a matter of individual choice.

The Buddhist Saṅgha is one of the first institutions of its time to focus on the nature of non-kin corporate life and develops internal structures of democracy, egalitarianism, and governance by law[124] that suit the new unaffiliated modes of giving. Several have argued that, at this time in the Gaṅgā Valley, two parallel systems of government coexist, monarchies and republics or *gaṇa-saṅghas,* and that the organization of the Buddhist monastic communities best reflects that of the *gaṇa-saṅghas.*[125] Although, over the course of time "the republican states lost their independence to one monarchical state or the other," the preservation of republican structure in the Saṅgha is arguably found in an array of technical political terms present in Pali texts.[126] The practice of *dāna* in a corporate structure—governed by consent of all rather than by an autocratic hereditary ruler, by a judicial system applying to each and every one with clarity and consistency, and by equal distribution of goods across the full spectrum of the membership—is a significantly different setting than that of Vedic culture. Giving in an environment where every one receives as needed and where the proper application of donation guidelines is decided by the group means that these guidelines have, in turn, to function successfully in preserving the particular character of the community.

Mavis Fenn has argued that the Buddhist Saṅgha represents the institutionalization of "communitas," such that communitas "is that feeling of a common human bond with others that arises in liminal situations where structure, characterized by differentiation and hierarchy, is absent or minimal."[127] The association of communitas not only with a voluntary poverty but with a poverty understood as simplicity rather than as deprivation means that, in the Buddhist case, guidelines for giving have to account for the continued maintenance of the receivers in this state of poverty, that both distinguish them from the pleasure-oriented householders around them and reflect externally the developing non-attachment of their spiritual state. The complex guidelines that become Buddhist *dāna,* then, help create and stabilize a religious life conducive to Buddhism's highest goal, at the same time as they help give Buddhism a competitive edge in the new market-place of religions.

ENDNOTES

1. In the wake of the collapse of the urban superstructure of the civilization in the Indus basin by the early second millennium BCE, complex societies begin to consolidate again in northern South Asia only around the tenth century BCE. Called materially the Early Iron Age and textually the Late Vedic period, this interval is bound by the appearance of Painted Gray Ware in the Upper Gaṅgā Valley, estimated beginning in the tenth century BCE, and the earliest appearance of Northern Black Polished Ware, suggested to be in the mid-sixth century BCE, further east in regions of the river. Erdosy, "Prelude to Urbanization," pp. 79-80; Erdosy, "Ethnicity in the Rigveda," p. 43. The earliest ceramic culture of the Gaṅgā Valley is Ocher Colored Pottery; it is succeeded by a culture producing Black and Red Ware and Black Slipped Ware, the precursor to Northern Black Polished Ware occurring in the middle and lower Gaṅgā Valley at a chronologically comparable period to Painted Gray Ware in the upper Gaṅgā Valley. Erdosy, *Urbanisation*, pp. 153-155; Erdosy, "City States," pp. 101-102; Thapar, *Lineage to State*, pp. 71-72.
2. Erdosy, "Prelude to Urbanization," pp. 80-81. Migration eastward and the settlement of people occurs along two routes, a northern route along the Himalayan foothills and a southern route along the south bank of the Yamuna and the Gaṅgā along the base of the Vindhyas. Thapar, *Lineage to State*, p. 70; Chaudhury, pp. 9-11.
3. Erdosy, "Prelude to Urbanization," pp. 83-84; Erdosy, *Urbanisation*, pp. 90-91; Ghosh, pp. 5-11.
4. Erdosy, "Prelude to Urbanization," pp. 82-83; Erdosy, *Urbanisation*, pp. 88-90.
5. This population is arrayed over "a two-tier settlement hierarchy whose central place coordinated the procurement, processing and distribution of vital raw materials." Erdosy, "City States," p. 99.
6. *Sapta sindhu* as an area (RV 8.24.27) probably refers to the land watered by the Indus River, its five tributaries (Beas, Chenab, Jhelum, Rāvi, and Sutlej rivers) and the Sarasvatī river to the east. See Erdosy, "Ethnicity in the Rigveda," pp. 40-42.
7. See *madhyamā pratiṣṭhā diś* 'the established middle region' of AB 8.14.3, inhabited, says the text, by the Kurus, Pañcālas, Vaśas, and Uśīnaras. In time, *madhya deśa* comes to be primarily the land of the Kuru-Pañcālas, where the later Saṃhitās and Brāhmaṇas arise, demarcated on the west by the desert and on the east by the region of the Kosala-Videhas. In ŚB 1.4.1.10-17, a tradition is preserved that describes the Brāhmaṇization of the Kosalas and Videhas from the Kuru-Pañcāla region (Thapar, *Lineage to State*, p. 70). For a discussion of this passage, see Erdosy, "Language, material culture and ethnicity," p. 18; Erdosy, "Prelude to Urbanization," pp. 75, 90, 97.

   The traditional division of India into five areas is to be found as a full doctrine in the Kāvyamīmāṃsā as well as in the Purāṇas, with the boundaries of *madhya deśa* (or *āryāvarta*) being given in such texts as Manu (2.19-22). Law, pp. xix-xxi, 1-3; Chaudhury, pp. 12-13.

8. The use of terms like *janapada* 'realm, region' to denote this connection becomes standard (CU 5.11.5; 8.1.5). With the use of the term *māgadha deśiya* (KŚS 22.4.22; LŚS 8.6.28) a connection is made between a *janapada* and the territory of its sovereignty. Erdosy, "Prelude to Urbanization," pp. 85-86.

9. This culture is marked by Painted Gray Ware and located in small-scale two-tiered sites. Erdosy, "Prelude to Urbanization," p. 95. The Vinaya passage used to locate Buddhist activity within the larger geographical area is in the Mahāvagga (Vin 1.197), where the main immediate division of space is between middle regions *(majjhima janapada)* and border regions *(paccantima janapada)* with named areas located in different directions *(disā)*. Here the eastward boundaries of the middle country are clearly expanded beyond older Vedic understandings. The use of *disā* to designate distant areas can be found in Vin 1.50; 2.217; D 3.197ff; S 1.33, 234; 3.106; 5.216.

10. Ghosh, p. 2.

11. This period is marked, chronologically, by the appearance of Northern Black Polished (NBP) Ware, a distinctive trade ceramic whose alkaline slip fuses to a surface lustre when fired at a high temperature. Based on radio carbon levels, Erdosy has identified three phases of this period, that fit with recent revisions of chronology regarding the date of the Buddha: early NBPW (ca. 550-400 BCE), middle NBPW (ca. 400-250 BCE), and late NBPW (ca. 250-100 BCE). Erdosy, "City States," p. 105; Thapar, *Lineage to State*, p. 72.

12. Supporting Erdosy's work, Bechert has argued for a "short chronology," based on Indian sources, that places the Buddha's death somewhere between 370-368 BCE, giving lifetime dates of approximately 450/448-370/368 BCE. This suits the ceramic chronology more comfortably than traditional "long chronology" dates for the Buddha attested primarily by Sinhalese sources, that place his death about a century earlier. Bechert, "Date of the Buddha Reconsidered," pp. 36, 36n.

13. Erdosy, "City States," p. 99. The earliest surviving inscriptions are those of the Mauryan emperor Aśoka (ca. 272-268—ca. 235 BCE).

14. This happened in the aftermath of Alexander's efforts in north-west Indo-Pakistan. On the role of Alexander's conquests in the creation of conditions favorable to Chandragupta Maurya, see Erdosy, *Urbanisation*, p. 138.

15. Erdosy, *Urbanisation*, pp. 124-130.

16. Erdosy, "City States," pp. 110-112; Ghosh, pp. 13-15.

17. Darian, p. 227. On the monetary system, money-lending, and banking in early Buddhist times, see Misra, pp. 266-68; Wagle, pp. 135-136, 145-150.

18. Thapar, *Lineage to State*, pp. 42, 73-76.

19. Darian, pp. 226-27.
20. Darian, p. 228.
21. Darian, p. 228.
22. Darian, p. 230.
23. Thapar, *Lineage and State,* p. 149; see p. 111.
24. The previous period, the Late Vedic, has been characterized, archaeologically, by a two-tiered pattern in which central sites manage the gathering and dispersal of raw materials. Beginning about 550 BCE, increased concentration of a growing population in the region, greater gradation within the settlement hierarchy, and increased dominance of single central sites appear. Erdosy, "City States," p. 99.
25. This classification is based on his work in the Allahabad district. Erdosy, "City States," p. 107; Erdosy, *Urbanisation,* pp. 116-118.
26. Added to this is the continued appearance of new villages, presumably established to provide service and support for the secondary centers and to continue support for the growth of the more complex settlement levels. Erdosy, "City States," pp. 107-108. Parallel settlement hierarchies can be found in such literature as the Artha Śāstra. See Erdosy, *Urbanisation,* pp. 120-121, 139-141.
27. That is, the places of the Aṅgas, the Magadhas, the Kāsis, the Kosalas, the Vajjis, the Mallas, the Cetis, the Vaṃsas, the Kurus, the Pañcālas, the Macchas, the Sūrasenas, the Assakas, the Avantis, the Gandhāras, and the Kambojas. A 4.252, 256, 260-61; see D 2.200-201. Of these, Gandhāra and Kamboja are in the north west, Kuru, Maccha, and Sūrasena in the Indo-Gangetic divide, Avanti and Ceti in central India, Assaka in the south, and Aṅga, Magadha, Kāsi, Kosala, Vajji, Malla, Vaṃsa/Vatsa, and Pañcāla in the Gaṅgā Valley. See Erdosy, *Urbanisation,* pp. 23-26. For discussions of the nature and structure of *janapadas,* see Erdosy, "City States," p. 115; Erdosy, *Urbanisation,* pp. 119-120; Ghosh, pp. 32-35; Wagle, pp. 29-37; Law, pp. 3-23; Chaudhury, pp. 6-7.
28. Erdosy, "City States," pp. 115-116; Erdosy, *Urbanisation,* pp. 137-39. On the natural resources facilitating the rise of Magadha, see Thapar, *Lineage to State,* p. 114.
29. D 2.202-203.
30. Vin 1.197; A 4.226; Wagle, p. 32.
31. Horner, in *Book of the Discipline* 4:xx. See, for example, Vin 1.197.
32. In early passages, the *nagara* is most often described as a city built with strong fortification, with ramparts, towers, and gates for the watchful guarding of the movements of inhabitants. D 1.193; M 2.33; A 1.178-79. This confirms archaeological evidence of city areas with fortifications appearing by 550 BCE throughout northern India, among them Rājagaha (the capital of Magadha *janapada),* Campā (of Aṅga), Ujjain (of Avanti), and V/Bārāṇasī [Rajghat] (of Kāsi). Another great city of the Buddha's

time, Sāvatthi, is fortified by around 400 BCE, and Pāṭaliputta (formerly Pāṭaligāma), that supersedes Rājagaha as capital of Magadha and later becomes the capital of the Maurya empire, is fortified around 300 BCE. Erdosy, "City States," pp. 109-110; Darian, p. 227; Erdosy, *Urbanisation*, pp. 106-116, 134; Ghosh, pp. 62-67. A comparison of Erdosy's four settlement categories might allign them respectively with the *gama*, *nigama*, *nagara*, and *mahānagara*.

33. Campā, Rājagaha, Sāvatthi, Sāketa, Kosambi, and V/Bārāṇasī (D 2.146). These are offered by Ānanda, the Buddha's attendant, as alternatives to the little wattle and daub *(kuḍḍa)* city of Kusinārā in the midst of a jungle *(ujjaṅgala)*, because they are places of greater wealth where the Buddha might be more properly honored (Wagle, p. 27). The Buddha refuses, however, and recalls the great urban past of Kusinārā.
34. M 1.106, 187-189, 211; 3.59, 60; A 1.159-160.
35. E.g., Vin 3.46; S 3.93; A 2.95; 3.209.
36. S 1.233; A 1.281.
37. Vin 1.39; 2.158.
38. M 2.97; S 4.173, 174.
39. Vin 1.110; 4.166.
40. M 1.276.
41. Vin 3.46; Wagle, p. 13.
42. Wagle, p. 13.
43. Vin 3.46; 200-201; 4.63-64; D 2.344.
44. D 2.338ff.
45. Vin 3.249-250.
46. M 2.205.
47. Vin 1.350; A 2.182.
48. See the discussion in Wagle, pp. 16-18.
49. See Wagle, pp. 18-19; Thapar, *Lineage to State*, p. 110.
50. Vin 1.149.
51. Wagle, p. 20.
52. As a derivation from the Sanskrit *ni* and *gāma* implies (Wagle, p. 21). Another derivation takes *nigama* from *nadī-gāma*, a village on a river, suggesting a specialized settlement where trade from river commerce takes place among large gatherings of people. Many early Indian centers occupied sites on the banks of rivers (Horner, *Book of the Discipline* 2:63n).
53. Tapar, *Lineage to State*, p. 90.
54. Vin 4.109.
55. D 2.98; see also M 1.519; A 2.115; 3.90.
56. Just about as consistently, the town name appears with the name of its

corresponding peoples, often one of the sixteen recognized *mahājanapadas*. There are, for example, *nigamas* such as Anupiya (Vin 2.180; D 3.1) and Uruvelakappa (S 4.327; 5.228) in the Malla region, Kammāsadamma (D 2.55; M 1.55; S 2.107; A 5.30) and Thullakoṭṭhita (M 2.54) in the Kuru region; Āpaṇa (M 1.359, 447; 2.146; S 5.225) and Assapura (M 1.281) in the Aṅga region; and Paṅkadhā (A 1.236), Daṇḍakappaka (A 3.402), and Kesaputta (A 1.188) in the Kosala region. Other towns are in the regions of other groups, such as Medataḷumpa (M 2.119) and Devadaha (S 3.5; 4.124) of the Sākyans, and Haliddavasana (M 1.387) and Sāpūga (A 2.194) of the Koliyans.

57. D 3.61; A 3.149-153, 369; S 1.89.

58. D 3.148, 167-68, 169, 172.

59. S 3.3, 42, 46, 138, 164, 173; 4.206, 207, 287, 330; A 1.178.

60. Erdosy, "City States," pp. 119-120.

61. See Erdosy's summary, "City States," pp. 121-22, Chakravarti, pp. 35-39, 64.

62. Heesterman, "Brahmin, Ritual, and Renouncer," in *Inner Conflict*, pp. 40, 32, 34-36, 41-42; see Kaelber, pp. 102, 105-107. Theories about the rise of the individual note several sources. While Olivelle *(Saṃnyāsa Upaniṣads*, pp. 32-33) argues that the new value placed on the individual derives from the "emergence of kingship and urban culture," the king being "the supreme individual in society," and is facilitated by a "similar individualistic mentality...among merchants, whose success depended less on following an inherited and ritualized pattern of behavior than on initiative and enterprise," Heesterman's argument about the individual nature of the *śrauta* ritual is also persuasive. Not only is it "man by himself and alone, not the gods or any other supernatural agency, who must realize the absolute static order by unquestioningly submitting to the exacting rule of ritual," but it is the specialized use of the fire drill which, emphasizing "the exclusive link with its owner,...makes [the sacrificer]...independent, allowing him to make fire where there" is none *(Broken World*, pp. 81, 101). As the *śrauta* ritual develops, moreover, a process evolves, the "individualization of the ritual," whereby the sacrificer no longer relies on an array of ritual officiants to create the world but only on his own ritual work. Now an interior process, the individualizing of the ritual not only places a premium on individual effort in the maintenance of moral order, but also leads, eventually, to greater hierarchy and fixity in social relations *(Inner Conflict*, pp. 32-44; *Broken World*, pp. 216, 218).

63. Collins, pp. 29, 30-33.

64. Olivelle, *Saṃnyāsa Upaniṣads*, pp. 20, 21, 32; Dumont, pp. 46, 50. See also Kaelber, pp. 108-109; Basham, *Ājīvikas*, p. 5; Erdosy, *Urbanisation*, pp. 144-45.

65. Olivelle, *Saṃnyāsa Upaniṣads*, pp. 46, 23-46; Gombrich, *Theravada Buddhism*, pp. 49-59.

66. See Olivelle, p. 14.
67. Such as the followers of Nigaṇṭha Nātaputta (the Jains), Makkhali Gosāla (the Ājīvikas), Pūraṇa Kassapa, Ajitakesakambalī, Pakudha Kaccāyana, and Sañjaya Belaṭṭhaputta: the six "heretics" of the Sāmaññaphala Sutta of the Dīgha Nikāya (1.47-86). See Basham, *Ājīvikas,* pp. 10-26; Chakravarti, pp. 46-49.
68. Fenn (pp. 100-117) distinguishes between two types of poverty in Pali texts: poverty as deprivation, which needs to be redressed by the king and then by society at large, and poverty as simplicity lived out by renunciants in the Saṅgha, an institutionalized form of Victor Turner's liminality and communitas.
69. S 4.330-31; A 1.295-97; Ps 2.147.
70. D 1.47-86.
71. The early formula, the simple 'Come, monk' *(ehi bhikkhu),* is in time replaced by a ritual structure marked off in two clear stages: the admission *(pabbajjā)* into the Saṅgha, whereby one becomes a novice *(sāmaṇera)* and begins preparation and training under a preceptor *(upajjhāya),* and the ordination proper *(upasampadā),* whereby one becomes a newly ordained monk *(nava).* Horner, *Book of the Discipline* 4:ix-xiii.
72. D 1.250.
73. D 2.76-77.
74. M 1.198, 238; 2.1-4; S 3.69; 4.398-400.
75. See Bhagvat, pp. 1-17; Misra, pp. 1-3, 37, 105-107; Olivelle, *Saṃnyāsa Upaniṣads,* pp. 36, 52-57.
76. M 1.387-392.
77. D 1.5-12.
78. D 1.165-177; 3.40-57; M 1.77-83.
79. M 1.513-14.
80. D 1.165-67; 3.40-42; M 1.77-79; 1.238-39.
81. Horner, *Middle Length Sayings* 1.335. M 1.281.
82. M 1.281.
83. S 3.93; See S 5.224; Itivuttaka, p. 89.
84. D 1.4. See Chakravarti's (pp. 50-51) discussion of the criticism made of renunciants for behaving too much like householders.
85. See D 1.237; S 3.240; 5.325; A 4.187.
86. A 3.128-130.
87. See D 3.146; S 1.100, 180-181.
88. A 3.103-105.
89. Therī no. 340.
90. A 3.108-110; 341-344; 5.121-22. The *saṃnyāsin* tradition evolving at the

time of the early Buddhist is also mindful both of the full range of settlement hierarchies over the area and of the need for considered behavior when entering them. One could enter a village, for example, only to petition food (NpU 145) and one could spend only a certain number of nights in each type of location: one night in a village, five in a town (NpU 158); one in a village, two in a burg, three in a town, five in a city, six in a holy place, seven at a sacred bathing place (NpU 159, 201); one in a village, three at a sacred bathing place, five in a town, seven in a holy place (PpU 284). The need to be free of fixed attachments to places is extended to persons as well, for while the ideal is the single mendicant wanderer, two persons formed a village, three a town, and four a city (NpU 202), or one a mendicant, two a pair, three a village, and any above a city (NpU 145).

91. S 3.9-12.

92. Vin 1.110; 3.184; M 1.106, 370; 2.171; A 1.182-84, 274; 3.95-99. Thapar (*Lineage to State*, p. 150) has said of this relationship: "A parallel monastic society can only survive when there is a well-ordered agrarian system and trade to provide the surplus since the monastery for its daily needs has a parasitical relationship with society."

93. S 4.330-331; Ps 2.147; see Misra, p. 76; Thapar, *Lineage to State*, pp. 152-53.

94. A 1.295-297.

95. Vin 3.213-15; Vin 4.258-9.

96. M 1.10.

97. M 1.29-30.

98. M 1.126-127.

99. Darian, p. 230.

100. Fenn, pp. 109-110. Because Buddhism wholeheartedly adopts the karma and rebirth system developing among its Brāhmaṇical colleagues, there are in fact no real "accidents of birth." It may be that the relationship between Buddhism and society is a reciprocally transforming one and that egalitarianism becomes a cultural value decisive in many arenas of activity. In economics, for example, "the egalitarian nature of Buddhism—far more than the compartmentalized caste system—paralleled the market-type relations necessary for expanded commercial enterprise." Darian, p. 234.

101. Horner, *Book of the Discipline* l.ix.

102. Horner, *Book of the Discipline* l.xv.

103. Vin 1.44; 4.102.

104. Vin 1.298; 2.212-215.

105. Vin 4.344-45.

106. Vin 1.45, 50, 194, 289, 298; 2.136, 214, 217; A 1.182-84; 2.125; 3.95-99.

107. Vin 2.212-215; 1.70-71; M 1.206-207.

108. M 1.28.

109. M 1.28.

110. Vin 4.4-6; A 1.242-44.

111. M 3.293-97; see D 3.89; M 1.462; 3.294; S 1.297; A 2.125; 3.95-99.

112. Vin 1.45; 4.164-65; M 1.469; S 1.200; A 3.117.

113. For example, the first one to return from the village after going on alms tour is to make ready the seats, the water for drinking and washing the feet, and the bowl for refuse. The last one returning is responsible for attending to the left-overs from the meal, either eating them himself or discarding them in such a way that no injury will occur to living things. He is also responsible for tidying up the seats, the drinking and washing water, and the refuse bowl, and for sweeping the floor. Any help needed in these duties has to be signalled for by hand, not requested in words (Vin 1.157-58, 352; 2.216; M 3.157).

114. In addition to obvious large-scale market activity, heaps of grain, for example, are kept near some villages and towns from which country folk can simply come and take away corn (A 4.163-64).

115. S 1.18-19.

116. When a town like Madhurā comes to be known as a place where alms are gotten with difficulty *(dullabhapiṇḍa)*, not only does this signify hardship for renunciant petitioners there but loss of reputation for the center, competing as it must in a world where attracting good people of all kinds is considerably more desirable than repelling them (A 3.256).

117. Vin 3.144-45.

118. Horner, *Book of the Discipline* l.xvii.

119. E.g., cows, horses, garments, gold (Thapar, *Lineage to State,* pp. 58, 64-66).

120. Darian, p. 230.

121. Darian, p. 232.

122. Wagle, p. 152.

123. Wagle, p. 107.

124. Misra, pp. 108-110.

125. Erdosy, *Urbanisation,* pp. 144-45; Misra, pp. 208-209; Thapar, *Lineage to State,* p. 116; Chakravarti, pp. 10-12.

126. Misra, pp. 208-210.

127. Fenn, p. 109.

CHAPTER 2

Redefining Relationships: The New Donor

Buddhism arises in the new urbanism of the middle Gaṅgā Valley as material resources increase, as renunciant options proliferate, and as the social dynamics of the supporting community become more complex. One of the chief players at this time is the *gahapati* 'householder' (and his wife or the *gahapatānī* 'housemistress'), terms not new with Buddhism but, as used in Pali texts, reflective of the momentous social changes taking place. Many factors contribute to these changes and one of them is the centrality of administrative and commercial organizations.[1] Market and industrial towns and cities are distinguished from villages by larger and denser populations, by the prominence of non-agricultural activities, and by being convergence points for more complex political and commercial affairs. The conspicuousness of both the ruler and the merchant, "each the ally of the other in history,"[2] means that the organization and investment of wealth takes place on a scale larger than ever before and that wealth becomes a critical medium in the disposition of human affairs. Against this background, the merchant plays a decisive role in the rise of Buddhism.

THE HOUSEHOLDER AS DONOR

The more central place of the merchant, and of commerce, is the result of an evolution of a family-centered system out of an older lineage-centered system. Thapar has charted the shift from a lineage culture of Ṛg Vedic times[3] in which there is a bifurcation between the rulers *(rājanya)* and the tribute-giving clans *(viś)*. At this time, lands are held in common, though worked by the *viś*, and, as a pastoral society, wealth often comes through raids on cattle. Late Vedic texts reflect a system of combined lineage and householding economies with a shift from pastoralism to agriculture. As the *viś* produce more, the sacrificial ritual draws off greater amounts of wealth, going from the *viś* through the *kṣatriya* (that is, the older *rājanya)* patrons to the brahmins.[4] As the *kṣatriyas* become more dependent "on the agricultural activities of the *viś* and the prestations that the *viś* can provide," storage of materials for the ritual and for other gift-giving settings increases. As the *gṛhapati* 'head of house' emerges from this older householding system where keeping goods for ritual use evolves, *viś* is replaced by *vaiśya,* suggesting "an altered status, the clan element decreasing and the individual status becoming more apparent."[5] In time, with the break-up of lineage-held lands into family holdings,[6] the *gṛhapati* is transformed from a household head within a clan system working the land "to a landowner, and subsequent to this,...[to] a participant in trading activities"[7]—in both cases, a household head being himself responsible for the storage of his own goods. During this period, Pali literature often uses *gahapati* as a functional equivalent of *vessa (vaiśya),* though the former is, at the same time, evolving into a term of substantially broader referent. Thus, with the eventual consolidation of the kingdoms of Kośala and Magadha and the emergence of a more complex economy and of commerce, the *gṛhapati/ gahapati,* now drawn from any of the three twice-born castes, comes to be in clear contrast to the *śūdra* as peasant cultivator and artisan.[8]

Early Buddhist texts reflect a culture in which Brāhmaṇic ritual is seen as the domain exclusively of ritual specialists[9] and in which non-Brāhmaṇic renunciants are in regular daily contact with ordinary folk during their alms rounds in the villages.[10] The old Vedic *gṛhapati,* once a fairly narrowly used concept, now emerges as the Pali *gahapati,* its old ties to wealth still intact, but with a wider range of social applications. The term *gahapati* comes to be used in two ways: as a general term referring to the broad category of non-renunciants, i.e., to those who simply 'live in a house,' and as a more specific, contemporary, term referring to powerful managers of property. *Gahapatis* form "the basis of Buddhist Society." Not only are they the fledgling mainstream in which Buddhism takes shape, but it is their patronage, their good counsel, and their general support that is sought by each emergent religious group. They are, as Wagle notes, "the prizes in the religious struggle."[11] Thapar suggests that the relationship between the *gahapatis* and new religions like Buddhism and Jainism is a mutual one. On the one hand, *gahapatis* provide essential material support in their patronage of young religious institutions. On the other, these young institutions provide a place for *gahapati* merchants and businessmen in a religious panorama that up until this point has been intensely exclusivistic. By giving support to Buddhism, for example, *gahapati* merchants gain socio-ritual standing and Buddhism, then, becomes their religion, a religion rooted among householders.[12] The world to the householder is now an open market, and Pali texts show that it is this group, with its broad caste constituency, that becomes the principal audience and principal source of patronage for the new religion.

The Gahapati in the Social Order

The shift to an economically viable family unit of smaller proportions than the older lineage renders the Pali *gahapati* (or *gihin)* a family man of a few but definite ties. Routinely accompanied by his wife the *gahapatānī*[13] 'housemistress' and his offspring the *gahapatiputta*[14] (normally a son), the *gahapati* is no longer just the Vedic householder keeping the household stores but often a figure of substantial social and economic importance as well. Consisting of heads of household, the *gahapati* group has specific social recognition as a distinguished collection of distinguishable individuals,[15] making names for themselves as the opportunity suits.

Reflecting the production of wealth through both agriculture and commerce—and the computing of this wealth in both grain and coin—the occupations of the householder vary.[16] Most householders, however, are involved in some sort of trade in the town or city, and trade is identified as the *dhamma* or duty of the householder, along with support and provision for his parents.[17] While there are passages that locate the trader among others fairly low in the social order,[18] texts most often treat the trade practised by householders as work of burgeoning intensity and significance. Householder traders contract debts, set up businesses, and repay their accounts;[19] they assess investments and act accordingly, putting themselves at risk for success or failure. There are four possibilities for someone in trade: either the work fails, or it does not turn out as intended, or it turns out as intended, or it reaps rewards beyond all expectation. In the text, these possibilities are understood Buddhistically, i.e., "*dānically,*" as they are kammically dependent on what the trader has given to renunciants in previous lives.[20]

The most prominent occupation of the householder, however, is that of *seṭṭhi*[21] (Skt. *śreṣṭin),* a role exemplified by such figures as Anāthapiṇḍika[22] and his brother-in-law, the great merchant of Rājagaha.[23] Although there is no detailed discussion of the *seṭṭhi,* the texts suggest that he is a trader of high order and of great prominence: banker, treasurer, merchant, or a corporate officer.[24] A leading figure in the business community, he has wealth, talent, and organizational skills that bring him into decisive circles of political influence.[25] As Narendra Wagle points out, the *seṭṭhi gahapati* belongs primarily to urban sites where there is a cash economy and where wealth accumulates for those at the crossroads of commerce.[26] G.S.P. Misra has argued further that while *gahapati* "denote[s] a class constituted of wealthy people from [the] businessmen's community," the *seṭṭhi* is "a distinguished personage holding some post of responsibility and distinct from other *gahapatis* of the place."[27] The designation "*seṭṭhi gahapatis* [then] would mean the leading middle class *gahapatis* as distinct from the brāhmaṇas by birth and the members of [the] ruling aristocracy."[28] While many are *gahapatis,* only some are *seṭṭhi gahapatis.*

At this time, the householder has a complex relationship to the *varṇa* or caste system currently emerging in Brāhmaṇic culture. Given that the *gṛhapati* becomes important in Vedic texts when the head of the household begins to store goods for ritual use, the *viś* are drawn into the *varṇa* scheme as the source of these goods. Because it is the household head who does the managing of what comes in, then, *gṛhapati* and *vaiśya,* though not strictly equable, become correlated. While Thapar argues that the Buddhist *gahapati* is seen to replace *vessa,* a substitution that "points to the final disintegration of the original *viś*,"[29] support for this—viz., two apparently interchangeable lists in Pali—may refer instead to different systems of activity.

The first Pali list reverses the order of the first two ranks:[30] thus, the traditional four-fold division of *brahman, kṣatriya, vaiśya,* and *śūdra*[31] is rearranged into a decidedly Buddhist order in this way: *khattiya, brāhmaṇa, vessa,* and *sudda.* In the other, the first two ranks are again reversed and the list shortened by one, *khattiya, brāhmaṇa,* and *gahapati,* giving an apparent substitution of *gahapati* for *vessa.* While the first list—*khattiya, brāhmaṇa, vessa,* and *sudda*—is a classification of the four *vaṇṇas,*[32] the second—*khattiya, brāhmaṇa,* and *gahapati*[33]—is distinct in several ways. First, the *gahapati* list is not used as a description of *vaṇṇa* ranking, suggesting instead of ritual status something else, such as socio-economic place. Second, unlike the first list it is applied to an economic term *mahāsāla* 'having great halls'[34] designating those who live in substantial residences and who, by inference, have a sizable income and are socially prominent. Third, its three members are one of the many sets of *parisā* 'company, assembly, congregation,'[35] a term applied to various categories of Buddhist doctrine.

The most important difference between the two lists is that while the *vessa* list is oriented toward ties of birth and heredity, the *gahapati* list is oriented toward associations made voluntarily and toward status that is earned. This conclusion is based primarily on the *vessa* list's application to the category of *vaṇṇa,* a demarcation relating to complexion color[36] and to status given primarily by location of birth,[37] while the *gahapati* list's application is highlighted by *mahāsāla,* a designation usually set within the context of acquiring great wealth and prosperous authority, and of individual distinction through honest effort and hard work.[38] The *vessa* list, then, suggests socio-ritual status or caste, and the *gahapati* economic status or class.

The very use of the two lists in the same texts is a symptom of a culture in transition, a culture that knows Vedic structures but is also forging new ones. Because "the dominant strata of urban society are not catered for, not even recognized by brahminism"[39] at the time of the rise of Buddhism, the new structures come to be based not on ritual rank (the *vessa* list) but on socio-economic place (the *gahapati* list). Because of their similarities, however, the two lists are textually homologized, a process confirmed by the overlap in trade and commerce of the activities of *vessa* and many of the prominent *gahapatis.*[40]

If the terms are roughly equivalent, then, why not have only one of them and avoid the confusion? In mature Vedic society, with its tendency to classify,[41] the management of trade is the specific purview of a specialized sector. As changes in the Gaṅgā Valley take place, wealth is more available and more desirable, and a term is now needed separate from Vedic *vaiśya* to designate a cross-cutting category of those garnering and managing wealth. Because Buddhism grows up in a society where "wealth creates the differences,"[42] the term *gahapati,* that is already in use across the upper three castes,[43] comes to be associated with the new wealth as it is available to all in a position to handle it. Strictly, then, *gahapati's* appearance in the second list is the canon's recognition that in terms of profession, the *gahapati* and the *vessa* are often functionally equivalent. More generally, however, *gahapati's* consistently broader usage in narratives is the canon's recognition that all householders, drawn from whatever social ranking they might be, are the economic base of Saṅgha support to whom wealth might accrue. The *gahapati* is the one who has managerial place within his family and a place in society not given by birth but earned; he is also the one who has wealth, uses it in a certain way and, in that, forms a special relationship with emergent Buddhism. Because it is the agency of the householder that supports the Saṅgha, anyone may give who can; ties of caste or lineage are not necessary in a setting where individual choice is the determinant.

The category *brāhmaṇa gahapatikā* further illumines the relationship of the *gahapati* to the *vaṇṇa* system.[44] Seemingly parallel to *seṭṭhi gahapati, kassaka gahapati,* and *dārukammika gahapati,* the 'brahmin householder,'[45] however, lives in special brahmin villages, *brāhmaṇagāma.*[46] Most of these brahmin settlements are in lands under monarchical rule, where early patterns of *brahmadeyya* land-ownership are most prominent.

> Brahmadeyya *is the royal gift of land or an estate to well-known brāhmaṇas and others, for the services, probably ritual in nature, which they rendered to the king. Some of the* brahmadeyya *lands are specifically described as brāhmaṇa* gāmas.[47]

It is normally in the context of these brahmin villages, Wagle argues, that brahmins are called *gahapatis,*[48] emphasizing that here brahmins are land-owners and managers of their own household wealth. The need to identify brahmin householders in particular stems from early control of goods by only *kṣatriyas* and *vaiśyas,*[49] who through these goods support brahmins within the ritual system. As the ritual system's influence wanes, and as brahmins acquire land-owning status, they are newly available as potential donors in their own right, now to renunciant wanderers and institutions.[50]

The Pali *gahapati* thus represents a new moment in the cultural evolution of north India. As society and the economy become more complex and as great wealth is procured through trade,[51] householders like the *seṭṭhi* become more prominent as patrons. With wealth, patronage, and householdership now associated with commerce, the classifying tendency of canonical redactors has to relocate the *gahapati* in relationship to the social schema idealized by Vedists, and that process makes it an alternate to the *vessa/vaiśya.*[52] Although the *gahapati* is the representative of his whole household, whether his profession be farmer or priest, that household becomes important in Pali texts primarily because it is prosperous and can provide the support requisite for the survival and spread of the Saṅgha. The most prosperous householders, however, are not necessarily those who have been prosperous of old, but often the newly wealthy businessmen who are looking for investments that highlight their own recent prosperity and prominence. While the *gahapati* does not belong restrictively "to either the Buddhist or the *brāhmaṇic* order,"[53] he does find new (though not exclusive) identity in this period of transition through association with the Buddhist Saṅgha. The term *gahapati,* then, is both an old marker of responsibility for the management of common household property separating him from subordinate members of the household,[54] and a new marker of the householder's conspicuous association with commerce: what ties both these together is his role in the acquiring, maintaining, and disposing of wealth.

Householdership, Wealth, and Donation

The wealth from agriculture, and in time from commerce,[55] becomes a central part of *gahapati* identity, and attention focuses on both the attitudes and practices of its management.[56] Wagle notes that the emergence of the "*gahapati* from the Vedic householder to a comparatively wealthier head of the household may represent the growing disparity of wealth within the society,"[57] and Pali texts document householder wealth as being substantial. Not only do *gahapatis,* like nobles and brahmins, have *mahāsālas*[58] 'great halls' built with flowing cash and generating community stature, but much *dhana* 'property'[59] as well, deriving from agriculture through an abundance of grain and evidenced in commerce by silver and gold.[60] In standard descriptions, they are eminently prosperous,[61] and have great wealth,[62] riches, many possessions, and much treasure.[63] One brahmin householder in particular, a certain Velāma, is legendary for the richness and variety of the things he owns: a story in the Aṅguttara Nikāya tells of the thousands of golden, silver, and copper bowls, thousands of horses decked out in golden finery, thousands of chariots covered with animal skins, ocher blankets, and golden trappings, thousands of cows with silver milk pails, thousands of jewel-bedecked young women, thousands of expensive, handsomely made couches, coverlets, rugs, awnings, and cushions, and glorious food that flows in rivers.[64]

The reason the early texts make so much of householder wealth is that by mutual consent and through an elaborately reciprocal system of transactions, this wealth gets diverted from householder life to suit Saṅgha needs and eventually to fill Saṅgha stores. The linchpin in the arrangement is the growing conception of the *gahapati* as donor. Many terms are used for the donor (e.g., *dātar* 'giver,'[65] *dāyaka* 'benefactor'[66] /*dāyikā* 'benefactress,'[67] *dānapati* 'liberal donor,'[68] and *bhattar* 'supporter'), whose prototype is the liberal giver celebrated in the Dānastuti sections of several Ṛg Vedic hymns.[69] Like the old king Serī who pronounces himself an habitual giver, a generous benefactor, and an extoller of donation,[70] many such early givers are known by name[71] who from their often sovereign status give gifts *(dakṣiṇā)* of great munificence to the poets, priests, and gods who then ensure the maintenance of a benevolent cosmos.[72] The donor-patron of the ritual system continues in the Brāhmaṇa period to be at the pivot of the sacrifice, for not only is it at his expense that the ritual is performed, but it is through him and his transformation that ritual effectiveness and its cosmic consequences in the material world are ensured.[73]

The figure of the donor takes on new dimensions as Vedic society begins to accommodate larger numbers of renunciants receiving daily sustenance from local families. Texts like the Gṛhya Sūtras, in the making at the time of the early Buddhist movement but reflective of a system some centuries older,[74] prescribe etiquette for the alms contract of two religious offices, the *brahmacārin* and the *saṃnyāsin.* This etiquette assumes that, as each of these petitioners presents a request for food, the member of the household most often present at the request and from whom the gift will come will be the housemistress, the *gṛhapatnī.*[75] Thus, as family members, usually men, increasingly decide to leave home for a period, either as celibate students or as full renunciants, women as representatives of the entire household[76] are in a conspicuous position to offer material support for this life-style. The old concept of the householder as donor is thus based in two central assumptions of Vedic religion: first, that hospitable giving to religious persons, whether in the context of a self-commissioned ritual or of an other-initiated alms request, is a proper, necessary, and worthy posture for a householder to take[77] and, second, that the category of donor, as established now by religious tradition, can be either the householder himself or more normally his wife, who in the Brāhmaṇic view acts on behalf of the whole household whenever she gives.

Turning to the Buddhist *gahapati,* his main role as donor gives legitimation to the fact that the Saṅgha has material needs and that these material needs can be met only through donation. Poignantly put, a monk's livelihood rests on his being dependent upon *(upanissāya)* the economy of villages and towns.[78] Thus, a mutuality of contract develops whereby any tension about life choices between householder and renunciant—in particular, the renunciatory option as signifying the "rejection of the religious primacy of the householder"[79] central to the Vedic view—vanishes amidst the complexity of their increasingly interwoven relationships. Householders provide the Saṅgha with food, robes, lodging, and medicine, and Saṅgha members, in return, nourish householders' less advanced but nevertheless quite authentic quest for realized spirituality.[80] Crucial in the development of the philosophical network affirming this contract is support for the goodness of the act of donation itself, hence the description of the *gahapati* donor as a *sappurisa,* 'a good and worthy person.'[81] Because the duty of the *sappurisa*[82] is to uphold the charitable aim of the householder, [83] the new relationship is one where householding and donation are synonymous.

What does being a donor mean to the householder? The widespread missionizing activity that leads to so many householders becoming donors is not a fully correspondent process,[84] for some *gahapatis* in the texts are not associated specifically with donation to the Saṅgha and some donors to the Saṅgha are not marked specifically as *gahapatis.* The tie between house holdership and donation is so strong, however, that from the donor side, especially, the forces drawing one in are particularly compelling. Helpful here are the distinctions Kenneth Boulding makes between two kinds of economies: the "exchange" economy of the open market in which there is a two-way or reciprocal transfer of wealth and money, and the "grant" economy of a more centrally planned system in which there is a one-way or unilateral transfer of goods.[85] Each of these economies sheds light on the householder side of donation to the Saṇgha.

In seeing donation as an "exchange," the donor's gifts of robes, food, lodgings, and medicine are given in return for the goodwill of the Buddha, the *bhikkhus* and the *bhikkhunīs,* for the teaching of the Dhamma, or for a promise of heaven or a good rebirth after death. While the promise, in the latter case, occurs in the present, the actual return on the exchange does not happen until the future, making this particular option a "deferred exchange,"[86] a trade made in expectation of a delayed but certain and assured reward. The element of exchange present in donation is best expressed in the reciprocal act of *dānadhamma-dhammadāna.* That is, while donors operate under the rubric of *dānadhamma,* the teaching about (that is, the obligation of) giving, renunciants act under that of *dhammadāna,* the giving of teaching in return for material support.

In seeing donation to the Saṅgha as making a "grant," however, other more complicated things are involved. Boulding, first, distinguishes between grants made from fear that are the products of threats and threat systems, such as tributes or taxes,[87] and those made from love that are the products of an integrative and relational system in which the donor identifies with the welfare of the recipient. Authentic philanthropy, he argues, is "the gift which is given out of a genuine sense of community with the object of the donation."[88] While there is a loss of utility to the donor from a gift thus given, this is more than made up for by the donor's appreciation of the new well-being of the recipient. The identification of the householder donor with the Saṅgha recipient, then, is most obvious in case of the majority of donors who are also Buddhist laypeople; that there is genuine appreciation by householder donors for the benefits of their gifts to Saṅgha members is, in fact, a theme found throughout the Vinaya and Nikāyas.

Boulding notes, second, that grants within an organization, like a family or university, often involve an internal transfer and that the ability to make such an internal transfer is a principal mark of status within a hierarchy. "The higher a person stands in a hierarchy...the more internal grants he has the power to control."[89] The converse, then, would also be viable: the greater the grant one is able to give, the higher the place in the hierarchy one is presumed to hold or, at best, the higher the status one is imputed to have. If the social order in which Buddhism emerges is taken as the institution providing for the internal grant transfer, the attribution of status is normally found at the beginning of textual narratives. In many cases, immediate notice in the narrative is given to the non-renunciant who provides either the audience for the teaching or the context of the ruling, but most importantly, the material support needed by the Saṅgha. Here, then, status for donors, often specifically *gahapati* donors, is conferred by their increasingly wide-spread reputation as well as through the texts which are compiled by the donees elevating these donors to prominence on the basis of the gifts.

Third, central to the grant economy is the integrative factor whereby the giver gives out of identification with the receiver. A grant, Boulding argues, is a sacrifice made in the interest of one's identity to someone or some thing that heightens that identity; and if there is very great sacrifice, that identity is reinforced even more. This process is, in fact, mutual, for grants work best when there is "the building up of integrative structures and communities...[and in which there are] groups of people who have some feelings of identification and benevolence toward each other."[90] Moreover, "the more an individual identifies with some cause, community, or organization, the more likely he is to support it and the greater will be his donations to it."[91] Those *gahapati* donors who are related by family ties to Saṅgha members already gone forth are especially relevant here, as the kin tie seems to remain strong for some time after the renunciation. Indeed, one clear expression of this tie would be to follow a relative into the renunciant life, but when that doesn't happen material support to the monastic community is given not only because a family member belongs but concomitant with his or her belonging.

In examining the pattern of relative-support for the Saṅgha, the greatest majority of donors turn out to be women—mothers, aunts, wives, and sisters of men who have now become *bhikkhus.*[92] There are also men who give when relatives belong to the Sangha, and here male relatives of the Buddha, such as Mahānāma, and of Nakulapitar, are noteworthy. These women, and men, are like the mothers of Vedic *brahmacārins* who give to sons petitioning at the doorway for food; their relatedness to the wanderer is central to the good feeling of giving as well as to any identification they have with the system as a whole. Clearly other patterns of strong identification with Saṅgha are at work as well (personal, ethical, and philosophical commitment being preeminent), but relational ties are some of the most enduring.[93]

Boulding suggests, finally, that grant economy plays a significant role in the redistribution of resources, and that this role is one that strives for an equilibrium among competing groups.[94] The dynamics of the new urbanism may be involved in shifting the balance of wealth away from the hands of tribute-supported *kṣatriya* rulers, and of brahmin receivers of great ritual *dakṣiṇās,* into the hands of the mercantile community. With the rise of the renunciant option, *gahapati* donation helps to bring another new lopsidedness into better balance as well: that between householders and renunciants. The potential for householder extravagance in secular life is thus curbed, and the Saṅgha becomes a significant institution available as an equalizer in drawing off householder surplus. Being a donor, then, means not only reaping spiritual rewards for giving a gift, but contributing to social equilibrium as well.

The Gahapati as Buddhist Lay

The integrative function of the donation process seen as grant economy is probably most obvious in the large number of householder donors who are also laymen *(upāsaka)* and laywomen *(upāsikā).* Thapar has observed that the social context of Buddhism is "an essential part of...[its] religious doctrine"[95] and this may well derive both from the collaborative efforts of individual householders and Saṅgha members as they put together workable Dhammic and Vinayic systems for donation, and from Buddhism's strong appeal to mercantile and other economically energetic groups. The degree of integration of donor and donee varies tremendously, however, and it is a mistake to assume that all *gahapati* donors are personally committed to Buddhism, just as it is to assume that all Buddhist laity are called *gahapatis.* As Wagle points out, the *gahapati* is aligned not only with Buddhism, but with many other groups of wanderers as well, for there are many who seek him out for his growing resources.[96] The variety of renunciant groups householders are committed to is great[97] and, since the donor often feeds whomever comes to the door,[98] it happens that householder followers of one group may feed renunciants of another.[99] The Buddha's views on such interfaith giving are tolerant and are themselves responsible for many conversions to Buddhism.[100]

Perhaps the most substantial non-Buddhist householder audience is from traditional brahmin communities. Many of these brahmins are defenders of Buddhism and some, in time, become disciples in the tradition.[101] Brahmin householders are not only part of the Buddha's audience but conspicuous donors to the Saṅgha as well. There is the brahmin in Andhakavinda, for example, who waits his turn with other country people to provide a meal for the monks. When in the course of two months no turn comes up for him, he becomes mindful of his own personal affairs going to ruin with the waiting, and goes to the monastery dining hall to see for himself what is currently missing so that he can prepare it. Since he does not see conjey and honey-balls, he gets permission from the Buddha, through the intercession of Ānanda, to offer them and does.[102] The continued presence and conservatism of Vedic culture among householders donating to the Buddhist movement is further evident in terms such as *gahapataggi,* referring to the sacred domestic fire maintained by the householder,[103] and *gahapatipaṇḍita,* 'householder scholar.'[104] The fluidity and plurality of this environment in which donors of varied persuasion can give as they will to whomever they will is exemplified by the brahmin village of Pañcasālā in Magadha, whose inhabitants have the distinction of being the only people to *refuse* to give alms to the Buddha even on a festival day.[105]

Pali narratives overwhelmingly identify the householder as the intended audience of Buddhism and, although Buddhism has great tolerance for variety in spiritual development, Dhamma is most specifically for the consumption, inspiration, and conversion of that broad category of *gahapati.* The most important type of *gahapati* for Pali texts, then, are the *gahapatis* who are also laymen or laywomen, for amongst them the exchange of Dhamma and *dāna* may be the most fortuitous. Successful outreach to the householder follows an ideal course: according to the Tevijja Sutta, a householder hears the Dhamma, acquires confidence *(saddhā)* in the three refuges, realizes all the hindrances of the householder life, and sees the contrasting freedom of life in the ocher robe. Forsaking all his wealth and property, and forsaking his relatives, the householder then cuts his hair, shaves his beard, dons the robe, and goes forth 'from the household life into the homeless state' *(agārasmā anagāriyaṃ).*[106]

The material well-being of the Saṅgha, however, depends on this process moving not swiftly but slowly, intense enough at the beginning to turn the householder toward commitment to Buddhism, but leisurely enough in the intervening time before renunciation to continue the householder's procurement of wealth and his use of it in support of the Saṅgha. The most frequent descriptions of the householder donor, then, are descriptions of him or her in this transitional time, applying some but not all effort to spiritual development and equal or more effort to the building up and proper use of his material resources. It is to the Saṅgha's benefit, then, to make this intervening period as desirable as possible: by giving it clear status along a recognized progression to enlightenment, as layman and laywoman; by developing doctrinal systems peculiar to lay needs, focusing in particular on merit; and by establishing an external symbol in the standard white clothes by which the Buddhist householder will be recognized by others.

The technical terms for layman and laywoman *(upāsaka*[107] and *upāsikā)*[108] are from *upa* 'up close' and *ās* 'to sit,' indicating both the direct receipt of teaching from the Buddha himself and the still-present need for a teacher—hence perfect terms for the committed, yet transitional, donor who links the uncommitted with the fully committed. Thus, the Pali portrayal of the *upāsaka gahapati* is as an unstable figure marked by transitional spirituality; the householder is always vulnerable both to temptation from the material world as well as from the full life of a renunciant. The canonical definition exemplifies this, for an *upāsaka/upāsikā* is someone who has taken the triple refuge—in the Buddha, the Dhamma, and the Saṅgha[109]—but who has not yet gone forth into the homeless state. Despite the "unsettled" place of the layperson, the Buddha tells the wanderer Vacchagotta that many hundreds of them have committed to his movement,[110] and they are known openly to the public because they are *odātavasana* 'dressed in white'—an auspicious symbol of purity and well-being[111] worn prior to rebirth in the fully spiritual life of the ocher-robed renunciant.

The key distinguishing feature of the layperson is that he or she hears the Dhamma,[112] the doctrinal formulation of the discovery that brings enlightenment with all its attendant implications. Although he isn't the only audience for the Buddha's sermons (certainly the monks and nuns hear Dhamma as do nonfollowers), the layperson acts as the mainstay listening-post for the missionizing activities of the early movement.[113] The "hearing" of hearing the Dhamma is crucial for, as in the Vedic context, "the respect and reverence in which the sacred scriptures are held" is based on their not being seen but having "to be learnt by hearing them from one's teacher."[114] The acquisition of knowledge through hearing is purer than through other means, for less interferes in the transmission and more authority can be imputed to the source. Buddhist Dhamma, however, works even without a teacher for it is pure and auspicious directly on its own;[115] if indeed there is any convincing in the hearing of the Dhamma it is because of the bare truthfulness of what is heard.[116] Just hearing the Dhamma, however, is not enough: one has to listen to it, to be mindful of it, and to take heart in it. [117] Because the Dhamma is always given out of compassion *(karuṇā)* and empathy *(anukampā)* for the specific vulnerabilities and needs of the audience,[118] the possibility for receptive hearing is heightened. Those who do become laypersons, however, have presumably heard the Dhamma correctly, for it cannot happen if hearers engage in certain trades that injure others[119] or are otherwise spiritually unprepared.

The results of authentically hearing the Dhamma vary. At the very least, a hearer finds pleasure *(abhinandati)* in the teaching and delights in it.[120] Often, hearing the Dhamma causes the curious to become laypersons and those who are already laypersons to go forth into the homeless state, that is, to be accepted into the Saṅgha as *bhikkhus/bhikkhunīs.*[121] It is especially advantageous, however, when hearing the Dhamma results in giving to the Saṅgha. In a transaction evocative of an exchange economy, the word of the Buddha can elicit generous sentiment and, then, support for the movement.[122] The exchange structure can be reversed as well: the donor can give a gift and in return receive a Dhamma talk. In a repeated formula, for example, the layman Udena sends a messenger to the Buddha, who is staying for the rains at Anāthapiṇḍika's monastery in Sāvatthi, with the request that the monks come to the monastery he has just built in Kosala: 'I want to give a gift, and to hear the Dhamma, and to see the bhikkhus.' This formula is then repeated throughout the narrative as Udena, angry over the monks' delay in arriving, proclaims himself to be a benefactor, a doer of good works, and an attendant on the Saṅgha (and is thus due the proper attention of a Dhamma teaching!).[123]

The exchange described by Udena, however—that initiated by a gift and followed by a Dhamma talk—is set out in a number of other places, including Visākhā's gift of a cloth for wiping the face to the Budddha who upon receipt delivers a talk to her. In giving the cloth, however, Visākhā does not ask for Dhamma; what she says is, 'may the Blessed One, O Lord, accept this cloth for wiping the face from me, that is for my prosperity and happiness over a long time.'[124] This appeal is interesting for two reasons. First, the use of the imperative at the beginning signifies a speech act, a performative utterance, such that the command given at the very event of Visākhā's handing over of the wiping cloth is what effects her future providence. Secondly, although she gives, expecting an exchange, what she wants in return is not necessarily Dhamma now but contentment in times to come. This transaction, again, is a deferred exchange or, better, an exchange with a continuing return over time—a gift that keeps on giving.

That some kind of worldliness remains a part of lay householder status is clear from the description *kāmabhogin* or 'enjoyer of pleasures.' While some see the phrase describing lay possession of wealth,[125] others see it describing lay pursuit of sensual pleasures.[126] In either case, however, it underscores again the transitional position of the lay: still bound to the material world and yet, when the phrase follows *odātavasana* 'dressed in white,' committed to the Buddhist mission. The training of the *upāsaka,* moreover, allows him to handle this liminal posture as best as he can. The white-clothed lay householder Sandhāna, for example, does not surprise the renunciant Nigrodha when he arrives in quiet, for Gotama's lay followers are known to be 'trained in quiet, trained in making little noise.'[127] This training begins with taking the vow of triple refuge and proceeds through the five precepts (vowing to abstain from taking life, from stealing, from sexual misconduct, from wrong speech, and from using intoxicants) to a self-contained posture of confidence, moral habit, and renunciation *(saddhā, sīla,* and *cāga)* in living out the Dhamma. Although clearly a social and pleasure-loving creature, the lay householder can work for spiritual advancement in ways that not only transform him internally but are visible to those around him.[128]

Hindrances of the Householder Life

To work for his own spiritual benefit as his sole endeavor is difficult for the householder for he is what the Buddha called *manussagāha,* still 'caught up by humans.' He lives in a mixed society, rejoices and sorrows with his fellows, finds happiness in their happiness and suffering in their suffering, and in this way makes a bond *(yoga)* with them in whatever befalls them.[129] His efforts to achieve a middle pose as a committed Buddhist, still of this world, are hampered by several restrictions, restrictions related to the circumstances he finds himself in as well as his own mental conditioning.

More than anything else, the householder's mentality is grounded in enjoying sense-pleasures.[130] Not only is this defect looked down upon and a source of criticism from others,[131] but a source of self-derision as well. More spiritually aware householders look around them and see that they take unfortunate delight, for example, in Benarsi muslin and sandalwood, in ornamental flowers and cosmetics, and in using gold and silver and, noting this, ask the Buddha to teach them another kind of happiness.[132] While householders know that they are enjoyers of pleasure *(kāmabhogin),* fond of pleasure *(kāmārāma),* delighters in pleasure *(kāmarata),* and rejoicers in pleasure *(kāmasammudita),* they also know that it will be hard for them to cross the 'precipice' *(papāta)* of actually giving these pleasures up—thus the radical difference between the renunciant and the 'many folk' *(bahu jana)*[133] who are bound to this world by *kāma.* A source of solace and satisfaction for householders, however, is given by Buddhist doctrine, for four types of happiness are available to the *kāmabhogin:* the happiness of owning, the happiness of wealth, the happiness of being without debt, and the happiness of being without blame.[134] And each of these types of happiness are so, curiously enough, because of the possibilities of *dāna.*

The grip of the householder life is expressed again by *rajopatha,* 'of the dusty path.'[135] Some interpretations focus on the narrow confinement of life in the house with its stuffy, oppressive, dirty air in stark contrast to open freedom of life in the 'gone forth' state with its clean, pure air. Others find the dust of passion here, and still others the dust of ignorance which conceals knowledge. What is clear from the passages, however, is that however obscuring and confining this dusty life might be, it is difficult to maintain. It is not an easy thing *(na sukara),* these passages say, for one living the household life to practice the spiritual path perfectly and purely.[136] While the answer for some is to give it up and go forth in ocher-robes, this is not always suitable for the householder nor is it entirely suitable for the welfare of the Buddhist movement. If everyone gives up the dusty life, there would be no one to support the pure life. Hence, Buddhist teaching has to provide a clear way through difficulties that will still allow the householder the greatest satisfaction and advantage in committing temporarily to staying precisely where he or she is.

The difficulties of householder life mount even more: not only is one still prey to pleasures and to the obscuration of knowledge, but to innumerable diversions as well. The householder by definition lives in sleeping quarters crowded with children *(puttasambādhasayana);*[137] and this proximity to the young, especially to his own, is a distraction filled with attachment. While he is obliged (by none other than the Siṅgālovada Sutta) to provide the basic necessities to those he lives with,[138] their acquisition is not always easy. But if the collection of necessities is difficult, more so is their protection, that often entails the maintenance of a strong bodyguard.[139] Moreover, the householder has to pay taxes (thus filling up the coffers of the king)[140] and is saddled with numerous administrative chores and with duties and responsibilities at every turn of his way.[141] Most of all, however, is the continuing bondage of his wealth,[142] a theme that pervades the discussion of householder hindrances and that, fortuitously, can be rectified by Buddhist lay ethics.

WOMEN DONORS ON THEIR OWN

As the householder moves onto center-stage amidst the changes of his world, and as *dāna* becomes the religious contract suitably accommodating him to these changes, his own household unit responds as well with the emergence of the *gahapatānī* or 'housemistress' as an independent agent. Not only are householder and housemistress distinguished one from the other in the giving of gifts to renunciants, but women are named as independent donors to the Saṅgha almost as frequently as men. The new autonomy of women in matters of *dāna* reflects a wider involvement of women in economic matters at this time[143] and has its immediate roots in the gift of food by the Vedic wife to renunciant petitioners who appear at the household door. In *dānadharma* "the utmost importance is given to the gift of food"[144] and, when petitioners come to the door, according to the prescriptions for the ritual transaction of *bhikṣā* or alms petition, it is normally the wife who gives out cooked fare into their waiting bowls.[145]

This formal pattern of the Vedic tradition is reflected in the Buddhist context from the beginning, and the featured role of women in the day-to-day practice of lay Buddhism toward the Saṅgha remains significant in Buddhist settings to this day.[146] While some see Buddhist disparagement of women as the norm in Pali texts,[147] these same texts can be read otherwise: as support for the enlightenment of women[148] and for the full participation of women in the lay life of Buddhist donation. The significance of the status of women donors in Buddhism is reflected not only in textual formulations of the alms petition, but in the requisites of the Vedic ritual as well,[149] where the full range of hospitality anxieties are rendered manageable in ritual form.[150]

Hospitality: Binding Vedic Women Donors to the Marital Unit

The Vedic pattern for women as gift-givers derives from both the *śrauta* (public) and the *gṛhya* (domestic) setting. In the solemn sacrifice, it is the guest reception (Ātithyā) of Soma that illuminates the efficacy of the ritual around two central points: the hospitality of the patron and his household in receiving and hosting guests, and the role of the sacrificer's wife in mediating relations with the guest and, most importantly, in representing the household in the gifting of its property. Although the fire god Agni is the frequent guest *(atithi)* of humans at the ritual from Ṛg Vedic time onwards, and although the brahmin officiant is the human "guest *par excellence*" at the ritual,[151] it is the herb King Soma[152] around whom the paradigms of ritual giving are most significantly woven.

In the Ātithyā ceremony, after ritual purchase of the plant and after Soma is brought forward to 'the house of the sacrificer' *(yajamānasya gṛha)* the fire is kindled[153] and Soma is received by the household:

> *(The sacrificer/household) offers hospitality for the continuity of the sacrifice. The wife touches (the Soma cart) from behind, for the wife is the mistress of the household goods; in this way (the household) offers what is approved by the wife. Verily that part of the sacrifice that is the wife makes a pairing. Now this touching (of the Soma cart) from behind by the wife is for the uninterruptedness of the sacrifice.*[154]

Here, the power and successful endurance of the ritual is clearly defined as dependent upon the hospitality of the sacrificer and his household, and the wife's approval is established as essential in the making of the ritual offering.[155] That the whole household is the agent in reception of a ritual guest—represented in the couple *(mithuna)* of husband and wife—is made clear again in a Śatapatha Brāhmaṇa passage:[156]

> *Thus they enclose him (Soma) on two sides by a (husband and wife) couple; wherever in this way a worthy one comes, there indeed all the household members bestir themselves. Thus, he is attended to.*

The ritual wife, as half of the couple, thus ensures the auspicious prosperity of the process by her full presence in the hosting.

The wife is indispensable to hospitality within the ritual specifically because of her relation to household property. Although subject in other ways to the overlordship of her husband, and although united symbolically as one with the husband in the marital unit,[157] the wife has power through use and disposal rights over, as well as responsibilities of care for, goods in the household domain. As seen, TS 6.2.1.1-2[158] declares that in the guest reception of Soma to 'the house of the sacrificer,'[159] the wife is essential to hospitality settings because it is she who is the 'mistress of the household goods' *(patnī hi pārīṇahyasyeśe)*, such that "her *permission* to give [household goods]...away to a guest is required" for a ritual's efficacy.[160] Stephanie Jamison has discussed this passage and the possible origin of *pā́rīṇahya* in "the moveable goods that the bride brought to her new home at marriage" as a way of focusing on the rights of dominion a wife may have over a wider range of goods and property in the household.[161] In the *śrauta* setting, she argues, the ritual wife is seen as guardian and manager of the household property and not only has to be present at the occasion of the ritual, but has to give agreement to ritual offerings as well. As indicative of a wider paradigm, *śrauta* hospitality offered to Soma comes to be emblematic of that offered to all guests, particularly to brahmin guests[162] and to the increasing numbers of wandering petitioners appearing at the household door.

The linkage between the Vedic housemistress and her household's hospitality obligations is clear as well in the *gṛhya* context. Identified fully with the house as her resting place and sanctuary, the housemistress is the representative of the hospitality of the domestic fire.[163] This is most conspicuous in the *bhikṣā* relationship ritualized in the appearance of the *brahmacārin,*[164] and later of *saṃnyāsin,*[165] at the door for food. In the case of the *brahmacārin,* the encounter at the door is governed by the identity of the donor and the identity of the petitioner, as well as by whether the student is coming at the time of his Upanayana or as part of the actual practice of his student hood. The donor, that is, the housemistress at whose house the student petitions for food at the time of the Upanayana, is identified by the majority of the Gṛhya Sūtras, first, as the student's own mother and, then, as a woman who will not refuse him.[166]

For food during his daily alms round, the student is to petition women in the reverse order of the initiation. Thus, the Śatapatha Brāhmaṇa enjoins the student to petition daily from women in whom he has confidence and, if no others are to be found, to petition from his teacher's wife and finally from his mother.[167] Manu actually prohibits the student from petitioning on a day-to-day basis from relatives of his teacher or from his mother's family unless there are no strangers' houses available, in which case he is allowed to begin with his mother's blood relations.[168]

The identity of the petitioner is announced by the student himself at the very moment of the encounter and, as given in Vedic texts, the announcement upholds the idealized social schema of the tradition. According to the Pāraskara Gṛhya Sūtra, a brahmin student is to petition from a householder woman by putting *bhavati* 'lady' at the beginning of his request, a *kṣatriya/rājanya* student by putting 'lady' in the middle, and a *vaiśya* student by putting 'lady' at the end.[169] Although other texts have formulae that can be applied either to a male or a female donor, the norm for the verbal petition is for use in approaching the householder wife.[170] For her part, the housemistress is enjoined by the Dharma Sūtras not to refuse alms that are requested by students for fear of violating those who are truly conscientious about their vows, to examine the qualities of those who petition and to be favorable to those who are worthy and, finally, to give according to her ability.[171]

In the Vedic encounter at the threshold door, then, the *pārīṇahya* model is at work: as dispenser of the household goods and as representative of the household in an *ātithya* 'hospitality' setting, it is the woman of the household, the *gṛhapatnī,* to whom the *brahmacārin* goes as giver of food on behalf of the household. That a woman as hospitality representative of the marital unit actually manages the property of the household is critical in the threshold encounter and, in this way, a woman's *dāna* identity is formulated early on by the structure of her marriage.

If the obligations of the Vedic relationship rest upon a view of hospitality in which the agent of that *ātithya* behavior is the household, represented by the presence and hospitable functioning of the housemistress, there are only a few rules obligatory to the behavior of the guest at the point of the encounter; most rest upon the host, that is, upon the hostess. The householder wife here does not act independently,[172] however, but instead stands in for the household itself for not only does she complete the household, but she is the one whose graciousness to others cements the bonds of a hierarchical and highly segmented society.

The *bhikṣā* encounter between the *brahmacārin* and his donor thus serve to reaffirm the social placement of the participants within the larger structures of Brāhmaṇic society. While the Upanayana petitioning brings the student into a newly distant and more formalized relationship with his own family, especially with his own mother, daily petitioning brings him into greater contact with other families in his wider social world. The formalized relationship of *bhikṣā* heightens his awareness both of caste boundaries and of the need for a solemn, purity-maintaining, etiquette. It also, importantly, underscores the traditional role Vedic women have in representing the household as a critical part of that etiquette.

Individual Agency: Buddhist Women Donors and Risk

The Vedic relationships of alms petition have formal parallels in Buddhist texts, but the Vinayic understanding indicates that much has changed, particularly for women. Similar to the case of the *brahmacārin,* the Buddhist *bhikkhu/bhikkhunī* is obliged by virtue of admission into the Saṅgha to take up the bowl and outer-robe and to go on tour for alms food once a day during the period before noon.[173] Pali accounts of the *piṇḍapāta/piṇḍacāra* prescribe in exceedingly careful detail the wearing of the robe, the walking amidst the houses, the comportment of the body as the renunciant meets the *gahapatānī* at the door, the holding of the bowl, and the careful focusing of the mind.[174]

In contrast to the Vedic paradigm, however, there is a shift in the Buddhist relationship from household obligations toward the renunciant to individual patronage of him or her, that is, a shift from responsibilities that impinge upon the donor to prescriptions given over to the monk or nun. Thus, instead of donor hospitality, the relationship is governed by renunciant dependence *(upanissaya)*: others are, by open acknowledgement, relied upon to supply food, robes, lodgings, and medicine.[175] Nevertheless, although set now in the context of voluntary patronage instead of obligatory hospitality, the Buddhist encounter remains an encounter primarily with the woman of the household. Thus, with formal pattern from the *brahmacārin* model, this patronage is, again, a style of matronage.[176]

Two elements are critical as the renunciant walks among the houses, clad properly in three robes and waiting silently for the *gahapatānī* to offer food: the anonymity of both the donor and the petitioner and the need for the petitioner to evoke the donor's goodwill. In the Cullavagga, the renunciant is enjoined to walk among the houses with his eyes cast down,[177] looking a plough's length ahead,[178] and not to look at the face of the donor of the alms. Based on the commentary, I.B. Horner notes that "the donor may be a woman or a man. One is not to look at his (or her) face at the time when the alms are being given."[179]

The contrast to the practice of the *brahmacārin* is striking. Not only is the Buddhist petitioner not to look at the face of the donor, and thereby not to notice the donor's gender (although the texts are clear that the donor is normally the mistress of the house), but there are also no prescriptions for announcing the status of the petitioner. Although certain unmistakable signs will signal to the donor that it is a Sakyaputtiya, a follower of the Sakyamuni, who has come to the door—the color, number, and hang of the robes, the material of the bowl, and the comportment of the body—there is no overt sign, and certainly no verbal formula, indicating the petitioner's status along the pathway. It is true that the donor accrues greater merit by giving to increasingly more productive 'fields of merit' *(puññakkhetta)*,[180] but external markers for these are rarely found in the texts prescribing the encounter. A later practice found particularly in the Theragāthā may prescribe, however, the self-identification of *arahants* with "I am an *arahant,* worthy of gifts," in order to compensate for the increased unfamiliarity of donors in an urban environment with the spiritual status of individual renunciants and, therefore, of the quality of merit resulting from seeds sown in particular renunciant fields. In the traditional Buddhist paradigm, rather than focusing on the social markers of those in the *bhikṣā* relationship (e.g., caste and gender), however, where a woman's place as woman vis-à-vis the household is heightened as in the Vedic paradigm, the tradition turns a blind eye to the externals of gender, in the case of both the donor and the petitioner, and focuses instead on the internal qualities of those in the transaction.[181]

While the downcast eyes reaffirm the anonymity of the threshold relationship, they also express a virtue crucial to the dependence of the renunciant upon the donor: humility. Because the merit to the donor increases with the spiritual advancement of the recipient and because the inner spiritual advancement of the recipient is thought to be visible in his or her external comportment, donors are more likely to give when the recipient's behavior fits their notion of worthiness. Downcast eyes, then, are a critical sign of deferential reliance upon the generosity of the donor and of a renunciant's need to keep these channels open.

Preserving the goodwill of the donor is effected, secondly, by a renunciant's ritualized "testing of the waters" in which he or she discerns how willing the donor, here explicitly the housemistress, might be to giving food. According to the Cullavagga, at each instance of petitioning food, a monk or nun has to do the following :

> *While standing, he [or she] should consider: 'Is she willing to give alms food or is she not willing to give?' If she lays her work aside, or rises from her seat, or wipes a spoon, or wipes a dish, or sets it out, he [or she] should stand still thinking: 'it is as though she is willing to give.'*[182]

The giving of specific signs—the transfer of attention, the getting up, the readying of utensils—indicates that the donor herself is open to the encounter and is willing to give on the basis of perceptions of the renunciant's integrity as well as out of her own goodwill. This shift from the obligation of hospitality to the search for goodwill not only lays the burden on the Buddhist petitioner to demonstrate each time anew, through signs of inner worthiness, the appropriateness of the dependent relationship but opens up an element of choice for the woman being petitioned.

The Jain case is reflective of the common formal pattern but applies a central Jain principle. Aptly, the Ācārāṅga Sūtra notes that the donor petitioned is normally a woman and, as with the *brahmacārin,* prescribes that the Jain renunciant approaches the donor with a verbal formula. To the householder's wife, sister, daughter-in-law or nurse, or male or female slave or servant, the renunciant says: 'Oh long-lived one! (or Oh sister!) will you give me something to eat?' Ever mindful of the need for *ahiṁsā,* however, if the woman, in agreement, moves to wipe or wash the hands or spoon or plate in water, the renunciant is to intervene by asking her not to, saying, 'if you want to give me something, give it as it is,' for washing might cause injury to waterborne creatures. The concern for *ahiṁsā* is so great that Jain renunciants have to choose carefully which donors to petition from,[183] how and with whom to walk, and the exact manner for acceptance of food into the bowl. Water is of particular concern for not only can the washing of hands in preparation for giving the food kill living creatures, but water to drink is, preferably, to be poured by the renunciant him or herself.[184] Moreover, any food that is suspected of containing live matter—in the form, for example, of seeds, sprouts, mildew or dust—is unacceptable for alms and has to be rejected by the petitioner.[185]

Jain injunctions are shaped throughout by the principle of noninjury. While the woman serves as donor,[186] as she has in other cases, the governing of her actions is not hospitality etiquette or a willingness prompted by renunciant's worthiness but the need to maintain *ahiṁsā* both in the process of giving and in the food that is given. This principle is visible in the issue of bathing:

while both *brahmacārins* and *bhikkhus* and *bhikkhunīs* are to bathe regularly and to wear clean clothes, Jain mendicants normally do not, hoping to avoid killing living beings lodged on their skin. This often gives rise to a smell that is notably disagreeable to householders.[187] Whether for reasons of *ahiṃsā* or of an indifference to the outside world,[188] the effect is to disregard a principle that Buddhists now hold so central, that is, the maintenance of goodwill in the donor.

Thus, the paradigm shift for Buddhist women is manifest in altered prescriptions for renunciant encounter. This shift has at least two aspects. First, the subordination of women to the marital unit, and the consequent definition of women as given by the structure of marriage, is loosening somewhat so that separation from the strict confines of the household becomes possible. No longer the religious unit having agency for ritual effectiveness, the household as represented in the Buddhist *gahapati* and *gahapatānī* is now more generally a social unit with significant economic implications. The redefinition of the household within a broader network of resources and responsibilities aligns its members with channels supporting the young religion and, as wealth can increasingly be directed in ways different from Vedic patronage, women's role in that redirection is often independent of consultation with her household.

Second, the shift away from defining women exclusively as the hospitality representative of the household is concurrent with the emergence of a new individualism,[189] best reflected in what Pali women do with wealth. In that the Buddhist prescriptions for the renunciant encounter place final agency in the hands of the housemistress at the door, she is unlike the Vedic wife who gives on behalf of the whole household. As the actual individual who comes to the door, she is the one who decides then and there whether giving or not giving is something she wants or is prepared to do. The element of choice in the Buddhist setting, and of the play of personal judgment and of inventive agency by a female donor, is strikingly illustrated in the story of Suppiyā. Hearing of a sick monk in need of a meat broth, Suppiyā goes in search of something in the market with which to make it. Finding none (this being a non-slaughter day, *māghata ajjā),* she remains intent upon making a medicinal gift to the monk and eventually cuts a piece of her own thigh for the simmering. When the broth is done, she has a servant bring it to the monk and herself goes to her room in weak confinement. Invited to Suppiyā's house by her husband, the Buddha then asks for her and, when she comes before him, the cut out of her thigh is healed immediately. The Buddha then returns to the community and berates the monk who has accepted the broth for not inquiring as to its origins, ruling finally against the use of human flesh as food.[190]

The separability of a woman's wealth and her independent use of it are illustrated in two further stories. In both, well-meaning parents use three piles of wealth, one of them belonging specifically to the mother, to entice the renunciant son back into the household life. In the case of the monk Sudinna, part of what he refuses is *mātumattikaṃ itthikāya itthidhanaṃ* 'the mother's portion, the wife's property due her because she is a woman/wife,'[191] and in that of the monk Raṭṭhapāla it is *mattikaṃ dhanaṃ* 'the mother's property.'[192] Significant to both stories is that the property of the wife is clearly differentiated and that the mother of each monk has given permission for this property to devolve separately upon the "errant" son should he choose to return to householder life.[193]

Some measure of the economic independence available to women is reflected in Buddhist encouragement to wives to learn the business of their husbands. In this instance, the Buddha's counsel to the daughters of the *gahapati* Uggaha is not only to guard and protect the material property of their future husbands and to manage deftly and sensitively the household staff, but to learn their husbands' crafts as well. The daughters respond:

> *We will be skilled and diligent at the domestic crafts of our husbands, whether they be of wool or of cotton, focusing on understanding the techniques therein in order to do it and to get it done.*[194]

On another occasion, a wife counsels her sick husband, that, having learned his crafts well, she will be able to support herself and her family prosperously through its proceeds when he dies.[195] The most notable example of women's economic independence, of course, is the great number of individual women donors to the Saṅgha who on their own give not only monumental quantities of food, medicine, and robes, but land and lodgings as well.

The possibility for a woman to be a donor of the four Buddhist requisites *(parikkhāra)* illuminates further the changes in the traditional *bhikṣā* relationship at the door. Although the fact that Pali households are normally marked by both the householder and his wife indicates the continued influence of the Vedic "unit" model of marriage *(mithuna)*, of the hospitable *(ātithya)* reception of guests, and of Vedic views on household wealth *(pārīṇahya)*, the ritual prescriptions for the renunciant encounter tell more. That the petitioner does not look at the face of the donor and that the donor may be a man or a woman,[196] suggests the new trend at work. If it is not important that the food giver at the door be a woman, then the understanding of the wife as manager and dispenser of household goods is of less importance than in the Vedic paradigm. What seems to be more significant is that whoever makes the donation does so out of individual support for the movement, rather than out of hospitality obligations reflected in female management of household goods. The positioning of a woman as a donor in her own right, then, is not ultimately the attribution of a higher status, but a sign that gender, in theory, does not matter in the *dāna* process. In practice, moreover, it means that women's identity is not bound by an accident of birth but open to redefinition through individual actions.

Having said this, one curious item from the Vinaya prescription remains. Buddhist discipline is not laid down as a simple list of rules, but often set within narrative contexts purporting to give an originating situation or a defining historical arena.[197] The classic prescription for the *piṇḍapāta/piṇḍacāra* in the Cullavagga is no exception and its narrative home is helpful in illuminating the new setting for women in the Buddhist world. According to the Cullavagga, there is once a time when a certain unnamed monk, who is dressed improperly and who walks amongst houses improperly, happens to come upon a woman lying naked on her back in the inner chamber of her house. The husband seeing the monk there accuses him of seducing his wife and beats him, waking the woman who then comes to the monk's defense. Hearing of this, the Buddha lays down rules for proper alms-touring,[198] that emphasize the monk's (or nun's) taking more stringent measures to reign in his (or her) senses and to guarantee donor-suitable comportment.

At first glance, this seems an odd mechanism by which to introduce alms-touring rules—until it's remembered that, in the Vedic paradigm, marriage is the establishing structure for a woman's *bhikṣā* obligations. The advantage of using this structure is that in marriage the natural, and potentially explosive, erotic tendencies of women[199] can be tamed and, in their domestication, the threat they pose to the social and moral order defused. The institution of marriage itself is then the context within which sexual pleasure *(rati)* can be expressed and the goal of children *(prajā)* pursued,[200] such that wives who allow these boundaries to frame their identity are honored and revered by their husbands.[201] The Vedic paradigm of the *bhikṣā* encounter, then, is founded on and circumscribed by the properly functioning institution of marriage: the two women specifically named in the defining and sustaining ritual of Upanayana *bhikṣā* are the wife of the father and the wife of the teacher. Although Dharma literature is especially mindful of the distracting and seductive powers of women,[202] these do not play into the threshold encounter with a renunciant, for it is here that the controlling model of the household unit is so strong that the untamed sexuality of the woman at the door is rendered moot by her married state.

In the Buddhist case, however, where the household unit is not necessarily the defining unit, the *bhikṣācara,* that is, the *bhikkhu* or *bhikkhunī* is instructed to be forever on his or her guard. Unlike Vedic prescriptions giving those households-not-to-beg-from as those whose heads do not have Vedic expertise, but saying nothing specific about certain women's households,[203] Buddhist prescriptions deride those who petition among prostitutes, widows, grown girls, eunuchs, and nuns[204] in order to protect, apparently, the monk from the untamed sexual powers of such people. More specifically, in giving rules for the renunciant encounter, the Cullavagga text works within the newer context in which the woman who meets the *bhikkhu* at the door, and who indicates her willingness to give by certain subtle actions in the kitchen, is doing so not necessarily as representative of the household unit but as an individual sympathetic to the new religion.

Appearing, then, in a role that is, for all intents and purposes, unprotected by the Vedic ramparts of marriage, the woman becomes a source of a more loosely contained sexuality against which the vulnerable renunciant now has to guard himself with all his mindfulness. Like the more general Vedic understanding of women, the canon's view of the individualized encounter is that, while it is the woman who tempts, it is the male renunciant who has to be on his guard.

While the *piṇḍapāta* rules set within this story of the naked encounter seem to be exclusively about the sexual seductiveness of women, they are in fact as much, if not more, about maintaining the goodwill of the donor. With the Cullavagga passage as the base for these procedural rules, this goodwill is certain to be preserved if the onus for the safeness of the threshold relationship rests upon the renunciant. That it is the responsibility of the renunciant for maintaining the sexual safeness of the donor-renunciant relationship is reaffirmed textually when the genders are switched; a number of times in the Bhikkhunī Vibhaṅga nuns are enjoined to keep their desires in strict control when around male donors,[205] indicating that bearing the burden of safeness in the threshold encounter is not, fundamentaly, a gender-bound issue.

The Encounter as a Non-Gendered Transaction

The transaction at the door is a central feature of lay-renunciant relations, in part because it serves the nutritional needs of monks and nuns. It is clearly more than this, however, for as a truly religious act it contributes to spiritual transformation as well. If this act does, in fact, effect fundamental change, and if the paradigm for giving is in fact the woman's posture at the door, it becomes important to examine what place gender has, if any, in shaping the transformational process of the alms encounter.

Most influential on the Buddhist understanding of the process is the view of "causal productiveness" developed within the context of the early Vedic ritual: the belief that there is a power set in motion by the ritual procedure that produces a future result, and the belief specifically that the individual is the beneficiary of his own ritual action at a later time. The formative threads of this early quest to understand the mechanisms of causality eventually produces the traditional Indian views on karma and rebirth *(punarjanman, punarmṛtyu* and *saṃsāra).* And out of this development in the *śrauta* and *gṛhya* contexts, significantly, emerge values instructive for male and female identity. In the influence of these threads on the Buddhist alms encounter, however, ambiguities arise due to conflictingly engendered ideas; but, whatever ambiguities there are they are solved with the rituals' loss of gendered properties when expressed in the Buddhist setting.

As noted, it is in the ritual efficacy associated with hospitable reception of ritual guests, such as Soma, that the causal process becomes associated with the identity of the Vedic wife. Representative of the household and manager of its property, the wife's proper action within the boundaries of this identity, ensures that the ritual process will produce the desired short-term fruit of prosperity for the household, and the desired long-term fruit of future spiritual advantage for, principally, the sacrificer. Here female identity becomes associated with the continued prosperity of the extended household as it upholds the socio-ritual obligations of its place within the Vedic schema.

The shaping of male identity takes place in a number of different contexts, each consistently delineating family lineage as the construct of enduring value. Two of these contexts are especially significant in understanding the eventual mechanism of causation taking place in the Buddhist encounter. In the first, speculation focuses on what happens at death and, in particular, where the person might go and how individual identity might be maintained. Ṛg Vedic funeral verses suggest the dispersal of parts of the body into appropriate natural elements[206] or the movement of the mind *(manas)* itself out toward natural habitats.[207] Attempts to control this process ritually, to the auspicious benefit of both the departed and the survivors, is paramount and, although the ideas about rebirth are sketchy, hopes for the human mechanism of control are increasingly elaborate. To the point, although the verses can be said of any deceased, their use in later ritual settings[208] suggests that the generic deceased is, in fact, a dead man; that is, person here means male person.

This concern for continuity after death, and for the mechanics of ensuring and controlling it, are developed in the 'rite of transfer' *(sampratti/sampradāna)*[209] whereby a dying father gives his own person up into that of his son. Working out of a Vedic heritage that holds that the son is both the symbolic immortality of the father here on earth as well as his actual continuity, [210] the rite of transfer as laid out in the Upaniṣads effects the transfer through a series of responsive utterances. In it, when the father pronounces 'I will place my speech in you,' the son responds 'I place your speech in me,' and this pattern of antiphonal utterances then moves sequentially through functions such as breathing, seeing, hearing, tasting, acting, moving, and thinking up to full transfer of the father into the son and the father's death.[211] In this way, the ritual ensures the continuity of the father through the son and, in time, of the son through his grandson in an ongoing lineage sequence, through the power of performative speech. The person as male person is linked uninterruptedly into a sequence of 'immortality' by the potency of the linked members' own verbal activity.[212]

Male identity established in the context of lineage continuity is the basis, second, for the ritual efficacy of the funeral and ancestral rites. The early notion of *iṣṭāpūrta,* for example, whereby the person unites with the fruits of his own and other's ritual action after death is tied primarily to the deceased's being male and to his connections with previously deceased male ancestors *(pitaraḥ)* and to still surviving male descendants.[213] Through the Śrāddha offerings, the son guarantees a happy life for his father after death as well as for several generations of immediately preceding fathers. Because the dead need the assistance of the still living in order "to emigrate from this world to that higher one, to pass from the dangerous condition of a disembodied spirit *[preta]* to the secure role of pitṛ among his own pitaraḥ,"[214] the negotiation of this passage in the *sapiṇḍīkaraṇa* rite requires regular nourishment for the creation of a temporary body necessary for the process. During the rites, for example, offerings of cooked white rice *(piṇḍa)* are needed for the remembering, part by part, of the *preta's* intermediate body and, through continued ritual manipulation of the symbolic nourishments of *piṇḍa* and of cups of water, and of the honorifics of incense, flowers, lamps, and white threads for clothing,[215] the deceased eventually moves to "the triple world of the immigrant dead."[216] In addition to providing for the transitional well-being of the newly dead, the postcremation Śrāddha rites establish and reaffirm the *sapiṇḍa* relationships, the ritual bonds between living men and preceding generations of deceased male ancestors. Although these rites can be performed as well for maternal relations, the Vedic standard focuses on the paternal lineage and on the subsumption of male identity within it.[217]

In these ways, then, female and male identity come to be defined within different but related constructs that stem from Vedic ritual. While the identity of the woman/wife is *ritualized in the hospitality etiquette* to be shown a guest (e.g.,to Soma, the brahmin guest, and the *brahmacārin),* as *based in the household,* the identity of the man/son is *ritualized in the rites of transfer* from a dying father and in the Śrāddha offerings by the son to paternal ancestors, as *based in family lineage.* In the one case (female identity), proper action affirms the structure of the community over space and, in the other (male identity), it affirms the continuity of the community over time. When these threads come together as formal Vedic remnants within the setting of the Buddhist renunciant encounter, the alms ritual as prescribed in the Vinaya not only combines them into a more complex understanding of the mechanisms of causality, but it brings together conflictingly gendered components. Specifically, the norm in the Cullavagga is that a female donor at the household door gives to a male renunciant who receives *piṇḍa.* The gender discordance here is that Vedic practice does not conspicuously call for a woman to give *piṇḍa* to benefit "the dead."[218] Through a now more complex construction, the Buddhist encounter solves this gender ambiguity by rendering the gender aspects moot.

Thus, one of the most important changes in the Buddhist ritual is the de-gendering of the offices of both donor and donee. On the donor side, the guest etiquette proffered by an obligated housemistress becomes donation offered by a willing follower, male or female; and, on the donee side, the ancestral dead served *piṇḍa* in hopes of prospering from an enduring male lineage becomes a humble renunciant, monk or nun. In this way, the degendering takes place in clear context of individualism, illumined sharply by the Buddhist doctrine of kamma, where one reaps exactly what one sows. Although in form, parallels to Vedic ritual persist, the meaning is sufficiently "Buddhized" such that, by doctrine, the donor and donee stand in for no one but themselves and can be either male or female: *gahapati* or *gahapatānī, bhikkhu* or *bhikkhunī.*

If view of causality not fully explained by the earlier mechanics of the ritual,[219] a new structure emerges that fits more constructively into Buddhist thought and that, for the discussion here, confirms the movement away from gendered categories. The image that comes into use, possibly from the expansion of agriculture in the Gaṅgā Valley, is that of the field. In this image, just as a farmer sows seed in a field and reaps a harvest, so a donor gives gifts to a renunciant and makes merit. Although seemingly simple, the sowing and reaping imagery becomes manifoldly complex as the relation between donors and the Saṅgha grows symbiotically, in such a way that there are many gradations of farmers/donors,[220] seeds/gifts,[221] and fields/renunciants.[222] Moreover, the act of sowing/giving[223] changes depending on the agent's nature, and the growing in the field depends on the frequency and quality of the rain and sunlight, ongoing attention to the field, and the timing of the harvest.[224] In all, the prosperity of the result, that is, of the harvest/merit—both of which are the foundations of enduring life—depend upon a great many variables.[225] For purposes here, it is enough to make two points. First, in the shift to a new image for describing the causal process of alms giving, Buddhism leaves behind gendered structures and uses instead an image in which the elements can be either male or female: though male with no feminine version, the *kassaka* as farmer does not need to be male to do the sowing; moreover, both the seed *(bīja)* and the field *(khetta)* are already neuter and are treated in Buddhism without thought to a gendered role. Second, the shift to a new image does not involve, after *de*-gendering, a second process of *re*-gendering. Although the traditional Hindu view casts the field cultivator as male and the cultivated field as female—with Sītā's father, the ploughing King Janaka, and mother, the furrowed Earth, as clear exemplars of this stereotype—these renderings are rare in Pali texts. [226]

As the context of householder life changes, so does householder religious affiliation with the Pali *gahapati* and *gahapatānī* emerging as much more open-ended and flexible religious consumers. Available now to a number of groups to provide resources, the householder and housemistress experience a new freedom in choosing their alliances. Moreover, since many are involved in trade and since the merchants are not well-provided for in the Vedic religious system, the availability of so many spiritual possibilities is tremendously invigorating. As one of these possibilities, early Buddhism responds with a clear, well-organized, and systematic schema for lay religious life, including teachings on proper relationships, good conduct, and values for using wealth.[227] While there is nothing doctrinally that prohibits lay meditation, day-to-day impediments prove significant,[228] and practices such as donation (as a part of good conduct) become the easiest and most opportune way for householder commitments to be effective. Donation is good for, as Harvey Aronson notes, harm does not ever come to a family from the practice of giving gifts.[229]

In spite of the Dhammic importance of giving, however, the householder life remains the antipodal symbol of monastic virtue. The *gahapati* and *gahapatānī* are by circumstance *kāmabhogins,* enjoying those very things that homeless wanderers vow to give up. Moreover, they are reminders to renunciants of what they once were but now can no longer be. The separation is sometimes artificial, however, for monastic renunciation is not fully authentic when texts focus on, for example, which donor gives the most sumptuous food[230] and how resplendent gone forth lodgings can be. And these gone forth cannot be too far gone with householder support so critical to the Saṅgha's material survival.

Whatever the spiritual defects of their place, however, householder husband and wife are treated with the utmost respect in Pali texts. There is honor in the family life,[231] an advantageous address[232] and, most importantly, the designation of *sappurisa* 'good person,' as someone who cares for the welfare of others.[233] To be a good person, one has to be able to act responsibly and in consonance with a set of ethical standards and this, perhaps, is one of the crucial elements represented by the new houseperson: that of the individual. In this setting, householders move away from conformity in a group to separately choosing affiliation and separately making free use of their wealth. Steven Collins, in fact, makes a case that the houseperson, as one who lives in a house, becomes the very symbol of individuality, for in the *saṃsāric* cycle the house or the abode comes to represent a station for the self in the pursuit of its perfection.[234] Householder individuality needs guidelines, however, and the emergent Buddhist institution gives these novice practitioners just that.

ENDNOTES

1. Reynolds, p. 71.
2. Ghosh, pp. 20-21, 41.
3. Thapar, *Lineage to State,* p. 17.
4. Thapar, *Lineage to State,* p. 41.
5. Thapar, *Lineage to State,* pp. 37-38. The term *gṛhapati* is associated with ritual wealth from very early times. In the Ṛg Veda, it refers to the fire-god Agni who as 'lord of the home' presides over the domestic hearth-place ensuring the continued reception of sacrificial offerings from human petitioners and the continued return-bestowal of blessings by the gods. Because the hearth-place is the crucible for the transmutation of offerings and blessings between man and god, its perpetual care guarantees the enduring presence of wealth in Vedic homes. For references to Agni as *gṛhapati* see, for example, RV 1.12.6; 1.36.5; 1.60.4; 2.1.2; 4.9.4; 4.11.5; 5.8.1,2; 6.15.13, 19; 6.16.42; 6.48.8; 7.1.1; 7.15.2; 7.16.5; 8.60.19; 8.102.1; 10.91.10; 10.118.6; 10.122.1.

   In one early and well-known case, *gṛhapati* actually refers to a human head of the household: 'lead us to suitable property *(vasu)*, 'sings the poet to the god Pūṣan in RV 6.53.2, 'to one we can count on, to the expected poet's pay *(dakṣiṇā)*, to a *gṛhapati* agreeable (to our service).' Here the householder is understood as the suitable, propertied, responsible patron of priestly prowess, whom Pūṣan, the god of prosperity, can provide for the skillful, unemployed singer.

By the time of the Śatapatha Brāhmaṇa, *gṛhapati* is a designation given to the principal sacrificer patronizing the ritual, who as lord of the home has primary control over the domestic wealth, some of which will then be given to the officiating priests as *dakṣiṇā*. See ŚB 11.8.4.1; 12.1.1.1.; Eggeling, *Śatapatha Brāhmaṇa* 4.xxv.

6. Thapar, *Lineage to State*, pp. 39, 42.
7. Thapar, *Lineage to State*, p. 157; Chakravarti, pp. 87-93.
8. Thapar, *Lineage to State*, p. 159.
9. Heesterman, *"Dákṣiṇā,"* p. 242.
10. Collins, p. 66.
11. Wagle, pp. 71, 74, 77.
12. Thapar, *History of India*, pp. 68-69.
13. E.g., M 1.125; A 2.57ff., 61. While the 'accompanying role' of the *gahapatānī* is historically parallel to that of the sacrificer's wife, the *yajamānapatnī*, the Pali housemistress is, in fact, much more involved, and often independently so, in the material support of the young Saṅgha.
14. E.g., D 1.62, 169, 250; 3.180; M 1.179; 2.171; S 4.347; A 1.117, 137, 274; 2.125; 3.210; 5.40. The form *puttī* is rare in the texts, occurring primarily in the Jātaka compound *rājāputtī*, 'princess,' leaving the *putta* here to function generally, without necessary reference to specific gender. Nevertheless, in normal usage *gahapatiputta* seems to refer primarily to the male offspring, first-born, who will become the next head of household, hence the 'householder's eldest son.' (See the gloss in Vin 4.224 on *gahapatiputta* as *nāma yo koci puttabhātaro*, 'whoever are brothers and sons.') Another term sometimes found in early texts is *kulaputta* (e.g., M 1.16, 193; A 4.284) meaning son of a good or respected family.
15. Wagle, p. 71.
16. Some are farmers *(kassaka gahapati* or *kassaka gahapatika)* (Vin 1.240-45), following the livelihood of a large majority of those living in small villages and rural areas. They make a living not only by tending cattle but also by cultivating cereals, especially evident in the increased production of rice *(sāli)* (A 1.241-42; see also Wagle, pp. 150-51; and Misra, p. 247). Other householders are wood workers or perhaps wood traders or sellers *(dārukammika gahapati)* (A 3.391), and still others like the householder "Firetools" are builders or master carpenters *(thapati)* (M 3.144-48). The increased use of iron for the clearing and cultivation of land directly benefits householders like these, whose own labors produce goods for a wider market. See Thapar, *Lineage to State*, p. 92.

17. Sn no. 404.
18. Among, for example, field ploughers, cowherders, archers, or servants to the king (A 3.229). See the discussion in Wagle, pp. 135-36.
19. D 1.71-72.
20. A 2.81-82.
21. Vin 1.273; S 1.92. See Chakravarti, pp. 73-79.
22. See Wagle, p. 147.
23. Vin 2.110-12; 146-48. Like other householders, *seṭṭhis* are also family men, for the early canon knows of the *seṭṭhibhariyā* the 'merchant's wife' (Vin 1.270-72) as well as the *seṭṭhiputta* the 'merchant's son' (Vin 1.275). Horner addresses the question of the *seṭṭhiputta* specifically and argues that while he is in fact a young merchant he is 'not yet the head of the firm, for his description as *putta* mean[s] that his father...[is] still alive.' Horner, *Book of the Discipline* 2.xlvii.
24. Horner, *Book of the Discipline* 2.xlvii; Thapar *Lineage to State*, pp. 94-95, 103.
25. Gokhale, p. 395; Misra, pp. 260-62.
26. Wagle, pp. 28-29; see also pp. 22, 82, 84, 118.
27. Misra, pp. 260-61.
28. Wagle, p. 29.
29. Thapar, *Lineage to State,* pp. 86, 88.
30. Thapar, *Lineage to State,* p. 85.
31. See RV 10.90.12.
32. E.g., Vin 2.239; D 1.91; 3.82-83; M 2.128-29, 150, 151; A 3.242; 4.202; see also M 2.132, 147, 149. See also M 2.89, 177-184; S 1.102, 166; 4.219; 5.51-52; A 1.162; 2.194; 3.214, 226, 229; 4.259. There are occasional passages where *brāhmaṇa* is the first in the list (M 2.177), and where the four (headed most often by *khattiya)* are followed by a fifth, lower, ranking, that of the *caṇḍāla.* (S 1.102, 166; A 1.162; 3.214, 226, 229). On the issue of Brāhmaṇic versus Buddhist ordering of the *vaṇṇa* ranks, see Gombrich, *Theravada Buddhism*, p. 49; Wagle, p. 133; and Misra, pp. 35-36, 166-67. Although the Dīgha has a lengthy discussion of the origin and characteristics of the *vaṇṇa* ranks, indicating that the categories are known to the compilers of the canon, the discussion is resolutely Buddhist not only in using the Buddhist caste order for ranking but also in giving a Buddhist take on the story as well: greed, desire, and the hoarding of goods play an important role in human evolution (D 3.80-98, see Thapar, *Lineage to State*, p. 120). The ranks in the first list (the *vessa* list of four members) also define different *kulas* or families (Vin 3.184-85; 4.80, 100, 177, 272; M 1.284. See Wagle, pp. 119-121.), different *maṇḍalas* or social circles (D 3.80-98) in which people of like birth exhibit like characteristics, and different wealths *(dhana* [M 2.84-86] or *sandhana* [M 2.180]) assigned to them as appropriate.

33. D 1.136-37; 3.16-17, 46; M 1.86; A 1.66; 2.74; 3.328. It intersects with the first, however, in its description of *kula* families (Vin 2.161 *[kula]* and M 3.177; S 1.94; A 2.86; 3.386 *[mahāsālakula]*).

34. D 3.258; S 1.71, 74; A 4.132, 133, 239. See the usage of *mahāśāla* 'possessor of a large house; a great householder' in CU 5.11.1, 3.

35. Vin 1.227; D 2.86; 3.236; M 1.72; A 2.133; 3.39; 4.80. This includes the well-known list of the 'eight assemblies:' of nobles, of brahmins, of householders, of recluses, of the celestial retinue of the Four Guardian Kings, of the thirty-three (Devas), of the Māras, and of the Brahmās (D 2.109; 3.260; M 1.72; A 4.307). As a list, moreover, it distinguishes categories of learned men *(paṇḍita)* (M 1.396; S 3.6, 7, 8), and often has other members appended to its end: *samaṇa* or 'recluse'(Vin 1.227; D 2.86; 3.236; M 1.72; A 2.133; 3.328), *titthiya* or 'member of another school' (D 3.44, 46. See the discussion in Horner, *Book of the Discipline* 2.xliii), *negamajānapada* or 'townsman and country man' (D 3.61; see also D 2.202; 3.167), and mother, father, child, brother, sister, and friend (M 2.120).

36. See the discussion in Wagle, p. 125.

37. A 1.162.

38. See the discussion in Wagle, pp. 28, 121, 126.

39. Gombrich, *Theravada Buddhism,* pp. 55-56.

40. See Wagle, p. 126.

41. See Smith, pp. 26-85.

42. Kalupahana, *Causality,* p. 133.

43. Thapar, *Lineage to State,* p. 159.

44. D 1.111, 112, 127; 2.202; 3.167, 172, 173, 177; M 1.285-290, 334-37; 400-401, 413; 2.54, 55, 56, 79, 80, 164, 165, 185; 3.116, 117, 176, 290-93; S 1.114; A 1.68, 110, 180; 2.74; 3.30; 4.340.

45. An alternate understanding renders the compound 'priests and laymen' or 'brahmins and householders.' Rhys Davids and Stede, p. 495; see also T.W. Rhys Davids, *Dialogues* 2.207n.

46. Such as the Kosalan villages of Sālā (M 1.285-290, 400-401; S 5.144-45), Verañjā (M 1.290), Manasākaṭa (D 1.235-253), Nagaravinda (M 3.290-93), Venāgapura (A 1.180), Opasāda (M 2.164), and Icchānaṅgala (A 3.30; 4.340), the Kuru town of Thullakoṭṭhita (M 2.54-55), and the Magadhan villages of Pañcasālā (S 1.113-14), Ekanāḷā (S 1.172-73; Sn pp. 13-16), and Khānumata (D 1.127).

47. Wagle, p. 18. These gifts of land are made out of the royal domain, not out of lands held by cultivators, and are often uncleared or only partially cleared lands (Chakravarti, pp. 24-26, 57). Some of the grants of land to brahmins are so large that the phrase *mahāsāla* indicating wealth is applied to them (Thapar, *Lineage to State,* p. 87). See D 1.136, 235; 3.16, 20; S 1.175.

48. Wagle, p. 19.

49. Thapar, *Lineage to State*, p. 158; see also Gombrich, *Theravada Buddhism*, p. 56; Wagle, p. 156.

50. Hence are wealthy "and influential Brāhmaṇa householders like Jāṇussoni, Aggika Bharadvāja and Dhanañjani and distinguished Brāhmaṇa teachers, like Pokkharasādi, Lohicca, Caṅki and others [who] became life-long devotees and disciples of Buddha." Chaudhury, p. 15.

51. Misra, p. 260.

52. Misra, pp. 167-68.

53. Wagle, p. 71; see also pp. 156-57.

54. Rhys Davids, *Dialogues* 2.207n; Chakravarti, pp. 66, 69, 82-84.

55. Thapar, *Lineage to State*, pp. 103-104.

56. Wagle, pp. 28-29, 126-28, 151-56.

57. Wagle, p. 154. Perhaps the most telling signs of the new prominence of wealth as a social marker are the stories of those who by contrast have little wealth—either through circumstance or through voluntary abandonment. In a story from the Suttanipāta, impoverished brahmins, bereft of cows and gold, look around at the new world of great human wealth and complain about their own meager circumstances—the Buddha's response, of course, is that they are ripe for a new spiritual pathway (Sn nos. 285, 301, 303). Voluntary forfeit of wealth also points out the propertied nature of the householder, for if and whenever a householder does lose his status as *gahapati* (if he enters the Saṅgha, for example), the biggest change is the loss of his wealth: as there is a rise in Buddhist confidence *(saddhā)*, the Dhamma teaches, there is a consequent decrease in wealth *(bhoga)* (Vin 4.179; D 1.62-63; 2.85, 86; M 1.179, 452; A 5.204; Sn no. 393). A story is told of the householder Potaliya in this regard who approaches the Buddha for teaching and is angry when the Buddha still calls him a "householder," since he thinks he has given up all of the requisite wealth and occupations and is now living a most simple life. The address "householder" is still to be used for Potaliya, argues the Buddha, because a modicum of ethical and mental wealth yet remains (M 1.359-368; see S 3.93).

58. D 3.258; S 1.71, 74; A 2.86; 3.386; 4.104, 239

59. As one of the seven treasures *(ratana)* belonging to the universal sovereign *(cakkavattin)*, the householder has *dhana* 'property.' See D 2.176-77; 3.59, 142, 177; M 3.175; S 5.99; A 4.89.

60. S 1.71; A 2.86; M 5.40.

61. D 1.136, 137; 3.16, 17.

62. D 3.188; M 2.71.

63. Vin 3.17, 18; M 1.451-52, 505; S 1.71; A 2.86; 3.386.

64. What makes this story so spectacular is not only that these things are given as gifts, but that this man Velāma is none other than the Buddha himself in a former life (A 4.393-94). In another story, a rich *seṭṭhi gahapati* from Sāvatthi dies intestate, childless and without heir. His estate, by the

principle of escheat, then reverts to his king, King Pasenadi of Kosala. Pasenadi, receiving the property, goes to the Buddha and bemoans the fact that so great an amount of wealth has belonged to so poor a specimen of humanity *(asappurisa)*, who has lacked the wisdom to spend it usefully. While this story has as its clear goal to teach the proper use of wealth, it also functions to enumerate in some detail what great and luxurious things householders can acquire in this life (S 1.89-93).

65. A 2.203. Archaeological work at places like Bodhgaya and Sānchi has revealed a number of inscriptions designating parts of each complex as the gift *(dāna)* of donor *gahapatis*. Even though monks and nuns *(bhikkhu/ bhikkhunī)* are responsible for many of these gifts, many others are attributed to lay men and women and to otherwise uncommitted householders. Ansari, pp. 101-103; Cunningham, pp. 150-172, 180-183, 222, 226.

66. M 1.236-37; A 1.26, 161; 2.64, 80; 3.32, 336; 4.81; Sn p. 87.

67. Vin 2.216.

68. D 1.137; A 3.39; 4.79-82; Sn no. 487.

69. Precise traditional listings of the Dānastuti portions of Ṛg Vedic hymns can be found in Kātyāyana's Anukramaṇī and in the Bṛhaddevatā. These listings do not agree fully, but agreement does occur in the following cases: RV 1.125; 6.27.8; 7.18.22-25; 8.2.41-42; 8.3.21-24; 8.4.19-21; 8.5.37cd-39, 8.6.46-48; 8.21.17-18; 8.46.21-24; 8.55 and 56.1-4; 8.68.15-19; 8.74.13-14. Several scholars have found "that in reality there are many passages which possess the marks of Dānastutis although they are not so recognized," and have put together their own lists. Patel, p. 20; see pp. 13-75.

70. *dāyako dānapatī dānassa vaṇṇavādī* (S 1.58).

71. E.g., Svanayu, Sudās Paijavana, Kaśu Caidya, Tirindira Pāraśavya, Kānīta.

72. These gifts include cows, horses, sheep, camels, dogs, chariots and rigging, gold coins and ornaments, and clothes. See Patel, pp. 64-75.

73. Heesterman, *Inner Conflict*, p. 27.

74. Ca. 1000-500 BCE.

75. See RV 10.85.26.

76. See ŚB 2.5.2.29; 3.3.1.10; KhGS 1.5.17.

77. Thapar, *Lineage to State*, p. 65.

78. M 1.369.

79. Olivelle, *Saṃnyāsa Upaniṣads*, p. 43.

80. Wagle, p. 154.

81. *Sappurisadānaṃ deti* (M 3.23). See Wagle, pp. 106-107.

82. M 3.37.

83. In Hindu law, the householder comes to be charged with the support, through gifts, of all other life stations, and who finds himself most at home in the present Kali Yuga, the age of liberality (Manu 3.77, 78, 80; 1.86).

84. N. Dutt, *Monastic,* pp. 96-132.
85. Boulding, *Love and Fear,* pp. 1-3; "Philanthropy," p. 57.
86. Boulding, *Love and Fear,* p. 2; "Philanthropy," p. 59.
87. Boulding, *Love and Fear,* p. 4.
88. Boulding, "Philanthropy," p. 61.
89. Boulding, *Love and Fear,* p. 3.
90. Boulding, *Love and Fear,* pp. 98-99, 27.
91. Boulding, "Philanthropy," p. 62.
92. For example, Sujātā (mother of Yasa), Suppavāsā (mother of Sīvalī), Mahāpajāpatī (aunt and step-mother to the Buddha), Ambapālī (mother to Vimalakoṇḍañña), and Veḷukaṇṭakī (mother to Nanda).
93. Note that the great *seṭṭhi* Anāthapiṇḍika and his brother-in-law, the great *seṭṭhi* from Rājagaha, are both extravagant, and sometimes rival donors—though each's generosity would probably be as large without competition from the other.
94. Boulding, *Love and Fear,* pp. 7, 8.
95. Thapar, *History of India,* p. 68.
96. Wagle, pp. 74-77; see also S. Dutt, p. 48, and Chakravarti, pp. 131-140.
97. A 1.217.
98. Gombrich, *Theravada Buddhism,* pp. 75, 79.
99. Vin 2.165.
100. In a well-known passage from the Majjhima Nikāya concerning the persuasions of the householder Upāli from the village Bālaka, the Buddha's own thoughts on donation and commitment reflect a characteristic openness and flexibility. Upāli is a follower of Nātaputta the Jain and is asked by his teacher to refute the teachings of the Buddha. In conversation with the Buddha, many topics are covered, including Upāli's long-time material support of the Jains. It is at this point in the teaching, on the very issue of *dāna,* that Upāli asks to be accepted as a Buddhist *upāsaka.* Upāli apparently has heard that the Buddha teaches giving-only-to-the-Saṅgha, for only such gifts are of great fruit but, when the Buddha úrges him to give to the Jains as well, the householder is struck by his tolerance and converts (M 1.371-387, esp. 379-80. See Vin 1.236-38; A 1.160-62). In her discussion of the Sīha story, Chakravarti (pp. 60-61) notes the Buddha's concern for continued support for all *samaṇa* life-styles.
101. There is once a brahmin woman named Dhānañjānī, for example, who has trusting confidence *(abhippasannā)* in the Buddha, the teaching and the Order and who speaks out on their behalf; for this she incurs the criticism of the Bhāradvāja brahmin youth Saṅgārava. (Vinaya texts note that the Bhāradvājas are among those brahmin families considered to be low *[hīna]* and not worthy of respect [Vin 4.6].) When the Buddha comes to town, however, Dhānañjānī is able to persuade Saṅgārava to go near

him, after which the young critic becomes a lay disciple (M 2.209-213). Again, many brahmins are impressionable hearers of the Dhamma, such as the young Vāseṭṭha and Bhāradvāja of the brahmin village Manasākaṭa in Kosala who ask about the doctrines of other sects, the brahmin Aggika Bhāradvāja of Sāvatthi who shows his prejudice against outcastes *(vasala),* and one brahmin of great wealth who is worried about what he sees as the current depopulation of the world, all of whom become committed followers of the Buddha (D 1.235-253; Sn pp. 115-123; Sn pp. 21-25; A 1.159-160).

102. Vin 1.220-22; see Vin 1.248-49. Again, a resident pupil of a brahmin woman from the Verahaccānī family visits the monk Udāyin and, after having an inspired talk, invites Udāyin to a meal with the woman at her home as a teacher's fee for his sermon (S 4.121-24). Again, a brahmin of Verañyā who hosts the Buddha and his monks during the rains grows upset when he realizes the entourage will leave before he has a chance to give his gifts *(api ca yo deyyadhammo so na dinno;* Vin 3.10-11). The Buddha consents (in silence) to the giving and the group stays on for feeding and the bestowal of robes. Finally, there is the case of the young brahmin named Māgha who comes to the Buddha and announces his own great munificence and liberality and worries whether such great giving will produce much merit *(puñña) (aham...dāyako dānapati vadaññū yācayogo;* Sn p. 87). The Buddha assures him that it will and then speaks of the characteristics of the recipients (e.g., worthy Buddhist renunciants) to whom gifts will provide the most merit for the brahmin.

103. D 3.217; A 4.41, 45. See Thapar, *Lineage to State,* p. 89.

104. M 1.176, 395-96.

105. The force of the narrative is not diminished by attributing the source of this stinginess to Māra's effect on the potential donors' minds.S 1.113-14; see Wagle, p. 19.

106. D 1.62-63, 250; M 1.179. Given stories such as these, it is unclear how Chakravarti (p. 148), who notes fully the strong relationship of *gahapatis* to the Saṅgha as lay (p. 84), can wonder about "the absence of *gahapatis* in the ranks of *bhikkhus."*

107. D 3.124-25; M 1.299; A 1.25-26; 4.233. Obeyesekere ("Theodicy, Sin and Salvation," pp. 31-32) argues that the *upāsaka* is the Buddhist analogue of the Hindu *vānaprastha,* each deriving out of similar socio-economic contexts.

108. D 3.124-25; M 1.493; A 1.26; 4.233.

109. Vin 3.189; Vin 1.18; M 1.378-79, 413; 2.213; 3.7; A 1.226; 4.220.

110. M 1.491-92. The *upāsaka* list of A 1.26-26: Tapussa, Bhallika, Anāthapiṇḍika, Citta, Haṭṭhaka, Mahānāma, Ugga, Uggata, Sūra Ambaṭṭha, Jīvaka, and Nakulapitar; the *upāsikā* list: Sujātā, Visākhā, Khujjutarā, Sāmāvatī, Uttarā, Suppavāsā, Suppiyā, Kātiyānī, Nakulamātar, and Kāḷī. The list of A 2.164: Citta, Haṭṭhaka, Khujjuttarā,

and Veḷukantakiyā. The *upāsikā* list of A 4.347-48: Bojjhā, Sirimā, Padumā, Sudhanā, Manujā, Uttarā, Muttā, Khemā, Somā, Rūpī, Cundī, Bimbī, Sumanā, Mallikā, Tissā, Tissā's mother, Soṇa, Soṇa's mother, Kāṇā, Kāṇā's mother, Uttarā the mother of Nanda, Visākhā the 'mother' of Migāra, the lay-disciples Khujjuttarā and Sāmāvatī, Suppavāsā the Koliyan's daughter, the lay-disciple Suppiyā, and Nakulamātar the *gahapatānī*.

111. D 3.37, 125; M 1.340, 490-94; 2.23; 3.261; S 4.301; A 1.73; 3.211, 213, 297, 384; 4.218; 5.185. See Beck, pp. 553-56, and Tambiah, "Ideology of Merit," p. 89.

112. Vin 1.15-18, 227-28; Vin 2.210; D 1.62-63, 211, 250; 2.85-86; 3.180-193; M 1.179, 285-290, 344, 397; 400-413, 483; 2.22-29, 106; 3.290-93; S 2.68-80; 4.123; 3.1-2; A 1.217-19, 261-63; 2.57; 3.203-219; 5.58. See Harrison, pp. 52-55, on hearing the Dhamma in Mahāyāna.

113. Whole sections of the Nikāyas are given over to material for or about the committed Buddhist householder (M 1.339-413; A 3.203-219) and/or layperson, and this material acknowledges clearly that, while the lay is "actively concerned with religious affairs," he isn't concerned only with religious affairs. Moreover, the material has to acknowledge as well that those committed householders who are brahmins "generally chose not to completely relinquish their membership of the brāhmaṇa order;" hearing the Dhamma seriously, then, means that "brāhmaṇa upāsakas...[have] to resort to various subterfuges in openly acknowledging the Buddha as their superior, even when they are intellectually convinced of his superiority" (Wagle, p. 73).

114. Jayatilleke, p. 58.

115. M 1.400-402.

116. M 1.402-404. Note here the words of the Buddha to Ānanda just before the former's death (D 2.154): *siyā kho pan' Ānanda tumhākam evam assa: "Atīta satthukaṃ pāvacanaṃ, n'atthi no Satthā" ti. Na kho pan' etaṃ Ānanda evaṃ daṭṭhabbaṃ Yo vo Ānanda mayā Dhammo ca Vinayo ca desito paññatto, so vo mam' accayena Satthā.*

117. The canon uses the term *sāvaka/sāvikā* 'hearer' or *ariyasāvaka/sāvikā* 'hearer of the noble doctrine,' to describe a disciple of the Buddha, normally a layperson in training but sometimes a monk (Warder, p. 181; Ergardt, p. 37).

118. Warder, p. 196; Aronson, *Love and Sympathy,* pp. 14-17. See M 1.400-413.

119. Wagle, p. 146.

120. D 1.223.

121. Vin 1.15-18, 236; M 1.493.

122. When the Buddha, for example, knows that the mind of Roja the Malla is ready and malleable, he gives him a progressive talk *(anupubbikathā)* on

Dhamma; Roja the Malla, now filled with confidence *(saddhā)* in the instruction, gives solid food and vegetables to the Saṅgha. When Roja wants to be the only donor of robes, food, lodgings, and medicine, however, the Buddha assures him he will be one among the many other well-appreciated donors (Vin 1.247-49; see also Vin 2.156). Again, Sīha the general hears a long Dhamma talk from the Buddha and then, with the Buddha's permission, serves him and the monks with his own hands, after which the Buddha speaks once more from his teaching (Vin 1.233-38). And again, the Buddha gives a Dhamma talk to Visākhā, who in turn gives a full feast to the monks of the Saṅgha the next day (Vin 1.290-94).

123. Vin 1.139-142.

124. Vin 1.296. *paṭigaṇhātu me bhante bhagavā mukhapuñchanacolakaṃ yaṃ mama assa dīgharattaṃ hitāya sukhāyā.* On gifts that "keep on giving," see Schopen, "Doing Business for the Lord," p. 532.

125. E.g., Rhys Davids, *Dialogues* 2.118.

126. D 3.126; M 1.491.

127. D 3.37.

128. A 4.220-22.

129. S 4.180.

130. Vin 4.288, 305, 337, 338; Vin 1.185, 191, 204, 287; Vin 2.105-107, 115, 123, 124, 133, 136, 137, 139; D 3.124; M 1.491-93; A 2.69; 3.391; 4.281; 5.176-182; S 1.78. See also A 4.369-370. Women householders as *kāmabhoginī:* Vin 2.266, 267, 271.

131. Vin 1.185, 190, 191, 204, 287; Vin 2.105-107, 115, 123, 124, 133, 136, 137, 139. The Buddha's criticism of *kāma* to the monk Ariṭṭha can be found in M 1.133.

132. A 4.281.

133. A 4.438.

134. A 2.69.

135. D 1.63, 250; M 1.179, 240; S 2.219; A 5.204.

136. S 2.219; A 5.205. See also M 2.56.

137. S 5.353; A 3.391; 4.281.

138. A 1.49. Note, however, that in the very same passage the struggle of the gone forth to renounce is detailed as well.

139. Vin 3.148-49; S 3.112; A 2.67-68.

140. D 1.61-62.

141. M 2.205.

142. M 1.452.

143. See, for example, the role of women in small trade (Wagle, p. 148).

144. Acharya, p. 28.

145. Manu 3.99-117; see ĀpDS 1.1.3.26.

146. Tambiah, "Ideology of Merit," pp. 66-67.

147. E.g., Chakravarti, pp. 31-35. See the discussion in Findly, *"arahant."*

148. Findly, *"arahant."*

149. Nath, pp. 191-195.

150. Jamison, *Sacrificer's Wife,* p. 254.

151. Guest, *atithi,* is derived either from *at* 'to wander,' as in an etymology favored by Grassmann (pp. 28-29; see Amore, pp. 21-22, 22n), or from *a-tithi* 'being or arriving without regular schedule, or unexpectedly,' as in an etymology suggested by Monier-Williams (p. 14), *tithi* being one of the regular days of the lunar month (p. 446). His rendition of *atithi* is: 'one who has no fixed day for coming.' Amore (p. 22n) notes that this is a folk etymology and renders *atithi* as 'outside the lunar days': "The guest was extraordinary, outside the ordinary cause-and-effect sequence, and therefore potentially very powerful" (Amore, p. 22).

    The concept of *atithi* 'guest' is first expressed in the Ṛg Vedic figure of Agni. As Knipe *(Image of Fire,* pp. 94-95) points out, the ritual fire Agni is in the paradoxical position of holding two positions at once: he is a guest of man in every household, being invited in anew each day, as well as the lord of the household, the householder himself, being responsible for the procurement of wealth and its proper management and distribution to appropriate recipients.

    As for the brahmin officiant, Heesterman argues that, in eating the sacrificial food, the brahmin "takes over the burden of death...for in order to be prepared the food must first be killed." Heesterman, *Broken World,* pp. 188-89, 155-56.

152. AV 6.96.1; CU 5.10.4; AV 6.15.3.

153. AB 1.15, 25; TS 1.2.10; KB 8.1; ŚB 3.4.1.1-26. Jamison's discussion of the wife's place in the ritual is substantial (pp. 38 ff.) and need not be recapitulated here.

154. An adaptation of Keith's *(Taittiriya Sanhita* 2.501) translation of TS 6.2.1.1-2: *ātithyaṃ gṛhṇāti yajñasya santatyai. patny anvārabhate, patnī hi pārīṇahyasya īśe; patniyā eva anumataṃ nirvapati. yad vai patnī yajñasya karoti mithunaṃ tad. atho patniyā eva (l) eṣa yajñasya anvārambho 'navacchityai.*

155. See, again, TS 6.2.9.2: *upānakti patnī hi sarvasya mitraṃ mitratvāya. yad vai patnī yajñasya karoti mithunaṃ tad. atho patniyā eva eṣa yajñasya anvārambho 'navacchityai;* "The wife (of the sacrificer) anoints (them) for friendship, for the wife is the friend of all. In this way that part of the sacrifice which is the wife makes a pairing. Now this touching (of the Soma cart) from behind by the wife is for the uninterruptedness of the sacrifice" (An adaptation of Keith's *(Taittiriya Sanhita* 2.510) translation).

156. An adaptation of Eggeling's (2.86-87) translation of ŚB 3.4.1.6: *eva etan mithunena anvārabhete; yatra vā / arhann āgacchati sarvagṛhyā iva vai*

tatra / ceṣṭanti. tathā hāpacito bhavati. Jamison gives a persuasive argument for *mithuna* 'coupling' as a sexual concept, related perhaps to an interpretation of *parīṇáh* as 'box' in the sense of female genitalia (see the charm for safe childbirth, KS 13.9). Of this she (p. 118) says: "If this was a common Vedic vulgar idiom, it may be that the expression "the wife is master of 'what belongs to the box'" conveyed a sexual meaning as well as a housekeeping one in the passages in question, and the transition from the cupboard to the bed in all three passages would be easier to understand." An economic interpretation, that focuses on marital rather than sexual 'coupling' as a unit of wealth, is also feasible. Not only is it possible that the wife's participation is essential to the efficacy of the ritual, personally for the *yajamāna* and cosmically for all, but also is the economic linchpin to the *dakṣiṇā* system.

157. See TS 1.1.10 ('I go as wife united with my husband,' *sampatnī patyāhaṃ gacche),* ŚB 5.2.1.10, HGS 1.7.24.4, and Manu 9.45 ('The husband is said to be one with his wife,' *etad ayo bharttā sā smṛtāṅganā).* Manu (9.18, 96) makes clear that neither husband nor wife can perform the *śrauta* ritual alone, and the Taittirīya Saṃhitā (3.2.8.4-5; 6.2.9.1-2) notes that efficacious rituals are produced by husband and wife participating together.

158. See parallel passages in KS 24.8 and MS 3.7.9 (88.5).

159. AB 1.15.

160. Jamison, *Sacrificer's Wife,* p. 117 (including italics).

161. "These she would have control of, and even when pārīṇahya came to refer to household goods in general, the old notion of the wife's ownership of what she literally brought to the marriage may have been preserved. This may in turn help explain why the wife's permission is needed to give away what she does not really own, hence part of the reason why she is so necessary to the exercise of hospitality." Jamison, *Sacrificer's Wife,* p. 118. Nath (p. 74) interprets the household goods the wife is mistress over as her *strīdhana,* wealth and goods peculiarly hers as a wife. The passage, however, as Jamison suggests, might bear a wider interpretation.

162. The guest is to be considered a 'friend' *(priya),* and it is to him and to the religious mendicant that offerings of food are due, for he comes only to places where there is a wife or a domestic fire (GGS 4.10.24; PGS 2.9.12; ŚGS 2.16.3). By definition, the guest is someone who belongs to a different village and who is only intending to stay over one night; if he comes in the evening he is not to be turned away and whoever comes into the house as a guest is not to go without the offer of cooked food (GDS 5.40; VDS 8.7; ŚGS 2.16.3; ĀpDS 2.3.6.5). Although the Pāraskara Gṛhya Sūtra suggests that the householder might eat before the guest, thus keeping the best portion for himself, this is frowned upon by most other schools who clearly state that the guest has to eat first (VDS 8.4,5; PGS 2.9.15; ĀpDS 2.2.4.11; 2.3.73; 2.4.8.2; VDS 11.6-11). The host also offers the guest a seat, water to drink, water to wash his feet, and a room (with a bed,

mattress, pillow, and cover) in which to sleep. The reward for such an honoring of a guest is stated to be freedom from trouble and future bliss in heaven (GGS 4.10.1-26; ĀpDS 2.3.6.6-20; 2.3.7.1-17; 2.4.8.1-14).

In the *śrauta* context, then, there are two ways a woman might be thought of as being an agent of *dāna*. First, the *dakṣiṇā* given to priestly participants comes from the husband and wife as a unit. Because it is as a pair that the two make an effective sacrifice, and because the *dakṣiṇā* symbolizes the regenerative power of the birth/disintegration/rebirth cycle of the sacrifice, the wife's presence in the completion of that cycle means that the *dakṣiṇā* comes as much from her as from the husband. Moreover, if, as the whole of TS 6.2.1.1-2 (see 6.2.9.1-2) suggests, her indispensability within the 'ritual pairing' of husband and wife *(mithuna)* is tied to her being mistress of the household goods *(patnī hi pārīṇahyasyeśe)*, then it becomes even clearer that the ritual *dakṣiṇā* is thought to be grounded within the economic parameters of the wifely role. That the *dakṣiṇā* is thought to be given by the union of the husband and wife, moreover, coincides with what seems true about early views on household property. The lack of discussion of women's possessions in Ṛg Vedic times, coupled with the increasing expansion of the parameters of a 'wife's property' *(strīdhana)* in later times (Kane 3:772), suggests that early on there is some version of joint ownership of the household wealth.

163. ŚB 3.3.1.10; KhGS 1.5.17; GGS 1.3.15.

164. In the Śatapatha Brāhmaṇa, the young student entering the *brahmacārin's* life during the Upanayana is obliged to petition alms according to prescribed rules for the initiation and then to continue petitioning alms until undergoing the final ceremonial bath that marks the end of studenthood (ŚB 11.3.3.5-7; see Manu 2.48). The Gṛhya and Dharma Sūtras then require that the young boy undertaking initiation vow to live by certain practices (e.g., tending the teacher's ritual fire, petitioning alms, sleeping on the ground, doing the teacher's bidding, and studying the Veda) (ŚB 11.3.3.3-6; CU 4.3.5; 4.10.1-2), and that *bhikṣā* continue as a daily practice with food being petitioned from a number of houses belonging to any but very low caste families and then brought back to the residence for announcement to the teacher who then gives permission to eat (ŚGS 2.6.4, 7, 8; ĀśGS 1.22.10; PGS 2.5.11; ĀpDS 1.1.3.25, 31-34; GDS 2.35, 39-40; VDS 7.14; BDS 1.2.3.18; Manu 2.51, 182, 183, 188). *Brahmacārins* are not allowed to petition from *apapātras,* that is, those born from a high-caste mother and a low-caste father, or from *abhiśastas,* that is, those who have committed certain heinous crimes (see ĀpDS 1.9.24.6ff).

165. For the *saṃnyāsin, bhikṣā* prescriptions are a function of the rite of passage in which he renounces the sacred fires, depositing them in himself *(ātmasamāropa),* and renouncing as well the ritual implements used in connection with these fires (ĀpŚS 6.28.11; ĀśŚS 3.10.6). Having renounced a dwelling place as well as fire, the *bhikṣu* is to live on alms gathered morning and evening (or, by some accounts, once a day) as he goes from village to village to randomly or accidentally selected houses. With a fully

concentrated mind, he is to 'continue to obtain alms' *(bhikṣāṃ liseta)* and, without eagerness, to accept only that amount of food needed to sustain life (Manu 6.50, 43, 55, 57; GDS 3.11, 14, 16, 17; VDS 10.6, 24, 25; BDS 2.10.18.4, 12, 22). For a full discussion see Olivelle, *Saṃnyāsa Upaniṣads* pp. 86-94.

166. ŚGS 2.6.5-7; ĀśGS 1.22.6-7; PGS 2.5.5-8; KhGS 2.4.27-30; GGS 2.10.42-44; HGS 1.2.7.15-19. The Pāraskara Gṛhya Sūtra enjoins the *brahmacārin* to petition from three women who will not refuse, or from six or twelve or an indefinite number (PGS 2.5.5-6), and the Gobhila Gṛhya Sūtra prescribes a total of three women or as many householder women as live in the neighborhood (GGS 2.10.43). The only Gṛhya Sūtra to prescribe a male donor is the Āśvalāyana which requires the student to petition from a man who will not refuse, or from a woman who will not refuse (AsGS 1.22.6-7). Manu then extends the range of possible female donors in the Upanayana from the student's mother to his sister and then to a maternal aunt, as well as to other local women who will not refuse (Manu 2.50).

167. ŚB 11.3.3.7; see GDS 2.37; BDS 1.2.4.7.

168. Manu 2.184. Basham (p. 122) discusses a practice among the Ājīvikas that is similar, but for different reasons: "the ascetic followers of Gosāla did not beg food of their female relations, because Gosāla himself was once disappointed at not receiving alms, presumably from his own kin."

169. This injunction appears as well in Manu and in various Dharma Sūtras (PGS 2.5.2-4; ĀpDS 1.1.3.28-30; BDS 1.2.3.17; Manu 2.49).

170. GDS 2.36; BDS 1.2.3.16; ĀśGS 1.22.8-9. See Jamison, p. 294 n. 61.

171. ĀpDS 1.1.3.26; 2.5.10.2; GDS 5.22; VDS 8.13; 9.18.

172. GDS 18.1; VDS 5.1; BDS 2.2.3.44, 45.

173. Vin 3.6, 242-48; 4.243-45; Vin 1.90-91; M 1.31, 108, 109, 146, 160, 171, 206, 227, 237, 336, 359, 456-57; 2.61-63; 104, 112; 3.247.

174. Vin 2.212-215; M 2.136-39.

175. The four *nissayas* 'resources' are *piṇḍiyālopabhojana, paṃsukūlacīvara, rukkhamūlasenāsana, putimuttabhesajja* (Vin 1.58), while the four *parikkhāras*'requisites'are *cīvara-piṇḍapāta-senāsana-gilānapaccay-abhesajja-parikkhāra.* Vin 1.248; Vin 3.89, 90, 132, 184, 211, 266; M 1.104-108, 126, 271; 2.101; 3.254; S 4.288; A 1.247; 2.26-27, 54-55, 65; 3.124-126, 130, 135; 4.114, 134, 366; 5.15, 67, 131, 201, 350.

176. I am indebted to John Nelson for this term. On the role of matronage in the rise and development of Buddhism, see Willis, "Nuns and Benefactresses," p. 73 and "Female Patronage," pp. 46-53.

Matronage achieves clearer definition as Hindu *dānadharma* evolves for, at a mature state, two types of gifts are recognized: in the first, those offered into the single *(gṛhya)* fire, into the three *(śrauta)* fires, and inside the *vedi* during sacrifices constitute *iṣṭa* giving, while "the dedication of tanks, wells, temples, places for public distribution of food," and gardens, as well as "gifts made at the time of eclipses,...on the sun's passage in a zodiacal sign or on the 12th day of a month" constitute the second, or *pūrta,* giving (Kane 2.2:843-44). As the range of possible Hindu donors is expanded in time to include women and *śūdras,* it is deemed that twice-born men can perform *iṣṭadharma* and *pūrtadharma,* while women and *śūdras* can only perform *pūrtadharma.* Acting independently, then, women are excluded from giving within the Brāhmaṇic ritual system, as they have always been, but they can now make independent gifts under the categories of gifting which lead to the ceremonial consecration or dedication of a monument, icon, temple, well, tank, or park—that is, anything established for the benefit of the public at large (Kane 2.2:845, 889). These categories are known as *utsarga* and *pratiṣṭhā.* Technically, *dāna* and *utsarga* differ in the following way: while in *dāna* the donor gives up all ownership and control over an item to a private receiver, in *utsarga* he or she gives up ownership over an item to the full benefit and use of the public; and as a member of that public, then, the donor or former owner can him or herself make use of the item so dedicated (Kane 2.2:893).

In the light of the type of gifts made by women and men to the Buddhist Saṅgha, that include large donations of lands and lodgings, it's possible, then, that the Dharma Śāstric structures might either inform or be informed by the early Buddhist ones. Note, however, that in the early Buddhist context giving almost consistently falls under the technical denotation of *dāna,* and not *utsarga,* for gifts to the Saṅgha, while made to the institution and not to individuals, are still not dedicated for the "public good."

177. Vin 2.213, 216.

178. M 2.137.

179. Horner, *Book of the Discipline* 5.303n.

180. M 1.446; A 1.244, 284; 2.117, 171; 3.134, 161, 248, 279, 387; 4.113, 290-91; 5.67, 198.

181. The anonymity of the *saṃnyāsin's* alms round is echoed here, for not only is he to stop at houses chosen randomly and accidentally (VDS 10.7), but, like the brahmin guest who is not to boast of his family background in order to get a meal (Manu 3.109), he is to make no humble salutations at all, so as not to fall into a hierarchically pre-defined relationship (Manu 6.58). Horner's *(Women,* p. 324) treatment of the Cullavagga passage, however, renders the Buddhist household almost identical to the Vedic: "She performed this function, her duty and privilege, because the home was looked upon pre-eminently as her sphere, and not because she was in any way the owner of the house."

182. An adaptation of Horner's translation *(Book of the Discipline* 5.302) of Vin 2.216 (See Frauwallner, p. 125: *ṭhitakena sallakkhetabbaṃ bhikkhaṃ dātukāmā vā adātukāmā vā 'ti. sace kammaṃ vā nikkhipati āsanā vā vuṭṭhāti kaṭacchuṃ vā parāmasati bhājanaṃ vā parāmasati ṭhapeti vā, dātukāmā viyā 'ti ṭhātabbaṃ.* There are striking similarities to the prescriptions for the *saṃnyāsin.* In going to the village for food, he is to beg

only once a day, eating food that is given without his asking (BDS 2.10.18.5, 12), waiting to go to a household late, after people have finished their meals—that is, after the smoke and embers of the cooking fire are out and the grinding pestle and dishes are put aside (GDS 3.17; VDS 10.8; Manu 6.43, 55, 56)—in the hopes that at that time he will not intrude. While the *saṃnyāsin* looks for signs of appropriate timing among the inanimate objects of the household, however, the Buddhist renunciant looks for signs given by the donor herself.

183. Jacobi, pp. 64-66, 91-93. As Vv (no. 70) indicates, however, washing the hands before eating is the custom in lay Buddhist households.

184. Jacobi, pp. 93, 159, 103, 117-19, 107-108.

185. Jacobi, p. 88.

186. Jacobi, pp. 101-102, 121.

187. Jacobi, pp. 124-25; but see p. 242.

188. Jacobi, pp. 24, 27.

189. On the foundational role of the king for the development of individualism, see Olivelle, *Saṃnyāsa Upaniṣads,* pp. 32-33, and on the developments internal to the *śrauta* ritual, see Heesterman, *Broken World,* pp. 81, 101, 216, 218, *Inner Conflict,* pp. 32-44.

190. Vin 1.216-220. Another, happier, story highlighting the independent-mindedness of a woman's giving is the account of Visākhā's request to the Buddha to be a permanent donor of eight items. Wanting to give eight gifts to the Saṅgha for life *(yāvajīvaṃ)*—rain cloths, food for the incoming, food for the out-going, food for the sick, food for the sick-tenders, medicine for the sick, conjey, and bathing cloth for the nuns—Visākhā persists and after a protracted time and much discussion, the Buddha grants her request (Vin 1.290-294).

191. Vin 3.17.

192. M 2.63.

193. Unusual here is that the normal devolution of a woman's *strīdhana* (goods that come to her as wife) in contemporary Hindu law is upon her daughters.

194. An adaptation of Hare's *(Gradual Sayings* 3.29-30) translation of A 3.37: *ye te bhattu abbhantarā kammantā uṇṇā ti vā / kappāsā ti vā, tattha dakkhā bhavissāma analasā, / tatrupāyāya vīmaṃsāya samannāgatā alaṃ kātuṃ alaṃ / saṃvidhātun.*

195. A 3.295-98.

196. See Vin 2.213-216.

197. Frauwallner, pp. 63, 65, 153-54.

198. Vin 2.215-16.

199. Manu 2.213; 9.5, 7, 12.

200. AV 2.36.3; TS 3.2.8; BĀU 6.4.3, 28; HGS 1.6.19.7; Manu 3.45; 5.153; 9.26, 27, 45.

201. Manu 3.55.

202. See ŚGS 4.11.1, 6, 10; 6.1.3; Manu 2.213.

203. Kane 2.1.309-310.

204. Vin 1.70.

205. Vin 4.2.213, 220-21, 233, 234.

206. E.g., eye to the sun, breath to the wind, limbs to the plants (RV 10.16.3. See Heesterman, "*dákṣiṇā*" pp. 242-43.

207. E.g., the four-cornered earth, the four-quartered sky, the ocean, the lights, the waters, the plants, the mountains (RV 10.58).

208. For RV 10.16.3, see AV 18.2.7; TA 6.1.4; 7.3; 9.2. For a discussion of *piṇḍa* offerings to female relatives, see Kane 2.2:794-795.

209. See Olivelle, *Saṃnyāsa Upaniṣads,* pp. 89-94.

210. The husband (as seed) entering the wife becomes an embryo entering its mother, to be born a new man again in the tenth month (See AB 7.13; Manu 9.106, 107, 137). In the "sniff kiss" ritual of KsU 2.10, the father on returning home from a journey sniffs the head of the son and pronounces his name, reaffirming the father's continuity through the son's viability. The Vedic value on sons is so strong, in fact, that it is a main argument against celibacy. Olivelle, *Saṃnyāsa Upaniṣads,* pp. 42, 49.

211. KsU 2.14. This rite of transfer is like one in BU 1.5.17 in which, at death, a father pronounces to the son that he is the *brahman,* the sacrifice, and the world, and the son responds acknowledging that he is the *brahman,* the sacrifice, and the world.

212. This rite of transfer is also used in the renunciation of a male ascetic who ritually dies to his family and who continues on for them in the person of his son (KsU 2.14). See again, Olivelle, *Saṃnyāsa Upaniṣads,* pp. 90-91.

213. See RV 10.14.8; TS 5.7.7.1; Kane 2.2:843-44; Varma, pp. 29, 31; Keith, *Religion and Philosophy,* pp. 250, 409, 478n, 573n-574n.

214. Knipe, "*Sapiṇḍīkaraṇa,*" p. 114. The Dīgha (1.97) and Aṅguttara Nikāyas (1.166; 5.269, 273) make clear that the *saddha* offerings to ancestors are well-known to the Pali compilers.

215. Knipe, "*Sapiṇḍīkaraṇa,*" pp. 115-117.

216. Knipe, "*Sapiṇḍīkaraṇa,*" pp. 117-122.

217. The use of lineage linkages as a structure for working out the mechanisms of ritual causality (through such things as performative speech and ritual manipulation) is evident again in the development of the two paths taken after death (BĀU 1.5.16; 6.2.1-16). The *devayāna* fathers, is taken by the man of action who has lived a ritually correct life and who is destined to return to and be reborn again in this world. See Varma, pp. 34-35; Olivelle, *Upaniṣads,* pp. xlvii-xlviii. In this context, rebirth is understood as follows: upon cremation, persons destined to be reborn go up to the moon in the form of smoke or vapor from where they return to earth as

rain; entering plants, they are eaten by men, become semen and take on new lives in wombs of women. Persons with liberating knowledge, however, break the cycle by passing through the opened lid covering the vault of heaven and escaping to immortality beyond the bounds of the universe. Like the Śrāddha rites, the construct of the *pitṛyāna* affirms the power of the lineage linkages active within the ritual, in whose setting not only the fruits of action ripen, but the center of male identity rests.

218. See Kane 2.2.1085-1090, where the norm of the Piṇḍapitṛyajña is for fathers, grandfathers, and great-grandfathers. Female relatives as departed ancestors are certainly known to Buddhist culture, however, as *petīs* figure prominently in the Petavatthu. That the renunciant at the door petitioning for alms is thought of as dead to his family is clear in S 1.209: *puna jīvaṃ mato hi so* 'though living again (as a renunciant) he is yet dead.' The Cullavagga itself (Vin 2.215-216) acknowledges the problem of women giving *piṇḍa,* as evident in the words used in the alms encounter prescription: while *piṇḍa* is used throughout the section for alms, at that point when the donor is specifically a woman—i.e., feminine forms used and woman's work in the kitchen described—*piṇḍa* is not used for alms and the less encumbered *bhikkhā* is used instead.

219. This is more fully discussed in the chapter on food.

220. *dānapati,* 'donor,' S 1.174; see A 4.237-39; Cp 2; Pv 1, 36-37; Thera no. 566. On the farmer (= Buddha as teacher) sowing seeds of discipline in his disciples, see S 4.315.

221. *bījāni vuttāni,* 'seeds sown,' S 1.21; see S 1.174; A 4.237-39; Cp 2; Pv 1, 36-37; Thera no. 566. On the seeds as Dhamma sown by the teacher in disciples, see S 4.315; see also A 5.212-214.

222. *sukhette,* 'in a fertile field,' S 1.21; see S 1.174; A 4.237-39; Cp 2; Pv 1, 36-37; Thera no. 566. On the disciple as field of varying quality into which teaching is sown, see S 4.315.

223. S 1.174; A 4.237-39. The image of ploughing, sowing, and yielding is used as well to describe the renunciant's own disciplined pathway, with the renunciant's body as field, confidence as seed, rain as discipline, insight as plough, pole as conscience, mind as tie, and mindfulness as ploughshare (S 1.172).

224. S 1.174; A 4.237-39; see A 3.243. In S 1.100, the donor is likened to a raincloud *(megha)* drenching the earth, as he gives showers of gifts.

225. This is more fully discussed in the chapter on merit.

226. The only gendered image is of the rain as god-king *(devarājā)* of the clouds (S 1.174; A 4.238), whose violent energy is endowed with strong virility (A 3.243); but this is clearly an old image inherited from the Vedic worldview of Indra the powerful storm god.

227. Little and Twiss, pp. 63-66.

228. Gombrich, "Intention," p. 92.

229. Aronson, *Love and Sympathy,* p. 9.

230. Vin 3.160; Vin 2.77.

231. A 4.45.

232. See references made to the houses and dwelling places of the *gahapati*: as *pāsāda* (Vin 1.16) and as *nivesana* (Vin 1.271).

233. Wagle, pp. 71, 105-110.

234. Collins, pp. 168-69.

CHAPTER 3

Resources to Requisites: Gifts to the Gone Forth

The most public aspects of the *dāna* contract are the negotiations about the propriety of certain material resources, that is, the gifts donors make to those gone forth into the homeless life. These negotiations are part of what Olivelle calls the "domestication" of renunciant ideals as they are "incorporated into the fabric of mainstream religion,"[1] and the process involves the development of truly Buddhist ideals out of the contexts of both Vedic antecedents and contemporary ascetic forms alternative to Buddhism.

GIFTS AND THE VEDIC PATRON

Vedic ritual practice is well-known in Pali texts, [2] and there is every reason to assume that Buddhists of the time live and work side by side with Vedic practitioners, and that they draw upon what they know from this tradition[3] to define a material life beneficial to their religious quest. Giving is an appropriate and expected Vedic activity, and both the terms *dāna* and *dakṣiṇā* are used in reference to gifts given to poets and priests participating in the ritual. Thus, RV 6.53.2 makes clear that material transaction is a central part of religious relationship: "Lead us to suitable property, to one we can count on, to the expected poet's pay *(dakṣiṇā)*, to a householder *(gṛhapati)* agreeable (to our service)." Deriving, perhaps, from *dakṣiṇā* ' right,' the hand that gives and that is said to have "munificent and beneficial powers,"[4] the *dakṣiṇā* is not strictly a salary but a gift, given by the sacrificer to all those priestly officials present at the place of the sacrifice, that itself helps to effect ritual ends.[5] Ordinarily, the specific items to serve as *dakṣiṇā* are agreed upon ahead of time, with certain *dakṣiṇās* deemed appropriate for certain rituals.[6]

Like *dakṣiṇā, dāna* appears in the Ṛg Veda—in particular in the Dānastutis, those sections of hymns designated as containing praises of gifts, of their givers, and of giving.[7] While the Dānastuti sections are probably later additions, they nevertheless show that the priestly office is a lucrative one[8] and that, in its early form, *dāna* is the preserve of a highly placed few. Developing out of the gifts named in the Dānastutis, and out of the *dakṣiṇā* from ritual patrons, are later Hindu gift *(deya)*-systems in which long lists of gifts are classified and ranked.[9] Of the gifting rituals in the Dharma literature, three contexts predominate: the *śrauta* ritual in which sacrificial patrons give to priestly officiants, the *ātithya* context in which hospitable householders serve visiting guests, and a general gift-giving setting for which the tradition prescribes optimal times, seasons, and occasions.[10]

As noted, the roles of women in early Indian practices of giving are considerable. Not only are they normally the ones at the household door passing out alms to petitioners, such as the *brahmacārin,* but the wife's permission and ritual yielding of property is necessary for the gifting of a household's materials to ritual guests. The relation of the wife to the actual gift, then, is significant. The phrase *pā́rīṇahya* 'mistress over the household goods' is attributed to the ritual wife and is a "rather startling statement"—for the use of the verb *īś,* standard for 'rule,' is a strong declaration "of control"[11] when applied to the *pārīṇahya,* household furniture and utensils.[12] The traditional Dharmaśāstric term for a wife's possessions or property is *strīdhana*[13] and while the understanding of the content of this property varies by school,[14] the important issue is not how much property a wife may actually own, but how much of it she controls and what kind of control she has.[15] The verb in the Taittirīya Saṃhitā is *īś* 'to rule over' and regardless of whether the contents of *pārīṇahya* 'household goods' is what is in the cupboard, and, hence, belonging to the whole household, or what is in the (traveling) trunk and, hence, belonging to the wife alone, the focus of ritual hospitality is the wife's control over the material resources of the household that is brought into the public ritual sphere of gift-giving.

Thus, the earliest form of *dāna* is the *dakṣiṇā* given by the sacrificer to the priestly participants in the ritual, either as a fee for services rendered or, following Heesterman, as a symbolic sharing and inclusion of all in the regenerative wealth of the ritual. And the giver of the *dakṣiṇā* is not just the sacrificer, but the sacrificer and his wife who operate as a unit in the agency of the ritual. Without the presence and regular participation of his wife, the sacrificer cannot successfully perform the ritual. In order to reap the proper cosmological and material blessings, his wife has to be present, has to participate at appropriate times, and has to be part of the offering of the *dakṣiṇā* to the ritual participants, for it is the sacrificer "who with his wife [is] eager to offer a good sacrifice."[16]

With further reflection on women's role in *ātithya,* can more be said about the *dakṣiṇā* itself? The list of things given as *dakṣiṇā,* for example, usually includes gold: gold pieces, gold lumps, and boxes of gold. Ordinarily, the gold is referred to generically—not shaped or fashioned or presented in any special form.[17] Some texts, however, are more specific. Atharva Veda 9.5.24-26 refers to gold ornaments; Chāndogya Upaniṣad 4.2.1-4 describes a gold necklace *(niṣka);* the Baudhāyana Śrauta Sūtra mentions a woman's gold ornaments; and later Purāṇic texts prescribe gold ornaments for the ears, neck, wrists, and fingers[18]—all specifically designated as items to be given to priests in the ritual context.[19] What is not known, however, is whether women's gold ornaments are what is normally meant when a *dakṣiṇā* of gold is given; whether they are only one of several kinds of gold items that can be given, taking their place among the lumps of gold, gold coins, men's ornaments, and gold trappings for animals; or if they are not to be included in the *dakṣiṇā* at all. But if they *are* used in *dakṣiṇā,* then the wife's *strīdhana* is important, for gold jewelry and costly clothes are among the oldest items said to make up a woman'sown property.

Thus, it's possible that gifts from the households of Vedic patrons may be drawn not only from traditional household property but from the wife's *strīdhana* as well. Pali texts retain the concept of *itthi-/itthīdhana* but expand its use: in the stories of Sudinna and Raṭṭhapāla, for example, the 'woman's property' becomes part of a legacy offered to bribe a renunciant son into returning to lay life,[20] and a woman's *itthidhana* can be used for gifting the Saṅgha as, for example, the gold neck ornament used for building a shrine given by the young Sesavatī.[21]

Materials of the Renunciant Environment

Certain features of the renunciant environment are relatively uniform across traditions, such as giving up the house, household belongings, and the household cooking fire, wandering except during the rainy season, and petitioning for food once a day. Other features such as what counts as acceptable foods and ways of eating, the proper treatment of bodily hair, and the appropriate manner of covering (or not covering) the body, are items "modified...to suit...[each tradition's] own needs."[22]

In general, certain categories of renunciants evolve, each with specific views on the materials needed to suit the particular state of renunciation.

> *1. The Kuṭīcara/caka, for example, petitions food from the house of his son, wears a sacrificial thread, a top knot, a loincloth and a patched, ocher outer garment (or a single garment) and carries a triple staff and a water jar.*
>
> *2. The Bahūdaka petitions from virtuous brahmin households, wears a sacrificial thread, a top knot, a loincloth, and a patched, ocher outer garment, and carries a triple staff and a water jar.*
>
> *3. The Haṃsa uses his hands as an alms bowl and petitions food from houses that have not been preselected, wears a sacrificial thread (but not a top knot) and a rag loincloth, and carries a single staff and a water jar.*

> *4. The Paramahaṃsa uses his hands as an alms bowl in petitioning from any of the four* varṇas, *wears no sacrificial thread or top knot, but does wear a loincloth and a garment (or a single garment alone or no garment), and carries no staff (or a single staff), no water jar, no sling, no shoulder yoke, no water strainer, no bowl, no shoes, and no seat.*
>
> *5. The Turīyātīta eats like a cow by taking food thrown to the ground with his mouth, wears nothing (being clad as he is at birth), and carries nothing.*
>
> *6. The Avadhūta eats like a python by waiting for someone to bring food without being asked, wears nothing, and carries nothing.*[23]

Worn over a loincloth when used, the outer garment of several of the classes is needed for protecting the renunciant's own body as well as for preserving modesty in front of other people.[24] It's normally made from clean scraps of cloth that are patched together and in appearance are discolored with age or dyed with ocher.[25] It's to be clearly distinguished from the white garments of worldly life.[26]

The utensils used by renunciants include a bowl made of clay, gourd, wood, or leaves,[27] and a water strainer that removes living beings from drinking water.[28] The water jar[29] is often a gourd and is carried in a sling tied to the staff and, like the staff, is one of the items not found in Buddhist practice, though is known in Pali texts.[30] Developed from the earlier tripod that carries a water container,[31] the *tridaṇḍa* staff consists of three bamboo shoots tied together.[32] Used by lower classes of renunciants, it becomes a single bamboo staff in the higher classes.[33] While the particularities of the material items assigned to each of the renunciant classes are important signs of the spiritual dynamics of the state in question, they are also significant markers to those still of the world. Not only are garments in the lower classes to be worn, in part, out of consideration for the general public[34] but, as the Mahābhārata notes, signs such as an ocher garment, shaved head, triple staff, and water jar are specifically instrumental in securing food.[35]

Early Buddhists are fully aware of the range of material and behavioral accoutrements prescribed for their renunciant colleagues in other traditions, many of whom openly practice asceticism. Descriptions of the eating habits of naked ascetics abound, with details of what counts as acceptable food and from whom it can be received, the manner and place from which food can be taken, and the timing and regularity of the alms petition. The variety of known clothing options in Pali texts ranges from full nakedness to garments of grass, bark, wood, feathers, animal and human hair, animal skin, and rags taken from corpses and dust heaps. Seating and lying arrangements include never using a seat, lying on iron spikes or plant thorns, and sleeping on bare earth.[36] Buddhist accounts of these practices carry implicit criticism on several grounds: first, such renunciants are extreme and immodest in both dress and behavior; secondly, they show a disrespect for the public setting of the practices; and, third, they show little concern for soliciting the goodwill of those from whom they petition. As Buddhist practice itself develops around the visible articles of three ocher-robes and a clay or iron bowl, other standards mark it out from the larger renunciant panorama: an inclusion of women and all social groups in its ranks, a grounding within a community of like-minded adepts, an avoidance of extremes and commitment to balance, and an open accommodation to the serendipitous nature of human experience.

From "Found Resources" to "Given Requisites": The Domestication of the Buddhist Renunciant

The Buddhist's relationship to the material world undergoes a change early in the tradition. In concert with the more extreme varieties of renunciant possibilities, Buddhism's earliest followers rely on the four 'resources' *(nissaya),* things found by happenstance along the way: meals of scraps, robes of rags, lodging at the root of a tree, and medicine of strong-smelling urine of cattle *(piṇḍiyālopabhojana, paṃsukūlacīvara, rukkhamūlasenāsana,* and *pūtimuttabhesajja).*[37] Reliance upon "found" items over time, however, has problems. First, there is increasing competition within a growing renunciant population for the limited resources of public space. Second, charges of theft are possible[38] that result from unclear claims of householder ownership over such things as land and its produce. And, third, there is an evolving Buddhist focus on finding a balance between extreme forms of practice, and this attention to adhering to a middle way includes an acceptance of the role of human culture as well as an affirmation of a dependence *(upanissaya)* upon that culture.

Consequent to this is the need for donors who can supply the materials for a moderate livelihood and who are committed to working out a transaction fully suitable to both parties. In Buddhism's willingness to change and adapt according to the fortuitous occasions presented to the early community, the shift from relying on chance 'resources' *(nissaya)* to dependable 'requisites' *(parikkhāra)* is a natural transformation. "As a more settled existence in monastic establishments displaced the wandering life," the four requisites "modeled on the four 'resources' supersede...the latter as more appropriate for a stable and permanent life-style."[39] These four requisites appear in the oft-repeated formula: *cīvara-piṇḍapāta-senāsana-gilānapaccaya-bhesajja-parikkhāra,* the requisites of robes, alms-food, lodgings, and medicine.[40]

In shifting to a relationship dependent upon donors, in which a regular, organized, and fully-agreed-to redistribution of goods takes place, the Buddhist community modifies the behavioral expression of its initial individualism. Monks and nuns are enjoined, of course, to live as islands unto themselves, as refuges unto themselves, and with none other for their support.[41] But needing material gifts to sustain an acceptable livelihood in the middle way means that non-reliance increasingly becomes a feature primarily of mental cultivation. At the heart of the Buddha's six year quest for perfection is the realization that a life-style of "easy maintenance,"[42] balanced between strict asceticism and indulgent hedonism, is the most suitable for developing the mindfulness needed to seek the truth, and thus becomes the ground for the Saṅgha's relationship to receiving the four requisites. At the same time, however, and in harmony with the shift from *nissaya* to *parikkhāra,* is the early tradition's commitment to accommodation which is flexible to changes in time and geography and responds to the peculiar exigencies of local material culture.

Overseeing the requisites as they come to and are used by the Saṅgha actively occupies the evolution of the young tradition. Developing the four categories of gifting—what they include, how they are given and under what circumstances they are given, and to whom they are offered—takes place over a lengthy period of time. The resultant codification in the Vinaya, supported by passages in the Nikāyas, represents extensive trial and error in the community's relationship to its *dāna* environment as well as a sharpening of the sense of Buddhist posture within the flow of human experience. Indeed, the ongoing need to detail and refine the donative process may well involve a substantial influence on the larger formation of Buddhist philosophic positions, as issues like the nature of experience, interdependence, rebirth, and mindfulness of the body are debated. *Dāna,* then—as its initial place in so many lists of the Buddhist path suggests—is formative for both renunciants and non-renunciants in grounding the Buddhist transformation of sense of self.

Pali terms for gift reflect Vedic influence on the tradition. *Dāna* [43] is the general term for gifts to a religious or a religious community with a focus on the purity and the good intention of the giver, while *dakkhiṇā* [44] is a more circumscribed term indicating the religious worthiness of the recipient. Practically, however, these two terms are comparable in early texts: the Buddha, for example, tells the householder Anāthapiṇḍika that there are two gift-worthy *(dakkhiṇeyya)* types of people to whom gifts *(dāna)* are given: the student *(sekha)* and the no-longer student *(asekha*), that is, one who has experienced *nibbāna*.[45] The most common early term for the food given as alms to petitioning monks and nuns is *piṇḍa,*[46] technically a rice ball given to the deceased ancestors, but in Pali texts a general term for whatever is put into the renunciant's bowl. The old term for sacrifice, *yañña,* is also used but now only marginally for the ritual. Instead, *yañña* is an offering to those spiritually advanced enough to be worthy of receipt—as the Cullaniddesa explains, *yañño vuccati deyyadhammo, 'yañño* is a meritorious gift.'[47] And *cāga* (Skt. *tyāga)* becomes a general gloss for *dāna,* defining a developed moral habit of abandonment of material possessions and, hence, of generosity. More secular words from tradition include *dhana*[48] for household possessions or property that is often made up of staples like food stores and animals; *bhoga* for wealth above and beyond a householder's necessities;[49] *bhojana* for food or a meal normally given by householders to renunciants;[50] and *lābha* for a gift made from what one has acquired.[51]

The dependence of the renunciant[52] upon the goodwill of the villagers, townspeople, and city-dwellers among whom he or she walks is a relationship of mutual requirement, for, reliant as the renunciant now is upon householders *(parapaṭibaddha),*[53] he or she nevertheless has to give something in return. And, in that, householders are enjoined to minister unto *(paccupaṭṭhita)* monks and nuns, renunciants are in turn to minister unto householders by teaching Dhamma.[54] Thus, the process of gifts-giving-rise-to-a-Dhamma-talk often happens in reverse, that is, a Dhamma-talk-giving-rise-to-gifts.[55] Whatever the sequential order of the elements of the "contract," however, it is clear that monks and nuns need what householders can give them and, whatever their other motivations, their own livelihood must be a central issue.[56]

The ministering unto renunciants comes to be a matter of tremendous encouragement by several early master gift-givers. Anāthapiṇḍika, for example, urges people along the road between Rājagaha and Sāvatthi to build monasteries, prepare lodgings, and provide gifts for the Buddha and his followers.[57] This sense of responsibility is codified in the Siṅgālovāda Sutta where Siṅgāla is given a great edifice of lay instructions that include the types of relationships he might enter into; among these are instructions for treatment of friends, relatives, teachers, servants and employees, and recluses.[58] Although Buddhist renunciants are not specifically mentioned, they belong to the category *samaṇa* and, in fact, when the Buddha tells Siṅgāla he should minister to *samaṇas* and *brāhmaṇas* he uses the same word *(paccupaṭṭhita,* 'minister unto, provide for') as is used in the Itivuttaka passage. Clearly, this teaching directs Siṅgāla to support the Saṅgha materially and, coming as it does at the end of the ethical instruction, might be said to be the instruction's concluding message, making sure that Siṅgāla responds to monks and nuns with perpetually open doorways and with perpetual attention to their material needs.[59]

The specific items available for giving by donors are detailed over time. When listing the four resources *(nissaya),* for example, the Vinaya adds, as extra, later items falling into the general range of each of the four categories.

1. meals of scraps of food
(piṇḍiyālopabhojana); *extra* (atireka,
i.e., acceptable and therefore not
deemed excessive):
meal for a Saṅgha (saṅghabhatta)
meal for a special person
(uddesabhatta)
invitation (nimantana)
ticket-food (salākābhatta)
food given on the waxing or waning of
the moon or on Uposatha day
food given on the day after
Uposatha (pāṭipadika)

2. robes of rags from a dustheap
(paṃsukūlacīvara); *extra: when*
made of linen, cotton, silk, wool,
coarse hemp, or canvas

3. lodgings at the root of a tree
(rukkhamūlasenāsana); *extra:*
dwelling place (vihāra)
curved house (aḍḍhayoga)
long house (pāsāda)
mansion (hammiya)
cave (guhā)

4. medicine of strong-smelling urine of cattle (pūtimuttabhesajja); *extra:*
ghee (sappi) *oil* (tela)
fresh butter (navanīta)
honey (madhu)
molasses (phāṇita)[60]

Over time, a range of other items become giftable as well.[61] In fact, so many types of material goods are allowed to monks and nuns of the Saṅgha, that some renunciants are actually called *bahubhaṇḍa* 'having an abundance of goods' and *bahuparikkhāra* 'having an abundance of requisites.'[62] Thus, reining in the use of goods becomes part of the diligence of the ongoing tradition.

THREE OCHER ROBES

The robe is the most highly valued and most highly regulated of all requisite donations. Because the Buddhist renunciant has specifically not taken vows of nakedness,[63] proper robes are necessary for ordination. One function of the robe—clearly different in color, number, and care—is to distinguish Buddhist renunciants from lay people, obvious in their white garments, as well as from rival renunciants.[64] Highlighting the radical spiritual basis of the posture of the gone forth, moreover, the robe provides visibility in its open declaration of other-worldly status, anonymity in that all renunciants look the same, permanence in that mistakes in the robe-donation process can't be hidden as easily as they can in the case of food, and donor-friendliness as it is washed and mended on a regular basis. The stated purpose of wearing a robe, finally, is to keep off cold and heat, to keep away insects and snakes, and to diminish the effects of wind and sun[65] and, in this way, it is in keeping with a life on the middle way.

The Charge to Wear Robes

As given in the Mahāvagga, the Buddha's first injunction on wearing robes occurs after his sermon to the five ascetics and after the conversion of the young merchant Yasa and his family. At this time, the Buddha is a new figure on the landscape and is inundated with requests for admission *(pabbajjā)* and ordination *(upasampadā).* Accordingly, he allows those monks already 'gone forth' to go out far and wide in order to admit and ordain new recruits by a given procedure: to have hair and beard cut off, to put on ocher cloth *(kāsāya vattha)* arranging an upper robe *(uttarāsaṅga)* over one shoulder, to pay homage to the other monks, and to recite the triple refuge.[66]

Buddhist renunciants are, originally, to wear *paṃsukūla* 'rag robes,' robes taken from the dust heap, preferably from in a cemetery.[67] The Buddha is said to have been content with any kind *(itarītara)* of robe material himself and to believe that the clearest reflection of living in dependence *(upanissaya)*[68] is to wear robes taken from the trash pile; robes that are worn thin; robes patched together from pieces of cloth from a cemetery or a shop; or a householder's old robe worn thin and strengthened with thread from a white gourd. Being content with any kind of cast-off material for a robe is consistent with a Buddhist life of non-attachment, and reflective of the virtues of simplicity and economy, as illustrated in the story of Mahā Kassapa's gift of his robe to the Buddha.

One day Kassapa offers his outer-robe *(saṅghāṭī)* of cut patchwork pieces, now folded into a square, to the Buddha to sit on as he rests at the foot of a tree. The Buddha remarks on how soft the material is and Kassapa responds by offering the robe to the Buddha, hoping that he will accept out of compassion for the senior follower. The Buddha then asks Kassapa if he is content to wear in turn the Buddha's coarse rag robes that are worn past wear[69] and, when Kassapa accepts the Buddha's offer, the exchange is made. The story raises the possibility of two lessons. First, the Buddha is testing Kassapa's non-attachment to a good robe of his own as well as his commitment to the standard 'rag robe' policy. Or, second, the Buddha himself finds Kassapa's robe pleasing and wants it for his own. Although the latter interpretation contradicts the teaching of being content with whatever robe is available, it affirms the teaching of the middle way where some minimal comfort between asceticism and hedonism is acceptable. Since the passage goes on to praise Kassapa's spiritual attaiments, however, this monk's non-attachment rather than any tendency to excessive comfort in the Buddha seems the best interpretation.

The rag robe rule is modified some years into the Buddha's ministry after he takes ill once and has to accept a valuable non-rag robe at the request of his physician Jīvaka. Mohan Wijayaratna suggests that there are two issues of concern: first, that Jīvaka is worried about the Buddha's overall health when using old rag robes and, second, that rag robes are getting increasingly difficult for growing numbers of Buddhist renunciants to find.[70] Whatever the impetus, from the time of Jīvaka's action onward, other Saṅgha members are allowed to accept gifts of new robes given by householders as well—such a robe being called a *gahapaticīvara* 'a robe given by a householder.'[71] The *gahapaticīvara* rule, however, is not obligatory and some monks choose to follow the older stricter rule of the rag robe—both of which groups the Buddha approves as he sees contentment arise with either choice.[72]

The Number of Robes

The normal allotment of robes to a monk is three *(ticīvara)* and, for this reason, a Buddhist is known as a *tecīvarika* 'a wearer of three robes.'[73] The reason for limiting the number to three is to prevent the accruing of robes in abundance that might then foster possessiveness.[74] Under normal circumstances, the three allotted robes are for the exclusive use of the individual renunciant for the Mahāvagga notes, in the context of ordination, that using a loaned robe is not allowed—only a robe that can be used solely and lastingly by the individual is acceptable.[75] In fact, a new robe is marked with a small colored dot so as to indicate the individual who is its proprietor.[76]

The three allotted robes are an inner robe *(antaravāsaka* or *nivāsana)* tied at the waist with a girdle, an upper robe *(uttarāsaṅga)*, and an outer-robe with a lining *(saṅghāṭī)* that can be folded in four and used as a seat.[77] Wearing extra robes is not allowed[78] except if the cloth is very thin, in which case each of the three robes can be doubled.[79] If an extra robe happens to accrue to a monk after his *kaṭhina* privileges have been removed, he is allowed to wear it for at most ten days, and then has to assign it to someone else.[80] All three robes have to be worn when a monk or nun is on tour in villages, towns or cities,[81] and when the text notes that a monk has picked up his bowl and robe *(pattacīvaraṃ ādāya)*[82] and has gone out walking, it is the outer robe that is taken up and worn to ensure some public modesty. The Rhys Davids describe the customs of wear as follows: when in his private quarters a monk wears only his inner robe, tied with a girdle, from the waist down; when he sets out to visit a village he puts on his upper robe, carrying his outer one over his arms; and, when just outside the village, he puts the third one on over the others.[83] The use of the outer-robe can be waived in five instances: when a monk is sick, during the time of the rain-retreat, when crossing a river to the other side, when dwelling in a place secured with a bolt, or if the *kaṭhina* cloth has been made and privileges are still in effect.[84]

Nuns are traditionally allowed five robes: the usual three worn by monks ('outer' *saṇghāṭī,* 'upper' *uttarāsaṅga,* and 'inner' *antaravāsaka)* and two others, a vest or bodice *(saṅkacchā)* and a bathing mantle *(udakasāṭikā).* Any woman wishing to receive ordination knows of these extra requirements beforehand, and a nun is then enjoined to wear her vest under her inner-robe when going into a village and not to bathe in the nude.[85] Because nuns can dirty upholstered seats when menstruating, they are forbidden to sit on them, but are allowed the use of the householder robe during their periods and, in time, the use of a loincloth and hip string.[86] Menstruation often abates, however, under the rigors of intense mediation, and references in the Therīgāthā that suggest a state of dryness in some women's experiences may point to this connection.[87]

The Material and Color of Robes

As the shift from found rag robes to donated robe cloth takes place, standards are developed for both the material and the color of robes. Traditionally, robes are made from six types of material: linen, cotton, silk, wool, coarse hemp, and canvas.[88] Although, ideally, the renunciant is to be indifferent to the quality of the material, distinctions in cloth are certainly known to them.[89] The use of a variety of quality of cloth materials reflects the Buddha's "take as given" approach as well as his expectation of the monastic recipient's equanimity in the face of whatever he or she may get as a gift. Mindful of this, rules are set down to prevent renunciants from petitioning any more desirable piece of cloth than would ordinarily come from the weaver.[90]

Modeled after the traditional rag robe made from pieced scraps taken off dust heaps *(paṃsukūlacīvara),* the robe worn by a monk or nun is not to consist of a single length of uncut cloth. Rather, large pieces of material given by householders are to be cut into several smaller pieces and resewn according to dimensions given in the Vinaya. The resulting robe then resembles a rag robe sewn similarly from small pieces.[91] The robe sewn from newly woven and dyed sections is often based on exacting models, and one such example are the many-seamed robes created by Ānanda for monks, at the Buddha's request, in a pattern of stripes and squares that follows a well-laid out field in Magadha.[92]

Wijayaratna suggests that the cutting up and resewing of the robe is meant "to reduce the original value of the cloth to a minimum: even a very costly piece of material loses its commercial value when it is cut up in small bits." Since the Saṅgha cannot refuse valuable cloths when given, in this way it can "transform...them into clothes [that are] in keeping with the spirit of renunciation."[93] This interpretation is consistent with the Mahāvagga reason for resorting to robes made out of cut cloth: that people *(manussa)* criticize the use of uncut cloth because it makes renunciants look like householders enjoying sense-pleasures. Other Vinaya texts, however, explain the use of pieced robes from donated cloth as a way of distinguishing Buddhists from contemporary rivals,[94] and a third interpretation, taken up in a later chapter, is that the labor of resewing robe material out of smaller patches secures renunciant "ownership" over the robe.

The signal color of the Buddhist robe is ocher, a dark, brownish-yellow or saffron color *(kāsāya, kāsāva)* otherwise named *siṅgivaṇṇa* 'the color of gold,' and *dantakāsāva* 'yellow, the color of teeth, or ivory.'[95] This color reflects an ancient Indian tradition in which gold specifies the transformative powers of the tawny Soma plant, the ghee-driven ritual fire, the brilliant enlivening sun, the golden egg of creation, and the illumination of religious vision and rebirth. The color of the robe cloth when given is normally white or off-white and is made ocher with dye from roots, stems, bark, leaves, flowers, and fruits.[96] Originally, monks experiment with robes of many different colors: blue-green, yellow, red, bright red, black, safflower plant orange-red, and Mahānāma plant yellow-red. These experiments include the use of ornamental borders and uncut cloth—but the Buddha eventually rules for uniformity based on traditional values.[97] The fixing of robe color and care, like all Saṅgha rules, is a flexible and changing process with nothing firmly established until the Buddha's own judgment, informed by earlier Brāhmaṇic tradition and the opinions of local people *(manussa),* clarifies it into a meaningful pattern.

The Acquisition and Care of Robes

Early on, the provision of robes and a bowl becomes a condition for ordination *(upasampadā),* and accompanies other conditions such as being at least twenty years of age from conception, being free of certain diseases, being without debt or state of bondage, and being present with parental consent.[98] A rite of official provision is given in the Mahāvagga whereby, just after being invited to choose a preceptor *(upajjhāya),* a monk is shown a bowl and robes with these words: "This is your bowl, this your outer-robe, this your upper-robe, this your inner-robe; go and stand in that place."[99] Giving a renunciant custody over these materials through a speech act is like a *saṃnyāsin's* act of "possession" who, when taking up his staff, waistband, loincloth, garment, and water pot, recites verses that direct the objects in question to provide essential support in his renunciant endeavor.[100] Although the Buddhist rite is not couched in specific expectations of detachment towards the objects, as the *saṃnyāsin* charge is, subsequent rulings on the handling of things like robes indicate that non-attachment is essential from the beginning.

The robes taken up initially by a monk or nun are, of course, not expected to last for the renunciant's entire lifetime, and a gift of new robes is one of the most significant, regular, and enduring acts of donation that can be undertaken by a donor. In time, and on the basis of extensive experience, codification of rules for the acquisition of robes focuses on curbing renunciant behavior to make sure that mindful non-attachment is preserved and that a renunciant does not get new robes from a donor in improper ways.[101] A renunciant is not to ask a householder or housemistress for a new robe, for example, unless he is related to them, except in the cases of his robe being stolen or destroyed.[102] He is not himself allowed to ask for yarn to have robe material woven by weavers[103] and, once a non-related householder or housemistress commissions material woven especially for him, he is not then allowed to go to the weaver and give him any extra instructions.[104] If a non-related householder or housemistress invites him to take material for a robe, then the most he can take is enough for an inner and upper robe.[105]

At some point the possibility of a robe fund *(cīvaracetāpana)* is instituted whereby donors can set aside things—such as gold, precious stones, ploughshares, cloths, threads, or cottons—that can be used in exchange for robes for renunciants, and rules develop accordingly.[106] Moreover, within the Saṅgha certain general rules apply with regard to the distribution of robes. A monk is not allowed to appropriate knowingly any robe material that is prepared for the Saṅgha at large.[107] Nor is a monk allowed to barter with other religious for better robes,[108] nor to hide a robe or any other requisite belonging to another monk,[109] nor to tear away in anger a robe given to another monk,[110] nor to accept a robe from the hand of a nun who is not a relation except in exchange.[111] Concerning this last, it is ruled that transactions that involve exchanges can take place only among five classes of non-related people: a monk *(bhikkhu)*, a nun *(bhikkhunī)*, a female probationer *(sikkhamānā)*, a male novice *(sāmaṇera)*, and a female novice *(sāmaṇerī)*.[112]

Robes can accrue either to the Saṅgha or to an individual renunciant. Although robes do come in to the Saṅgha at a variety of different times of the year, the official moment for acceptance of robe material from donor householders is 'at the right time, in the right season, in a timely fashion' (see *kālacīvara, cīvaradānasamaya)*, i.e., at the annual donation of cotton *kaṭhina* cloth at the end of the rainy season.[113] Thus, at the end of the rain retreat, Vassāvāsa, and on the day after Pavāraṇā, a yearly ritual in which all monastic misunderstandings and lapses are laid aside, *kaṭhina* cloth is brought to the community by laypeople and is given to the Saṅgha.[114]

During the rains, monks and nuns receive alms from nearby local householders,[115] and substitute for their old and shabby robes, cloths for the rains *(vassikasāṭikā)*[116] to wear within the residence. With the conclusion of the rains and the injunction to go out once again on tour,[117] the thin, worn-out, insect-eaten, and stained robes of pre-retreat times need to be replenished or replaced.[118] Although a monk or nun may not need three new robes every season, the ceremonial distribution of new robe material every year is designed, among other things, to keep the renunciants' appearance pleasing and acceptable to potential donors, as well as to provide a clear, well-designated channel for giving to those who are disposed to do so. It may even be that having so marked a ceremony for the donation of robe material to the Sangha actually raises householder sensibility to the possibility, and perhaps even desirability, of *dāna* and thus serves to bring about an even greater amount of materials given. Gifts from donors to renunciants who have spent the rains in residence is a normal occurrence at the end of the season,[119] and can come in on the day of Pavāraṇā before the actual 'invitations' are made by the monks for making amends;[120] but special robes given before the full moon of the month of Kattika, while accepted, have to be laid aside until the proper time for accepting robes[121] occurs.

Kaṭhina cloth is a special ceremonial cloth given by householder donors to the Saṅgha at the end of the rains. This is the one monastic ceremony in which the lay are integrally involved and, Gombrich notes, "it is the only Buddhist festival which is celebrated in virtually identical form in every Theravādin country" today.[122] On the designated day at dawn, the unsewn *kaṭhina* cloth (rags, used cloth, or newly made cloth, sufficient to make at least one of the monks's three robes) is brought to the monastic residence by the donors, offered to and accepted on behalf of the Saṅgha by an experienced, competent monk *(vyattena bhikkhunā paṭibalena)* who has remained within the monastery for the duration of the rains retreat.[123] It is then washed, marked, measured, cut up, and sewn into proper robes all in a single day.

Elaborate rules are given for the making of *kaṭhina* cloth into *kaṭhinacīvara:* the material is washed clean, the robes are made out of separate cut pieces, and the robes are sewn, strengthened, hemmed, and bound properly, using a special *kaṭhina* frame in a special hut.[124] Moreover, the robes are to be made with the proper mental attitude and conduct, allowing no round-about talk for getting cloth from donors and no postponement in the handling.[125] *Kaṭhina* robe material is "regarded as the property of the Saṅgha"[126] and, because of this, each monk, upon receipt, must give special thanks to the Saṅgha for its use. The distribution of *kaṭhina* cloth within the Saṅgha entails some discussion. A renunciant can only accept his portion of the robe material at the residence where he has spent the rain retreat.[127] Robe material is only *kaṭhina* cloth if given at the right time (if not, it is forfeited back to the Saṅgha), and distributed properly;[128] and distribution cannot be held back if all who are fully ordained within the *sīma* boundary are, in fact, present.[129]

Kaṭhina cloth brings with it five privileges for monks and nuns that last for four months: 1) going to families for alms food without asking (their prior) permission;[130] 2) walking for alms without taking all three robes, the outer-robe being left aside;[131] 3) participating in a group meal *(gaṇabhojana);*[132] 4) using, but not appropriating, as many robes as is required;[133] and 5) having available the use of whatever robe-material accrues to the Order.[134] *Kaṭhina* cloth can be worn for any length of time as long as the *kaṭhina* quality is there; at the end of the season the relaxed quality of *kaṭhina* rules is gone and renunciants have to return to their regular robe practice. *Kaṭhina* privileges can be taken away or removed prematurely under any one of eight detailed conditions given in the Mahāvagga.[135] With the conclusion of *kaṭhina* privileges, a monk's robe material is considered to be 'settled' *(niṭṭhita),* he having "his set of three robes made up and ready to wear"[136] now under normal conditions.

Whenever there are unusual or problematic cases, the regular, orderly life of the Saṅgha remains as the organizing principle of redress. The community has to respond, for example, to situations where expected robe-material does not accrue to the Saṅgha by the end of the robe season,[137] to the instance of a solitary monk alone for much of the year being given robes for the Saṅgha,[138] and to the time when a monk spends the rain retreat at two residences, in order to get more robes than his allotment.[139] These exceptional cases allow the Saṅgha to establish standard rules and procedures for robe acquisition that acknowledge the orderly process of Buddhist life, and to solidify its relationship with householder donors in a formal and celebratory context. As Wijayaratna notes:

> *The monks and nuns taking part in the ceremony represented the Community, and would give such robes to those who have spent the Retreat according to the rules. For monks, the ceremony represented a formal act of the Community; for lay people, it symbolized the culminating point of their hospitality towards the monks during the rainy season.*[140]

Robe materials and related textile pieces do accrue to the Saṅgha at times other than at the end of the rain retreat.[141] While Horner calls these "unusual circumstances,"[142] the Buddha's ruling on the eight channels for the giving of robe material suggests that it is routine for the Saṅgha to receive cloth other than at the conclusion of the rains.[143] Moreover, the giving of other textile pieces such as mats and blankets is governed less by seasonal protocol and more by use; the Buddha routinely rules on the appropriateness of these goods based not on the time of giving but on the moderation or extremity of their luxury.[144] Thus, the convention of accruing most robe material as *kaṭhina* cloth at the end of the rain retreat might have developed 1) as a practical matter to respond to the clothing needs of the renunciants as they head back out on extended tour, and 2) as a way of deterring any attachment to the accumulation of individual robes. It does not preclude, however, incidental gifts of robe material at other times of the year.

The care and treatment of robes is a paramount concern for, unlike some renunciant traditions where random, dirty rags are a mainstay, Buddhist robe cloth is washed before being patched together into regulation robes, and washing and mending continue to be part of the normal care of each of a monk's or nun's clothing allotment.[145] The attention given to robes is, in part, an acknowledgment that the renunciant's day-to-day livelihood is a matter of social convention, whether it be the social convention of the internal monastic community or the larger community of city and countryside and, in part, an acknowledgement that individual pursuit of the middle way touches every part of a person's life. Although traditional work is forbidden that precludes, for example, nuns from spinning yarn,[146] the maintenance of already worked materials is expected.[147] When robe transactions of maintenance take place between renunciants of different genders, however—e.g., handling, washing, dyeing, and sewing—they can only be done if the two renunciants are related.

As the most personal of all the materials used by Buddhist renunciants, the care and treatment of robes reflect the general values of the Buddhist quest undertaken within a like-minded community. Dependence upon a donor's gift of robes allows non-attachment to develop and provides freedom from the worldly concern of work. Governance over the initial distribution of robe material by the Saṅgha ensures fair and just allotment and discourages individual hoarding. And full care and treatment of his or her own robes by the individual promotes self-sufficiency, mindfulness, and development of a balanced life on the middle way.

THE ALMS TOUR AND SPECIAL MEALS

While the gift of robes is a momentous event in the material life of the Buddhist renunciant, the gift of food is a regular feature of daily routine. In going forth, a renunciant gives up the tools for making a living, be it the bow and quiver of the warrior, the sickle and flail of the farmer, or the wheel of the domestic cotton spinner. The renunciant can no longer work to provide for basic personal necessities, that is, to earn a living. Although some manual labor around the monastic residence is allowed, such as sweeping and repairing, and although later on some farming and cow-tending accrue to the monastic complex, in general, work—such as performed by the householder—is deemed incompatible with the religious life. Attending specifically to the production and preparation of food is inappropriate, and the provision of sustenance is dependent solely upon those the renunciant moves among.

The Charge to Petition Alms

In two early traditions about the first gift of food, both are made to the Buddha and both occur at the time of his enlightenment. According to the Mahāvagga story, two merchants Tapussa and Bhallika, on their way from Ukkalā to the place where the Buddha is, happen upon him sitting at the foot of a tree as he emerges from a period of contemplation *(samādhi)*. Urged by a certain divinity, Tapussa and Bhallika approach the Buddha at a respectful distance and ask him to accept some rice cakes and honey balls, that the act may provide blessing and happiness to them for a long time. The Buddha doesn't know what to do, however, as he has only his bare hands; the four Great Kings then send a bowl of rock crystal and, with this bowl, the Buddha accepts the merchants' food. At the meal's conclusion, he receives them as the first Buddhist lay disciples.[148] The Jātaka tradition says that Sujātā, the daughter of the landowner Senānī from a village near Uruvelā, is the first to give food. When her wish for a son is fulfilled, Sujātā needs to make good on a vow for a food offering to the god of the nearby banyan tree. Her maid happens upon the Buddha and, thinking him the god, tells her mistress who brings a meal of milk-rice in a golden bowl that sustains the Buddha during his days of contemplation.[149]

The Buddha's early formal teaching on food and its acquisition is set within the narrative of a brahmin's complaint. This brahmin notices the sumptuous feasts prepared for the Sakyaputtiyā monks[150] in Rājagaha and decides to go forth himself in order to live in a similar leisurely way. When the luxurious meals dwindle away, the other monks ask him to go out for alms food *(piṇḍa)* but he balks and confesses that he has actually gone forth for his 'belly's sake.' The Buddha rebukes him and prescribes, as one of the conditions of Buddhist life, living in perpetuity on meals of scraps *(piṇḍiyālopabhojana).*[151] Thus the purpose of taking alms is made clear by the Buddha: "The alms which are sanctioned by me for you, let that suffice to sustain the body in life, to keep it going, to prevent injury, [and] to aid you in living the holy life."[152]

The importance of food in the shaping of spiritual life is paramount as renunciant groups of the time form their identities.[153] For Buddhists, food is important because it maintains strength[154] and supports the body. While food can encourage the five hindrances *(nīvaraṇa),* it can also support the seven limbs of wisdom *(bodhi).*[155] Had the complaining brahmin-turned-monk of the 'belly's sake' story known more about the uses of food in the spiritual quest, he would have been better off for, in his desire for the pleasures of food, he doesn't see that ordinary food like gruel has physical advantages essential to life on the middle way—keeping hunger and thirst at bay, regulating flatulence, cleaning the bladder, and helping to digest other food.[156]

The norm for the Buddhist renunciant during the non-rainy months[157] is, in taking up the bowl and outer-robe *(pattacīvaraṃ ādāya),* to go out once a day on a tour for alms food during the period before noon. Sometimes this tour or gathering is called the *piṇḍapātika,*[158] sometimes the *cārikā,*[159] and sometimes the time of being away or of walking *(car)* for alms *(piṇḍāya).* The alms petitioner then is a *piṇḍapātika.*[160] After gathering the day's food, the renunciant goes back to the residence, eats the meal, and turns to one of a number of things: resting, hearing instruction from the Buddha,[161] sitting in quiet contemplation,[162] going into the forest for quiet contemplation,[163] meeting with other renunciants for discussion,[164] or going back out on preaching tour.[165]

The Alms Bowl

The use of a bowl *(patta)* for alms food is enjoined upon renunciants at an early stage. Originally, followers of the Buddha put their hands out as they walked for food and collect it in their cupped palms like other petitioners. The Buddha, however—perhaps to distinguish his followers from rival groups or to maintain standards of cleanliness and respectability—rules that no one can be ordained who is not provided a bowl at the time.[166]

The bowl is a crucial part of a renunciant's spiritual identity, signifying abandonment of all worldly concerns and full dependence upon others for sustenance. It is also a personal item to be maintained by each renunciant, and there are no formal provisions for regular giving of bowls after the original rite of provision at ordination.[167] Although bowls are not normally thought of as gifts provided by donors, if a renunciant's bowl gets broken he or she can ask for a new one but only if the old one is already mended in at least five places. Taken up thus, the bowl is to be used throughout the renunciant life in the proper way, that is, only for receiving and eating food.

The Saṅgha oversees the assignment of bowls in times of emergency and, under the supervision of the *pattagāhāpaka,* 'the assigner of bowls,' harmonizes these assignments according to seniority rankings. If a bowl, for example, is received in exchange for an old bowl mended in less than five places, the new bowl is forfeited to the Saṅgha by the offending monk and, under the supervision of the assigner of bowls, is passed from the elder monks down to the youngest, in order of seniority, each choosing the newly available bowl or the one already in provision. The bowl left over at the end becomes the bowl of the offending monk. In this spirit, asking for many bowls without cause and hoarding extra bowls are clearly not allowed.[168] At death, however, a bowl can be passed on through the Saṅgha to another who will use it, or cast it off as appropriate. Bowls are to be made out of two standard materials, iron and clay. The Buddha rules against bowls that are gourds, water-pots, and skulls as well as against those made of gold, silver, pearls, beryl, crystal, bronze, glass, tin, lead, copper, or wood, presumably for reasons of health and safety, but certainly for reasons of attachment.[169] The Buddha makes other rulings as well: only ordinary, unadorned, circular bowl-rests of tin and lead can be used to prevent bowls from rubbing; bowls are to be put away clean and dry after each use, out of the sun and in a safe place; and some paraphernalia like stands and bags are allowable to ensure the proper storage of bowls.[170] Thus, a balance is maintained between minimal survival and luxurious extravagance.

Touring and the Encounter at the Household Door

The convention of taking the bowl, setting out on alms tour, and receiving food belongs to a larger South Asian phenomenon: that of renunciants walking for alms *(bhikṣācaryaṃ caranti).* These renunciants, who no longer desire sons or wealth or the worlds and who no longer have need for learning, live the life of a child by 'begging for alms through a village' *(grāmam bhikṣitvā).*[171] In discussing the significance of mendicancy, Olivelle notes two issues. First, in renouncing a fixed residence, a wanderer, thus begging, "negated the established custom of winning one's daily bread through labor." In this way, a donor householder's 'useful' life is contrasted with, and ultimately rejected by, "the recluses who led 'useless' lives." Second, among all of the other things renounced by the wanderer is the renunciation of the sacred fire, and since this includes the domestic kitchen fire, in "renouncing fire the *parivrājaka* rejected the most central element of life in the world, and with it gave up the right to cook his own food. He could not use fire for the secular purpose of cooking and reject its sacred use, for no such distinction ever existed in ancient India."[172] Initially, Buddhist mendicancy assumes the appropriateness of these two principles but, as it develops, it responds with a greater sense of compromise and adaptiveness, seeking the middle ground between extreme isolation from the household world and complete immersion within it: renunciants increasingly provide services to donor householders and are increasingly able to take some responsibility in the handling of their own food.

The *piṇḍapāta*[173] is the alms tour Buddhist renunciants make through villages and market towns[174] for the purpose of receiving donated food in their bowls. The etiquette of going for, receiving, and eating food requires that, every day during the months outside the rainy season,[175] at the right time,[176] the renunciant walks among the houses of people who are acceptable donors.[177] A renunciant is to be properly dressed in three robes and to move carefully and unhurriedly, paying proper attention to the seniority of others with him. His eyes are to be cast down, not looking to see if the householder donor is a man or woman; he is to make little noise and no laughter; and he is to control his body in a still, straight manner. Standing for food,[178] a renunciant is to wait patiently for signs that the donor, usually the housemistress, is willing to give: laying her work aside, rising from her seat, and taking and wiping a spoon or dish. Accepting what is given and only what is given,[179] the renunciant all the while holds his bowl evenly to receive the food.

On the alms tour, certain values are maintained with consistent regularity. The shaved head and matching three robes preserve the anonymity of the renunciant whose individual worldly identity is now replaced by a public uniform associated with the Saṅgha. The visual sameness presented to donors and among themselves creates a context of equality in which only spiritual differentiation is noted. The silence of the *piṇḍapāta* allows for the cultivation of mindfulness, preserves the equality of the petitioners, encourages the development of donor goodwill, and circumvents the power play of male ritual speech in a now non-gendered transaction. With the regularity of the humble presence of renunciants at the household door, there evolves on both sides a sensitivity to the subtle but effective mechanics of the encounter that maintains both essential Buddhist values as well as householder commitment.

The interdependence of the alms encounter is the arena in which traditional rules and etiquette emerge. Though not contributing in obvious ways to the ongoing maintenance of society,[180] Buddhist renunciants nevertheless strive for the adaptive middle ground in all things, mindful that some return on the material support given them is important. Providing exchange services not only in their teachings,[181] many of which are especially geared to issues of householder life, they are also model public persona. Good manners while on tour and while receiving and eating food are both an effective advertisement for the wholesome truthfulness of the Buddhist Dhamma (and hence a draw for donors), as well as a paradigm for good behavior among the public who value the etiquette of place and decorous humility. Just as donors have to learn how much to give and the care with which to give it,[182] renunciants have to learn how to garner donor goodwill.[183] A monk is not allowed to eat anything not actually given by a donor, though an exception is made for fruit only if, ordinarily, someone is found who will act as its donor.[184] Again, mindful of the need for non-attachment, a monk is not to eat alms food procured through the intervention of a nun, unless there has been a prior arrangement with the householder or unless the nun is a relative of his.[185] It is of interest that the public and private posture of renunciants is in part the product of good-intentioned and sometimes intrusive counselling and complaining done by donors, as they observe the minutiae of what they determine to be deviancy in monastic behavior. And it is part of the brilliant social policy of the Buddha and his followers that adapting to these householder voices becomes a way of life in the formation of food and eating etiquette.

The Buddhist alms tour has ties to the Vedic tradition of ancestor rites, primarily through the use of the word *piṇḍa.* Food eaten by Buddhist renunciants is referred to by several terms, *anna/aṇṇa, āhāra,* and *bhojana,* but the most common one in mendicant contexts is *piṇḍa*—a term that comes into Buddhist use loaded with Vedic baggage. In the Mahāvagga's directive about the four resources *(nissaya),* the food monks and nuns should eat is *piṇḍiyālopabhojana* 'meals of scraps of food.'[186] Moreover, the alms tour is the *piṇḍapāta, piṇḍacāra,* and *piṇḍāya carati;* the alms seeker is the *piṇḍacārika* or *piṇḍapātika;* the alms donor is the *piṇḍadāyika,* and the state of the *bhikkhu* and *bhikkhunī* is *piṇḍapātikatta* 'characterized by alms gathering.' Although *piṇḍa* is a ball or lump of food in general, [187] its most recognized use is in the Śrāddha rites performed regularly in honor and for the benefit of the, primarily male, dead. While there are obvious ritual antecedents for food gifts to Buddhist renunciants, either in the sacrificial food (ghee, milk, rice cakes, and meat) offered to the gods on the ritual ground, or in the food given as *dakṣiṇā* to the priests, one of the most illuminating antecedents to the Buddhist *dāna* system may well be the role of *piṇḍa* in the Vedic funeral and ancestral rites.

The encounter at the household door, originally formalized as between the housemistress and the monk around the transfer of *piṇḍa* into the waiting bowl,[188] draws from at least two Vedic patterns: the hospitality etiquette shown by a household to a ritual guest and the rituals of lineage preservation enacted prior to and after the death of a father. In the first case, Pali traditions of hospitality[189] derive from old ritual treatments of the fire god Agni, the herb god Soma, and the brahmin priest as guests at the ritual in which, at least by classical ritual times, the sacrificial patron's wife represents the household in receiving the guest and in proffering gifts of favor and goodwill. The hospitality etiquette of the public domain extends as well into the domestic domain in the feeding of the *brahmacārin* at the door and in the welcoming of the brahmin guest into the home.[190] As Amore suggests, this brahmin guest finds expression in the *bhikkhu,* "the wandering...true guest *(atithi),* the mysterious, powerful man whose sudden appearance represents...the intrusion of the sacred into the profane."[191]

The centrality of the householder wife in the Vedic patterns, and then formally in the early Pali milieu, is based upon her having management responsibility for the household wealth. Important as a representative of the household in honoring a guest, the wife is also important in permitting the use of household property for his honoring; her presence is significant in this way, for, without her engagement in the hospitality offered, a great insult ensues to the guest.[192] Thus, it is likely that the developments taking place in Vedic and Hindu views on women's ownership and control over property are known to and interdependent with the culture of Pali texts. The shift that seems to take place in Buddhism is that, while women continue to have management roles and hospitality obligations in terms of the household goods, they are also developing more autonomous, individualized roles in terms of religious giving in which their own personal decisions and commitments are at stake—and this is clearly evident in the formulation of the *piṇḍapāta* encounter.

In the second case, the household encounter draws on rites of transfer and ancestral rites that seek to preserve lineage and augment family prosperity. Reflecting basic values of the continuity of the male line through the father's perpetuity in his son, his son's in his grandson's and so forth, both the Upaniṣadic rite of transfer[193] and the Śrāddha ceremonies work to provide cohesion for the ancestral lineage over generations. Allowing not only for the "recovery and recuperation for the mourning family"[194] but also for the passage of the deceased into the world of the ancestors *(pitṛ),*[195] the Śrāddha rites begin the day after the death when a lump of cooked white rice *(piṇḍa)* is placed on a small altar of earth by a river or temple tank. The *piṇḍa* represents the *preta,* the restless spirit of the newly dead in its subtlest form, and is accorded veneration of incense, flowers, a ghee lamp, and white threads symbolic of clothes. Each day, for ten days, a cup of water with sesame seeds is poured over the *piṇḍa,* with the number of cups increasing by one each day, and in so doing the *preta* is given nourishment for the creation of his new intermediate body.

> *And each day of the rites results in a new portion of the preta's intermediate body, the head being created on the first day, then in succession the neck and shoulders, the heart and torso, the back, the stomach, the thighs and bowels, the lower legs and skin, the knees and hair, the genitals, and on the tenth day of the offerings, the preta receives digestive powers so that the sufferings of hunger and thirst now experienced by the "body of nourishment" duly created may be allayed by continued offerings of piṇḍas and water from the living.*[196]

With the tenth-day creation of the *preta's* full intermediate body, the period of ritual impurity for the survivors ends, and they can now, in their new state of purity, provide "the worship and ritual payment of the priest who...[has] served as ritual surrogate for the dead" and "the requisite feeding of invited brāhmaṇas who represent the company of the ancestors."[197] There then follows up to a year of daily rituals culminating in the actual day of *sapiṇḍīkaraṇa* and the recently dead's "release from 'pretahood'." At this time, the ritual requires the cutting of the *pretapiṇḍa* into three slices and the blending of each slice into one of the three *piṇḍas* of the ancestors, accompanied by their names and by verses indicating a union with the "company of ancestors" and a passing "from the preta to the pitṛ stage."[198]

The Śrāddha rites contribute to the theory of rebirth. In the Śrāddha, O'Flaherty argues, the *piṇḍa* is "offered to the dead ancestors in limbo as a transitional food mediating between death and rebirth." Symbolic of seed and, in its inclusion of milk and butter, of "the commingled substances of human procreation," the *piṇḍa* is eaten by the ancestors and by the living wife, and "the embryo that she conceive[s then becomes]...the new body of the deceased ancestor."[199] Ritual treatment of the *piṇḍa*, then, brings about new life, and the quality of that new life depends upon the correct precision of the ritual. Through the transfer of the *piṇḍa*,

> *the parents give the child both his substance...and his merit, or karma..., in one process. The householder* (gṛhastha) *is thus precariously balanced in the middle, supporting the male line of the past (his* piṇḍa*-consuming ancestors) and of the future (the sons who, he hopes, will feed* him *after death, and whom he must nourish with his own bodily substance before their birth.)*[200]

Thus, the Buddhist *piṇḍapāta* ritual includes a formal synthesis of Vedic hospitality etiquette and the Śrāddha rites. The centrality of the concept of *piṇḍa*, both as an offering to the dead for his own as well as the donor's benefit and as a link in the causal chain of individual efficacy, is clear from the widespread use of the term to refer to alms food. Although other terms are used for the food eaten by renunciants,[201] *piṇḍa* appears to be one of the ones used exclusively in the alms food setting. Passages prescribing behavior for the alms tour such as the one in the Cullavagga[202] use several terms for alms food, particularly, *piṇḍa,* and *bhikkhā,* and it is significant to note that in this passage *piṇḍa* is used in the general references to the alms tour, while *bhikkhā* is used in those specific places prescribing interaction with the woman of the household.

Several things are clear. First, that those passages in which *piṇḍa* is found usually include other terms such as *bhikkhā,* reflects a transitional stage in which there is both an incorporation of the older Vedic heritage and a shifting into newer contexts. Second, the appearance of *piṇḍa* is not accidental, for the Buddhist *piṇḍapāta* draws upon Śrāddha rituals in defining and significant ways. If, as suggested previously, the inclusion of elements from two ritual forms—the hospitality etiquette of a woman's household duties and the lineage-preservation rituals of fathers and sons—creates a conflict (the housemistress hosting a guest is in conflict with the son giving the dead food for rebirth) then passages like that of the Cullavagga reflect that conflict. For *bhikkhā* to be used in discussing renunciant interaction with women at the door and *piṇḍa* to be used only with other prescriptions reflects a tradition clearly aware of the problem it has in connecting a female donor directly with the giving of *piṇḍa.*

What might be said, then, about the significance of *piṇḍa* within the Buddhist alms tour? To be sure, *piṇḍa* is daily food to nourish and sustain the bodies of the monks and nuns, much as it serves to nourish and maintain the spiritual bodies of the *preta* and *pitara.* At the very minimum, then, *piṇḍa* is just another word for food. But the fact that it is used, and not some other word like *anna,* means something—for example, that it is not ordinary food but rather ritual food given to figures in a transitional state meant to keep them in that state until further maturation takes place. This maturation, however, is not necessarily the direct product of eating the *piṇḍa,* nor might the *piṇḍa* serve to ward off any negative advances by those who eat it toward those who give it, as it is in Vedic rites.[203]

It is more likely that, in the milieu of the interiorization of the sacrifice, the Buddhist renunciant provides a field or arena for the transmutation of food into a new rebirth, not for himself but for the donor. Collins argues that food, as an instrument of continuity, is found in the notion of consciousness "as a 'food' for the sustenance of future life." Based on the Vedic view that "the Fathers need...food to continue their shadowy existence, and the 'store' of good deeds was seen as a kind of nourishment for the next life, equivalent to food in this world," Buddhist doctrine sees food as necessary for both the creation and maintenance of the body and as a location of desire,[204] a central ingredient in continued rebirth. Because this view of food supports one of the recognized goals of the Vedic funeral rites, the desire (through *piṇḍa)* to assure rebirth,[205] the notion of the Buddhist renunciant as a field where this transmutation is to take place means that *piṇḍa* is like a seed planted in the field and harvested by the planter, through the workings of merit, in a new rebirth.

From the point of view of the Buddhist donor, then, gifts of food as *piṇḍa* are more than just selfless gifts of nourishment to renunciants but, in the proper contexts, acts calling forth all the good effects of *piṇḍa* within the linkages of rebirth. From the point of view of the renunciant, the receipt of *piṇḍa* is more than just the receipt of nourishment but, in the proper context, the offering of his or her field to the donor for the transmutation of the donor's gifted *piṇḍa* into a better rebirth. Both O'Flaherty and Knipe point out the tension in the Śrāddha ritual between the desire to prevent and the desire to assure rebirth: for the Vedic householder who wants rebirth through sons, the Śrāddha provides it, and for the ancestor who wants to prevent the dissolution of his after-life, viz., prevent *punarmṛtyu* 'repeated deaths,' the Śrāddha provides it.[206] In this way, the *piṇḍa* channel establishes an exchange of benefits for both Vedic parties.

The Buddhist adaptation of *piṇḍa* rites has to do, first, with grading the quality of the field, based upon the worthiness of the recipient in terms of merit production for the donor. From this, perhaps, there comes an explanation for why there are in the Theragāthā, for example, monks who, breaking their silence, say to donors at the threshold, 'I am an *arahant,* worthy of gifts.' This may be a straight-up way of telling the potential donor that the field of merit now at the door is of the highest quality, the most worthy of receiving gifts. While the Buddhist pattern of silence at the household door is designed to generate donor goodwill in an overall package of decorum and humility, there seems to be, in this later reflection of the encounter, a regressive recovery of an older pattern that responds, oddly, to newer needs within society. In the older pattern of the Vedic student on alms tour, self-identification by the student takes place at the door in order to establish caste, and perhaps family, affiliation with the housemistress as she comes to give out food. This model is abandoned in Buddhist practice of the alms tour because of the emphasis on anonymity and egalitarianism expressed in the uniformity of shaved heads, ocher robes, and silent modesty. In the increasingly urban context, however, the ever larger crowds of strangers may breed a considerable lack of familiarity with renunciant individuals and groups. Thus, in this denser and more mobile population, self-identification by monks may become a necessary practice for donors who are concerned about the quality of the merit field they are giving to. In this way, the older Vedic pattern of fixed and identifiable categories that has fallen into disuse is now reflected in a newer, "second generation," Buddhist practice of compensatory recognition of *arahants* in an environment where renunciants may be becoming increasingly unfamiliar to donors. That the Vedic term, *dakkhiṇeyya* 'worthy of gifts' is used in this self-identification formula further supports the connection of this practice to its older ritual heritage. Thus, the tradition goes back in order to go forward.

The adaptation of old *piṇḍa* rites to Buddhist practice has to do, second, with the gender dynamics of, normally, a housemistress as superintendent over the specific seed sowing process.[207] If meeting the housemistress at the door is the normal encounter of the Buddhist *piṇḍapāta,* it is so with a transformed dynamic. While the obligation of the Vedic *bhikṣā* relationship highlights the role of the wife as the representative of the household in its hospitality obligations, in the Buddhist case the downcast eyes negate the importance of gender in the donor, much as the shaved head of the renunciant does in the case of the monk or nun. There is no doubt that the formal Vedic hostess-guest relation is a pattern for the encounter at the Buddhist door, but the hospitality of the *ātithya* rite is transformed by living in *upanissaya* 'dependence' on or 'interdependence' with, and, in its recentering of obligation from the donor to the donee, the voluntariness of the alms encounter is highlighted. In the new context of individualization that heightens the issues of freedom and selectivity, and concomitantly that of responsibility, the donor can choose now whether to give or not—whether to offer seed or not into this particular field—and to then bear the commitment for this religious affiliation. Moreover, the encounter now focuses on the internal spiritual life of both the donor and donee for whom external comportment in both cases gives unmistakable signs of internal status. Going for food, then, is not just going for food, but involves both the housemistress and the renunciant in a state-of-the-art measure of life on the middle path.

Acceptable Food, Acceptable Eating, and Acceptable Handling of Food

The original posture of Buddhists is to be content with any kind of food given.[208] This follows the Buddha's own experience of finding spiritual satisfaction not in extreme pleasures of the palate nor in fasting, but in some balanced pattern of eating that does not focus concern on the content of the meal. Soon, in the cases of both alms petitioned and invited meals, the most common reference to nourishment given is to *khādaniya* 'hard or solid food' and *bhojaniya* 'soft food.'[209] This pair of terms is usually preceded by *paṇīta,* often translated as 'sumptuous' but suggesting 'heaped up or abundant.' The latter reading focuses on the wealth of the householder donor and his or her ability to give, rather than on renunciant greed or delight in pleasant food. Nevertheless, the Vinaya does preserve stories of renunciant attachment to good food and its negative consequences.[210]

In general, Buddhist food rules tend to be more lenient than those of some other renunciants who are more fastidious about what they'll accept. There are certain guidelines, however, that develop in the early community—in spite of the fact that Buddhists eat from almost all food groups[211]—the most notable being those that deal with meat. Meat is an issue of some discussion but it's not, in general, prohibited by the Buddha, especially if prepared and given by a donor householder.[212] If the meat served to renunciants, however, is seen, heard, or suspected to come from an animal especially killed for the occasion, it is prohibited,[213] and raw meat as well as human flesh and flesh from elephants, horses, dogs, snakes, lions, tigers, panthers, bears, hyenas, and wolves is prohibited as well.[214] The Buddhist middle ground here is evident once again: while there are market days declared to be no-slaughter days in recognition of the non-violent sentiments of some fellow ascetics,[215] Buddhists are allowed to eat meat given in alms; and while others kill for their own sustenance, Buddhist renunciants on their own practice *ahiṃsā*.[216]

The acceptable eating of food is a matter of some discussion. Renunciants are to go out for and eat their food in only one session *(ekāsanabhojana)*, being *ekabhattikas* 'one meal eaters,' a practice that is optimal for good health, spiritual wellbeing, and comfort, [217] and they are to go early in the forenoon, but not too early,[218] and to return not too late in the day.[219] Eating at the wrong time means eating between noon and sunrise;[220] eating at the right time means eating between sunrise and noon.[221] Buddhist renunciants are enjoined to accept only the little amount of food that will satisfy them,[222] though they are allowed to take back the extra to share with others,[223] keeping only one bowlful for themselves. A renunciant is not, however, allowed to eat food that has been laid aside and stored, i.e., accepted one day and then eaten the next, nor is he allowed to eat what is not expressly given to him, such as food given to the departed, nor himself to give food to a naked ascetic or to a male or female wanderer *(paribbājaka/paribbājikā)*.[224] After moderate eating,[225] leftover scrap can be thrown away as long as it is cast where there are no crops or in water where there are no living creatures.[226] When finished, the renunciant puts away his seat and bowl and sweeps the eating area.[227]

The act of eating receives attention as well. If there are two or more different types of food, the renunciant is to take a little of each with each mouthful, turning the food around in his mouth two or three times so that it is completely chewed before swallowing.[228] He is not to open his mouth with food still in it; he is not to put his whole hand in his mouth while eating; he is not to talk with a mouthful; he is not to eat by tossing balls of food into his mouth; he is not to break up the whole lump of food to eat it; he is not to eat stuffing his cheeks; he is not to eat shaking his hands about; he is not to scatter his food while eating; he is not to eat sticking his tongue out; he is not to eat smacking his lips; he is not to eat with a hissing sound; and he is not to lick his fingers, his bowl, or his lips.[229] While he experiences the full flavor of the food as he eats, he is not to experience greed or revulsion, accepting the full quality of the food just as it is given. As he accepts water for his empty bowl, the bowl is held evenly and, in cleansing it, there is to be no noise or scattered water, the handling being mid-way between care and unconcern. When finished, the renunciant is not to hope for another meal or to decry the quality of the previous; he is simply to continue deliberately with his day.[230]

In time, there is a shift away from the vulnerability of total dependency to a position in the middle, seen especially in the policy for cooking and storing food. Originally called *anagni,* 'without (kitchen) fire,' because of the totality of the renunciant vow,[231] the Buddhist renunciant is prohibited from all cooking[232] and from eating food that he or she has stored,[233] as these are marks of the new householder life for whom surplus food raises the necessity of wide-spread and long-term storage. During a famine, however, the Buddha allows his followers to cure and cook food that is brought to them by householders, though this concession is lifted with the return of prosperity.[234] In time, renunciants are permitted to store food in a *kappiyabhūmi*[235] 'a place for what is allowable, an outhouse.'[236] The Cullavagga, in fact, describes a situation in which food stored for monks becomes too abundant and is allowed by the Buddha to be offered to the nuns; the reverse is also allowed, that is, food grown to abundance as stored by nuns can be offered to monks.[237]

The Group Meal, The Invited Meal, and Regular Diners

Although the community is the basis and moderator of life, individual activities such as eating are primarily self-directed. This posture reflects the value placed on self-discovery and internal development, but its practice is hindered by a natural tendency to commensality. Eventually, the Buddha allows a 'group meal' *(gaṇabhojana),* an eating together by monks in a group of four or more (a three-monk meal being a *tikabhojana),* if it takes place in one of seven conditions: at a time of illness, at the time of the giving of robes, at the time of the making of robes, when embarking on a journey, when embarking on a boat trip, when there is a great scarcity of food, and at a meal-time of all recluses *(samaṇa).*[238] That this rule takes seven emendations to get right[239] is thus a good example of the incremental nature of disciplinary evolution.

In time, donor householders begin to invite renunciants to special meals *(bhatta)* either by themselves, in selected groups noted by tickets *(salākābhatta),* or as the whole Saṅgha *(saṅghabhatta).*[240] Alms petitioning is not mandatory, despite Devadatta's hope to make it so, and this new phenomenon grows out of an increasing awareness that the Buddhist endeavor is a joint one, encompassing all living creatures, and that no seeker can live in true solitude but does indeed have to depend on others, both for his sustenance and for his spiritual development: interdependence, thus, is the true mark of experience. These new special meals are not only a codification of philosophic teaching but a more formalized version of the social contract between donor and renunciant. They also serve to heighten, even more, the increasingly clear distinction between the early Buddhists and other religions of the time.[241] When a donor in the Buddhist context wants to give a meal, for example, he or she issues an invitation the day before (but sometimes on the day of) the meal *(uddesabhatta);* it cannot be a personal invitation, but has to be addressed to the Saṅgha as a whole—the group then decided who's to attend. Consent to the meal is given in silence. All the various dishes for the meal are prepared by the donor's household very early in the morning and, at the time when it's ready, an announcement is made to the renunciant recipients who, having already dressed, take their bowls and robes and go to the place of the meal, normally the dwelling of a householder. Each renunciant sits down in an appointed seat, is served in his bowl by the donor's own hands, and eats. As a sign that he or she is finished eating, the renunciant withdraws the hand from the bowl and moves away to a respectful distance. The meal is formally finished with the giving of thanks, and sometimes with a Dhamma talk.

More rules delimit conduct for the invited meal. In responding to an invitation from a donor to eat at the house, the renunciant needs to be clear not only about the actuality of the invitation, but about keeping to proper time, coming not too soon nor too late.[242] While a meal to which renunciants are invited is still going on, no renunciant can turn others away even though they arrive late.[243] Renunciants are to eat their meal straight through as given, and to take up invitations to meals in the order in which they are offered. Doing otherwise is to eat an 'out-of-turn meal' *(paramparabhojana)* that is prohibited except under special circumstances.[244]

In another development, renunciants come to be supported by particular donor families *(upaṭṭhākakula)* for their meals.[245] Although this can lead to greater familiarity on the part of the renunciants, approximating the empathic ties householders have amongst themselves, disciplinary vigilance seeks to preserve a normative modesty and detachment. The donation of perpetual meals to the Saṅgha is of continued interest to donors[246] and while it means a regularity of renunciants to host for a meal it does not necessarily mean a regularity of the same renunciants. Thus the Saṅgha exhibits a willingness to adapt to the permutations of a diverse human community and its needs. The general posture, however, is to insist upon moderate and modest behavior as renunciants practice their religion under the watchful and resourceful good graces of donor householders.[247]

A PLACE TO SIT AND LIE

The third requisite is that of lodging *(senāsana)*, a place for sitting and sleeping. The Buddha's original injunction, proclaimed again to the young monk at his ordination, is for renunciants to use the root of a tree *(rukkhamūla)*[248] as a resource *(nissaya)* for resting, in keeping with the ethic of using what is found without imposing any intrusive changes or interferences upon surroundings. The Buddha himself experiences enlightenment at the foot of the Bodhi Tree where, according to the Mahāvagga, he stays in contemplation for seven days. [249] In time, the tradition allows more elaborate lodgings: a dwelling *(vihāra)*, a curved house *(aḍḍhayoga)*, a long house *(pāsāda)*, a mansion *(hammiya)*, and a cave *(guhā)*.[250] Eventually, the norm for group lodgings is recognized as either the *āvāsa*, that is built and maintained by renunciants themselves in the countryside, or the *ārāma*, that is provided by donors nearer to towns and cities. With the latter, temporary encampments evolve into places of more settled monastic life.[251]

The Peripatetic Ideal and Changing Conditions of Residence

The role of the rain retreat in the shift from a wandering to a more anchored life-style is crucial. During this time, monks and nuns gather separately for temporary but fixed residence either in the countryside, where they themselves "staked out, built and maintained" settlements on their own, or near towns and cities, where they reside in lodgings provided to them by householder donors.[252] No renunciant is refused entry into the rain-retreat,[253] but exceptions are allowed for renunciants to leave the rain-retreat for up to seven days. As Horner notes:

> *Even as life must go on, so the Order's business must go on. And the life of this smaller world within the larger one could not close down entirely for a third of each year; monks were too much involved with the world outside, they were dependent on it..., and had commitments towards it, and their lives were too much interlocked with those of the laity to make this feasible.*[254]

The seven days excused absence, then, is allowed to a renunciant if requested to go on business by any one of seven peoples (a monk, a nun, a female probationer, a male or female novice, or a male or female layperson).[255] Renunciants are also allowed to leave the rain retreat for up to seven days in the case of illness of a fellow renunciant or a relative, or in other emergency cases involving the spiritual status and discipline of colleagues.[256] Cutting short the rain retreat is allowed when there is danger from wild beasts and reptiles, and from robbers and demons; when nearby villages that give alms food or the lodgings of monks are destroyed by fire; or when nearby villages or lodgings of monks are carried away by a flood.[257] The safety and security of livelihood within a residence are paramount to the keeping of the rain retreat, and it is not to be kept among unsympathetic people of little confidence *(assaddhā)* in the doctrine,[258] or in hollow trees, in the forks of trees, in the open air, in houses for the dead, under a sunshade, in a water-container, or in any place that does not afford proper and suitable lodging.[259]

In time, the Vassāvāsa is inaugurated by an obligatory ritual, the Vassupanāyikā, whereby monks vow to look after themselves and their lodgings, to perform due religious ceremonies, and to remain in the settlement for three months. It is brought to a conclusion by the Pavāraṇā that normally takes place on the fourteenth or fifteenth day of the month of Kattika.[260] The need for such a closing ritual becomes clear when, at the end of these intimately settled months, renunciants have developed gripes and animosities amongst themselves or have done or thought unwholesome things to someone else in the group that the Buddha doesn't want repressed in silence once wandering begins again. The Pavāraṇā is a gathering designed to bring out any hidden grievances, resolve them, and create a friendly and harmonious setting in which renunciants can pass out of the rainy season. With this in mind, the Buddha asks each monk on this 'invitation day' to go before his fellows all seated on the floor in solemnity and respect and, by raising his joined palms, to invite comments from them about anything seen or heard or suspected about any grievous aspect of his behavior, so that out of compassion *(anukampā)* amends can be made.[261] Olivelle argues:

> *The earliest form of the* pavāraṇā *may well have been the first occasion for such a public confession within the Buddhist* saṅgha. *The* pāṭimokkha *confession at the*

> uposatha, *I feel, is an extension and an elaboration of this* pavāraṇā *confession. The main difference between the two is that in the* pāṭimokkha *it is the guilty* bhikkhu *who confesses his faults, while in the* pavāraṇā *he invites the others to indicate his faults.*[262]

The argument that the Pavāraṇā is the earliest form of Buddhist confession, laying the groundwork for the fortnightly Uposatha at which monks hear a recitation of the rules contained in the Pāṭimokkha, confess to any wrongs, and receive appropriate redress,[263] is intriguing in that it gives a practical explanation for the appearance of confession in what, by all accounts, is a complicated evolution for the Buddhist Uposatha.[264] In "the extension of the residence at an *āvāsa* from three months to the whole year," Olivelle notes, the Pāṭimokkha confession, "as an extension of the *pavāraṇā,"* then, would have the same rationale, *"viz.,* to make the life at the monastery friendly and harmonious."[265]

As the custom of returning to the same *āvāsa* and *ārāma* year after year develops, the rain retreat settlement becomes a domicile "of a semi-permanent character."[266] Chakravarti emphasizes that the growing importance of regular donations and of the ethical emphasis on giving are key in the appearance of settled patterns of living. "The transformation of the *saṅgha* from an association of eremitical *bhikkhus* to a settled monastic organization made *dāna* one of the central concepts of Buddhism, particularly in relation to the lay supporters of the religion."[267]

In contrast, Wijayaratna sees the wandering and settled lifestyles as contemporaneous rather than sequential: the rain retreat is not necessarily "a bridge between two different periods in the history of the Buddhist monastic Community: first wandering and then sedentary life." Rather, the "institution of the Retreat served...to connect two different styles of life: traveling and being settled in one place," for "even after being given places to live, the Master and his disciples did not abandon traveling."[268] While travel continues to be a part of renunciant life, canonical texts confirm that donor-given *ārāmas* are an increasingly prominent feature. In fact, the continued importance of the life of travel depends upon there being numerous monasteries at well-spaced intervals, for when the Buddha charges his followers with going out in separate directions to teach the Dhamma, "these monasteries made their wandering easier."[269] Two conclusions then emerge from Pali narratives: that the renunciant life balanced between wandering and settling is commendable, and that a renunciant may, tolerantly, occupy almost any place along the wandering-settled continuum.[270]

The original purpose of lodging is to ward off cold and heat, to mitigate the effects of wind, sun, and any dangers of climate, to keep at bay insects and snakes, and to provide the renunciant with the benefits of seclusion.[271] The Buddha is said to have been content with any kind of lodging during the non-rainy eight months of the year—at the foot of a tree, out in the air, or in some temporary shelter.[272] Pali narratives confirm this contentedness with whatever little comes his way, for he and other renunciants stay in the woods,[273] on the banks of rivers,[274] on hillsides,[275] in mango groves,[276] and in bamboo groves.[277] For meditating, he enjoins monks filled with mindfulness and self-possession, to choose a spot deep in the forest, at the foot of a tree, on a hillside, in a valley, in a hillside cave, in a cemetery, in a wooded grove, in the open air, or on a heap of straw[278] as places to continue and advance their practice, and yet rebukes those who think that simply going to these places is enough to gain spiritual prowess.[279]

The need for a fixed residence during the three to four months of the rain retreat is clear from an early point, given considerations of weather, *ahiṃsā,* and community life. Choosing a good site for a rain retreat is important, and King Seniya Bimbisāra, for example, ruminates on this at length in finding lodging for the Buddha: not too far from nor too near a village, suitable for coming and going, accessible to those who want to come and hear the Dhamma, not crowded in the daytime, quiet at night, and with privacy and seclusion.[280] Such a place will be an *āvāsa,* a temporary "monks' colony staked out by the monks themselves"[281] with clear natural markers like rocks, trees, and hills indicating the boundary *(sīma)*,[282] to be dismantled at the end of the rain retreat, or an *ārāma*, a more permanent lodging within an enclosure in or near a town or city. The *ārāma*, 'pleasure park,' is normally the private property of a well-placed urban householder laid out as an orchard or garden, often with buildings already on it, that is given over to the Saṅgha *(saṅghārāma)*. Once given over, the donor continues to maintain the property, erecting new buildings, maintaining old ones, and providing robes and food for those dwelling there.[283] In time, he or she might even staff the premises with monastery attendants *(ārāmika)* who, if there are enough of them, establish special villages to live in with their families.[284]

Inside the boundaries or enclosure of an *āvāsa* or an *ārāma* are living places of the individual renunciants. A *vihāra* is a single hut or room used by each renunciant, as well as a place where groups of renunciants might meet; later, it designates a larger lodging or monastery for housing a number of monks or nuns.[285] It is distinguished from the *kuṭī* as the latter is a single-roomed hut or cabin nor formally part of a larger establishment.[286] Within his individual cell or dwelling place, each renunciant is allowed a bed or couch to lie on, a spittoon, and a chair. The inclination to make these furnishings excessively comfortable with covers, mattresses, and decorated upholsteries is curbed by popular outrage at the pleasurableness of such things (so much like householders!), so textile accoutrements are kept to a minimum, using only what is practical and necessary for minimum comfort.[287] The use of fine furniture, even if given to the Saṅgha, is curtailed as well, in the light of the trend to simplicity and usefulness, and in the face of householder criticism.[288]

Aside from providing places of lodging for renunciants, the settlement, whether temporary or permanent, needs to provide a place for congregational meeting where practices such as the Uposatha observance can be held. Originally, the Uposatha is held in successive monks' cells, but the Buddha allows the Saṅgha to argee on an Uposatha hall of their choosing, that is to be kept clean, well lit, and properly arranged.[289] In time, a regular common meeting hall is provided for, called an *upaṭṭhānasālā*,[290] that can be given specifically by a donor. The brahman Ghoṭamukha, for example, is encouraged by the monk Udena to have just such an assembly hall built for the Saṅgha at Pāṭaliputta.[291] Other rooms and parts of buildings come to be allowable as well, including fire halls (or 'kitchens'), huts for allowable items (or 'warehouses'), privies, enclosed places for walking, heated bathing rooms, lotus ponds, and temporary sheds. All of these a layperson can provide for the Saṅgha[292] or they can be built by the monks themselves.

Building and Caring of Lodgings

In building a place for Buddhist renunciants, care has to be taken that preparing the site does not entail destruction of living creatures, that it does not disturb any ancient religious sites, that it is placed with open spaces around it making it accessible to walking and to carts, and that it is properly marked and measured.[293] In designing the construction, tradition eventually allows doors with bolts, locks, and keys, roofs of grass, leaves, tiles, stones, and plaster, windows, curtains, shutters, and grass matting on the floor; privacy through the use of curtains, half-walls, and inner rooms; awnings, covered terraces, and screened verandas; pegs and stretched lines for hanging things; and furnishings, fences, porches, and water drains.[294]

Minimal decoration of buildings and their contents is also allowed. After hearing that members of other sects decorate their sleeping places with whitewash, covering the ground with black and the walls with red chalk, the use of three colors (white, red, and black) is allowed on *vihāra* surfaces, as well as depictions of wreaths, creepers, and swordfish-like teeth—in painting or carving. Not allowed, however, are figures of women, men, or animals. Textile covers for furnishing can be marked with line decorations and outlines of the hand, perhaps as a way of identification or to prevent misplacement.[295] Later texts note the decoration of monasteries with tapestries of many colors,[296] and representational images eventually make their way into monastic complexes.

Given that all monks and nuns are provided due lodgings but that they also have to be responsible users of such property, the specific assignment of lodgings becomes an increasingly weighty task, beginning with the assignment of lodgings for the rain retreat. Consequently, the Saṅgha designates one reliable person to be an assigner of lodgings *(senāsanagāhāpaka),* who is always mindful of what is needed and what is available. Three times for the assigning of rain retreat lodgings are given: the 'earlier' *(purimaka),* on the day after the full moon of the month of Āsāḷhī when some monks begin the rain retreat; the 'later' *(pacchimaka),* a full month after the full moon of Āsāḷhī when late arriving monks begin the retreat; and the 'intervening' *(antarāmuttaka),* on the day after Pavāraṇā when monks are assigned lodgings for the next retreat, one year hence. Although monks are distinctly prohibited from making reservations at two lodgings for the same period, Prebish argues that the very allowance of such 'reservations' is crucial in the early transformation of renunciant life. "With reservations already made one year in advance, they were assured of a satisfactory dwelling for the next year's rains."[297]

In time, as monks and nuns continue to travel to preach the Dhamma, and because established monastic lodgings make this easier to do, etiquette for a newly arrived renunciant emerges. When entering a monastery *(ārāma)* an incoming monk has to take off and put away his sandals, lower his sunshade, and uncover his head. He is to go to where the others are, not disturbing the old or sick monks, to put away his bowl and outer-robe, to sit down on a suitable seat, and to inquire about drinking and washing water. He is then to ask about available lodging, where to go for alms, and what families are learners (so as to suit his Dhamma talks); once in his assigned lodging cell he needs to clear, clean, and dry the furnishings, to put away his own things, and to keep the place neat and tidy by sweeping.[298] Cleanliness within the *vihāra,* for either new or present monks, is emphasized throughout the Vinaya, and several passages give minutely detailed instructions for the laying aside of bowl and robe, the moving of furniture and fabric coverings, and the washing, drying, dusting, and sweeping of all parts of the dwelling. Particularly worrisome are the appearances of dust, cobwebs, stains, and litter, and particularly onerous is the task of cleaning the bathroom and privy.[299]

The treatment and use of lodgings is carefully regulated as well. Movable furniture and fabrics can be stored in a shed after use and before going on tour, if one is staying out in the open air during the non-rainy season.[300] The care of furniture and fabrics belonging to the Saṅgha but used by the renunciant is up to each individual but, when neglected, constitutes a *pācittiya* offence (requiring expiation).[301] In a dwelling belonging to the Saṅgha, renunciants are not allowed to encroach on sleeping space that is intended for a monk earlier arrived.[302] Again, in a dwelling belonging to the Saṅgha, renunciants are not allowed to throw another out in anger,[303] and have to be careful that parts of furnishings they are using do not bring harm to another person.[304] Maintenance on the residence as a whole can be assigned out, but when a poor tailor from Vesālī has trouble making repairs to a renunciant lodging, the Buddha allows a monk to be put in charge of repairs as an overseer. Likewise, a donor wanting to build a lodging for nuns has first to contact a similar *bhikkhunī* overseer who has been put in charge of repairs.[305]

Giving Lodgings

Lodgings are considered to be the greatest gift a donor can give the Saṅgha: 'the gift of a dwelling to the Saṅgha is praised by the Buddha as the very best.'[306] While the gift of land, on which lodgings might be built, is late in being added to the materials of Vedic *dāna,* it is consistently "eulogized as the most meritorious of all gifts"[307] from the time of its Buddhist debut.[308] Gifts of land and lodgings are an important and very public act of support for the young movement, and the merchant householder Anāthapiṇḍika beats the drum for householder donations as he goes from Rājagaha, where he is on business, back to his home in Sāvatthi. Having just become a lay-disciple himself and having just decided to provide the Saṅgha with a rain retreat in Sāvatthi, he tells all comers: 'Masters, build monasteries, prepare dwelling-places, furnish gifts; an Awakened One has arisen in the world, and this Lord, invited by me, will come along by this road.'[309] Anāthapiṇḍika's influence is tremendous—as is the charismatic appeal of the Buddha—and there are almost always donors ready to provide lodgings for the Sakyaputtiyā whenever they need them, whether the donors are family to the renunciants[310] or not.[311]

If the lodging is not already available but has to be built especially for the Saṅgha, the role of the donor varies. Renunciants can, of course, build their own lodgings, either without a benefactor using things found and not owned by others, or under the auspices of a benefactor[312] who will help with building provisions. In either case, two objectives govern the process: "monks should not stray from a simple way of life, and they should not abuse the generosity of their benefactors."[313] When monks give their own labor to building for the Saṅgha, there are some limitations of site and access, but not so when donors are in charge; in both cases, however, the Saṅgha has to approve the site.[314] The timing of a gift of dwellings is important and donors, like the householder Udena, are urged to wait until after the rain retreat unless the gift is urgent, in which case it can be made in the presence of monks already resident at the site.[315]

The provision of lodgings is a significant moment in the institution and the Cullavagga narrative that describes the appearance of the very first man-made lodgings specifically for the Buddhist community reveals that this provision is and is meant to be primarily donor-driven. The great merchant of Rājagaha, brother-in-law to Anāthapiṇḍika, goes to Veḷuvana (which is still just a grove) one day and sees monks going from place to place out in the open. When he asks if monks would live in dwelling places *(vihāra)* if he provides them, the monks ask the Buddha. The Buddha then rules that five types of dwelling *(leṇa)* are allowable (dwelling, curved house, long house, mansion, and cave) and the monks return to the merchant with the ruling saying to him: 'Give whatever you consider appropriate.'[316] The merchant then has sixty dwellings built in one day, and, even though each of these huts is probably "so small and flimsy that sixty could be put up in a day,"[317] their appearance spurs the building of other dwellings for the renunciants by the 'people' *(manussā)*.[318] Because lodgings are so much harder to give, entailing substantial resources and labor, they are almost always a gift that needs donor initiative. (Note how the monks leave it to the merchant to do what he judges best.) While renunciants can appropriately appear at the household door for food, and reasonably assume new robe material will be given at the appropriate time, they cannot make such assumptions for lodgings. Such a gift is a momentous event of time and place for the Saṅgha—and for the donor as well, for it often provides him or her with a bit of fame and immortality, especially if the donor's name is attached to the residence.

ALLOWABLE MEDICINES

The last of the four requisites is medicine *(bhesajja),* to which a whole chapter of the Mahāvagga is given over. The Buddha's original injunction to renunciants is to use the strong-smelling urine of cattle *(pūtimutta)* as medicine,[319] presumably applied as an external astringent or antiseptic. Animal urine is one of the ingredients, along with dung, ashes, and clay, allowed in the treatment of snakebites—to be used if someone makes them allowable, or to be taken by the renunciants themselves.[320] It is also an important ingredient "in numerous recipes and therapies" found in early Āyur Vedic texts.[321] Because it is easily available to wandering renunciants—not needing to be given in donation nor taken in violation of the principles of *ahiṃsā*—use of animal urine as medicine is a common feature of the renunciant traditions of early Buddhist time.

In the shift from *nissaya* 'resources' to *parikkhāra* 'requisites,' the tradition allows expanded use of medicines during sickness *(gilānapaccaya-bhesajja),* medicines that can be given by donors along with the other requisites of robes, food, and lodgings. The five items originally allowed as medicine (now for internal use) include clarified butter, fresh butter, oil, honey, and molasses.[322] These are items that are to be taken internally and that also count as nourishments *(āhāratthaṃ)* but not as substantial food sources *(āhāra).* The Buddha adds these when he sees monks at Sāvatthi who, vomiting from an autumnal affliction, are grown thin and yellowish.[323] The nutritional value of food as a whole and the specific health benefits of particular foods are known from very early times,[324] and the Buddha's ruling on the medicinal as opposed to the food value of the five standard medicines is important because the Buddha also rules that no soft or solid food *(bhojaniya, khādaniya)* can be eaten after noon. The five medicines, however, can be taken both during the 'right time' *(kāle,* that is, from sunrise until noon) as well as during the 'wrong time' *(vikāle,* that is, from noon until sunrise); this constitutes a clear priority given monastic health over other concerns regarding food. Medicines are not to be taken for their nutritional value (and certainly not for pleasure), however, but only for good reason *(paccaya)* of health,[325] such as for warding off of injurious sensations and for freeing up the person for the best possible state of being.[326]

As in other early medical traditions, early medicinal items are "based on a systematic classification of foods."[327] The five medicines to be taken by renunciants who are ill are defined in the Suttavibhaṅga as follows: clarified butter and fresh butter that are prepared from cows, she-goats, buffaloes, and those animals whose meat is suitable; oil that is from sesame seeds, mustard seeds, honey-tree seeds, castor-oil plant seeds, and tallow that is from bears, fish, alligators, pigs, and donkeys; honey that is from bees; and molasses that is from the sugar-cane plant. Given pre-prepared by donors, these items can be stored for at most seven days, then have to be thrown out, and can only be used for the purpose given, that is, for medicine—not for food, nor for bodily enjoyment, nor for the lighting of lamps.[328] Other items eventually accepted as medicines, to be used only for good reason of health, include certain types of roots, astringent preparations, leaves, fruits, resins, salts, ointments and ointment powders, unguents, broths, and gruels. Also allowed are other accoutrements needed for the preparation and administration (internal or external as appropriate) of healing items: viz., grindstones, mortars and pestles, cloth sifters, ointment vessels, boxes and sticks, materials for vaporizing, sweat treatments and blood letting, compresses, and bandages.[329] Some items, such as the four great foul things *(mahāvikaṭa)* to be used for snake bites (e.g., dung, urine, ashes, and clay), are addressed separately as donated items: if someone is there to make them allowable then they are formally offered, if not then the renunciant can take them himself.[330] Renunciants know that the return to good health after a period of sickness does not depend only upon proper medicine, but also upon a good diet and careful nursing.[331] The real cure, however, comes from freedom from mental afflictions,[332] something that householders cannot donate to the Saṅgha.

Buddhist medicine develops in the renunciant environment where knowledge of healing techniques is an acceptable study. Zysk argues that "ancient Indian physicians...[are] shunned and denigrated by the dominant orthodox brāhmaṇic society,...[and] found refuge in the less orthodox communities of renunciants and mendicants who did not censure their philosophies, practices, and associations." As wanderers, they "gradually became indistinguishable from the *śramaṇas*" and only much later are these physicians and their lore "incorporated into the mainstream Hindu religious tradition."[333] It is because knowledge of the healing arts is present among wandering ascetics already, Zysk argues, that medicine becomes one of the four Buddhist *nissayas*, for some of the early materials and techniques of Buddhist and Āyur Vedic medicine are commonly available to all those wandering on the fringe.

The giving of medicine by donors is a natural derivative of the giving of food, and it is perhaps because some medicines become classified with, but differentiated from, other foodstuffs that donations of medicine are recognized equally with the other requisites. Because medicines and medical items are usually the products of human culture and not, as in the case of urine, found in nature, and because renunciants cannot work to procure them, it is critical that medicines be donated by householders. As the Saṅgha develops in size and complexity, medicines continue to be one of a renunciant's necessities and they grow "into an entire pharmacopoeia, including numerous foods and incorporating culinary traditions derived perhaps from the laity."[334] The monk Pilindavaccha, who receives the five kinds of medicine into the community, is known 'customarily' as a 'receiver' *(pakatiyā lābhī)* and, receiving them, gives them out among his compatriots. Storage for medicines becomes a part of the more general discussion of storage for Saṅgha materials and it is quite possible that the Saṅgha member appointed as *appamatta-kavissajjaka*, 'disposer of trifles,' is in charge, among other things, of the drugs and medical supplies given over by donors and used at a given residence.[335] While renunciants depend upon householders for the giving of medicine, zealous donors are encouraged to give within the established *dāna* boundaries. Suppiyā's gift of a meat broth made from flesh of her own thigh, for example, is a gift well outside expectations of self-sacrifice and of appropriate food-stuff and results in a severe rebuke for the ill, and thoughtlessly accepting, monk.[336]

Because of his or her having gone forth from home into homeless life, the Buddhist renunciant depends upon the generosity of the householder donor to supply the four requisites *(parikkhāra)* of robes, food, lodging, and medicine. Originally, these four are items that can be found anywhere; they are available in the environs all around the wanderer, without having to make trouble for the donor: rags, foodscrap, trees, and cows. In short time, however, partly because of the variety of renunciant needs that emerge, partly because of the structures already in place for householder gifts to wanderers, and partly because donors feel a desire or obligation to give to the renunciants they identify with in some way, a more complicated context for supplying basic needs emerges. What makes the early Sakyaputtiyās stand out is that the Buddha (and the subsequent Saṅgha leadership) is eminently adaptable both to the circumstances the followers find themselves in, and to the concern of interested householder parties as they criticise and promote the evolving Saṅgha. Without the traditions's early willingness to compromise and to be flexible, the Buddha's followers would not thrive as they do. His commitment to the middle way ensures the survival and growth of his community and, ultimately, allows Buddhism to change shape as time and geography continue to shift their way through it. As Gombrich notes, for example, the Buddha's original teaching on food is that "one should treat oneself well enough not to be distracted from spiritual life by hunger, and moderately enough not to be distracted by over-indulgence."[337]

Buddhist inheritance from the Vedic tradition includes, in addition to specific vocabulary and mechanics of practice, an assumption about proper behavior to religious persons: that sharing the wealth with those perceived to be more exclusively dedicated to spiritual goals is a commendable and expected thing to do for those engaged in the householder life. While the specific things given as *dakṣiṇā* to brahmin priests may differ somewhat from those given as one of the four *parikkhāra* to Buddhist renunciants (the most obvious example being precious metals and currency), in both cases the gifts are substantial, requiring some sacrifice on the part of the donor. In the specific case of alms food, the *piṇḍa* offered is not on its own consequential, but it is in most cases a daily affair and it is given at some presumable cost to the householder. Moreover, Vedic heritage is eminently present in this giving and receiving of alms food, for the etiquette of the renunciant petitioner at the door has sure foundation in the Soma guest reception and in the touring practice of the young Vedic student.

There may be most divergence, however, in the purpose of the gifts, for the *dakṣiṇā* to the priest is payment for services rendered or, alternatively, as Heesterman argues, an expression of the "generative alliance between the giving and receiving parties."[338] The gift of Buddhist *parikkhāras,* however, is at first glance at least more mundane for, returning to the case of the young householder boy Siṅgāla, the donor is asked to minister unto renunciants in five ways, the last two being by keeping an open door to them and by providing for their temporal needs.[339] With renunciant dependence on householder donations an acknowledged and life-long position, there is substantial departure from the *dakṣiṇā* relationship of priest to patron where such dependence is less public, and from the *brahmacarya* relationships of youth to household where arrangements are by design temporary. No wonder, then, that Gombrich can say: "The existence of the Saṅgha, and hence of Buddhism, depends, in theory at least, on the generosity of the laity."[340]

As the peripatetic life of the Buddhist renunciant becomes more settled, the involvement of the donor becomes more active. Donor initiative is more crucial as "monks and nuns were forbidden to work to buy...items or to produce them," and the alms round is increasingly "replaced by the acceptance of offerings brought to the monastic communities."[341] It makes great sense, then, to tie the ritual life of early monks and nuns increasingly to the possibility of donation, a link evident, for example, in the very definition of those who can attend the Uposatha: "On every Observance Day we who live depending on the same field and village each and all gather together on the same day."[342] What makes this renunciant dependence viable, however, is an ethic that gives all aspects of donation a Buddhist significance—an ethic specifically designed to ensure the survival of the Saṅgha.

ENDNOTES

1. Olivelle, *Saṃnyāsa Upaniṣads,* p. 20.

2. This is clear from periodic reminders throughout the canon: ritual fires burning in homes of brahmins (Sn p. 21), the Agnihotra sacrifice maintained with loyal regularity (Sn p. 79; see Olivelle, *Saṃnyāsa Upaniṣads,* p. 25), and brahmins known to be worshippers of fire (A 5. 263). King Pasenadi, for example, is a patron of the Vedic ritual at which five hundred each of bulls, oxen, heifers, goats, and rams are scheduled to be led to the sacrificial pillar (S 1. 75-76). Brahmins from the Bhāradvāja (M 2.196; Sn pp. 115-116) and Verahaccāni (S 4.121) families regularly interact with the Buddhist community, and a number of brahmins—Sela (M 2.146; Sn pp. 104 - 105), Caṅkī (M 2.165), Kāpaṭhika (M 2.168), and Saṅgārava, for example ((M 2.210)—are known to be versed in the three Vedas, in vocabulary, in ritual, in phonology, in exegesis, and in grammar. Practicing brahmin women are also prominent: as worshippers of the god Brahmā (S 1.140-142), as teachers of resident pupils (S 4.121) , and, significantly, as converts to the new Buddhist movement (M 2.209-210). Vedic observances of sacrifice and austerity are known to have as their goal "dwelling in the Brahmaloka by acquisition of merit" and Vedic gods, in particular Indra (Sakka), are familiar figures in local lore (N. Dutt, *Monastic Buddhism,* pp. 4-7). In all, as O'Flaherty states: "There is such constant interaction between Vedism and Buddhism in the early period that it is fruitless to attempt to sort out the earlier source of many doctrines; they lived in one another's pockets..." (O'Flaherty, pp. Xvii-xviii).

3. S. Dutt *(Monks and Monasteries,* p. 73) for example, discusses the Buddhist Uposatha's ties to the Vedic New and Full Moon sacrifices, and Frauwallner argues at length (e.g., p. 62) for the modeling of Vinaya teacher lists on similar Vedic ones "in order to bestow on the own [Buddhist] tradition an authority similar to the Vedic one." See the discussions in Schopen, "Doing Business for the Lord," p. 553 and Schopen, "Monastic Law Meets the Real World." pp. 110, 121-122.

4. Heesterman, *"dákṣiṇā,"* p. 256. Alternately, the cow *go* is the 'abundant

one,' *dakṣiṇā,* and the cow is the usual and expected gift given. See Macdonell and Keith 1.336.

5. Symbolically, according to Heesterman ("*dákṣiṇā,*"p. 257), "the dakṣiṇā is the material manifestation of the cyclical course of the universe as it is represented in the ritual." The birth, disintegration, and rebirth of the sacrificer necessarily involves all parts of the sacrificial universe, and those who receive *dakṣiṇā* do so not because of "the importance of the services rendered" by them but because they are all a part of this universe. The *dakṣiṇā,* then, as the Śatapatha Brāhmaṇa notes in 4.3.4.2, is the means of invigorating the sacrifice and of ensuring its success.

6. Items found in the Ṛg Veda include cows, horses, camels, chariots, young girls, food, gold, and garments. The cow takes precedence from the beginning, and a Ṛg Vedic hymn, 10.107, that divinizes the *dakṣiṇā,* lists in order four items that are most valuable as gifts: the gifts of cows that bestow heaven on the donor, of horses that bestow the world of the sun, of gold that bestow immortality, and of garments that bestow long life. By the time of the Śatapatha Brāhmaṇa (ŚB 4.3.4.24-27), however, the order of this list has changed—gold, cows, garments, and horses—indicating a shift from a martial culture to a more mercantile one.

7. Patel, pp. 13-30.

8. Eggeling, 1:xi.

9. In one, a group of nine are considered best (food, curds, honey, protection, cows, land, gold, horses, and elephants); a group of four are considered average (learning, house for shelter, domestic items such as cots, and medicine); and another group considered poor (shoes, swings, carts, umbrellas, vessels, seats, lamps, wood, fruits, and other items, some of which might be old or worn out) (Kane 2.2:847). Other traditional lists of ranked gifts are known as well, often different one from the other, however, by what counts as the 'best gift' *(atidāna;* e.g., cows, land, learning) or what the reward is for giving the best gift (e.g., heaven, happiness) (Kane 2.2:848). Some items, moreover, are designated as unacceptable gifts (in receipt particularly by brahmins), such as certain types of animals, weapons, poisons, and alcoholic drinks (Kane 2.2:851).

10. Holy places, natural and man-made, are auspicious venues for gifting, with the home being the principle auspicious location (Kane 2:2:847, 851-54). In the latter, the general gift-giving ritual prescribes that both the donor and donee should come bathed and properly dressed and, when both are properly seated, "the donor should utter the name of the subject of gift, its presiding deity and the purpose for which he makes the gift, and say 'I make a gift to you of such and such an article,' pour water on the donee's hand, and when the donee says 'give' the donor should sprinkle water on the subject of gift and place it into the hand of the donee, who utters the syllable 'om' and says 'svasti.' The dakṣiṇā is given to the donee" (Kane 2.2:855). Formal receipt of larger items, such as a house or land, are made by the donee's walking around or entering the gift.

11. Jamison, p. 117. MS 3.7.9: *pátnī vái pārīnahyasyeśe pātnyaivá rātám ánumataṃ kriyate,* 'The wife is master of the household goods. Thus, the gift (of them) is made with the approval of the wife.'

12. The word *pārīṇahya* is used in three Saṃhitā prose texts as well as in the Mānava Dharma Śāstra (MS 3.7.9; TS 6.2.1.1-2; Manu 9.11) to designate 'household goods.' Jamison discusses its derivation from *parīṇáh,* a container or box, as follows: "the 'household goods' may be literally 'those belonging to the cupboard'...or 'those belonging to the trunk'....If the latter is the source, the striking attribution of property-ownership to the wife might be explained. The *pārīṇahya* might originally have been the moveable goods that the bride brought to her new home at marriage.... These she would have control of, and even when *pārīṇahya* came to refer to household goods in general, the old notion of the wife's ownership of what she brought to the marriage may have been preserved" (Jamison, p. 118).

13. Note that this is the same term used in Pali texts *(itthi-* or *itthīdana)* to describe household possessions or property often comprised of basic holdings. Note as well that the word used for 'woman/wife' is not the *patnī* 'wife' of the sacrificial system (as in *yajamānapatnī)* or the *patānī* of the Pali householder (as in *gahapatānī),* both of whom have horizontal linkages to the husband, but *strī* 'woman, female' who has vertical linkages to children (being derived possibly from *sū* 'generate, enliven'). The vertical linkage may be at issue here because of important discussions with regard to a deceased mother's property in which daughters are favored. The preference for daughters as heirs, in all schools, may well be an attempt to provide equity in a system where daughters are allowed to be excluded in the devolution of a father's estate.

14. Ordinarily, *strīdhana,* includes all wealth a woman receives either while betrothed or married, either in her father's house or her husband's, and given by either of the two families (Kane 3:778). Kane argues that the actual amount of property owned by Vedic women increases over time: while in the Ṛg Vedic period such property is meager, as the Brāhmaṇic period develops, "such kinds of property went on increasing in extent and value" (Kane 3:772). While *strīdhana* as an operative concept is not present in the Ṛg Veda, the wedding hymn (10.85.13, 38) indicates that the bride takes bridal gifts with her when she shifts into her husband's house; Sāyaṇa's explanation of *vahatu* here is as "cows and other objects given for pleasing the girl to be married" (Kane 3:770).

15. While some, like Jaimini, use this to establish a woman's ownership over certain property (see Kane 3:770-71), the passage itself is not clear on the issue of ownership; what it does do is to establish some supervisory responsibility for the wife over domestic property, whether it is hers, her husband's, or jointly owned. Moreover, it does not elaborate on how she is to manage or dispose, only that she can. Manu must have the sentiment of this passage in mind when he declares that a husband should allot to his wife the collection and the expenditure of all of this wealth (9.11).

16. Keith'translation of TS 3.2.8.5
17. E.g., RV 1.126.2; 6.47.23; 8.5.38; 10.107.2, 7, 8; TS 1.4.43; TB 2.2.5; AB 39.6; ŚB 4.3.4.7, 20-24; 5.5.1.8.
18. Kane 2.2:871.
19. See Macdonell and Keith 1.336.
20. Vin 3.16; M 2.63. An alternate reading for *mattika* given in the notes is *mātumattika*.
21. See Dhammapāla's commentary to Vv no. 35.
22. Olivelle, *Saṃnyāsa Upaniṣads,* p. 12. For a full discussion see Kane 2.2:930-975.
23. See ĀśU 100-102; NpU 174-178, 203-207; BhU 233-236; TaU 241-242; BSU 254-55; ŚU 324. See also the bovine and canine ascetics known to early Buddhists, M 1.387-392.
24. PhU 46.
25. LṢU 20, 21; KśU 33, 40, 41; JU 68, NpU 141, 145, 186; PpU 282; ŚU 327, 328.
26. NpU 148. Other types of covering are worn as well: e.g., garments made of antelope skin (ĀrU 11; NpU 204; PpU 282), bark (KśU 33; TaU 242; PpU 283) and, on rare occasions, grass and leaves (ŚU 328).
27. ĀrU 11; LSU 22; ŚU 327. Metal bowls are forbidden (BSU 270; see KśU 38).
28. ĀrU 6; LSU 21; KśU 41; JU 70; ĀśU 101-102; ŚU 323.
29. LSU 21; KśU 41; NpU 145, 169; BSU 252.
30. S 1.167; A 5.263.
31. Olivelle, *Saṃnyāsa Upaniṣads,* p. 125n.
32. LSU 21; KśU 41; JU 70; ĀśU 101-102; NpU 145, 154, 174, 192; BhU 234; BSU 254; ŚU 323-24.
33. BU 90; NpU 160, 175, 180; BSU 255. Wooden staffs are also used: PhU 50; NpU 180.
34. PhU 46.
35. See Kane 2.2:935-36.
36. D 1.165-177; 3.40-57; M 1.77-83; 238.
37. Vin 1.58. See Vin 2.274, 278; D 3.137, 141; A 1.117; 3.271; 4.353; 5.73; Sn 753, 877; Thera nos. 1057, 1146-49. Living within the 'aṣ-is-found' environment is a staple of the *saṃnyāsin* mode: eating only to sustain life; living only on whatever one happens to receive; and wandering homeless by sleeping on chance river banks, at the foot of trees, in mountain caves or in temples.
38. Vin 3.41-45.
39. Zysk, p. 40. The shift from resources *(nissaya)* to requisites *(parikkhāra)*

is reflected in a Dhamma talk given to the monk Anuruddha, who is told by the Buddha that with mental cultivation he will see his rag robe as a luxurious householder's garment, his alms scraps as a tasty feast, his tree root lodging as a well-built house, his grassy seat as a softly covered divan, and his ammonia medicine as a sumptuous extra (A 4.228-235).

40. Vin 1.248; Vin 3.89, 90, 132, 184, 211, 266; Vin 4.122; 1.104-108, 126, 271; 2.101; 3.254; S 4.288; A 1.247; 2.26-27, 54-55, 65; 3.124-126, 130, 135; 4.114, 134, 366; 5.15, 67, 131, 201, 350; Sn no. 339. See Prebisch, *Buddhist Monastic Discipline,* p. 4.

41. *atta-dīpā bhikkhave viharatha atta-saraṇā anañña-saraṇā, dhamma-dīpā dhamma-saraṇā anañña-saraṇā* (D 3.58; see also Sn nos. 35-75).

42. Misra, p. 97.

43. D 2.357-58; M 1.404; 3.24; S 1.18; A 1.91-92. See the similar use of co-derivatives of *dā, dinna* (e.g., M 1.401-402) and *deyya* (S 1.18).

44. D 1.51; 2.88, 266; M 3.253-57; Thera no. 566; Therī no. 287. For a discussion, see Amore pp. 32-36.

45. A 1.63.

46. D 3.1, 16; M 1.31, 108-109, 160, 173, 206-207, 227, 237, 336, 359, 371, 420, 447, 481, 501; 2.29, 61, 104, 112, 185; Thera nos. 381, 579.

47. Sn nos. 461, 484; Nd2 no. 523. The Cullaniddesa enumerates a list of fourteen gifts *(deyyadhamma),* rendered in a slightly different order in the Mahāniddesa (no. 373).

48. D 3.67.

49. D 3.78.

50. D 1.9.

51. D 3.46.

52. Vin 3.184. See the discussion in Prebisch, *Ethics,* pp. 34-35, 38, and Zysk, p. 40.

53. A 5.87.

54. Iti 111.

55. See S. 2.269-270, where laypeople, pleased with the monastic preaching of doctrine, do their duty by giving gifts.

56. Rājavaramuni (p. 34), however, gives this issue secondary place when he says, the "monks' task of working for the good of the people [is] both as an act of compassion and in terms of the necessarily reciprocal nature of their relationship."

57. *ārāme ayyo karotha vihāre patiṭṭhāpetha dānāni paṭṭhapetha* (Vin 2.158).

58. D 3.180-193.

59. *anāvaṭa-dvāratāya āmisānuppadānena* (D 3.191). As Rājavaramuni (p. 38) goes on to point out, however, many benefit over time from offerings to the renunciants of the Saṅgha: "... donated food generally benefits

not only the monks, but also a number of people who come to seek shelter in the monasteries. This tradition is said to have originated at the time of the Buddha, and in the course of time monasteries have become places where the destitute, orphans, and students live, obtain sufficient food, and receive moral and educational training from the monks.

60. Vin 1.58.

61. In addition to the three robes, a variety of textile goods are allowed, viz., a loin cloth for the rains, a piece of cloth to sit on, a sheet, small cloths for itching and for wounds, a towel for wiping the face, bags for various incidental uses, a bathing cloth, a canopy, a ground covering, a screen-wall, a mattress, a pillow, and a rug. Moreover, monks and nuns are allowed an alms-bowl, a water-strainer, sandals, a razor, needle and thread, a small knife, a bag for medicine, a bag for sandals, a duster to sweep the lodging, as well as a host of things for modestly furnishing a place to live. A second list of items suitable for giving to the Saṅgha, called "a standard set" by Rhys Davids and Stede (p. 318), includes eight items of food, drink, clothing, carriages, flowers, scents, ointment, seats, lodging, lamps, and oil.

62. Vin 1.305.

63. This rule is first set down when some come to ordination without a robe, having walked naked for alms food (Vin 1.90-91, 93-95, 305-306; D 3.9, 40-41; M 1.77-83, 238, 281, 342-43; 3.124-26; A 2.205-207; see Gombrich, *Theravada Buddhism,* p. 98). Says Wijayaratna (p. 33): "The members of the Buddhist Community...and its founder, were not willing to acknowledge nudity as a virtue, nor to imitate the mode of dress of any other ascetics."

64. ŚGS 2.1.15-17; ĀśGS 1.19.10-12; GGS 2.10.7-10; ĀpDS 1.1.2.33-37, 39-41; 1.1.3.1-10; 2.9.21.11-12; 2.9.22.1; GDS 1.7.15-21; 3.18.18-19, 34, VDS 9.1.

65. D 3.130; Vin 1.287-89.

66. Vin 1.22.

67. Vin 1.253, 282-83; 305-306; D 1.166-67; 3.40-41; M 1.77-83; 2.102; S 2.202-203, 221, 281; A 1.240-41, 247; 2.26. Note that *paṃsukūla* are also listed as garments of non-Buddhist renunciants.

68. *...paṃsukūlikā lūkhacīvaradharā; te susānā vā saṃkāra-kūṭā vā pāpaṇikā vā nantakāni uccinitvā saṃghāṭiṃ karitvā ahārenti...gahapatāni cīvarāni dhāremi daḷhāni yattha lūkhāni alābulomasāni* (M 2.7; see also A 2.27).

69. *sāṇāni paṃsukūlāni nibbasanāni* (S 2.221). The term used for compassion here is *anukampā,* a significant posture of Buddhist renunciants towards others.

70. Wijayaratna, pp. 34-35. He (p. 35) explains the Buddha's acceptance of a householder-robe as follows: "It looks as if the Master was only waiting to be asked by devotees to allow monks to wear robes given by lay people. If the Buddha and his disciples had started from the first days to beg for robes made with unused pieces of material, and to accept them,

this would undoubtedly have hindered their popularity....For the Buddha, the time was now ripe to change the habits of the Community."

71. Vin 1.280-81; M 1.31; 2.7; S 2.202; A 3.391.
72. Vin 1.280-281; see Misra, p. 124.
73. Vin 3.195; Vin 1.253, 287-290; M 1.353; 2.102, 117; S 2.187, 202.
74. Vin 1.288; Vin 3.198, 262-64.
75. Vin 1.90.
76. In dark green, brown, or black (Vin 4.120-21).
77. Vin 1.288-89; see Misra, pp. 125, 185. Thera no. 367 mentions Gotama making a bed by spreading his *saṅghāṭī* out in the open air.
78. Vin 3.195-96; Vin 1.289.
79. Vin 1.290, see Misra, p. 124.
80. Privileges attending the giving of cloth to the Saṅgha at the end of the rains and lasting for four months (Vin 3.195-96, 202-205; Vin 1.289).
81. Vin 3.198-202; 4.281-82; Vin 1.109-111. The Buddha's attendant Ānanda, however, who is often criticized for not paying closer attention to important matters such as these, is said to have gone into a village one day for alms wearing only two robes. He confesses his unmindfulness to the other monks who see him, and then hears from the Buddha about the five occasions on which the outer robe can be omitted -- none of which fit his case (Vin 1.298; see also Vin 3.262-64).
82. See the discussion in Horner, *Book of the Discipline* 2:xviii-xix.
83. T.W. and C.A.F. Rhys Davids, *Dialogues* 2:162n.
84. Vin 1.254, 298.
85. Vin 4.278, 282-83, 323-24, 345; Vin 2.272.
86. Vin 2.270-71. If she retains a householder robe for use during menstruation, a nun then has in fact to use it, and use it for that purpose (Vin 4.303).
87. Therī nos. 1, 41; see nos. 496, 497.
88. Vin 1.58, 281; Vin 3.196. See Vin 4.25.
89. See, for example, the interchange on the worthlessness of rough fiber cloth and the great value of material like cloth from Benares (A 1.246-49), and the metaphor used for the adept well-prepared to take on Dhamma practice: 'just as a clean cloth without black specks will take on dye properly' *seyyathāpi nāma suddhaṃ vatthaṃ apagatakāḷakaṃ sammad eva rajanaṃ patigaṇheyya* (Vin 1.16, 181, 225, 237; Vin 2.156-57; D 1.148; see D 1.76).
90. Vin 3.257-260.
91. Wijayaratna, p. 36. The making up of robe-materials by monks is called *cīvarakamma* and the proper time of sewing robes is called *cīvarakārasamaya* (M 3.110).

92. Vin 1.287.

93. Wijayaratna, p. 36. A Vinaya of the Mahāyānists notes that the shaven head, robes, and alms-bowl of the monk is designed to destroy his pride, as it places him in a similar social location with a young outcaste *(caṇḍāla)* (N. Dutt, *Mahāyāna*, p. 315).

94. Vin 1.287; see Frauwallner, p. 98.

95. S 2.220; Thera nos. 961, 966, 969, 973; D 2.133-34; Vin 1.287. The use of the ocher color is reflected early on in a verse from a Soma-related hymn, RV 10.136.2, in which the long-haired, visionary, silent sages *(muni)* are said to be dressed in dirty yellowish- or reddish-brown garments *(piśaṅgā vasate malā;* in an alternate rendering, the sages wear ocher mud). This color is found in the garments of the Vedic *brahmacārins* (ĀśGS 1.19.11) as well as in the garments of later-stage renunciants in the Vedic and Hindu traditions (BDS 2.6.11.21). The establishment of *kāsāya* as the norm for Buddhist robes, thus, may be a continuation of the ocher of the Ṛgvedic *muni's* garment, having become a normative sign of the renunciant wanderer, or a standardization of the yellowed color of old rag robes taken off of trash heaps. In either case, the color suggests several associations: with the golden drink of Soma and, through Soma, with the sun and immortality (RV 9.74.1; 9.113.7, 9, 10, 11); with the light and warmth of the ritual fire Agni who is the transformed and the transformer, but also the internal heat of austerity *(tapas)* that cleanses, burnishes, and purifies (Knipe, *Image of Fire*, pp. 128-133); and with new life and rebirth as reflected in the golden egg theories of creation of the Upaniṣads (CU 3.19). The Vedic ritualist, then, might well be homologized with a new embryo and, through the ritual use of garments and of color symbolism, reborn to effective religious life (AB 1.3). Following this the Buddhist renunciant, thus clothed in ocher, can be understood as part of an ancient Indian lineage in which the sacrifice is interiorized and the spiritual heat of one's own hard work and discipline brings (or gives the promise of) full ripening and maturity.

    Beck (p. 559) notes another correlation of yellow in her discussion of color in south Indian ritual: that of yellow with the *vaiśya varṇa* (white/brahmin; red/*kṣatriya;* blue/*śūdra*). "Yellow is the colour of saffron and tumeric, both very cooling substances...[tumeric] has a very strong association with fertility and prosperity." Smith (p. 31) then discusses in some detail the correlation of the *vaiśya* with productivity, prosperity, and abundance. It is a long shot, however, to argue the choice of yellow for Buddhist robes from the socially correlated color symbolism of their merchant donors.

96. Originally, ocher coloring is made from dung or yellow clay, but it is not good color and not always healthy (Vin 3.240; Vin 1.285-6; M 3.126).

97. Vin 1.306.

98. Vin 1.93-94.

99. Vin 1.94. *ayan te patto, ayaṃ saṃghāṭī, ayaṃ uttarāsaṅgo, ayaṃ antaravāsako, gaccha amumhi okāse tiṭṭhāhīti.*

100. ĀrU 9-10; NpU 169-170; BSU 252-253.

101. D 3.224.

102. Vin 3.210-13. The Buddha does allow the nun Thullanandā to bargain with King Pasenadi for a heavy cold-weather cloth that was not expensive (the upper limit being four 'bronzes,' *kaṃsa,* in value) and for a light cloth (of up to two and a half 'bronzes' (Vin 4.255-57).

103. Vin 3.256-57.

104. Vin 3.257-260.

105. Vin 3.213-15.

106. If a robe fund is set up by non-related householders or housemistress for getting a robe for a certain monk, for example, then that monk is not allowed to initiate with any of the donors a premature request for a robe (Vin 3.215-19). If a messenger from a king, someone in his service, a brahmin, or a householder comes with a robe-fund for a certain monk, that monk is not allowed to accept the fund but only a robe in its place. If an attendant to the monk (either a worker at the monastery, *ārāmika,* or a layperson, *upāsaka)* is designated by the monk who is in need of a robe as an intermediary, the monk is allowed to remind the attendant several times of his need and, if to no effect, he is allowed to stand in reminding silence for it up to six times. If this course does not produce results, the monk is allowed, himself or through a messenger, to release the robe fund back into non-renunciant use (Vin 3.219-223). In addition to the robe fund, another means, the *chandaka* or voluntary collection, is mentioned particularly in connection with securing robe material for nuns. This collection is made by laypeople and can be exchanged for robe material for nuns, but cannot then be substituted by them for some other item such as medicine (Vin 4.250-53; see Horner, *Book of the Discipline* 3:228n).

107. Vin 3.265-66.

108. Vin 3.240-42.

109. Vin 4.122-24.

110. Vin 3.254-55.

111. This last rule is the result of an incident in which the monk Udāyin presses the nun Uppalavaṇṇā to give him her inner robe—even after she pleads that 'we women...get things with difficulty,' *mayaṃ...mātugāmā nāma kicchalābhā* (Vin 3.208; see 4.175).

112. SV 1.207-210; see also Vin 4.121-22; see Vin 1.297.

113. Vin 3.203; 4.74, 100, 245-46, 284-87.

114. The rain retreat normally lasts for three months of the four month-long monsoon rainy season and in Pali texts is said to begin at one of two times, either the day after the full moon of the month of Āsāḷhī or a month after the Āsāḷhī full moon, and ends on the full moon of the month of Kattika (Vin 1.137; see Horner, *Book of the Discipline* 2:153n) sometime

in October-November. Each monk or nun, then, chooses whether to observe the first three months or the second three months. The purpose of the rain retreat is for the protection against injury of monks and nuns during times when roads are often impassable and rivers flooded; for the protection against injury of other living things such as young stalks and small animals and insects from renunciants walking in wet weather who may inadvertently kill them (Vin 4.296-97; Vin 1.137-38); for providing a settled and sequestered context within established natural boundaries for the renewal of Saṅgha collective life through discussion, teaching, ritual and meditation (Vin 1.104-106); and for providing a focal point for the donation of gifts, especially robes, in large quantities to the community.

The Mahāparinibbāna Sutta (D 2.98-99) says that monks begin the rainy season around Vesālī by each going to where his friends, acquaintances, and intimates are residing *(samantā Vesāliṃ yathā-mittaṃ yathā-sandiṭṭhaṃ yathā-sambhattaṃ vassaṃ upagañchum;* see also S 5.152). S. Dutt (p. 54) remarks that the communal living together within boundaries during the rains "seems to have been the practice of no other sect" than the Buddhists; and since they are "professed almsmen, the Bhikkhus would naturally make their *vassa* settlements in localities where alms were available." As Misra (pp. 122-23) notes, during "these three months the Saṅgha was completely dependent upon the gifts of the laity of the particular place and would have been frequented very often [by them] to hear religious discourses."

115. Vin 4.296-97; Vin 1.137, 253-54.

116. Vin 3.252-54; see Horner, *Book of the Discipline* 4:426n.

117. Vin 4.297.

118. Vin 4.245. The Buddha, in fact, is said to have introduced the *kaṭhina* procedure upon seeing rain-bedraggled monks approach him in Sāvatthi having spent the season in Sāketa (Vin 1.253).

119. Vin 3.11.

120. Vin 1.168.

121. Vin 3.260-62.

122. Gombrich, *Theravada Buddhism,* p. 100 For *kaṭhina* rules of the Mahāsāṅghikas and Mūlasarvāstivādins, see Prebisch, *Monastic Discipline,* pp. 64-75, and compare Frauwallner, pp. 99-103. For the rules of Mahāyānists on dress, see N. Dutt, *Mahāyāna,* p. 315.

123. Vin 1.254-55; M 3.124-26; see Horner, *Book of the Discipline* 4:356n. Note Frauwallner's (p. 185) comment here on the problems of the *kaṭhina* text.

124. Vin 2.116-17.

125. Vin 1.254-55.

126. Bhagvat, p. 144.

127. Vin 1.300-301.

128. Vin 4.245-46. Horner *(Book of the Discipline* 3:217n) notes that robe-material "accruing not at the right time might be accepted by a monk, but then should be made up quickly" (Vin 3.203), but that in this case it appears "as if Thullanandā and her nuns had had their kaṭhina robes made up before these other nuns arrived at Sāvatthi, and that she took possession of the material given by the laity, and in having it distributed, ignored these incoming nuns."
129. Vin 4.284-85.
130. See Vin 4.98-101.
131. See Vin 4.198-202; Vin 1.298.
132. See Vin 4.71-75. In time, a group meal is allowable after the making of *kaṭhina* cloth (Vin 1.254).
133. See Vin 3.195-97. When robe-material is settled and the *kaṭhina* privileges removed; then a monk is allowed to wear an extra robe for at most ten days.
134. Vin 1.254.
135. Vin 1.255-265; Vin 4.287-88.
136. Horner, *Book of the Discipline* 2:4n. See Vin 3.195-97; M 2.437-447.
137. Vin 4.286-87; Vin 1.306-310.
138. Vin 1.298-300.
139. Vin 1.153-55.
140. Wijayaratna, p. 39.
141. Vin 1.280-81.
142. Horner, *Book of the Discipline* 2:26n.
143. Vin 1.309.
144. Vin 2.123-24, 174; see Wijayaratna, pp. 50-52.
145. Wijayaratna, p. 33.
146. Vin 4.299-301.
147. In finishing a robe, a renunciant has to remember that robes cannot be as large as a well-farer's *(sugata)* robe (that is, six by nine spans) (Vin 4.173-74), and very specific instructions are given for sewing, especially if it is of *kaṭhina* cloth (Vin 1.254-55). For mending robes, small knives (or scissors), needles and thread, and needle cases are allowed (Vin 2.115-16; M 3.126); rough darns, fixing misshapen corners, patching, and binding are allowed (Vin 1.297); but unsewing a poorly sewn robe for a fellow renunciant and then not resewing it again is not (Vin 4.279-281). Monks are allowed to mark new robes with a small dot or smudge *(kappabindu)* in dark blue-green, mud, or black color in order to recognize who normally uses them (Vin 4.120-21). And monks are to wear their robes as the Buddha does: neither too high nor too low, neither plastered to the body nor flying free from it, neither caught by the wind

nor unprotective of dust (M 2.139). Finally, provisions are made for the washing of robes; but if a nun is to wash robes belonging to a monk, the two have to be related, though her assistant does not (Vin 3.205-207). Related to this last is the prescription for sewing or causing to be sewn, a nun's robe: a monk can do it only if she is a relative (Vin 4.59-62).

148. MV 3-4; see also MV 90. Misra (p. 180) discusses the specific food offered by Tapussa and Bhallika to the new Buddha, and describes *mantha*, especially, as of a "portable nature," not surprising in the case of the two merchants.

149. J 1:68ff.

150. Sakyaputtiyā, 'sons of the Sakyan,' a common early name for the followers of the Buddha, the Sakyamuni. See Vin 1.44; D 3.84.

151. Vin 1.57-58. See the description of thievery in Vin 3.89-90, that gives, as one example, the over-zealous alms tour through countless towns and villages to bilk admiring householders of alms.

152. D 3.130: *yo vo mayā piṇḍapāto anuññāto, alaṃ vo so yāvad eva imassa kāyassa ṭhitiyā yāpanāya vihiṃsūparatiyā brahmacariyānuggahāya— 'Iti purāṇañ ca vedanaṃ paṭihaṅkhāmi navañ ca vedanaṃ na uppadessāmi.* Trans. by T.W. and C.A.F. Rhys Davids, *Dialogues* 3:122.

153. The centrality of food to the interconnections of the cosmos is clear in texts like the Upaniṣads (See BĀU 1.5.1-2; AU 1.3.1-10; MU 6.9, 11).

154. S 1.32; M 1.247. For a discussion of food and spirituality, see Wijayaratna, pp. 72-73.

155. S 5.64-67.

156. A 3.250.

157. The Mahāvagga (Vin 1.57-58) indicates that during the rainy season monks and nuns may not go on tour for alms but do procure alms food themselves from the local village they have taken residence near for the season. Thus, although there may be some question of violating the principle of not walking around in wet weather during which living things can be injured or killed, the destruction of life, as inferred from this passage, is kept to a minimum.

158. M 3.88, 109; S 1.76; 3.94; 4.105; 5.108; A 1.182; 3.320, 348; 5.89. *Piṇḍapāta* can also refer to the food itself (Vin 3.1.89; A 3.348).

159. Vin 3.89; 2.296-97; Vin 1.137. In its more general designation *cārikā* 'wandering' refers to the tour taken by the Buddha and/or his fellow monks through towns and countryside for the purpose of spreading Dhamma. Saṃyutta Nikāya 3.94-99, in fact, describes just such a *cārikā* the Buddha dares to take alone and unattended.

160. Vin 2.197; M 3.7, 109; S 1.76; 3.94; 4.105; 5.108, 109; A 1.182, 279; 3.95; 5.48, 49; Sn no. 414.

161. S 1.75-76; 5.108-109.

162. M 3.88; A 3.320-22.

163. S 4.105-107; A 1.182-85.

164. M 3.88-89; A 5.88-91.

165. M 3.109-110; S 3.94-99.

166. Vin 1.90-91. The Ājīvakas are not allowed an alms bowl being called *hatthāpalekhana,* those who lick food from their hands after eating (D 1.166; 3.40; M 1.77, 238, 307; A 1.295), and the Jains are allowed bowls of gourd, wood and clay (See Misra, p. 125). There is a story of a young man Pukkusāti who asks the Buddha for ordination *(upasampadā)* but, having no bowl or robe, is sent out to secure them as prerequisites. On the way, however, Pukkusāti is hit by a swerving cow and dies, but is said, with this, to have resolved all five fetters, not to be reborn again in this world (M 3.247). The oddity here is that Pukkusāti has already gone forth from home into the homeless life and is already called 'venerable' *(āyasmant).* The need for a robe as well as a bowl reflects the time when Buddhists are ordained without one and walk naked for their food like other renunciants (Vin 1.90-91).

167. Vin 1.94.

168. Vin 3.242-47.

169. Vin 4.243-44; Vin 2.114-15, 112; Thera no. 862. The *saṃnyāsin* is not allowed a bowl of metal, only a bottle-gourd or a bowl of wood or clay (Manu 6.44, 52-54. BSU 270, ĀrU 11, LSU 22, ŚU 327; Thera no. 127 also notes the early practice of using a funeral pot *(chavasitta)* as a bowl). The narrative setting for the rule against wooden bowls describes a donor, the great merchant from Rājagaha, who mischievously decides to have a bowl carved from an expensive block of sandalwood and to give it to whomever can retrieve it through the use of his psychic powers from atop some bamboo poles. Although there is a successful Buddhist claimant, Piṇḍola the Bhāradvāja, the Buddha rebukes him for his display of power before householders and, as an aside, forbids bowls made of wood (Vin 2.110-12). The bowl Piṇḍola wins seems to have been of substantial size, and the Suttavibhaṅga notes that three sizes of bowls are allowed—small, medium, and large—the size defined by the amount of food the bowl can hold (Vin 3.243; 2.243-44).

170. Vin 2.112-14.

171. KBU 2.1. In the domestic version, the young student of traditional Vedic texts practices *bhikṣācarya* in very specific detail: petitioning from precisely set Vedic households, he is supposed to maintain purity and proper etiquette throughout as he encounters the housemistress at the door (ŚGS 2.6.4-8; ĀGS 1.22.4-10; PGS 2.5.1-8; KGS 2.4.27-30; GGS 2.10.42-44; HGS 1.2.7.14-19; Manu 2.182-85; 188-190). The *saṃnyāsin,* likewise, in a practice consonant with the Buddhists, undertakes *bhikṣācarya* with equally strict governance: he is to wander alone, in silence, with no thought to what is offered to him. Waiting to petition until the householders' meal is finished, he is to accept only what is needed to sustain life and to eat the little portion given standing or sitting in solitude (BSU 264-66; Manu

6.41-44, 51, 55-57, 59).

172. Olivelle, *Origin,* p. 15.

173. Vin 2.77, 215; D 2.1, 102; M 1.68. The Buddha himself, before his enlightenment, practices *bhikṣācaryā* in the streets of Rājagaha, for example, and, after his enlightenment, goes to Kapilavatthu to seek alms from his Sākyan relatives. When he begins to formulate practice for his own followers, his initial injunction is to eat off scrap.

174. D 3.257.

175. Vin 4.296-97.

176. I.e., before noon (see Dhammapāla's commentary to VV no. 71).

177. The Mahāvagga (70) mentions several groups monks cannot beg alms from: prostitutes, widows, grown but not married girls, eunuchs, and nuns.

178. Vin 2.212-15. The Cullavagga (Vin 2.111) describes the great *seṭṭhi* of Rājagaha as taking the bowl of Piṇḍola, filling it with food, and handing it back.

179. M 3.33. Gombrich (p. 101) notes that on alms tour Buddhist renunciants "do not even thank for the food, since it is they who are doing the favor by giving the laity a chance to earn merit; but they may say a few edifying words."

180. See Olivelle, *Origin,* p. 15.

181. See S. Dutt, p. 48.

182. See Dhammapāla's commentary to Vv nos. 74, 84.

183. Vin 4.81-82.

184. Vin 1.212, 215.

185. Vin 4.66-68, 175-77.

186. Vin 1.58.

187. In its earliest citation, RV 1.162.19, it refers to a piece of flesh from the sacrificed animal.

188. Vin 2.216.

189. *Ātitheyyā* (A 1.93; 4.63-64).

190. As Amore details his characteristics, the 'true guest' for the Dharma Śāstras is ideally a brahmin from another village, a knower of the Veda, not involved in commerce, and intending to stay with the householder for only one night. The host's obligations are then to give him proper shelter and food, with 'proper' depending on the learnedness of the guest.

191. Amore, pp. 19-24.

192. Jamison, pp. 1-4.

193. KU 2.14.

194. Knipe, "*Sapiṇḍīkaraṇa,*" p. 112.

195. Knipe, *"Sapiṇḍīkaraṇa,"* p. 111.

196. Knipe, *"Sapiṇḍīkaraṇa,"* p. 115.

197. Knipe, *"Sapiṇḍīkaraṇa,"* p. 116.

198. Knipe, *"Sapiṇḍīkaraṇa."* p. 114.

199. O'Flaherty, p. 6.

200. O'Flaherty, pp. 12-13 (author's italics).

201. *Anna, bhatta, bhikkhā, bhoga,* and *bhojana,* in the Buddhist context and *bhikṣā* and *bhojana* in the *saṃnyāsin* context, for example.

202. Vin 2.215-216.

203. O'Flaherty (p. 12) notes that the *piṇḍa* offering is used "to appease potentially angry or harmful ancestors." The renunciant powers of Buddhist *iddhi,* especially as held by someone "dead" to the concerns of the ordinary world, may inspire just such fears in donor householders, but this is unlikely, for householder fear of Buddhist renunciants is not a normative feature of the Pali narratives.

204. Collins (pp. 208-210) correlates *āhāra* with *upādāna* 'grasping,' the ninth state in the *pratītyasamutpāda.*

205. O'Flaherty, p. 4.

206. O'Flaherty, pp. 3-4.

207. See Misra, p. 246.

208. M 2.7-8; A 2.26-29. The Bṛhatsaṃnyāsa Upaniṣad contains teachings on what constitutes acceptable food for *saṃnyāsins* (BSU 266-68).

209. Vin 3.237; 4.232-5, 310-11; Vin 1.44, 217-18, 222-23, 229, 232-33, 237, 243, 291; Vin 2.147, 164; M 1.353, 393, 448, 461; 2.50, 64, 93; 3.145; S 4.122, 288; A 3.30, 37, 341; Sn p. 111.

210. In one, some followers of Mettiya and Bhummajaka who are newly ordained receive inferior food at a house known to give good food. They complain that Dabba the Mallian, the monk who apportions the invited meals out to the monks at the Rājagaha residence, has set the householder against them and they lodge charges. Fortunately, the Buddha rules in Dabba's favor and the greedy monks are punished (Vin 3.160-64; Vin 2.76-80). As noted above, monks who specifically ask for and eat *paṇīta* food, defined as including ghee, fresh butter, oil, honey, molasses, fish, meat, milk, and curd, commit an offense, and it is ruled that they are only allowed to do so when sick (Vin 4.87-89: *sappi, navanīta, tela, madhu, phāṇita, maccha, maṃsa, khīra,* and *dadhi).* The Cullavagga, moreover, describes a time when monks gluttonously eat *paṇīta* food and, oddly, become very sick and have to be treated by Jīvaka Komārabhacca, the Buddha's doctor (Vin 2.119).

211. For an extended discussion of food, including "favorites," see Misra, pp. 179-185.

212. Vin 1.222. According to Misra (p. 182), the "*Vinaya*...[is] not specific to any flesh as a people's most favorite choice, though goat's flesh...[is] seemingly the general non-vegetarian diet."

213. Vin 1.238; M 1.368-69.

214. Vin 3.58; Vin 1.216-220; D 1.5.

215. Vin 1.216-220.

216. A 1.214; see the discussion in Wijayaratna, pp. 70-71.

217. M 1.124, 437, 473; 2.91, 125, 141; 3.34; D 1.204; 2.72; A 4.389; 5.205.

218. M 1.84; 2.1; 3.7; A 4.37.

219. Vin 1.70.

220. Vin 4.85-86, 273-75; M 1.448, 460-61, 473-74; 3.34; A 4.389; 5.205; Sn nos. 386-88, 971.

221. Vin 4.271-72.

222. Vin 4.222; M 1.12-13; see Vin 4.69-71.

223. Vin 4.79-81. One of the classes of renunciants to receive alms food brought back is the monk on solitary retreat who is to see no one except the bringer of his alms food.

224. Vin 4.89-92. An alternate to Pācittiya 41 prohibits a nun from giving food to a householder *(agārika)* or to a male or female wanderer (Vin 4.302-303).

225. M 1.273.

226. M 1.12-13, 207. As food becomes a more regulated part of monastic life, scraps can also be given over to scrap-eaters or, if left over from a sick monk not up to eating a full share, to other monks.

227. Vin 4.91-92; 4.82-83.

228. M 2.138; Vin 4.94-95.

229. Vin 4.194-97; Vin 2.213-14. Compare to rules found in the Āpastamba Dharma Sūtra (8.19.5-12).

230. M 2.138-39; Vin 2.212.

231. Olivelle, *Origin*, p. 15.

232. Vin 1.210-11.

233. Vin 4.86-87.

234. Vin 1.211-12, 238; see Vin 3.207-210 where a nun roasts meat. See Horner, *Book of the Discipline* 2:37n.

235. Vin 4.239.

236. Horner, *Book of the Discipline* 4:75n. Or, "a place for doing certain operations some of which were allowable only in times of scarcity" (Horner, *Book of the Discipline* 4:327n).

237. Vin 2.269-270. Note that monks and nuns can share food with each other but cannot give to householders *(agārika)*, to naked ascetics *(acelaka)*,

or to male and female wanderers *(paribbājaka/paribbājikā)* (Vin 4.91-92, 302-303).

238. Vin 4.71-75. For meal and food rules of the Mahāsāṅghikas and the Mūlasarvāstivādins, see Prebisch, *Monastic Discipline,* pp. 78-93, and compare Frauwallner, pp. 93-95. For those of the Mahāyānists, see N. Dutt, *Mahāyāna,* pp. 315-17.

239. Horner, *Book of the Discipline* 2:xxvii.

240. Vin 1.57, 220, 229, 231, 237, 248, 291; Vin 2.157, 164; D 2.88, 95-98; M 1.236-37, 369, 393; 2.50, 92-93; S 4.289; A 3.36-37; Sn pp. 102-105. See Dhammapāla's commentary to Vv no. 16. Bhagvat (pp. 68-69) suggests that the allowing of invited meals comes about because of a relaxation of "the control over palate" coupled with meals offered to monks in Vesālī (Vin 2.119) and by the Ājīvakas (Vin 2.165). Says Gombrich (p. 102): "Once laity are allowed to bring food to the monks—and the monastic regulations could hardly stop them—one can see that the line between receiving food *ad hoc,* the original intention, and arranging meals on a more regular basis becomes hard to draw."

241. See D 1.165-66 for other contemporary practices.

242. Vin 4.98-101.

243. Vin 2.165.

244. Vin 4.75-78.

245. Vin 4.98-101.

246. See Dhammapāla's commentary for Vv nos. 18, 55.

247. This is done by preserving what S. Dutt calls "the sacramental character of...[a renunciant's] begging," with the hope that hewing to form will develop keen sensibilities (S. Dutt, p. 36; see also Wijayaratna, p. 60).

248. Vin 1.58. Nuns are said to have only three resources, for sitting at the root of a tree, or forest-dwelling, is forbidden to them for reasons of safety (Vin 2.274, 278).

249. From there he moves to the foot of the Goatherd's Banyan tree for seven days, to the foot of the Mucalinda tree for seven days, to the foot of the Rājāyatana tree for seven days, and then back to the foot of the Goatherd's Banyan tree for some time before resuming his tour of the countryside (Vin 1.1-4).

250. Vin 1.58. Rules from a Mahāyāna Vinaya on lodging are less detailed, and can be found in N. Dutt, *Mahāyāna,* pp. 318-319.

251. S. Dutt, pp. 54-55. Horner *(Book of the Discipline* 2:46n) distinguishes the two as follows: "*ārāma* was a whole monastery, consisting of the grounds and the buildings; *āvāsa* was the 'colony' or place in which the monks lived."

252. S. Dutt, pp. 54-55. There is often some tense discussion with householder donors when there are rival invitations to the Saṅgha for spending the rain retreat in or near a personal residence (see M 2.50-51).

253. Vin 1.138.

254. Horner, *Book of the Discipline* 4:xvi-xvii.

255. The particular case for the setting of this rule is the request by the layman Udena to have monks come to him, receive gifts *(dāna),* and preach Dhamma (Vin 1.139-142).

256. Vin 1.142-148.

257. Vin 1.148-49.

258. Vin 1.149.

259. Vin 1.152-53.

260. The full moon day when the *komudī* 'white water lily' flowers blooms, *cātumāsinī,* 'during the fourth month' (Vin 1.175-78; D 1.65-66).

261. Vin 1.159.

262. Olivelle, *Origin,* p.40.

263. Vin 1.101-104.

264. The Buddhist Uposatha—at which all monks, who live depending on *(upanissāya)* the same field and village (M 3.10) for the four requisites or who later are all members of a given residence within a certain boundary *(sīma),* hear the Pāṭimokkha rules recited by a senior monk—derives from a Vedic Vrata day preparatory to the New and Full Moon sacrifices (Darśapūrṇamāsa). On this Vrata day, named the *upavasatha,* the sacrificer prepares for the Soma sacrifice by fasting, abstention, and quiet withdrawal to a room with the sacrificial fire (see Misra, p. 119). Although these *upavasatha* days are originally meant for the householder patrons of the ritual, they are adopted, in a form isolated from the ritual, by *paribbājakas* or wanderers from other sects who use them for the rehearsal of their own doctrines. The Mahāvagga (101-104) indicates, in fact, that the Buddha originally enjoins the monks to observe these fortnightly days, in imitation of the *paribbājaka* practice, by rehearsing the Dhamma as a way of attracting new followers, but that he later prescribes the text of the Pāṭimokkha and turns the observance into a confession, to take place twice a month marking the nights of the new and full moon in an observance hall called an *uposathāgāraṃ* (Vin 1.106-108), to which only monks and nuns can, and are required to, come (Vin 1.104-105). See Vin 1.114-15; A 4.204-208, 248-259, 388-390, and Prebisch, *Monastic Discipline,* pp. 17-27 for a discussion of who attends the Uposatha and of the ritualization of the declarations of harmony and purity. Moreover, S. Dutt (pp. 72-73) notes that the Pāṭimokkha is the "first clear charter" of the Saṅgha, thought of as the 'root' or *mūla* of the Vinaya: "This confessional *Uposatha...* was introduced long after the currency among the Bhikkhus of the *Pāṭimokkha* code. But the incorporation of the *Pāṭimokkha* with the *Uposatha* was the final reaffirmation of the character of the Saṅgha as an Order."

It is likely then, that three separate developments are woven together to produce the Uposatha recital of the Pāṭimokkha: first, the Vedic Vrata day prior to the Darśapūrṇamāsa as a fortnightly observance of quiet, preparatory, withdrawal time (that is, Uposatha); second, the development of the Pāṭimokkha rules as the root charter for monastic behavior (see Misra, p. 29); and, third, the practical confessional tradition begun with the yearly Pavāraṇā reflected in the Uposatha as it comes to be the occasion of the recitation of the Pāṭimokkha. As Horner *(Discipline* 4:xvii) notes: "The recital of the Pāṭimokkha was to 'remove' offenses, by confessing them, during the nine dry months of the year; the Invitation was to remove any offenses that monks had committed during the three wet months." Laypeople then keep Uposatha days by giving gifts and by hearing the Dhamma.

265. Olivelle, *Origin,* p. 40.

266. "With donations coming in a liberal measure for the monks' maintenance during the months of stationary life, the rule of wandering almsmanship lost its urgency and much of its mandatory character" (S. Dutt, pp. 54-55).

267. Chakravarti, p. 58.

268. Wijayaratna, p. 21.

269. Wijayaratna, p. 28.

270. The story of the monk Dhaniya is a good example of what can happen when the life balanced between wandering and settling is ignored, for Dhaniya does not put away his grass and wood hut built on the hillside as his compatriots do after the rains end, but continues to live there season after season. Although the Suttavibhaṅga goes on to discuss the monk's eventual theft (Dhaniya inappropriately accepts wood belonging to the king from the overseer of the king's lumber yard in order to build a new hut), it also suggests an underlying agenda: desiring a life-style too much like householders leads to trouble—in Dhaniya's case, stealing materials to ensure a permanent abode (Vin 3.41-45).

271. Vin 2.147; D 3.130.

272. M 2.8; A 2.26-29. While the *saṃnyāsin* tradition prescribes a life of homelessness (LSU 21; KśU 41; PhU 51; JU 71; NpU 154, 158, 202; PpU 284), fixed residence can be taken up during the rainy season (ĀrU 8; KśU 33; NpU 141, 158-59, 198; BSU 26.9; PpU 284-85) and overnights of small duration can be taken in selected sites: for example, one night in a village, three in a town, five in a city, six in a holy place, and seven at a sacred bathing place (NpU 202). Moreover, the *saṃnyāsin* can live in a deserted house, in a temple, on a haystack, by an anthill, under a tree, in a potter's shed, in a shed for the fire ritual, on a river bank, in a mountain cave, in a cellar, in a glen, in a tree hollow, in a lonely spot, by a waterfall, in an open field, or in a forest (JU 70-71; NpU 154; BhU 236.

273. Icchānaṅkalavanasaṇḍa (D 1.87).

274. Nerañjarā *tīra* (D 2.112); Aciravatī *tīra* (D 1.235).

275. Gijjhakūṭa *pabbata* (D 1.175; 2.72, 81).

276. Pāvārikambavana (D 1.211); *uttara* Manasākaṭa *ambavana* (D 1.235).

277. Veḷuvana Kalandakanivāpa (M 2.1, 29). See a longer list in D 2.116-17.

278. *araññа, rukkhamūla, pabbata, kandara, giriguha, susāna, vanapattha, abbhokāsa, palālapuñja* (M 3.3, 35).

279. M 1.440-41.

280. Vin 1.38-39.

281. S. Dutt, p. 58.

282. Vin 1.106, 108-111.

283. S. Dutt, p. 59.

284. Vin 1.206-209; Vin 174-75.

285. Rhys Davids and Stede, p. 642.

286. Another term for the single cell or private room for a renunciant is *pariveṇa* (Vin 1.49, 216, 247; 2.167, 210; 3.69, 119; 4.52, 252). "In general, the larger *āvāsa* may be said to have contained, besides such "rooms" as the uposatha hall, the refectory, the warming-room and so on, a number of *vihāras.* These were the separate rooms or dwelling-places, each given over to one monk or if he had a *saddhivikārin* to two, to live in and use as his quarters, while staying at that particular *ārāma*... Several cells or rooms, *pariveṇa* or *vihāra,* suitable for not more than one monk to sleep in, lead off some of the large caves at Ellora and Ajanta" (Horner, *Book of the Discipline* 2:46n).

287. Vin 4.39-40, 169-170; Vin 1.192-94. Other, more elaborate, furnishings for the dwelling place are discussed in Vin 2.148-51, with the Buddha consistently taking the middle road of accommodation, emphasizing practicality and minimum comfort.

288. There is a monk, Udāyin, however, who is known to have a well-appointed and pleasing *vihāra* with nicely designed furnishings and well-placed water supplies. So many people come to look at it that it becomes crowded, and Udāyin inadvertently rubs up against a brahmin lady causing her husband to complain loudly. Although the resulting ruling is against a monk coming into physical contact with a woman, the passage implies criticism of domestic extravagnce for monks as well (Vin 3.1.119-127).

289. Vin 1.107, 118-9.

290. Vin 3.1.70; 2.15, 42; Vin 1.49, 139; Vin 2.153, 208.

291. M 2.163.

292. Vin 1.139-140; Vin 2.159.

293. Vin 3.1.149, 152-57; 4.34-35, 47-48.

294. Vin 2.117, 148-154.

295. Vin 2.117, 151-52; 4.47.

296. See Dhammapāla's commentary to Vv no. 46.

297. Prebish, *Monastic Discipline,* p. 9; Vin 1.137.

298. Vin 2.174-75, 207-210.
299. Vin 2.217-222.
300. Vin 4.39-40.
301. Vin 4.41-42.
302. Vin 4.42-43.
303. Vin 4.44-45; 2.166-67.
304. Vin 4.45-46.
305. Vin 2.159-160, 166, 172-74; 4.32-33, 211.
306. Vin 2.147.
307. Kane 2.2:858.
308. Attested substantially in copper plate and stone inscriptions from non-Buddhist settings (Kane 2.2:861-62), gifts of land in the Buddhist setting may be based, Chakravarti argues, on "the tradition of gifting *brahmadeya* lands to *brāhmaṇas* by the kings of Kosala and Magadha" (Chakravarti, p. 570.
309. Vin 2.158. Translated by Horner, *Book of the Discipline* 5:222.
310. M 3.109-110.
311. Vin 1.226-27.
312. Vin 3.148-157. There is a description of just such a temporary dwelling made by the monk Dhaniya, the potter's son, out of wood and grass on the slope of a mountain (Vin 3.41-45).
313. Wijayaratna, p. 24.
314. Rules for nuns' lodgings exemplify the increasing care that goes into formulating donor- renunciant relations over gifts of buildings. Donors wanting to give a nuns' dwelling, for example, need first to know that there is a nun in charge of repairs (Vin 4.156), and the acceptance of such a dwelling will ordinarily be done by monks on the nuns' behalf (Vin 1.140); moreover, repair to a nun's cell can be done through a voluntary collection, if no other sources are available (Vin 4.254).
315. Vin 1.139.
316. *Yassa dāni kālaṃ maññasi* (Vin 2.146-48).
317. S. Dutt, p. 94.
318. Vin 2.148.
319. Vin 1.58, 96; M 1.316; A 2.26-27.
320. Vin 1.206.
321. Zysk, p. 40.
322. Vin 1.58, 96, 199.
323. Vin 1.199.
324. Rao 2:91-94.

325. Vin 4.85-86; Vin 1.199-200. See Gombrich, *Theravada Buddhism,* p. 100 for a discussion of the modern Sri Lankan practice of taking "medicine"around six in the evening.

326. D 3.130.

327. Zysk, p. 41.

328. Vin 3.251-52; Vin 1.200; Prebisch, *Monastic Discipline,* p. 70; Frauwallner, pp. 92-93; N. Dutt, *Mahāyāna,* p. 318; Rao 2:123-24. Renunciants cannot change their minds concerning the specific medicine needed when the procurement by the donor involves buying from a shopkeeper. Thullanandā, for example, who states her medicinal need for ghee is not then allowed to exchange the ghee for oil as the purchase is already made (Vin 4.248-49).

329. Vin 1.200-206.

330. Vin 1.206.

331. M 3.263-64; A 1.120-22.

332. A 2.142-43.

333. Zysk, p. 33.

334. Zysk, p. 40.

335. Vin 1.209; Vin 2.177; Vin 4.38, 155; Zysk, p. 40.

336. Vin 1.216-220.

337. Bechert and Gombrich, p. 81.

338. Heesterman, *"dákṣiṇā,"* p. 245.

339. D 3.191.

340. Gombrich, "Intention," p. 95.

341. Zysk, p. 41.

342. Horner, *Middle Length* 3:60; M 3.10.

CHAPTER 4

Giving Gifts

Giving indeed is virtuous, sirs;
Giving from little store is virtuous;

Giving with confidence is virtuous;
Giving of what is well won is
virtuous;

And giving with discrimination is
also virtuous.[1]

DĀNA IN BUDDHIST ETHICS

Buddhism's adaptation to contemporary life pays significant attention to questions of social engagement: what is the Buddhist basis for active work among others? for example, and what teachings can respond most easily and beneficially to skillful behavior by and within international communities? The view that Buddhism can provide momentum for broad involvement in compassionate action in the wider world is not, in and of itself, a central theme of Pali texts.[2] To the degree that there *are* questions of a good society, of civic equity, of social justice, and of righteous living in the broad community in this early period, such questions are located in the canonical discussions of the act of giving.

If the Buddhist pathway, ordinarily, begins with being a layperson, and if lay ethics are grounded in the teachings on *dāna,* then discussions on *dāna* inform those on other ethical issues and serve as a cornerstone for the life of full Buddhist commitment. Even so, however, early texts do not focus *per se* on the building of a just community, on the development of a common sense of responsibility, or on issues of public policy. Rather, all social change is thought to begin with inner personal change, such that real peace in the world comes about only with individuals mastering their own unskillful tendencies. In this way, Buddhist ethics, as founded in *dāna* and as practiced at the heart of the tradition, is based in activating transformation in others, one by one.

The actions of giving and receiving are at the heart of Buddhist *dāna*. Pali texts understand a "person" as a collection of actions performed over time to which conventional society gives a name and recognizes by a certain form. The term "donor," then, does not describe a separable essential thing called an individual, but a "person" only so because of his or her action "in relation to" some other: thus, a *dāyika* is a giver, someone "who gives," and who gives in the fullness of detail that that action entails. Likewise, a "donee" is someone who "receives" in the fullness of detail that that action entails and, because of accepting donations, a *bhikkhu* or *bhikkhunī* is, as a receiver, someone "who shares in" the material lives of non-renunciants by accepting what these householders have to offer. Being thus "in relation to," givers and receivers are identified most profoundly by the nature of the action that takes place between them, such that the fulsome acts of giving and receiving are foundational acts in relation to others, because they are acts performed one by one have the overall possibility of transforming larger communities.

Tambiah notes that the monk is "different from the layman" and that connecting these different agencies is "a particular pattern of transactions."[3] This pattern of transactions develops into a complex arena of reciprocity whose guidelines fall under Buddhist teachings on donation. Not formally set forth in any systematic fashion, *dāna* teachings are, however, found throughout the canon and, collectively, deal with all aspects of the contractual nature of donor-renunciant reciprocity: views on proper acquisition and distribution of wealth, ideal givers and receivers, the concept of merit and its relation to kammic understandings of causation, and the specific rewards acquired by merit-producing householders. A crass approach to this reciprocity interprets the *dāna* teachings as a persuasive enticement to those who have for giving to those who don't, while a self-righteous approach downplays the specificity of the *dāna* teachings as too material a concern for the committed Buddhist. The teachings, however, are there in the canon in all their exquisite detail and are forthright and practical in their assessment of the varied human responses to wealth. The Buddha knows he has to provide for the Saṅgha, and an ethical structure that sets forth *dāna* in a context of natural human tendencies is the only way to do it.

There is a clear consensus that economic concerns are basic to the early Buddhist institution.[4] In many ways, the *dāna* story is the story of how the members of an institution, now beyond living by means of "whatever turns up," get enough material resources to stay in business. The Buddhist doctrine of *dāna* becomes the preeminent strategy of a young religious movement, composed of *bhikkhus* and *bhikkhunīs* 'sharers' of the household wealth, to get and keep the donor's attention so that its own survival is assured. This the institution does, first, by cultivating the donor's goodwill, second, by letting the people or more specifically the donors have a creative and substantial say in shaping the institution and, third, by creating a soteriology that makes giving central, and that provides a clear status-producing system of merit.[5] While, ultimately, the mature Buddhist movement hopes to target the populace at large with its *dāna* doctrine, in younger times it does not have as its object all the people but only those in potentially direct relation to the Buddhism renunciant.

Dāna in Early Buddhist Ethics

While *dāna* is a part of the Indian heritage from at least the time of the Ṛg Veda, it is only in the period of the Upaniṣads, when giving to wandering renunciants allows the development of new philosophic options, that *dāna* comes into its own as a recognized virtue of religious life. The bestowal of *dakṣiṇā* upon brahmin priests, so well praised in the Dānastuti sections of Ṛg Vedic hymns, certainly recognizes the importance of giving as the economic foundation of perpetuating the priestly system (and therefore the ritual and cosmic order), but it is not singled out and developed as a religious virtue until the era of the rise of Buddhism. It is only with passages such is Chāndogya Upaniṣad 3.17.4 that *dāna* becomes, with other religious ideals, a trait worthy of personal development that can lead to human perfection. In this remarkable passage that characterizes human life as itself an interior sacrifice, the "writer gives an account of a sacrifice which can be performed without any ceremonial and in spirit even by hermits."[6] "Thus, austerity, giving, rectitude, non-violence, and truthfulness are the gifts of" the priests,[7] it teaches, making the act of *dāna* itself, rather than its objects, the crucial focal point of a person's behavior.[8]

The Ṛg Vedic practice of *dāna* focuses on ritual praise as it is offered to the gifts, the donors, and the acts of giving to officiating brahmin priests.[9] During the later Vedic period the understanding of *dāna* becomes more complex, due in part to three concurrent developments: first, the *śrauta* system expands and solidifies into an institution of great precision and detail requiring the presence of many priests, and hence more *dakṣiṇā* to be offered; second, the practice of *brahmacarya* and the later-life *āśramas* becomes more widespread giving rise to greater numbers of men (and a few women) being dependent on households for sustenance and material support; and, third, the retreat into the forests of Upaniṣadic times makes the renunciant life a clearly recognized and acceptable posture. An adaptable theory of giving practice thus becomes necessary and, while Vedic development of *dāna* theory continues focusing on types of gifts, types of donors, gifting times and venues, and gift-accompanying rituals, relatively little attention is paid to the virtue and posture of giving and to the realities of donor life that, on a day-to-day level, characterize the qualities of the donation act. These issues are taken up in Buddhism, however, where at least as much concern is given over to the inner transformation in both partners to the act, one by one by one, as it is to the purely material benefit.

Dāna Teachings in Pali Texts

While it is clear that late Vedic and early Buddhist materials are densely and irretrievably intertwined,[10] it is also clear that Buddhist teachings on donor-renunciant transactions break radically from their Vedic past in their sweeping focus on householder wealth, as well as in their admonitions to procure it through proper means and to use it for the benefit of others. Forging this balance between securing the material needs of the Saṅgha and appealing to those who might wish to renounce the material life and go forth into more spiritual pursuits is the curious role of the new householder ethic. In that it provides guidance on the appropriate place of wealth at all stages of life, it helps mediate many precarious personal choices and effects, on a person-to-person basis, a substantial ethical revolution.

The preeminence of *dāna* to the Buddhist householder life, and in particular to the Buddhist lay life, is clear from the beginning, for the very first act of non-renunciants—by Tapussa and Bhallika, and by Sujātā—towards the Buddha is to give food.[11] Teachings on *dāna* are, ordinarily, part of a gradual or progressive instruction designed to move householders forward in a regulated fashion toward successively more elevated values. Progressive talks begin with discourses on giving, then move through instruction on moral habit and heaven, and finally address involvement in the Buddhist path. Properly received by donors, progressive teachings bring an understanding of the impermanence of experience and, eventually, to ordination into renunciant life.[12] Isolated discourses on *dāna* occur as well, and one in the Saṃyutta Nikāya called 'Virtuous' *(sādhu)* summarizes the whole *dāna* teaching in a discussion by the gods. Here, giving is best if it is from wealth well and honestly won; gifts from very meager possessions measure eminently better against much greater gifts from greater stores; gifts should be given out of confidence in the Dhamma not out of greed for any return, nor out of whim; wise giving is done with discretion in the choice of gifts and in the worthiness of the recipient; giving to others brings good, in the form of merit, to oneself; and merit brings the reward of heaven and a good rebirth. The passage ends, however, with a cautionary note from the Buddha: giving is good, but attention to the Dhamma is even better.[13]

Giving appears in other formulations is well. The three

standard bases of merit (the three activities that produce merit for the householder) are giving *(dāna),* moral habit *(sīla),* and mental cultivation *(bhāvanā).*[14] Of these three, *dāna* is most central to householders' lives, for giving gifts is the first way allowed by the Buddha to get merit, and householders continue to give gifts as one of the easiest merit-making actions to perform. Another list of merit-making actions covers the *dāna* of the alms tour: families viewing wanderers at the door beget merit by the new calmness of their thoughts, by offering the renunciants a seat, by abandoning stinginess as they go forward to give food, by sharing food as they are able, and by asking questions about and listening to the Dhamma. This passage is especially interesting because it teaches a method for the spiritual advancement of householders where, through each of the five items, receptive members of a family move one step forward along the pathway.[15]

Another teaching, the instruction of the four bases of 'sympathy' *(saṅgaha),* describes the development of a kindly disposition towards others through giving *(dāna),* kindness *(peyya),* doing good deeds *(attha),* and equal treatment of fellows *(samāna).* It is significant in two ways. First, it is a teaching enjoined upon renunciants not upon lay—upon monks and nuns who, presumably, have nothing to give. The teaching works, however, in that *dāna* is defined here as *dhammadāna* 'the giving of Dhamma,'[16] a gift impossible for any ordinary householder, or even a lay householder, to give. Dhamma is a gift only for renunciant giving, and is perhaps the only thing they can give, but a gift nevertheless, confirming that *dāna* at least in this one case is a practice carried over into the life of the 'gone forth' as well.

This teaching is significant, second, because the sequence of four practices indicates that broad social engagement is, if not a central feature of Buddhist life, at least an issue to which Buddhist leaders are attentive. While the emphasis on action towards others, and on compassion and equity as markers of that action, cannot be evidence that broad-based social policy-making is taking place at this early period, it does, however, provide foundation for contemporary practices of social engagement along Buddhist lines. That these teachings are for renunciants, moreover, highlights the potential for issues of social engagement to be present through even the most advanced spiritual levels, and to inform every phase of Buddhist life up to its final fulfilment.

Dāna is often glossed by *cāga* or 'renunciation,' the abandonment of material things over to someone else. With this gloss, there are five 'growths' that are enjoined upon householders who trust in the Buddha's teaching for their support: confidence *(saddhā)*, moral habit *(sīla)*, learning *(suta)*, generosity *(cāga)*, and insight *(paññā)*. These growths, including generosity, are specifically entrusted to the wide network householders have: wives, sons, relatives, and friends.[17] In a variant on this, householders work for the four 'attainments' of *saddhā, sīla, cāga,* and *paññā,*[18] interior states achievable within the ordinary context of a non-renunciant life. When called 'treasures,' this list grows to seven—*saddhā, sīla, hiri* ('modesty'), *ottappa* ('remorse'), *suta, cāga,* and *paññā*[19]—and is a list specifically enjoined upon the disciple *(ariyisāvaka)*, the layperson who has formally taken the triple refuge,[20] but who lives at home.[21] Presumably, it is here at home where a householder's practice of these treasures can best serve the spread of the Dhamma as well as the maintenance of the Saṅgha's material needs.

In later Pali literature, *dāna* appears in the standard doctrine of the perfections *(pāramī)* while this doctrine is "still in a developmental state."[22] The lists of ten perfections in the Buddhavaṃsa[23] and of seven in the Cariyāpiṭaka,[24] that pertain to the spiritual posture of the Bodhisatta, both begin with *dāna* and, at least in the Buddhavaṃsa case, add elements needed for the long run of the Bodhisatta career, viz., *viriya* (energy) and *khanti* (patience). All *pāramī* lists also include both *dāna* and *sīla* (as numbers one and two) indicating a more universal draw for the Bodhisatta than for either the renunciant or the non-renunciant of earlier Buddhism alone.

While *sīla* is a virtue enjoined upon both renunciant and non-renunciant,[25] *dāna* is primarily a non-renunciant virtue, encouraged of the ordinary householder as well as of those under *upāsaka/upāsikā* lay vows. In only one case, that of *dhammadāna*, the gift of teaching, is *dāna* a virtue encouraged of renunciants as well. The Bodhisatta of later literature also conspicuously begins the perfections with *dāna*—the same *dāna* as the early householder on whose shoulders the material needs of the Saṅgha rest. The Bodhisatta's *dāna,* however, because of many new applications and interpretations, is not specifically a "giving" to established Buddhist institutions but a giving across the broad range of experience.

Why is *dāna* normally the first item of each list of endeavors for the nascent spiritual life? It is the first item addressed in a progressive talk given to householders, and it is the first and probably most frequented action of merit-making for lay. (Moreover, and not inconsequentially, it is the initial practice in the various lists of later Pali *pāramīs* for the Bodhisatta.) Two answers may be given. Soteriologically, the Buddhist understanding of the source of human suffering is attachment, attachment to a world experienced thoroughly as impermanent. Since nothing can be done about the impermanent nature of experience, the focus of spiritual discipline that hopes to relieve suffering has to be on the abandonment of attachment. This being so, the practice of *dāna* as the initial stage for the householder, is the first step in reorienting the self vis-à-vis desirables in the world: by giving over some of what one has for the benefit of others, one acts out later more complex modes of renunciation and nonattachment. At the very beginning, then, a householder is doing what will not come to completion until the very end of the Buddhist career, giving up attachment to things of the self. Sociologically, *dāna's* first place position allows immediate attention to the redistribution of requisite materials of the world into the hands of the Saṅgha, thus ensuring the physical survival of the institution out of which teaching and missionary work is done: without *dāna,* in other words, practiced one by one, Dhamma would certainly be lost. The preeminence of *dāna* in householder teaching, then, is to provide a foundation, spiritual and material, upon which all other transformative elements naturally depend and without which there would be no tradition to follow.

AN UNDERSTANDING OF WEALTH

It is no surprise, then, that, in a society with an "extensive cash economy" and where there is "a tendency amongst the cities to vie with each other in respect of wealth and prestige,"[26] the texts of the period reflect an attunement to issues of affluence. This attention concentrates on the two "peoples" of Buddhism, renunciant and non-renunciant, for its teachings: while monks and nuns are not allowed to accept any kind of monetary unit or means of exchange, householders are enjoined to acquire wealth fairly and honestly and to dispose of it through worthy channels.

Money and Renunciants

The initial teaching for renunciants is very straightforward: a monk (or a nun) is not allowed to accept "money," gold and silver, to have another accept it specifically for him, or to have it kept in deposit specifically for him,[27] and he is, further, not allowed to make any effort to procure money by himself.[28] Moreover, in a ruling on the 'robe fund' *(cīvaracetāpana),* the Buddha teaches that 'you may accept a robe, but you must never accept money to buy it;'[29] and, in building a residence, a monk may seek out the materials himself, but never the money with which to buy them.[30] Renunciants are not allowed to engage in trading where money will be involved in the transaction,[31] and they are not allowed to be involved in bartering, except under certain conditions.[32] They can exchange things like robes, however, as long as it is only among five classes of people: monks, nuns, probationers, and male and female novices.[33] Although renunciants are not allowed to accept money,[34] there is no injunction against touching it—especially if it consists of precious materials left behind in the monastery by someone who has visited.[35]

The way of getting around the renunciant prohibition against accepting money is the special designation of a householder as a *kappiyakāraka,* someone who makes allowable those things not normally allowable to renunciants. This figure first appears in the discussion of the use of dung, urine, ashes, and clay as medicine, where, lacking someone to formally offer these foul and polluting items, thus making them allowable,[36] renunciants can take them themselves. In the case of money, however, the householder *kappiyakāraka* is especially useful, for householders can deposit coins in his hands and he can then use them to procure allowable items for the Saṅgha.[37]

Although Pali teachings on accepting money is very clear it is still problematic, for it is precisely over the issue of accepting gold and silver coins that the stalwartly conservative monk Yasa, one hundred years after the death of the Buddha, according to tradition, ferrets out the renegades who think it is perfectly fine, among other things, to take money from the lay. This then precipitates, according to the Cullavagga, the second Buddhist council (at Vesālī) and the splitting off of more liberal disciplinary factions[38] from the relatively orthodox tradition represented in the early Pali texts.

Wealth and Non-Renunciants

The teaching on wealth for non-renunciants is more complex, and depends on there being a substantial household stock, that is, a surplus out of which donations to the Saṅgha can be made. The discussion of the *gahapati* householder shows that the most important characteristic of this emergent group is a newly affluent situation. Moreover, it makes clear that this wealth increases the range of business and trading activities open to them, and that this wealth also increases what can be used for the support of immediate dependents, of elderly parents, and of other petitioners in need. Among householders of wealth, business ventures are launched requiring loans and repayment of debts;[39] shopkeepers are expressly encouraged to attend closely to their work so as to maintain a good profit, and are enjoined to be shrewd, clever, and confidence-inspiring.[40] Moreover, material profit to a family is carefully monitored, its diminishment due, teaches the Buddha, to not caring for what is lost or gone to ruin, to living in excess, and to the immoral behavior of those in authority.[41]

This last is significant for the one in authority monitoring the profit of a family can be either a woman *(iṭṭhi)* or a man *(purisa)*, reflective of the increased independence and control women have over household wealth, as well as of the more conspicuous designation of certain properties as belonging to the wife *(itthidhana).*[42] Young girls marrying into their husband's household are enjoined not only to be competent in and understanding of their husband's craft, but also competent in managing the work of the household staff and in guarding and protecting the wealth and property brought in against theft and waste.[43] This material guardianship, then, reflects the very definition of the mother and wife *(mātā ca bhariyā).*[44]

Again, when the householder Nakulapitā falls very ill one time, he is worried that his wife will not fare well should he die. She counsels him, with the Buddha's support and approval, that on the contrary she is quite capable of managing the family's textile business and the household, as well as of supporting herself and the children, should they be left alone.[45] In fact, the supervisory responsibilities of women in families is so important that the Buddha has to caution against a wife's tight-fisted stinginess[46] and in favor of material open-handedness.[47] Wealth is considered to be one of the five powers of women,[48] in spite of what might be seen as her economic dependence on the husband, and the fact that women have and control wealth in the family is certainly a formidable consideration as the Buddha looks to householder property to teach about its proper handling.

Acquiring Wealth

As Russell Sizemore and Donald Swearer note, the basic canonical attitude toward wealth "is an affirmation of the provisional value of material prosperity."[49] In this way, wealth becomes an intricate and positive part of non-renunciant life. The Pali texts make clear, however, that intertwined as wealth is in householder life there are *in*-appropriate ways to acquire it, as well as *in*-appropriate ways to use it.

All discussions of a householder's wealth assume that it has been fairly and honestly won *(dhamma laddha),*[50] and not acquired through means such as theft. The Nikāyas repeatedly point out that wealth arriving through robbery and thieving is ill-motivated (being the product of greed)[51] and pointless, for the robber invariably is caught and subjected to punishment: flogging, caning, burning, losing body parts, being fed to the dogs, and other forms of tortuous and fatal desserts.[52] The robber, who breaks into houses or who lies in wait along lonely highways, has to rely upon rough terrain, entangling vegetation, bribery to powerful figures, and solitary work habits to ply his craft—all elements antithetical to the Buddhist posture of openness, disciplined work, and community support.[53] Robbery and thieving must, indeed, be a significant fact of life in early Buddhist times for not only are wives perpetually enjoined to guard the family wealth from theft, but robbery is one of the five dangers (the others being fire, flood, greedy kings, and dispossessed heirs) one is subjected to as a householder in one's on-going accumulation of riches.[54]

Wealth well-won, however, is wealth acquired through diligence,[55] gotten by following the law,[56] and realized without violence[57] or greed.[58] It is wealth achieved through industry, maintained through vigilance, and presided over throughout with a serenity that's mindful of, but not affected by, either gain or loss.[59]

> *...even so, Tigerfoot, a clansman experiencing both gain and loss continues his business serenely, neither unduly elated nor unduly depressed.... This is called the even life.*[60]

Wealth well-won is wealth of one's own earning,[61] not of someone else's, and it is wealth that is often quite difficult to gather and even more difficult to protect.[62] Wealth well-won is, in part, the result of a worker's good reputation for should his reputation go down, his income would as well.[63] Wealth well-won comes through substantial effort; it is engendered by the great strength of one's arms and secured through the great outpouring of one's sweat. Only wealth acquired in this way can bring the householder perfect happiness *(sammā sukhaṃ pariharati),*[64] making the results of wealth lawfully gained, then, quite considerable. Perfect happiness for the worker brings a happy environment for the worker's family; and wealth well-won provides him with security against the five grave misfortunes of fire, water, greedy kings, robbers, and enemies and heirs.[65]

Using Wealth

Wealth is not only to be fairly and honestly accumulated, however, but it is to be turned to good and proper use as well. As Rājavaramuni notes, this good and proper use is two-fold: wealth is both "a resource for achieving the social good," and also a means of creating "favorable circumstances for realizing individual perfection."[66] Neither one of these good and proper uses can be achieved if the disposition of wealth is approached with greed or carelessness,[67] however, or with great susceptibility to the intoxication of sensual worldly pleasures.[68] Wealth will do no good if one comes to it mean-spiritedly, planning to do evil things, or holding the wrong views; one cannot dispose of wealth with disrespect, by abusing or reviling alms petitioners, or by raging in anger against them and obstructing their gifts.[69] Such a disposal of wealth by one is filled with delusion and this delusion will bring nothing but loss.[70] The experience of the monk Devadatta is used as a good example of this, of someone so fond of gain, honor and fame, that he brings ruin upon himself and misfortune upon others.[71] The Buddha teaches that selfishness can be expressed through any one of five forms—one's residence, one's family, one's wealth, one's social rank, or one's possession of the Dhamma[72]—and that such expression of selfishness can bring nothing but wasteful exhaustion of one's beloved acquisitions.

Wealth is often frittered away and there are several ways for squandering one's wealth. The Dīgha Nikāya lists six such habits (being addicted to intoxicating liquors, roaming the streets at night, frequenting fairs, excessive gambling, having evil friends, and being idle),[73] while the Aṅguttara Nikāya list has four (wildness with women, alcohol, dice, and association with wicked friends).[74] Moreover, wealth is poorly used when the wealthy man doesn't make himself happy or content with it, when he doesn't share what he has with others, or when he doesn't do meritorious things.[75] Wasted or unused wealth has no good purpose, for no one's happiness or contentment is increased thereby. Not even for a single second does piled-up wealth bring happiness unless it is used directly for someone else's well-being.[76] The beneficial uses of wealth, then, are the real focus of the Buddha's teaching on *dāna,* and they rest upon the assumption that householders can have and enjoy wealth most by doing good things with it. According to the canon, a householder should alot his income as follows: one quarter for daily expenses, one quarter for savings, and one half for appropriate investments, and it is from this last allotment that gifting to others comes.[77]

The key is that the user of wealth be a good, true, and worthy person, a *sappurisa,* "defined as one who care[s]...for the welfare of mother and father, son and wife, slaves, and household servants" and who acts "for the benefit and welfare of"[78] these dependents, as well as of those religious people needing assistance. Among the general discussions of the *sappurisa*[79] are those that describe the mission of his or her life: the good person is born into a family for the precise purpose of bringing prosperity, benefit, and happiness to many people. Just as the rains bring to perfection the crops, so the good person brings to perfection those around him, and especially those who depend upon him. In order to do this, the good person has to have at his disposal many material resources, and with this in mind the Buddha teaches: 'For many let the good person pursue wealth.'[80] The pursuit of wealth allows the good person to provide for the material well-being of others, and he is enjoined, among other things, to give gifts from this wealth in a certain way: the *sappurisa* gives a gift *(dāna)* respectfully, with his own hand, with consideration, in purity, and with a view to the future.[81] The good person, then, is the model for the proper use of wealth.

A person's wealth can be newly arrived at riches or property long-held by his or her family[82] but, whatever it is, it is from this individual accumulation that gifts come. The best gifts are those given from meager holdings, for the rich can afford to give much but the poor cannot, and a tiny gift from a tiny store measures commendably against the less generous offerings of the affluent.[83] Generous gifts from wealthy donors, however, are obviously much celebrated, and it is clearly an important boost for the Saṅgha to receive a few large donations from well-placed supporters.

Giving or using wealth properly is known as 'wealth gone to its proper place, securing good reward, and finding good use.' It has three categories: 1) using wealth to provide oneself with happiness and ease, 2) sharing it with others, and 3) doing meritorious deeds with it.[84] Using wealth, first, for oneself aims to bring about the highest happiness *(sammā sukha)*[85] in the person: a material comfort and ease that keeps one secure from want and danger, available for community life with others, and well-disposed and prepared for the practice of lay Buddhist life. Using wealth, second, to share with others means providing material needs and comforts to those kin, employers, and friends who are dependent and who need the same security from want and danger, the same availability for community life, and the same openness to Buddhist practice as oneself.[86] And using wealth, third, for meritorious deeds means providing the four requisites of robes, food, lodgings, and medicine to renunciants, most particularly Buddhist renunciants, to whom gifts provide merit for the donor.[87] These renunciants, to be sure, have to be worthy, and no use of wealth is appropriate if it is a gift to one who is lazy, undisciplined, and unfocused on his own spiritual progress. Wealth used as gifts to renunciants is given by one of high and noble aims and of clear and intent mind, who greets renunciants respectfully and peacefully and who puts no obstacles in the way of those who come to the door looking for food.[88]

Rājavaramuni argues that, as a cornerstone of lay Buddhist ethics, wealth is understood "as a resource for achieving the social good." Centering on the *sappurisa,* the

> *wealth of a good man is also the wealth of the society. It is, therefore, conducive to the social good and thus becomes a resource for all the members of that society. In other words, acquiring wealth is acceptable if, at the same time, it promotes the well-being of a community or society.*[89]

In addition to being an act conducive to the social good of other householder dependents, however, the proper use of wealth also helps to "create favorable circumstances for realizing individual perfection."[90] Although a secure and supportive material environment is only an initial advantage to the disciplined development of the mind and the careful nurturing of wisdom in the individual, proper acquisition and use of wealth is clearly seen as a significant, though not necessary, prerequisite to more mature stages of the spiritual quest in that it allows a certain freedom from disadvantaging distractions.

Proper use of wealth, finally, effects a redistribution of material resources. In a period of greater accumulation of resources and of greater trade and communication, Buddhist teachings on the use of wealth provide for a more egalitarian allocation based on new definitions of who should receive it. In an era where householder traders and businessmen are increasingly affluent and a greater range of society has such acquisitions available to them, that is, where more people are getting richer, Buddhist teaching calls for the leveling off of this affluence by diverting it to needy religious. Thus, the teaching meets the need for the survival of the Saṅgha and can be said to be essential to the institution of early Buddhism. Although "wealth is only a means, not an end" in Buddhist ethics,[91] it is a brilliant move to make it so central early on in the householder context, and to treat it with such emphatic approval and flexibility.

In his discussion of Max Weber's work on religion in India, David Gellner describes "the ideological resources [needed] to produce a capitalist spirit" as "an active rational to this worldly asceticism." Although Weber's claim for the Indian context is "that non-European civilizations could not have developed capitalism endogenously because they lacked" these resources,[92] Gellner points out that the early Buddhist context speaks to the contrary.

> *The urban origin of Buddhism, its original appeal to the middle classes, its universalism, and sociological egalitarianism, its rejection of magical means to*

> *salvation, and its ethical stress on carefulness...might make one think that Buddhism is an Indian Protestantism.*[93]

Like its application to the nineteenth and twentieth century Sri Lankan phenomenon, the term "Protestant Buddhism" [94] can be applied equally well to the period of emergent Buddhism recorded in Pali texts. Gombrich says of the modern development: "As had happened when the Buddha first preached, the urban middle class seized the religious leadership; Buddhism for the second time began a Protestant reformation."[95] The early reformation, then, as recorded in Pali texts, engenders a type of ascetic self-denial which, though it lauds the fair and honest gathering of wealth, does not encourage joy in the pure possession of wealth, but rather enjoins the self-divestiture of that wealth for higher ends.[96]

THE CONFIDENT GIVER

Giving gifts from wealth well-won is most effective when the act is pure and without stain or defilement.[97] And to emphasize the purity of giving is to highlight the particular state of the giver for, at this point in *dāna,* the material and spiritual posture of the donor becomes crucial to the power and impact of the transaction. [98] Operative here is more than just the old Vedic notion of hospitality *(ātithya)* whereby a householder is beholden by duty to provide for a guest. Rather, the gift given by the giver is most efficacious if it is the right type of gift given under the proper circumstances, if it has certain clearly visible beneficial results, and if the donor has the proper mental state at the time of the giving.

Reasons for Giving

Why should donors give? Under the rubric of the practice of giving *(dānadhamma),* two kinds of gifts can be made: the material *(āmisadāna)* and the spiritual *(dhammadāna).*[99] While *dhammadāna,* the gift of Dhamma, is an act for renunciants who are, ordinarily, the only ones experienced enough in the teaching to give it, *āmisadāna* is an act reserved for non-renunciants who have and can give material wealth. In giving, the non-renunciant is celebrated as the 'giver of good or pleasing things' *(manāpadāyin),* a title implying, first, that he has luxurious foods and accoutrements at home and, second, that when he gives good things he receives good things in turn *(manāpadāyī labhate manāpaṃ)*—that is, what he gets subsequently are the just rewards of an efficacious act of donation.[100] This sentiment, that out-going good brings in-coming good suggests sympathetic magic where, through the principle of similarity between what is manipulated and what is desired as a result, the action becomes efficacious. Although principles of this kind of analogy are at work in the Vedic ritual—one lights a fire at the right time, with the right people, and speaking the right mantras if one wants the sun to come up—more important in Buddhist giving is the mental posture of the donor.[101]

In support of a utilitarian view of *dāna,* good giving has certain visible results. These 'fruits of giving' *(dānaphala)* are final effects that are visible to others aware of a donor's activities. They are taught by the Buddha as part of conversations he has with the general Sīha, who wants to know what's in *dāna* for him. The visible results of giving for the donor *(dāyaka)* or generous person *(dānapati)* include becoming beloved and dear to many people, being followed by the peaceful and the good *(sappurisa),* having an auspicious reputation *(kalyāṇa kittisadda)* spread far and wide, being able to enter any group of people self-possessed and untroubled in mind, and being reborn in a happy heaven upon the break-up of this life's body.[102] To this list of advantages of practicing giving, a related passage adds that the donor does not stray from the prescribed Dhammic pathway for householders *(gihidhamma).*[103]

The specific reason why such fruits are beneficial to a donor is not because they feed or aggrandize his or her sense of self-importance but because—with a reputation going abroad for great generosity—*arahants,* those who have arrived at the supreme experience of the Buddhist life, are more likely to come visiting on their alms tour. The donor with a bad reputation is less likely to find himself or herself in such a spiritually fortunate situation.[104] Renunciants are discouraged from going to visit families with bad reputations, that is, who display any one of nine disadvantageous characteristics: they do not rise up pleasantly, or greet pleasantly, or offer a seat pleasantly; they hide their seats, or give little when they have plenty, or give mediocre food when they have good food; and they give without respect or care, or do not sit to hear the Dhamma, or do not listen attentively to the spoken word when offered.[105]

Clearly, it is important to have a good reputation for giving: to be known as someone who gives clean and plentiful things, who gives on time and repeatedly, who gives with respect and discrimination, and for whom giving brings calmness and dignity.[106] The reputation issue is a significant one for, though the Buddha points to its role in bringing accomplished renunciants to the door for food (thus allowing the householder to get even more merit in a *quid pro quo* exchange), the reputation may, in fact, be important for social reasons as well. To be known abroad as a *dāyaka* 'giver,' a *kāraka* 'worker, and a servant of the Saṅgha *(saṅghupaṭṭhāka)* as Sīha is, certainly brings high regard for the householder. And, in the "grant economy" understanding, such elevation in social stature among colleagues, acquaintances, and plain folk has (according to Pali texts) an accumulative effect: the more and better one gives, the more one is henceforth put in a position to give—that is, the greater spiritual reward one is allowed to accrue through giving.

Conversely, to not give does more than simply keep the status quo as it is—that is, a reputation for nothing and no beneficial social or spiritual effects—it also has a spiral effect, this time a downward generating disastrous effect for society. In a passage reminiscent of Arjuna's lament for the world if he is made to fight at the end of chapter one in the Bhagavad Gītā, the Dīgha Nikāya paints a dismal scene for the world if there are no donors. Not giving to those in need breeds poverty, which breeds thieving, which breeds violence and the destruction of life. Out of this decline, the life-span of humans diminishes and social distinctions *(vaṇṇa)* deteriorate. The actions of those not generous then gives rise to wicked behaviors, such as abusive speech, lust, greed, incest, impiety, familial disrespect, war, and the complete law of the jungle. To arrest these developments and, in particular, to prevent the passing away of the word for 'wholesome' *(kusala)* from the human language, people need to return to the wholesome way *(kusala dhamma)* that counts among its several practices that of *dāna.*[107] It is only then that the proper results of giving—that is, having a great number of *arahants* at one's door—take place as a sure, outward, and visible sign that one is a true Buddhist donor.

States of Giving

Both the gifts given and the results of giving are marks of the Buddhist donor, but nothing so marks him or her as the mental posture out of which the gift is made, the mental posture of the *sappurisa,* the good person. In developing a stance for proper giving, the donor needs to be in the process of overcoming the *kilesas* or defilements—craving *(rāga),* hatred *(dosa),* and confusion *(moha)*—becoming in this way without passion, without hatred, and without confusion.[108] The donor is to give without stinginess and without frivolity,[109] and is not to give on impulse, out of defect, out of confusion, out of fear, because of ancient family tradition,[110] or because of the perceived rewards of heaven, a good rebirth, and happiness in this life. A list in the Dīgha Nikāya gives eight grounds from which authentic Buddhist giving should not arise. Giving should *not* take place, for example:

1. because an object of hospitality has approached,
2. because of fear,
3. because the person has given "to me,"
4. because the person might give "to me,"
5. because giving is considered to be virtuous,
6. because one cooks and the other does not,
7. because of the great fame that will go abroad and
8. because of the spiritual benefit that will accrue.[111]

Each of these negative reasons suggests the continued influence of attachment, self-centeredness, or the pull of duty, without any hint of a transforming consciousness at work. Moreover, the donor is not to give with specific reference to an individual receiver in the Saṅgha, but rather—as demonstrated in the story of Mahāpajāpatī who wants to give only to the Buddha, her former "charge"—the donor is to give only for the sake of the Saṅgha as a whole.[112]

Giving instead should be a joyful affair. As the Buddha tells Nandiya the Sakyan, the truly liberal giver should always think to himself that, while all around him people are overcome by stinginess, "I live at home cleansed of the blight of stinginess, open-handed, pure-handed, delighting in self-surrender, one to ask a favor of, rejoicing in dispensing charitable gifts."[113] It is a great good fortune for a householder to be able to live a life of giving *(dāna),* of following the teaching *(dhammacariya),* of caring for relatives, and of doing kindly deeds.[114] Living the life of great good fortune means giving in a certain way, and three qualities of this posture stand out as especially significant.

First, the Buddhist donor gives out of 'compassion' *(anukampā)* for the receiver,[115] out of concern for his needs and out of interest in his spiritual well-being; in the same way, the receiver takes the gifts out of compassion for the donor, in the hope to foster a context for beginning religious growth.[116] The other-orientedness and reciprocity of *anukampā* in Pali texts foreshadows the great role that *karuṇā* has in later periods of Buddhism when it is no longer only the second of the four *brahmavihāras* 'sublime states'[117] but the spiritual and ethical basis out of which the Bodhisattva works. Early on, however, *anukampā* is the operative term for compassion, rendered by Aronson as 'sympathy' or the condition of 'being moved' *(kampa)* 'in accordance with [others]' or 'in response to [others]' *(anu).* In the context of *dāna,* he argues that the Buddha and his disciples, in showing *anukampā,* "created a situation in which individuals could enjoy the immediate satisfaction of a wholesome mind while creating the causes for a pleasurable future."[118] Although Aronson makes no mention of it here, giving gifts out of *anukampā* by the donor is certainly as necessary a component of any efficacious transaction as the *anukampā* of the receiver.

Second, the Buddhist donor gives out of 'devotion' *(pasāda)* to the receiver. As the Rhys Davids note of the term *pasīdi,* there may not be an easy translation for this word or its variants, *pasāda,* and *pasanna.* The terms, they argue, "are expressions of the satisfaction akin to aesthetic gratification felt by the believer in whom faith, confidence, amounts to a passion, akin to religious love."[119] Jayatilleke translates *pasāda* as 'mental appreciation,'[120] while others routinely treat it as an equivalent of *saddhā* and translate them both as 'faith.' The phrase *aveccappasāda* usually applied to the Buddha, the Dhamma, and the Saṅgha, for example, is rendered as 'perfect faith in,'[121] 'unfaltering faith in,'[122] 'unshakable faith in,'[123] and 'unwavering loyalty to'[124] its objects, while *pasanna* modifying *citta* 'heart' has been rendered as 'pure'[125] or 'devout.'[126] As a term which describes the lay Buddhist householder donor,[127] *pasāda* defines the directionality of the giver's attention and the strength of his commitment to the three refuges, as well as the pleasurably heightened quality of his state of mind. Good giving has to come out of *pasāda,* but the very act of giving further confirms "devotion's" validity to the giver.

The Sappurisa and Saddhā

The most frequent description of the act of giving, however, is that it is done in *saddhā* 'confidence,' with a certainty, trust, and conviction in the Buddha, the Dhamma, and the Saṅgha, that will at some point be verified in authenticating personal experience. The centrality of giving as an expression of 'confidence' is found in the Aṅguttara Nikāya's designation of the characteristics of the 'confident' person: striving to see those who are moral in habit (that is, more advanced Buddhists), desiring to hear the true Dhamma (that is, from the very same), living at home practicing liberal generosity, being pure-handed, taking pleasure in giving over, being amenable to begging, and taking pleasure in sharing gifts.[128] And just as habits of *dāna* are markers of the confident lay, so also is *saddhā* the centerpiece of *dāna* doctrine, that is, *saddhā* "is" the charitable attitude, as noted throughout the canon. As C.A.F. Rhys Davids says in an introduction:

> *...the reader cannot fail to see how praiseworthy 'giving'* (dāna) *is often recorded as being; he will also hear sometimes that in Buddhism it is faith that matters little as compared with knowledge; in other words, Buddhism is not a religion of the Creed. Let him check these standpoints by noting how, at the outset, this volume* describes *'faith'* (saddhā) *in the* very terms of creed - *viz., by the formula affirming the reality and functions of the Exalted One; how, a little further, it is made clear, that charity begins, not at home, not with the sick and needy, but with the Order of monks. So much surer is 'merit' to the donor—so Buddhism came to teach—when the recipient is 'worthy of offerngs.'*[129]

While the author of this passage appears cynical in attributing self-interested motives to the compilers of Buddhist doctrine, she is right in pointing out that the teaching clearly directs whom one should give to, and that *dāna* has something centrally to do with *saddhā*. On the first point, the objects for using one's wealth are stated as, first, oneself (ensuring comfort and happiness conducive to the practice of the Buddhist life), second, others who are dependent on the householder and with whom one, because of this, shares wealth, and, third, those worthies (i.e., Buddhist renunciants) to whom giving produces merit. Charity indeed, then, is to begin at home. On the second point, the problems of doctrine as creed become ameliorated by our understanding of *saddhā* not as 'faith' but as 'confidence' in the truthfulness of the Dhamma, to be experienced fully in time by the confident giver.

The *sappurisa* 'good person' is one who gives gifts through confidence: *saddhāya dānaṃ deti.*[130] Throughout the texts the householder recipients of the doctrine are reminded that the most efficacious gift grows out of *saddhā,* confidence or conviction in the trustworthiness of the teaching,[131] and that, in using one's wealth to give robes, food, lodgings, and medicines to the Buddhist renunciant community, the most significant gift is a 'gift made through confidence' *(saddhādeyya).*[132] Glossed in the commentary as 'what is given while one is confident of the deed, the fruit, (the rewards in) this world, and (the rewards in) the next,'[133] the focus of the phrase in the early literature is less on the confidence the giver has in the future rewards of the act and more on the confidence the giver has in the present worthiness of the objects of the act and especially in the appropriateness of the very act itself.[134] In fact, *saddhādeyya* is less about giving out of confidence in the reward and more about giving out of confidence in the truth of the doctrine.

Saddhā is a posture enjoined upon all within the Buddhist fold. Routinely the Pali narratives describe the non-renunciant figures as the 'confident clansman' [135] and the 'confident householder',[136] and say that the pious layman and laywoman most often act out of 'confidence.'[137] Beginners are known as householders 'young in devotion,'[138] and the progressive nature of the development of *saddhā* is evident in lists like that of the householder attainments,[139] of the lay attainments,[140] of the noble-follower attainments,[141] of the noble-follower powers,[142] and of the noble-follower treasures.[143] These lists are certainly for non-renunciants, for all but one includes *cāga,* the giving over of worldly property, something a renunciant cannot do since he has none. The fact that *saddhā* is the usual element to head the lists means that it has some important role in making all the other elements efficacious for final human perfection and that it is the foundational element underlying all other aspects of the quest.

The acquisition of *saddhā* is said to come about when one hears the Dhamma,[144] for a receptive listener is filled with confidence as he or she hears the teaching from the Buddha or one of his disciples. Acquiring confidence, the householder practices in that confidence until such time as he or she is ready to renounce, and it is said to be because of *saddhā* that one decides to go forth.[145] A common phrase appearing in several variants throughout the canon, then, is *kulaputtā saddhā agārasmā anagāriyaṃ pabbajitā* 'sons of respectable families having gone forth from home into the homeless life out of confidence'[146] in the Buddha, the Dhamma, and the Saṅgha.

In that "the bhikkhu-life generally commenced out of *saddhā*,"[147] *saddhā* continues to be the basis of monastic practice as well,[148] and renunciants even in the most advanced stages are known as those 'living in conformity with the teaching and with confidence' in the three refuges.[149] Renunciants work on the three attainments *(sampadā)* and the three growths *(vuddhiya)* of *saddhā, sīla,* and *paññā,*[150] and are said to practice, among other sequences, confidence, modesty, conscience, great learning, firm exertion, mindfulness, and wisdom.[151] A number of discussions about such sequences address the renunciant who, in bringing to completion each of the various progressive stages and in successively mastering each element of the path,[152] moves through the three preliminary stages of advancement (as a *sotāpanna* stream-winner, a *sakadāgāmin* once- returner, and an *anāgāmin* non-returner) and emerges into the final fruit of *arahant*-hood.[153]

The foundational role of *saddhā,* as a crucial basis of both lay and renunciant progress toward perfection, rests in its centrality to Buddhist 'right view' *(diṭṭhi).* As Collins notes, the "Buddhist term for the appropriate attitude here is *saddhā,* commonly translated as 'faith'."[154] The "function of faith" is not, however, "as the main part of the 'credo;'"[155] rather, a

> *more precise rendering would be 'confidence (in the truth of doctrines not personally experienced),' since in Buddhism and all Indian religion it is always said to be in principle possible for any individual to experience personally the truth of such doctrines.*[156]

Saddhā as confidence or conviction[157] is, in the early stratum of Pali texts, *saddhā* primarily in the Buddha as Tathāgata, and, in seeing *saddhā* as 'confidence' rather than 'faith,' this means that the Buddha does "not want his own statements accepted on his authority nor rejected, but seem[s]...to demand that they be tested and accepted if they [are]...found to be true and presumably rejected if they [are]...found to be false."[158]

In analyzing the Aṅguttara Nikāya's Kālāma Sutta[159] as a kind of empiricism, for example, K.N. Jayatilleke goes on to argue that its central doctrine is that

> *we should not accept the statements of anyone as true on the grounds of authority, [but rather] we should test the consequences of statements in the light of our own knowledge and experience in order to verify whether they are true or false.*[160]

Hoffman argues, however,"that *saddhā* [is]...not always consequent to checking,"[161] that is, is not necessarily a form of empiricism, and that it is important to see that Buddhist "progress in understanding the nature of religious belief consist[s]...in part, in ceasing to see it as an experimental (empirical in the strong sense) matter while seeing it as nevertheless experiential."[162] Central to this is underscoring *saddhā's* progressive nature whereby the focus is not on testing the claim of truth of teaching *per se,* but on realizing the efficaciousness of confidence within the advancement of the spiritual life of the person. *Saddhā* is not belief in a creed, then, but a posture of confidence in the trustworthiness of the teaching that informs and effects progress along the way leading to the supplanting of that confidence by authentic personal experience.

This progress in the Dhamma is understood by Hoffman as based in *saddhā's* "pragmatic efficacy" that is seen to express itself in three levels of application. He calls *saddhā* a "pro-attitude" that, in its first phase for the householder is a "listening orientation, a willingness to hear the Dhamma," that does not assume any intellectual agreement, but simply a willing assent to approach the teacher. In its second expression, *saddhā* is one of a number of qualities needed for progress along the path and, in its third, a "realized confidence," "necessary after becoming enlightened if one [is]...to teach the doctrine effectively." *Saddhā,* then, is "of continuing significance...from beginning to end"[163] of the Buddhist career in that it actively facilitates Buddhist growth at each stage. *Dāna* is a part of that growth for, as a kind of initial discipline grounded in confidence, it successively feeds into later spiritual postures of material abandonment, renunciation, freedom, and other-orientation.

The central posture of giving, then, is confidence such that when the text says "he gives a gift through confidence,"[164] this giving is an expression of a Buddhistically confident attitude, central to right view. Most agree that the overall focus of Buddhist ethics is on the psychological aspects of the action, that is, on its 'intention' or 'volition' *(cetanā).*[165] The traditional Abhidhammic understanding is that the *kamma* system is driven by *cetanā:* "Deliberate intention to do a deed plays an essential role in determining the ethical quality of that deed,"[166] and "intentionality becomes of crucial importance in determining the effects which a given deed will have."[167] The Kathāvatthu, in fact, describes the Theravādin position as holding, first, that *dāna* is not only the act of giving and the gift itself, but the mental state of liberality as well, and, second, that the reward to the giver does not increase with the utility of the gift.[168]

The focus solely on intention for much of the discussion of kamma, however, seems to contravene what Pali texts, in fact, portray: that, in terms of the efficacy of a *dāna* action, pure intention can be compromised by the size of the gift and by the worthiness of the recipient.[169] Gombrich points out that this "ethic of intention [has]...taken some blows because it [is]...to some extent counterintuitive." It seems obviously better, he argues, in the modern setting "to do good...than merely to mean well," and this is precisely what the early narratives show us, that donors are intensely interested in what they give, to whom they give, and the welcome with which their gifts are received. Because in actual religious practice, "an act must surely be better if you have something to show for it,"[170] the ethic of pure intention must be seen to fit together with a more "prudential attitude," that is, doing good deeds, in part, because they have positive effects.[171]

In understanding *dāna* anew as pure intention, the doctrine, that the worthier the recipient the greater the reward that is reaped, must be reexamined. Here, it can be said that because one chooses whichever recipient one wants, choosing the most worthy is a function of one's *cetanā,* thereby locating efficaciousness in the intention of the action rather than in the qualities of the renunciant. A similar argument may be made concerning the size of the gift. Since it is not absolute size that is reward-worthy, but the proportion of one's own stock represented by the gift, the abundance of the gift, again, is a function of one's own choosing. In this way, a donor can act out of good intention knowing that good reward is coming—secondarily—but, nevertheless, as a matter of course. Here, then, "prudence and true morality...coincide."[172]

ENDNOTES

1. S 1.21
2. Except in such *suttas* as the Cakkavatti-Sīhanāda Sutta of the Dīgha Nikāya, where concern for society's provision of sufficient resources for all people is paramount.
3. Tambiah, "Ideology of Merit," p. 42.
4. Chakravarti, p. 118.
5. Thera no. 566.
6. Radhakrishnan, p. 396.
7. This passage is even more remarkable in that verse 6 represents the earliest reference to the figure Kṛṣṇa, here Devakīputra, to whom Ghora Āṅgirasa has communicated the present material.
8. In this period, *dāna* becomes so important a focus as a practice in itself that eventually Manu characterizes *dāna* as the only proper religious life of the Kali Yuga: Kṛta *(tapas),* Tretā *(jñāna),* Dvāpara *(yajña),* and Kali *(dāna)* (Manu 1.86).
9. These early gifts tend to be items most valuable to both priest and noble, and include such things as young girls, cows, horses, camels, chariots, armor, gold and food.
10. O. Flaherty, p. xviii.
11. Being previously a giver *(dāyaka)* as opposed to a non-giver *(adāyaka)*

makes all the difference in terms of one's current life-span, complexion (caste), happiness, fame, and power. It is only after the winning of arahantship that those who are previously donors or non-donors are indistinguishable one from the other (A 3.32-34).

12. Vin 1.19; Vin 2.251; D 1.110, 148; M 1.379. The use of these different *kathās* in the Pali texts is fuel for later Mahāyāna teachings "that Buddha does not preach the Truth in a uniform manner. After observing the mental proclivities and capabilities of the persons to whom he desired to impart religious lessons, he selected discourses appealing to their minds, and thus initiated them into the truth." N. Dutt, *Mahāyāna*, p. 69.

13. S 1.20-22, 32; see also M 3.253-57; A 2.62-70; 4.236-248.

14. D 3.218; A 4.241. This list is later extended to ten (*dāna mayaṃ, sīla mayaṃ, bhāvanā mayaṃ, apacitisahagatam, veyyavaccasahagataṃ, pattānuppadānaṃ, abbhanumodanā, desanāmayaṃ, savanamayaṃ, diṭṭhijjukammaṃ*) and commented upon by Buddhaghosa (see Amore, pp. 109-110; Gombrich, "Intention," pp. 94-97, 111:note 9).

15. A 3.244-45.

16. A 4.364.

17. A 3.44.

18. A 2.66; 4.282, 284.

19. A 4.4-6.

20. A 4.245-47.

21. A 4.6.

22. Amore, p. 94.

23. *Dāna, sīla, nekkhamma* ('renunciation'), *paññā, viriya* ('energy'), *khanti* ('patience'), *sacca* ('truthfulness'), *adhiṭṭhāna* ('resolution'), *mettā* ('empathy'), *upekhā* ('equanimity').

24. Missing are *paññā, viriya,* and *khanti* (see Amore, pp. 94-96, for a discussion), three *pāramitās* present in the later standard listing of the six perfections of the Mahāyāna Bodhisattva: *dāna, śīla, kṣantī, vīrya, dhyāna,* and *prajñā* (see N. Dutt *Mahāyāna*, pp. 11-13, 306-307; Hirakawa, pp. 69, 75, 94).

25. Moral habit *(sīla)* for non-renunciants is found in such contexts as the *anupubbikathā*, the *puññakiriyavatthūni*, the five *vaḍḍhis*, the four *sampannas*, and the seven *dhānas*—all contexts where it is found with either giving *(dāna)* or generosity *(cāga)*. Moral habit *(sīla)* for renunciants is found, for example, in the Dīgha Nikāya's list (D 1.5-12), treated in minor *(cūla)*, medium *(majjhima)*, and major *(mahā)* fashions, that begins with the five precepts—no injury, no stealing, no sexual relations, no intoxicants, and no falsehoods— and proceeds through a host of detailed behavioral injunctions (many focusing on the material requisites) enjoined upon the Buddhist renunciant.

    The Pāṭimokkha is the accepted code of moral behavior for renunciants from the very early period, but in time the progress of an adept's development becomes codified under the three trainings of *sīla, samādhi,* and *paññā* (the original teaching includes a fourth *vimutti* 'freedom'; D 2.122-23) a triad made central to Buddhaghosa's work on the path *(magga)* of purification *(visuddhi).* See N. Dutt, *Monastic,* pp. 130-31, 148-158.

26. Wagle, p. 28.
27. Vin 3.236-39.
28. Vin 1.245.
29. Wijayaratna, p. 78; Vin 3.219-223.
30. Vin 2.294-98.
31. Vin 3.239-240.
32. Vin 3.240-42; Vin 2.174.
33. Vin 3.207-210; 4.59-60.
34. Vin 3.236-39.
35. Vin 4.161-64.
36. Vin 1.206; Vin 4.89-90. See Wijayaratna, pp. 79-80, 85.
37. Vin 1.245.
38. Vin 2.294-98; A 2.53. See Wijayaratna, pp. 85-88.
39. D 1.71-72.
40. A 1.115-18.
41. A 2.249.
42. Note here the cases of the monks Sudinna and Raṭṭhapāla both of whose mothers place their properties next to the stock of wealth from the father and paternal grandfather in order to entice their sons to return to householder life (Vin 3.16-21; M 2.62-64). See the discussion of relationships between parents and sons in Wagle, pp. 81-85.
43. A 2.36-38; 4.269-271.
44. A 4.93.
45. A 3.295-98.
46. A 2.57-59.
47. Such as is routinely shown by women like Mallikā (A 2.202-205), and by the wife of the merchant householder of Rājagaha to Jīvaka upon her cure (Vin 1.271-72).
48. The other four *balas* being beauty *(rūpa),* kin *(ñāti),* sons *(putta),* and moral habit *(sīla)* (S 4.246).
49. Sizemore and Swearer, "Introduction," p. 14; see also Green, pp. 224-226.
50. S 1.21.
51. D 3.92.
52. A 1.47-48.

53. A 3.128-130.

54. A 3.259.

55. This characteristic, the winning of wealth through diligence, is the first of five achievements attained by a householder practicing moral habit *(sīla)* (Vin 1.227-28; D 2.86).

56. S 1.21; 4.331-27; A 5.176-182; Sn 87.

57. S 4.331-37; A 5.176-182.

58. A 1.190, 195-97.

59. A 4.281-82; 2.67-68.

60. Hare, *Gradual Sayings* 4:189.

61. *Attavetanabhato 'ham asmi* (Sn no. 24).

62. Vin 3.148-49.

63. D 1.125.

64. A 2.67-69; 3.45-47.

65. A 2.67-69; 3.45-47.

66. Rājavaramuni, p. 45.

67. S 1.20, 34, 57, 96.

68. M 2.72-73; S 1.73-74.

69. S 1.96.

70. D 3.235-36; M 2.72; A 1.189-191; Sn no. 114.

71. A 2.73.

72. D 3.234.

73. D 3.182. For a discussion, see Warder, pp. 182-83.

74. A 4.283.

75. A 5.176-182. One particular merchant householder of Sāvatthi, for example, is just such an unfortunate. When he dies intestate, his wealth goes to the Kosalan king Pasenadi who complains to the Buddha that the estate is very large and that the deceased man is a stingy person who hasn't used his great properties to make his family, his friends, his colleagues, or his dependents happy in any way. Such a mean man *(asappurisa)* allows his riches to go to waste rather than to use them more properly for another's enjoyment *(bhogā sammā aparibhuñjamānā parikkhayaṃ gacchanti no paribhogaṃ)* (S 1.90; see also A 3.45-46).

76. A 5.84. See Sizemore and Swearer, "Introduction," p. 13; Green, p. 230.

77. Thapar, *Lineage to State,* p. 109.

78. Wagle, pp. 105-106. Woodward and C.A.F. Rhys Davids prefer "very man" for *sappurisa.* Woodward, *Gradual Sayings* 5:vi. See D 1.71-72.

79. Vin 1.56; D 3.252, 274, 276, 283; M 3.20-24, 37-45; A 2.217-222. He is equated at times with one who is *ariya* 'noble' (M 1.8; A 2.239).

80. Hare, *Gradual Sayings* 3:39. A 3.47.

81. M 3.24.

82. M 2.180.

83. S 1.20-22. Giving according to one's means is a consistent theme in the *dāna* stories of the Vimānavatthu. See Falk, "Exemplary Donors," pp. 139-143.

84. S 4.331-37; A 5.176-182. For a discussion, see Rājavaramuni, pp. 43-45.

85. A 2.67-69; 3.45-46, 259.

86. D 1.51; 3.188, 190; A 1.116-18; 2.68. For a discussion, see Wagle, pp. 105-110.

87. D 1.144.

88. S 1.96. In this way, the householder who makes proper use of his wealth can say: "I have enjoyed my wealth. Those serving me / And those dependent on me have escaped / From dangers. I have made the best of gifts, / Nay, done th' oblations five. The virtuous, / Composed, who live the good life, I've supported. / That aim which to win householders wise / Should long for, wealth, I've won. I've done a deed / Never to be regretted,—pondering thus / A mortal man in Ariya dhamma firm / Is praised in this world, then in heaven rejoices" (Woodward, *Gradual Sayings* 2.77. A 2.68-69).

89. Rājavaramuni, p. 45.

90. Rājavaramuni, p. 45.

91. Rājavaramuni, p. 52. Sizemore and Swearer (p. 19) caution against seeing Buddhist doctrine as social policy: "The focus is on the virtue of the giver and the dynamics of giving rather than on some generalized norm of structural justice, but it is recognized that individualized choices and actions will have social consequences."

92. Gellner, p. 528.

93. Gellner, p. 539.

94. Obeyesekere, pp. 43-63; Gombrich, *Theravada Buddhism*, pp. 172-197; Bond, *Buddhist Revival*, pp. 45-74; Tambiah, *Buddhism Betrayed?*, pp. 5-14.

95. Gombrich, *Theravada Buddhism*, p. 174.

96. See Gellner, pp. 528, 534.

97. M 3.24.

98. In fact, the states of both the giver and receiver are so important to the process that four types of purity of gift *(dakkhiṇā)* are soon identified: when the gift is made pure by the giver *(dāyaka)* but not by the receiver *(paṭiggāhaka)*, when the gift is made pure by the receiver but not by the giver, when the gift is made pure by both, and when the gift is made pure by neither (D 3.231-32; A 2.80-81).

99. A 1.91.

100. A 3.49-51.

101. Nevertheless, calling on old views, when the Aṅguttara Nikāya speaks of the five 'timely gifts' *(kāladāna)*—viz., gifts to those newly arrived, to those going away, to those who are sick, in times of scarcity, and at harvest time—it also notes that it is specifically the abundant gift *(vipulā dakkhiṇā)* that brings the best peace (A 3.41).

102. A 3.38-40; 4.79-82.

103. A 3.41; see M 2.197.

104. A 4.79-80.

105. A 4.387-88.

106. A 4.243-44.

107. D 3.67-74.

108. M 1.236-37.

109. S 1.18-20.

110. A 4.236-37.

111. D 3.258.

112. Vin 1.212-13; M 3.253-57.

113. Woodward, *Gradual Sayings* 5.215. A 5.336; 1.226.

114. Sn no. 263.

115. M 2.205. See Weiler's discussion of *dāna* and the "Buddhist act of compassion," pp. 239, 245-46.

116. A 3.49-50.

117. E.g., *mettā* 'empathy,' *karuṇā* 'compassion,' *muditā* 'sympathetic joy,' and *upekkhā* 'equanimity.'

118. Aronson, *Love and Sympathy,* pp. 3, 10. In another context, however, Aronson discusses *anukampā* as a mental state of the householder: "'Sympathy' refers to a broad spectrum of fraternal concerns at *any* level or strength. It generally seems to refer to unconcentrated states of minds. The audience Buddha addressed understood the notion of sympathy. It was an emotion easily discovered in their experience." Aronson, "Motivations," p. 5.

119. T.W. and C.A.F. Rhys Davids, *Dialogues* 3.97n.

120. Jayatilleke, p. 385.

121. Rhys Davids and Stede, p. 86.

122. Woodward, *Kindred Sayings* 4.211. S 4.304.

123. D 3.227.

124. Woodward, *Kindred Sayings* 5:337-38, 342-45; S 5.392-94, 399-403.

125. S 1.32.

126. A 2.44.

127. S 4.304. The term *ariyasāvaka* 'a noble follower' applies here also (S 5.392, 401).

128. A 1.150.

129. C.A.F. Rhys Davids, in E.M. Hare, *Gradual Sayings* 4:xiii.

130. A 3.172.

131. S 1.20-22, 32, 58-59, 96; A 2.44; 3.39; 4.79-82.

132. Vin 3.111; 2.30; Vin 1.298; D 1.5, 9; A 3.141; 4.131-34.

133. *Kammañ ca phalañ ca idhalokañ ca paralokañ ca saddhahitvā dinnāni,* Dh A 1.81. See Horner, *Discipline* 1:193n.

134. The Chāndogya Upaniṣad, for example, uses *śraddhādeya* giving 'gifts of confidence' to describe Jānaśruti, a *bahudāyin* 'generous giver' and a *bahupākya* 'preparer of abundant food' who builds rest houses everywhere thinking 'everywhere they will eat my (food) *(sarvata eva me'tsyanti;* CU 4.1.1). Here the intent of the phrase rests on the interior posture out of which Jānaśruti gives: a posture of willing work on behalf of others and of willing handing over of his own wealth for the benefit of others. While one could argue that his motivation for building the rest houses ('that everyone will be eating my food') belies a concern only for his reputation, a this-worldly reward, the point of the passage is that, even though the great light of Jānaśruti 'has spread like the sky,' all that Jānaśruti has and is (food and reputation) is nothing but the whole world: the generous giving of food and its eating, then, is important only because through it 'this whole world (i.e., Brahman) becomes seen' *(sarvam asyedaṃ dṛṣṭam bhavati;* CU 4.1.1 - 4.3.8. For a discussion of *śraddhā* in the Upaniṣads, see Gupta, pp. 492-513).

135. *Saddha kulaputta* (Vin 3.185; D 2.140; 3.113; M 1.465; A 3.42-43).

136. *Saddha gahapatika* (M 1.448, 461).

137. S 4.250, 297-300; A 4.236. Giving out of a mental posture of confidence is a consistent theme of the *dāna* stories of the Vimānavatthu.

138. *Taruṇa pasanna* (Vin 1.222-24).

139. *Sampadā: saddhā, sīla, cāga, paññā* (A 2.66-67).

140. *Sīla, saddhā, cāga, paññā* (S 5.395).

141. *Saddhā, sīla, suta, cāga, paññā* (A 3.53-54).

142. *Bala: saddhā, viriya, hiri, ottappa, sati, samādhi, paññā* (A 4.3-7; see S 5.196-200).

143. *Dhana: saddhā, sīla, hiri, ottappa, suta, cāga, paññā* (A 4.3-7; see S 5.196-200).

144. D 1.62-63, 250; M 1.179.

145. D 1.62-63, 250; M 1.179.

146. M 1.16, 32, 123, 161, 179, 192-97, 200-202, 462; S 2.281; A 2.125; 4.359; 5.129.

147. N. Dutt, "Place of Faith," p. 643.

148. A 2.164; 3.112, 433-34.

149. *Dhammānusārin, saddhānusārin* (M 1.226).

150. A 1.287. A 4.114 gives a list by which a monk measures himself as follows: *saddhā, sīla, suta, cāga, paññā.* Hare has translated *cāga* as 'self-surrender' *(Gradual Sayings* 4:76) rather than as 'generosity.'

151. A 4.38.

152. A 5.10-11; 4.314-16, 358-363.

153. S 5.200-203; A 5.120.

154. Collins, p. 89. See Findly, "Ānanda's Hindrance," pp. 262-63.

155. Ergardt, p. 5.

156. Collins, p. 89.

157. Norman, pp. 326-27; Katz, p. 101.

158. Jayatilleke, p. 390.

159. A 1.188-193; see also M 2.170.

160. Jayatileke, p. 391.

161. Hoffman, *Rationality,* p. 89.

162. Hoffman, *Rationality,* p. 97. See Findly, "Ānanda's Hindrance," pp. 265-66.

163. Hoffman, "Efficacy," pp. 399, 405-406; see Hoffman, *Rationality,* pp. 79-81.

164. *Saddhāya dānaṃ deti.* The *'āya'* ending here can be any one of several cases. Because the gift is given both 'because of' and 'infused with' confidence, the more encompassing preposition 'through' works best.

165. For *cetanā* as *kamma,* see A 3.415.

166. McDermott, "Karma and Rebirth," p. 182.

167. McDermott, *Early Buddhist Concept,* p. 71.

168. KV 339-347.

169. Gombrich, "Intention," pp. 95-97.

170. Gombrich, "Intention," p. 97.

171. Gombrich, "Intention," p. 94.

172. Gombrich, "Intention," p. 94.

CHAPTER 5

Receiving Gifts

THE WORTHY RECIPIENT

Like all relationships, giving is two-sided, and the great purity of the transaction depends as well on the purity of the recipient.[1] The Aṅguttara Nikāya states that on each side of the gifting negotiation, the two agents have three things to uphold in order to bring the negotiation to a successful closure: the ideal giver is happy before giving, of peaceful heart while giving, and of uplifted mind after giving. Likewise, the ideal receiver is free of passion or becoming so, free of hatred or becoming so, and free of delusion or becoming so while receiving the gift.[2] Already built into the characterization of the confident giver is that he or she gives with discrimination, that is, with a distinct idea about the wise choice of a recipient. In this way, Pali texts are clear about who the best recipients are, and it is no surprise that these recipients turn out to be the Buddhist renunciants of the local community, now given sociological status as those most deserving gifts.

Being Gift-Worthy

Monks and nuns are known as *dānapathāni* 'channels for gifts'[3] or pathways through whom gifts come to the Saṅgha. The best channels for gifts to the Saṅgha are those who are of exemplary behavior and of sound Buddhist view, and who have an even-minded attitude towards the gifts they receive. The monk or nun who is designated as an accepter of robe material *(cīvarapaṭiggāhaka),* for example, has to have five characteristics: he or she cannot be swayed off course by partiality, hatred, stupidity, or fear and has to be able to keep track of what is taken and what not.[4] Likewise, receivers of gifts need to be persons of good moral habit and of self-control,[5] and have to have abandoned the five attributes of sensual pleasure, malevolence, sloth and drowsiness, flurry and worry, and uncertainty.[6] In choosing a worthy recipient, moreover, a donor also looks for a particular attitude toward gifts. Of the Buddha, for example, the Dīgha Nikāya says: he lives forsaking the gift not given *(adinnādānaṃ pahāya)*, giving up all gifts not given *(adinnādānā pativirata)*, and accepting only what is given *(dinnādāyī)*.[7] The best recipient does not hope for gifts, nor is he made complacent or disdainful by receiving them,[8] but stands by in unhurried calm to receive a gift when offered. Of this paradoxical posture, Gombrich says:

> *The more a monk demonstrates his indifference to worldly comforts, the more he impresses the laity and comes to be regarded as worthy of their material support. Indifference to comforts thus causes them to be provided.*[9]

Renunciants are seen as channels for gifts because they are designated as *dakkhiṇeyya* 'worthy of receiving gifts,' and an excellent demonstration of the reciprocity of this relationship is found in an injunction to a brahmin woman:

> *Tasmiṃ pasannā avikampamānā*
> *patiṭṭhapehi dakkhiṇaṃ*
> *dakkhiṇeyye*
>
> Being of unwavering confidence,
> give your gift to him who is worthy
> to receive gifts.[10]

The confident giver, then, needs a gift-worthy recipient in order to make that confidence efficacious. Gift-worthy recipients can include one's parents—under the second proper use of wealth, that of sharing it with others—because one's parents are compassionate *(anukampaka)* and are one's teachers of old.[11] They can also include, specifically, religious figures who have achieved states of taming, calming, and cooling the self.[12]

Most often, however, the *dakkhiṇeyya* is a Buddhist renunciant who is at some stage of his spiritual progress. One list of seven "gift-worthies" includes those freed both ways, those freed through wisdom, those freed with testimony of the body, those realizing the view, those freed through confidence, those following the teaching, and those following confidence.[13] Another list of eight gift-worthies names those on the path of the streamwinner, the once-returner, the non-returner, and the *arahant,* as well as those who experience first hand the fruits of each of these four stages.[14] A list of nine gift-worthies names the above eight and adds the *gotrabhū* 'one become of the clan,'[15] defined in the commentary as one "endowed with exceedingly powerful insight and thought, with immediate prospects of attaining to the state of the Streamwinner and the Way."[16] Finally, a list of ten gift-worthies combines elements from all the other lists: a Tathāgata, an *arahant,* a fully enlightened Buddha, a solitary Buddha, one freed both ways, one freed through wisdom, one freed with testimony of the body, one who has realized the view, one freed through confidence, one following the teaching, one following confidence, and a *gotrabhū.*[17]

The term *dakkhiṇeyya* is commonly used to describe *arahants.* In the Theragāthā, a number of individual renunciants (e.g., Rāhula, Vaḍḍha, Mahāpanthaka) proclaim somewhat arrogantly, 'I am an *arahant,* worthy of gifts, of the triple knowledge, seer of the undying *(=nibbāna),*'[18] or 'I am an *arahant,* worthy of gifts, being completely freed, without attachment.'[19] That these statements by the gift-worthy can be part of a formal dialogue at some formal moment of gift-giving and receiving is suggested by two verses in the section on Moggallāna. Theragāthā no. 1177 calls Moggallāna 'pain-free, with fetters gone, of the triple knowledge, beyond death, worthy of gifts, the unsurpassed field of merit for people,'[20] and in no. 1179 someone, perhaps a donor with a gift, responds to him by saying, 'homage to you...whose fetters are annihilated. You, sir, are worthy of a gift.'[21] It is the case that the annihilation of the fetters *(āsava)* is not necessary for one to be 'worthy of a gift,' but it is most unusual to have a renunciant, especially a perfected one, announce himself in this immodest way to a donating householder. Such worthiness should be apparent simply from the general comportment of the petitioner.

The traditional attribution of the phrase *dakkhiṇeyya* to a renunciant takes place with a standard formula:

> *bhikkhu āhuneyyo hoti pāhuneyyo*
> *dakkhiṇeyyo añjalikaraṇīyo*
> *anuttaraṃ puññakkhettaṃ lokassa*
>
> The monk is worthy of offerings, worthy of hospitality, worthy of gifts, worthy of salutation, the unsurpassed field of merit for the world.[22]

This exact same formula is used for the Saṅgha:

> *esa Bhagavato sāvakasaṅgho*
> *āhuneyyo pāhuneyyo dakkhiṇeyyo*
> *añjalikaraṇīyo anuttaraṃ*
> *puññakkhettaṃ lokassāti*
>
> This community of hearers of the Lord is worthy of offerings, worthy of hospitality, worthy of gifts, worthy of salutations, the unsurpassed field of merit of the world.[23]

In his study on merit, Amore understands this formula as a bridge between Buddhism's Vedic roots and the new interpretations of the Sakyaputtiyās. Amore suggests that the term *āhuneyya* 'worthy or deserving of offerings' reflects the Buddhist renunciant's heritage in the brahmin priest's performing sacrifices,[24] with several important differences: while the priest is a knower of the three Vedas, the Buddhist has knowledge of the three supernormal spheres,[25] and while the priest performs a great range of sacrifices, the Buddha allows only "those which involve practicing charity or making oblations for the family."[26] Although Amore notes that there is an equivalent Sanskrit term, *āhavanīya*,[27] he does not follow up this crucial lead.

Āhavanīya refers to the eastern fire within the Vedic ritual ground corresponding in sacrificial analogy to the sun, the heavens, and the place of the gods. The term, in fact, is used at times in Pali literature to designate one of the three ritual fires—*āhuneyyaggi, gahapataggi, dakkhiṇeyaggi*[28]—and this designation becomes critical in understanding the Buddhist alms petitioner as the transformative agent of meritorious yield to the donor. Just as offerings given into and consumed by the Vedic ritual fire are the catalyst producing blessings desired by the patron, so also food gifts placed in the bowl of the renunciant and consumed by him are the catalyst producing meritorious reward for the donor.

Likewise, the Buddhist renunciant as *pāhuneyya* 'worthy or deserving of hospitality' has Vedic roots in the early understanding of the guest/host relationship at the ritual, that is, "the Buddhist wanderers [are]...worthy of the same unreserved hospitality originally due only to Brahmans."[29] Although Amore rightly points to the importance of guest etiquette in the domestic contexts of ancient India, as well as the dire consequences of failing to perform rituals of hospitality when someone, especially a learned brahmin, comes to the door he allows this to lead him away from the original sacrificial core of this term. The very first and chronologically earliest guest *(atithi)* is Agni, the ritual fire who is the guest of men invited to participate in activities on the consecrated ground.[30] Agni consumes the gifts of food offered into him and in his satisfaction effects the desired ends of the sacrifice: the recreation and maintenance of the cosmos as well as the patron's personal aims such as long life, many sons, prosperous harvest, and victory in conflict. The need to understand *pāhuneyya* in the sacrificial, rather than in the secular, setting is clear from its probable origin in the root *hu* 'to offer.' As in *āhuneyya,* then, Agni the guest is the very agent of transformation, the causative link between the technical performance of the ritual and the acquisition of sacrificial goals.

With *dakkhiṇeyya,* there is a shift in referent from the fire to the brahmin priest, but there continues to be an interest in the power of the ritual machine to produce results. As the fee for the sacrifice, the *dakṣiṇā* (also called *pūrta)*[31] is paid to all those participating in the ritual, and its giving (also called *pūrti)* produces reward for the donor: as RV 10.107.8 notes, bountiful donors do not die nor come to naught but rather, through their gifts, achieve this whole world and heaven. The mechanism for the production of this reward through the *dakṣiṇā* is examined by Heesterman who notes that, in the distribution of the *dakṣiṇā,* the patron-sacrificer gives over parts of himself and thus establishes a bond: *śraddhā* being "the mutual trust between the god and his devotees."[32] *Dakṣiṇā* is, then, both a binding force and an agent of productivity for, as "the result of a purely impersonal mechanical process,"[33] the *dakṣiṇā* has life-giving, life-quickening powers.

> *Dispersing himself—the* dakṣiṇās
> *represent parts of the sacrificer's*
> *body—among those to whom he*
> *stands in a marriage-like relation,*
> *he ensures renewal of concentration*
> *and eventual rebirth.*[34]

It is this "cosmic circulation of the dakṣiṇā wealth"[35] that is hinted at in the attribution of *dakkhiṇeyya* 'worthy of gifts' to the Buddhist renunciant for, in receiving alms food, he or she has to be able, i.e., worthy, to effect a beneficial result for the householder standing at the doorway. This attribute then makes the Buddhist renunciant *añjalikaraṇīya,* 'worthy of salutation.'

In discussing *dāna,* Little and Twiss use the phrase "the duties owed holy people" as descriptive of the relationship between giver and receiver.[36] The actual Buddhist context, however, describes something more complex than just transactions forced upon unwilling actors. Rather, early Buddhist teachings on *dāna* weave together a brilliantly conceived series of encouragements and enticements about giving. Householder donors are inspired to make good use of their wealth by giving to Buddhist renunciants and to the Saṅgha; and by giving more and more, a donor attracts more and more renunciants to his door. The social effects of acts of *dāna* include the redistribution of newly expanding wealth and the meeting of the material needs of the Saṅgha, while the personal rewards to the donor include a good reputation, resulting in a chance to augment it and one's merit even more.

What, however, is the role of the spiritual state of the recipient in this transaction? Little and Twiss argue that in Buddhist doctrine "the character of an act" is "determined more by the spiritual state of the recipient than by the degree of his material need."[37] For Buddhism, to emphasize this is to channel a donor's giving specifically to Buddhist renunciants rather than to any others who might be in material need. Emphasizing the spiritual state of the recipient is beneficial for the donor as well, however, for, good reputation aside, the real reward to the donor is future well-being—a reward more clearly assured by the heightened ability of the recipient to be an agent of the transmutation of the offering. That Buddhist renunciants be *āhuneyya, pāhuneyya,* and *dakkhiṇeyya* (with all their power-infused Vedic pasts) is not just cosmetic dressing in the contract, but is in fact what makes the donative contract viable for the donor. One could argue that this doctrine of the suitability of the recipient runs counter to the doctrine of the role of intention *(cetanā)* in the efficacy of an action. After all, if "generous intention [is]...all that count[s]...why should people give to the Saṅgha rather than to anyone else?"[38] Note again, however, that it's the worthiness of the recipient *chosen* by the donor where efficacy is seen to reside.

The final component of the worthy recipient formula is that he or she be an *anuttaraṃ puññakkhettaṃ lokassa,* 'an unsurpassed field of merit for the world.' This phrase occurs primarily within the formula itself, as an attribute of both the individual renunciant and of the Saṅgha as a whole, and it is this phrase about the 'field of merit' that brings to completion the transactional structure of the whole. With its inclusion in the formula, it becomes clear that the very unsurpassable *(anuttara)* quality of the renunciant has much to do with the resultant reward for the donor. In one of their interviews, the Buddha tells King Pasenadi that a gift to a moral person brings great reward, while a gift to an immoral one does not;[39] and, to the brahmin householder Māgha, he says that merit accrues to the donor of the four requisites *'precisely because of* the worthiness of the recipient of the gift' *(dakkhiṇeyyehi).*[40]

Grades of Gift-Worthiness

Individual recipients of gifts are ranked in order according to their consequent merit for the donor and, in a discourse called the 'Analysis of Offerings,' the Buddha gives the following list that begins with the most efficacious:

1. A gift to a Tathāgata, an *arahant,* a fully perfected Buddha, yields an incalculable and immeasurable amount.
2. A gift to a solitary Buddha *(paccekabuddha)* yields an incalculable and immeasurable amount.
3. A gift to a Tathāgata's disciple *(sāvaka)* yields an incalculable and immeasurable amount.
4. A gift to one striving to become an *arahant* yields an incalculable and immeasurable amount.
5. A gift to a non-returner yields an incalculable and immeasurable amount.
6. A gift to one striving to become a non-returner yields an incalculable and immeasurable amount.
7. A gift to a once-returner yields an incalculable and immeasurable amount.
8. A gift to one striving to become a once-returner yields an incalculable and immeasurable amount.
9. A gift to a stream-winner yields an incalculable and immeasurable amount.
10. A gift to one striving to become a stream-winner yields an incalculable and immeasurable amount.
11. A gift to one without passion *(vītarāga)* for sense pleasures yields a hundred thousandfold of crores.
12. A gift to an ordinary person of moral habit *(puthujanasīlavant)* yields a hundred thousandfold.
13. A gift to an ordinary person of immoral habit *(puthujanadussīla)* yields a hundred thousandfold.
14. A gift to an animal yields a hundredfold.

When the Saṅgha is the recipient of gifts, the following ranking pertains, again beginning with the most efficacious:

1. Saṅgha of monks and nuns with the Buddha at the head.
2. Saṅgha of monks and nuns after the Buddha's *parinibbāna.*

3. Saṅgha of monks.
4. Saṅgha of nuns.
5. A portion of the Saṅgha of monks and nuns, self-specified.
6. A portion of the Saṅgha of monks, self-specified.
7. A portion of the Saṅgha of nuns, self-specified.

According to this *sutta,* all gifts to the Saṅgha bring incalculable and immeasurable yield to the donor, and the Buddha makes clear to Ānanda, to whom this discourse is spoken, that gifts to the Saṅgha are always more advantageous in terms of fruit than gifts given to specific individuals. In these graded ways, the recipient purifies the gift of the donor whose yield from the gift is of even greater fruit if, as well, he acquires his wealth well and gives it in confidence.[41]

The worthiness of the recipient then stands at the center of the gift transaction, and his efficaciousness is understood to be pivotal to the donor's reward: out of confidence and with devout heart the donor is to give lavish offerings to those most deserving of gifts *(dakkhiṇeyya)* because they are good fields of merit *(sukhetta);* giving thus, the confident one, becoming wise *(paṇḍita)* and with heart freed *(mutta citta),* wins the happy world *(sukha loka)* that is free of suffering *(avyāpajjha).*[42] With the process thus highlighting the worthy recipient as one of the crucial elements in the measure of yield for the donor, two analogies emerge as ways of expressing the mechanism involved, one sacrificial and the other agricultural.

First, one of the terms describing the renunciant, *āhuneyya* 'worthy of offerings,' has its origins in the *śrauta* ritual such that the renunciant is homologized with the ritual fire. Just as the *āhavanīya* fire consumes the offerings placed in it, ripening, maturing and transforming them for future benefit to the ritual patron, so also the renunciant consumes gifts given to him, transmuting them for future benefit to the donor. That the Buddha himself is thought of as the consumer of sacrificial foods is evident in verses from the Suttanipāta: 'the Tathāgata deserves the sacrificial cake,'[43] for example, and 'May the Lord take my (sacrificial cake), may the Lord enjoy my sacrificial cake.'[44] Here the Buddha is characterized as a perfected 'field of merit' *(puññakhetta)* who in eating the sacrificial cake causes great fruit for the giver.[45] Likewise, in the Therīgāthā, a three-way correlation is made among an ascetic, an unsurpassed field of merit *(puññakhetta anuttara),* and an extensive sacrifice *(yañña vipula).*[46] Finally, and most telling, is a verse in the Theragāthā spoken by the monk Nadīkassapa: 'I sacrifice to the fire most worthy of gifts, I pay homage to the Tathāgata.'[47] While these passages are no doubt of historical significance in that they indicate the continued influence of Vedic culture where Buddhism flourishes, they are also of soteriological significance, for they verify that the image of a consuming and transforming fire is used in early Buddhism to describe agency in spiritual maturation.[48] Here, in *dāna,* then, imagery of fire can represent the powerful instrumentality of the renunciant as the gift bears fruit.

A Good and Fertile Field of Merit

The most common analogy for the efficacy of the renunciant in the *dāna* process, however, is, second, that of the 'field,' *khetta,* in which the worthy recipient is a 'good field,' *sukhetta.* Just as fields that are undulating, rocky, salty, without good top soil, and without proper watering conditions do not flourish when seeds are sown in them by the farmer, so also religious persons who are not well-disciplined do not produce good yield when gifts are given them by the donor.[49] Conversely, however:

> *As, in a field, perfected, when the seed*
> *That's sown is perfect and the deva rains*
> *Perfecting it, grain to perfection comes.*
> *So, perfect alms in perfect precept given*
> *Lead to perfection—for one's deed is*
> *perfect.*[50]

Gifts given to those wort hy of gifts bring forth great fruits, just as good seeds do when sown in fertile fields.[51] In this way, just as the earth is available to all for sowing seeds for crop, so also is the Buddhist renunciant available to all for giving gifts for spiritual yield.

Field imagery, and all of its agricultural attendants, is also used for Buddhist teaching: just as a bad field will not flourish when sown with seed, so also an unreceptive student will not grow in Dhamma when he hears it spoken. Here, however, other reasons for failure to thrive are suggested: perhaps the seed is bad, for example (i.e., the teaching is wrongly conceived), or has been improperly sown (i.e., has been wrongly taught). The possibility that both parties are as responsible for failure as they are for success,[52] seen here in the teacher model, is an idea not found so explicitly, however, in the donor model. Although there is much discussion devoted to improper acquisition and use of wealth and improper posture while giving, the lack of attention given to "bad seed" and "poor sowing" imagery in the context of the success or failure of the *dāna* transaction may be due most to a conscious sensitivity not to insult the Buddhist donor overly much.

Rather, the giver and receiver have a second analog in the field image: not only is the donor the sower of seed but the fertilizing rain, whose thunderous drenchings (= lavish gifts) pour down on the fields, its fullness filling hills and valleys and satisfying those seeking food and drink. Moreover, as this donor/rain cloud pours down in abundance, he cries 'give! give!' *(detha detha)* to others who might give as well,[53] thereby extending the Buddhist mission into the world much as Anāthapiṇḍika does in announcing the arrival of the Tathāgatha and in urging others to build buildings all around. Water imagery also describes the great return to the generous donor in a passage on the 'flood of merit, flood of righteousness.' Here the giver receives a yield measuring in the hundreds and thousands of gallons of water, torrent upon torrent—'an incalculable, unmeasurable, great mass of merit'—flooding him and confirming to him that the recipient of his gift is, in fact, an unsurpassed *(anuttara)* field of merit.[54]

The doctrine of the efficacy of the field of merit is thus an important one for the material livelihood of the Saṅgha. As McDermott notes:

> *Alms...are necessary for the continued survival of the order as then constituted. By thus presenting the order as the supreme field of merit, and emphasizing the rewards to be reaped through its continued support, the Buddhists are able to ensure that the giving of alms to the saṅgha became a somewhat more attractive practice.*[55]

The "worthy recipient as field of merit" notion not only encourages donors to give gifts but it suggests that the converse is true as well: that those renunciants who are the recipients of a great many gifts are, necessarily, especially worthy recipients and thus especially efficacious fields of merit. Although Buddhist teaching does not specifically make this point, a monk named Upananda who receives many robes is told by his fellow renunciants: 'You, reverend Upananda, are of great merit, [for] much robe-material has come to you.'[56] Amore suggests that there is probably a pronounced rivalry among religious sects of the time for material support,[57] and to be able to make the case that a certain group is especially worthy and efficacious means greater success among the competition.[58] Being a worthy field of merit also has a disciplinary effect on the renunciant for, as Katz notes, it "provid[es]...strong motivation for the monk to progress spiritually in order to fulfil the *puññākkheta* role."[59] Despite the focus on spiritual growth taking its own course, it's probably hard for a young and inexperienced renunciant to resist the thought of acting like a especially fertile field (i.e., an *arahant)* and thus bringing in many gifts to the Saṅgha.

Such discussion about the social importance of renunciants as efficacious fields of merit revives the issue of *dāna* as a *quid pro quo* process. Katz remarks that in their role as *puññakkhetta* renunciants are in a "passive modality,"[60] that, in fact, they don't do anything active for the donor, but are important primarily for who they *are* rather than for what they *do* as they stand before the householder at the door. Taking the field image seriously, it is the sower and the seed that are the active agents for productivity; the field simply provides the context for fertile germination. Being such a passive venue, the field doesn't gain or lose anything by having seeds sown into it (forget for the moment the passage of nutrients in and out of the soil), but merely offers itself for the beneficial purposes of the activities of others. The process of sowing and reaping is confined to the effective arena of the sower, with the field, like the sun, being a helpful element conducive to but not actively operative in the maturation of the produce. Renunciants, then, are not said themselves to activate yield for the donor, but only to provide the best possible milieu for activitation to occur. But renunciants *do* need to offer themselves. It is clear that the more spiritually advanced the recipient of the gift is the greater the fruit that accrues to the donor,[61] that is, 'whatever merit or what accompanies merit... there is in this gift, let that be for the happiness of donors...Whatever attaches to the gift-worthy recipient... that will be for the donors.'[62] Because of this, Buddhist teaching obligates renunciants, and especially advanced renunciants, to present themselves to donors so that great yield is in fact possible. The alms tour is not just for satisfying basic bodily needs, but is to foster merit-making for the donor. Thus, it is out of their compassion *(anukampā)*[63] for the less advanced state of the householder that renunciants do not stay aloof from society but pass among the people as ready fields.

Nuns and Gift-Worthiness

As in many arenas of early Indian culture, the disparities between options for men and for women are considerable, and one of the most significant in early Buddhism is the status renunciant women have at the household door, a status reflected in the early absence of the term *arahant* as applied to specific nuns. Although many scholars assume that those early Buddhist women who experience full enlightenment as described under the technical rubric of *nibbāna* are also, like their male colleagues, called *arahants,*[64] this, in fact, is not the case. I have shown elsewhere[65] that the application of the term *arahant* to enlightened women in early Buddhist communities doesn't take place in the Vinaya and the four Nikāyas, as it does for men experiencing enlightenment, but takes place only in later texts and commentaries. While the term is not applied to them—although that of *therī* 'senior nun' within Saṅgha hierarchy is—many women known to the early canonical compilers by name deserve to be called *arahants*, or some feminine version of the term. This is so because, by accounts ascribed to them, they experience the full range of elements traditionally associated with the transformative event of *nibbāna*: e.g., realization of the three knowledges, seeing past rebirths, freedom from further rebirth, bearing the last body, leaving death behind, becoming quenched, and finding unsurpassed rest from exertion.[66]

Why, then, is the term *arahant* not applied to enlightened women—an omission that prevents them from being included amongst the most worthy recipients of gifts from donors? It is ordinarily assumed that the title *arahant* is exclusively a soteriological term, describing a person in terms of spiritual achievement: in this case, that he (or she) has achieved the highest goal of the tradition's quest, the end of the cycle of *saṃsāra.* This soteriological orientation of the term *arahant* is in contrast with the sociological setting of terms like *therī* and *thera* that are applied to nuns and monks who are beyond the novice *(nava)* and mid-ranked *(majjhima)* levels in the Saṅgha and are now eldresses and elders. Being a *therī* or *thera* is a rank of seniority and not necessarily one of spiritual advancement, and places the holder in positions of community honor and respect, as well as of duty and responsibility. These senior renunciants, precisely because of their seniority, are often required to adjudicate allocations of material resources and problematic issues that face the Saṅgha on a routine basis.

Unlike *therī* and *thera,* however, the canonical title *arahant* is thought to take a different measure of the person, that of his internal advancement and wisdom, completely separate from any place or office he may hold in his daily communal life. Vedic origins of the term, however, evidence something quite different. One of the glosses for *arahant* in the canon, especially in the Theragāthā, is a phrase spoken by the monk at the household door: 'I am an *arahant,'* he says, 'worthy of gifts.' This phrase appears at least three times in this text[67] in the context of other traditional markers of the *arahant,* as well as several times elsewhere in the canon. [68] Because the term *dakkhiṇeyya* has such strong ties to the Vedic ritual system, returning to some Vedic references for *arh* becomes important.

Most references to Ṛg Vedic *arh* are related in some way to giving and to the disposal of material things. While there are a few references to *arh* as 'ought,'[69] most focus on the ritual relationship between gods and humans that makes the transfer of beneficial objects between them obligatory.[70] There are, as well, very explicit Ṛg Vedic passages in which *arh* is paired with *dā* 'to give,'[71] and all of the Ṛg Vedic *arh* contexts show the complex gift dynamics of the early ritual: not only must gods and humans give each other gifts to maintain the ever-needy, ritual-based, goods-driven cosmos but both parties, gods and humans, *are worthy to give as well as to receive gifts.* Worthiness to give gifts stems from wise acquisition and use of them; worthiness to receive gifts stems from meritoriousness, in the Vedic context based on poetic or ritual prowess.

In the Śatapatha Brāhmaṇa, there are two important references to *arh* in the hospitality rite (Ātithyā) of the Soma sacrifice.[72] In the first, in the ritualized haggling over the purchase of Soma, the herb is said to be worth *(arh)* much more than the bargainers have offered. In the second, Soma is a guest ritually honored as a worthy person *(arhat)* by the household's representative, the sacrificer's wife, who offers him cooked food so that he will not get angry and, thus without anger, will make the ritual's outcome prosperous. These Śatapatha Brāhmaṇa passages emphasize two critical components of the early understanding of the term: that *arh* is associated with an obligation to give and an entitlement to receive, and that whoever is an *arhat* belongs to the guest-host relationship in which the *arhat*-guest receives, and what he receives is cooked food.

In Pali texts the ritual proclamation of *bhikkhus*—'I am an *arahant,* worthy of gifts *(dakkhiṇeyya)'*—is, thus, a natural, Vedically conservative statement. It is also a theme supported by numerous passages that associate *bhikkhus* as *arahants* specifically with receiving gifts, with the donor's obligation to give gifts, and with the great merit that comes to donors from giving to them.[73] From these, it must be part of the Pali *arahant's* Vedic heritage to be defined as being worthy of gifts. If this is the case, then, the canonical term *arahant* is not just a soteriological term, focusing on the spiritual status of the holder of the title, but a sociological one placing certain monks, to put it crudely, at the top of the donative food chain.

Where are women renunciants in all of this? The term *dakkhiṇeyya* 'worthy of gifts' belongs to a standardized formula with strong ties to Vedic ritual that is applied in alternative versions to the *bhikkhu* and to the *sāvakasaṅgha*.[74] Although women's versions of this formula are hard to find, women do not appear to be explicitly excluded from it. The graded list of worthies to receive gifts does not distinguish by gender—except in the case of the *bhikkhunīsaṅgha* that by norm comes after the *bhikkhusaṅgha*[75]—and, thus, there is nothing doctrinally that prohibits or discourages donors from giving gifts to women renunciants. The problem is more likely a function of the social environment in which women renunciants seek material resources: an environment, Vedically sanctioned, that is hostile to an independent and public identity for women.

One key to the problem is a passage from the Saṃyutta Nikāya that designates five difficulties peculiar to women that distinguish them from men.[76] Two difficulties are cultural—that they have to leave their families at marriage and have to serve men—and three are biological. Of the biological difficulties for women, two constitute choices women can make—pregnancy and childbirth—while only one, that of menstruation, is a necessary constituent of women's bodies. Jamison has shown that the ever-present and insistent nature of a woman's menstrual periods becomes an important factor in Vedic ritual: while the sacrificer's wife has to be present throughout the ritual to make it procreatively and economically viable, her menstruations can make her temporarily polluting. Because a wife must be absent from the ritual during her menses, Jamison continues, creative ritual ways are found—such as using a piece of the wife's clothing in her place—to circumvent the uncontrollable and troublesome changes in the body of a main ritual participant.[77]

Once she becomes a Buddhist nun, a woman continues to present certain problems for the community because of menstruation. This problem remains until she becomes dry, either through the natural development of menopause or the physiologically altering influences of meditation. The Vinaya notes, for example, that special clothes are allowed to menstruating nuns for the purpose of cleanliness,[78] and nuns are explicitly cautioned about sitting on seats lest they soil them with menstrual blood. Not only is it impossible for the monastic communities to be unaware of *bhikkhunīs* in menstruation, but it is impossible for donors to be unaware as well—at least of the possibility, if not of the fact, that menstrual blood may be present at the household door encounter.

The problem for donors in giving to women renunciants, then, might be this: that the *dakkiṇeyya* formula identifies the gift-worthy renunciant as, among other things, a field of merit in whom a seed is sown and from whom a fruit is harvested by the donor. This field is supposed to be *anuttara* ('unsurpassed'), that is, fully a *sukhetta* ('good field') and in no way a *dukkhetta* ('bad field'), conditions indicating fertility based on soil quality and weather conditions, but implicating seed quality and skillful planting as well.[79] While the pollution of a menstruating women and the kammic infertility of a field are seldom linked, a wife's absence from the Vedic ritual during her menstruation does, nevertheless, signify a socio-ritual context in which premenopausal women are considered inauspicious, or even ineffective, as means or fields of merit. The persistent influence of Vedic culture on the Buddhist canonical tradition, then—e.g., through the *dakkhiṇeyya* formula as it ties gift-worthiness to unsurpassable effectiveness as a field of merit—may cause nuns to fall short in donors' eyes as merit-producing fields.

Returning to the *arahant* question, the donor attitude that women renunciants may not be as fully worthy of the same gifting as men may have influenced the dynamics of internal monastic practice. Although completely open to the full soteriological possibilities of perfection for women, Pali texts may well bow to the conventional views and values of society in order to keep material support coming in to the Saṅgha. While women renunciants are gift-worthy in that they do actually receive the four requisites of robes, food, lodgings, and medicine, they are apparently not considered gift-worthy enough to be granted, by the early tradition, the title of *arahant*.

By way of postscript, there is brief evidence in the texts that women renunciants have a harder time securing material resources than their male colleagues do. There are, for example, certain prohibitions that seem to be of a practical nature—rules that forbid nuns from going into villages alone, and that admonish them to walk only in safe places.[80] Moreover, there is a phrase that occurs several times in the Vinaya that actually indicates that nuns may be discriminated against in the donation process. This phrase occurs when a merchant householder is shocked that a nun should have to give up food to a monk, and says, 'women obtain things [only] with difficulty' *(kicchalābha mātugāma)*.[81] Although this passage supports an argument that women in the early period are less successful than men in the donation process, evidence for such a conclusion is not fully present in other parts of the canon. Nancy Auer Falk and Karen Christina Lang[82] make a case that, as the tradition develops, material resources for the *bhikkhunīsaṅgha* become very low, and this process causes or contributes to the demise of the nuns' Saṅgha in India. This conclusion is supported by donor inscriptions at places like Sanchi where there are many women donors but the primary beneficiaries of donor support are normally men. In the *dāna* transaction of the early tradition, then, the confident giver provides resources for the gift-worthy recipient in a process that is fully and unhesitatingly respectful for men renunciants but not quite so for women.

THE ROLE OF FOOD IN THE FIELD OF MERIT

What is the effective mechanism of change that brings about the rewards so hoped for by the donor? The traditional Buddhist image is of a farmer planting a seed in a field from which fruit grows for eating, that is, of a donor giving a gift to a renunciant from which merit arises for the donor's future benefit. Or, more suggestively, a worker earns cash to be used to purchase an item, that is, a donor earns merit to be used to attain a future return. While the second image, with its emphasis on 'merit,' resonates more harmoniously with the new urbanism and contemporary growth of trade at the time, it does not resonate as fully as the "renunciant as field" image does with *dāna's* older agriculturally-based heritage, an image that posits the monk or nun as an arena in which the alchemy of transformation takes place.

Food (pinda) and the Preta's Body

The doctrine of rebirth has its origins, in part, in what Knipe calls "the vedic-upaniṣadic notion of the redistribution of cosmic elements,"[83] based in verses like RV 10.16.3,[84] where parts of the deceased are ritually sent into the cosmos: e.g., eye to the sun, breath to the wind, and body to the plants. Again, in the Upaniṣads, the idea of the "order of mergence" notes that upon dying the person's voice merges into mind, mind into breath, breath into heat, and heat into the highest deity.[85] Along with the development of ideas about the deceased merging part by part into the natural cosmos is the notion that food has a central role to play. "This whole world is in fact food and the eater of food," says the Bṛhadāraṇyaka Upaniṣad, and in the Maitrī Upaniṣad, "this indeed is the highest form of self, namely food, for this life is constituted by food."[86] Based on the evidence of the senses, moreover, writers of the Upaniṣads observe that food is probably at the core of the transformations involved in rebirth, for creatures come into being from seed as a form of food, "by food alone they live, and then into it also they go at the end." Thus, the ritual transmutation of food is understood to traverse a course through the sacrificial fire to the sun and then back down to earth by means of its rays into new plants[87]—or, alternately, through the smoke of the fire to the world of the fathers to the moon, space, air, rain, and then earth.[88]

The liturgical use of food in religious transformations has many variations and one of them is based on a ritual exchange in which food is given, the gods eat, and give blessings in return. In the Bṛhadāraṇyaka Upaniṣad, for example, the 'transformer' is now the "great unborn self, who is the eater of food and giver of wealth."[89] This exchange context of food transactions continues, with some modification, into early Buddhism as a central feature of daily practice, for as Tambiah notes: "Food given away means that food will return to the donor in this world; it also means food for him in the other world and in his series of reincarnations."[90]

The mechanics of the *sapiṇḍīkaraṇa* in the Vedic ancestral rites then reflect the views that, first, there is a fragmentation and a reaggregation of the human body in death and after and, second, that the living's manipulation of food can both affect these processes for the deceased *and* bring reward for themselves. It is through the ritual reassembly of the *preta's* body over the course of ten days by means of the *piṇḍa* and sesame seed water that the deceased's briefest subtle body ("the vague ghost in the tree")[91] becomes the intermediate body of the *pitṛ*.[92] Moreover, in giving food to deceased ancestors, the living are acting on the Vedic desire to keep the afterlife from falling apart for the deceased and thus to keep him in heaven and prevent the suffering of repeated experiences of death and rebirth.[93] The dead's need for assistance from the living to move from this world to the next (from *preta* to *pitṛ)* is clear in the *sapiṇḍīkaraṇa,* and the mechanics of that assistance requires that descendants give ancestors food and merit: food through the actual *piṇḍa* and merit acquired from performing the *śrāddha* ritual, both of which effect the transformation of the deceased. These gifts not only allow the *preta* to move on, however, but they also keep the living from being harmed by the *preta* if and when he is dangerous.[94] There is another transfer as well, however: the wife of the sacrificer can eat the *piṇḍa* offered to his ancestral grandfather if she wants a son, signifying the transmutation of *piṇḍa* as "food" into *piṇḍa* as "seed" or "embryo." Thus the sacrificer has not only to support the male line of the past in his *piṇḍa*-consuming ancestors but of the future as well in his descendants. These he must nourish with the food of his own body before their birth in the hopes that they will, in turn, nourish him after his own death. In this way, then, the *sapiṇḍīkaraṇa* affirms the clear Vedic position that food is "the usual medium of merit transfer."[95]

The Idea of the Womb-Being

When karma theory becomes integrated with the ancestral *piṇḍa* system, some adjustments are made. The parents are "said to retain their role in providing the substance, but the merit [is]...attributed to the soul's previous existence(s)." In the case of the Buddhists, however, there is a need to rethink the mediation between the body given by the parents and the person's own kamma, a role given over in some discussions, to the *gandhabba*[96]—the "being to be born,"[97] the "being who is coming into the womb...the being about to enter the womb...about to come into that situation, being driven on by the mechanism of *kamma*."[98] Food is understood as an instrument of continuity, and consciousness *(viññāṇa)* is understood as the cause, or the food, of the appearance of rebirth in the future. The *gandhabba* spirit, Collins argues, descends at the moment of rebirth as consciousness and, conditioned by consciousness, as name and form *(nāmarūpa).*

> *In technical terms this is 're-linking consciousness,' in 'popular' language it is the* gandhabba, *or the 'being seeking rebirth,' or 'the being about to enter the womb.' In the latter case, it is at the moment when these elements have already been conjoined, and the psycho-physical unity of the embryo ('name and form') is thus formed, that there is said to be descent.*[99]

Rebirth takes place only when the three essential conditions are present, the union of the mother and father, the proper timing of the mother's menstrual period, and the presence of the *gandhabba.*[100] As consciousness, Kalupahana notes, the *gandhabba* is the psychic factor that survives the physical end of the body and that, in association with "biophysical factors in the womb" helps "in the development of the new personality." Thus consciousness is food for beings in the process of rebirth.[101] Hoffman cautions against seeing early Buddhist rebirth in terms of a spirit or 'disembodied consciousness,' and argues for *okkamati* as 'develops' rather than 'descends,' so as not to countenance "the possibility of disembodied consciousness existing quite apart from the material world."[102] Rather, he underscores Kalupahana's insistence on the unbroken continuity of life as well as on the argument of *gandhabba* as the death consciousness of the dying person: "It is the personality that survives physical death and, in conjunction with the new biophysical contributions of the parents, gives rise to a relatively new psychophysical personality."[103]

Feeding the Renunciant

How are these matters reflected in the *piṇḍapāta*, the alms round, of the Buddhist renunciant? In the light of his Vedic heritage and in the spirit of changes in the Buddhist philosophical outlook, the renunciant echoes three Vedic figures: 1) the brahmin officiant at the ritual, 2) the deceased ancestor as *peta*, and 3) the fire god Agni. Concerning the brahmin officiant, Heesterman notes that he is one of two main figures at the ritual: while the sacrificer is "charged with the evil of death to which he [has]...to submit in order to be reborn," the brahmin officiant is "to take over the death impurity of the patron by eating from the offerings and by accepting the dakṣiṇās."[104] By eating the offered sacrificial food and accepting the gifts from Vedic patrons, the priest serves to transfer the evil and impurity of death over to himself thus allowing purity for the sacrificer. According to Tambiah, contemporary Thai Buddhist monks "not only [act] as mediators between death and rebirth, but also take upon themselves, or absorb, the dangers and pollution of death. Their religious status makes them immune to these dangers."[105] The Pali *arahant*, the most gift-worthy recipient of *dāna* is, by definition, free from rebirth and thus no longer oriented toward the polluting touch of death. By the discipline of his life-style and the advanced quality of his mind he is beyond the binding ties of the household life: "There is no fear of death for me, there is no passion for living."[106]

The renunciant is homologous, second, with the deceased ancestor as *peta*, for both eat *piṇḍa* for nourishment to ensure proper progress on their spiritual journey, after having "gone forth from the village;"[107] both now are forever "lost" to the householder world, both "dead" to life in the home. As Knipe points out, at certain points in the *sapiṇḍīkaraṇa* ritual, the priest "served as ritual surrogate for the dead" performing "the necessary role of silent, watchful stand-in for the preta." While this performance of his, as the ritual presence of the deceased may, be *too* good in its avaricious claim on the finances and emotions of the living, the living put up with it.

> *...when he receives all the lavish* dakṣiṇās *in the form of gold, utensils, bed, linens, clothes, food, and paraphernalia intended to maintain the deceased and satisfy his every need for the coming year, the* mahāpātra *always begs, cajoles, and argues for more. And more he receives, lest the deceased take offense.*[108]

The Vedic priest's ritual role as stand-in for the *preta*, then, offers another link to the Buddhist renunciant's receipt of gifts of food. With visual attention focused on a bowl *(patta)* filled with offered food,[109] the donor/sacrificer feeds alms to the renunciant/*peta* for the latter's own physical nourishment hoping, thus, to create a materially beneficial foundation for his, the receiver's, further spiritual maturation. In both cases, the *piṇḍa* serves to prevent rebirth, for in the *arahant's* case *parinibbāna* will be final. The donor/sacrificer also gives for his own benefit, for the gift of the *piṇḍa*, as food and seed, not only ensures his own rebirth but a rebirth that is good and wholesome. The *dāna* teachings note that the gift of food that produces merit is in turn itself the 'food of happiness' *(sukhassāhāra)*,[110] that is, the cause of future reward.

This cycling of food through the process of rebirth, whereby the priest/*preta*/renunciant eats *piṇḍa* and rebirth for the donor results, is understood Vedically in three ways: first, the gift or *dakṣiṇā* offered represents the sacrificer himself, for "it is in the last resort oneself that one offers;"[111] second, the sacrificer holds on to the *dakṣiṇā* as it courses through to the world of the gods;[112] and, third, the food offering (here *prasāda)*— "given to the god to keep him 'alive' in limbo, like a *preta,* to give him the power to act"—is then recycled back as "a form of power granted to the worshipper in return."[113] While Pali texts are unclear as to the exact mechanism by which the gift of food results in future reward for the donor, the Vedic view that the nature of the gift relates clearly to what is expected as a reward is probably resonant here: for, in the notion of *piṇḍa* as food, there is basis for the continuity of life and, in *piṇḍa* as embryo, there is basis for a new (and good) rebirth. In this way, the term *piṇḍa* is not just a random word for food or gift in Pali texts, but a very specific term whose Vedic heritage is understood as significant on the practising level of the householder donor. The concept of *"piṇḍa,"* then, is a Vedic remnant echoing meaningfully for householders about how the reconstitution of the self after death is tied to food given to renunciants/*petas.*

Finally, the renunciant is homologous to the Vedic fire god Agni who carries the food offering to the gods, transforms that offering by fire, and effects heaven for the ritual patron.[114] Like Agni, the oblation-eating fire, the renunciant presents himself as an arena, a "field," where the transformation of the donor takes place. Just as the ritual fire burnishes the offering with its *tapas* 'inner heat'[115] and gives a ripened, cooked product in return, so the renunciant receives the gift-seed planted in him where it grows and matures through merit as a reward.[116] This image may be problematic in that the *bhikkhu* as *arahant* is kammically barren, that is, can no longer produce kamma, though still experiences the fruit of past kamma. How, for example, can the renunciant be a field if the field is kammically fertile only for others and not for himself? Again, using the Agni homology, how can the renunciant cause a gift to ripen like the heat-generating fire, when the *arahant* has lost heat, has become cool, has been blown out in *nibbāna*?

The quality of the fruit depends on the quality of the seed, but it also depends on the quality of the field, the growing medium. The paradox lies in the fact that the more advanced the renunciant the more fruit to the donor, that is, the more fertile kammically he is for others; but the more advanced the renunciant the more barren, less kammically fertile, he is for himself. The solution lies in the field image itself, in what Collins calls "causal efficacy as a process of husbandry."[117] While the field provides the context for the ripening, it is the seed that is to mature on its own, for it is "a natural process of seasonal change which [brings]...the crops to ripening."[118] The active ingredient in the process is the seed, the passive one the field, and nothing can speed up or slow down the transformative course, for it is governed by factors internal to the seed itself. Moreover, although the *bhikkhu* as *arahant* no longer "produces" seeds to be planted, his body (field) is still fertile enough to be involved in the "ripening" of his own past seeds. And, perhaps because *this is* the *kammic* activity of the *arahant's* body, and because it leads to *parinibbāna,* this field is the most auspicious for the donor.

If the renunciant provides a condition for good ripening, then one characteristic takes on renewed significance: his gift-worthiness. It is the quality of the renunciant as *dakkhiṇeyya,* as worthy of receiving gifts, that is homologous to the fertility of the field and to the heat of Agni. Though disinterested in the gift of food, the renunciant accepts it out of compassion *(anukampā)* for the householder donor, and because it is necessary for maintaining his own health. As the donor gives the renunciant food, the renunciant offers himself up as a venue for the donor's kammic process. While the quality of a donor's merit is thought to accrue from the act of giving itself,[119] from the choice of gifts, and from the choice of recipients, this merit remains a function of *cetanā,* 'intention, on which the choices are based—a *cetanā* grounded in confidence in the quality of the merit field chosen to receive the gift. Thus, the Theravādins are able to do two things: first, to retain an intention-based understanding of kamma, deriving from the individualization and interiorization of the Vedic sacrifice[120] and, second, to ensure the survival of the Saṅgha (and its spiritual hierarchy) by designating gift-worthiness as an important condition of the ripening process. In this way, then, the socio-ritual contracts of the *śrauta* system (patron : priest/*preta*/ Agni), rethought in the *dāna* practices of Buddhism (donor : renunciant), are ethicized by locating efficacy for merit-producing householders in, among other things, the personal spiritual quality of the recipients.

TWO POVERTIES AND *DĀNA*

In her article on poverty in Pali texts,[121] Mavis Fenn identifies two notions of poverty, both with implications for *dāna*. One is an involuntary poverty of economic and material deprivation, and the other a voluntary one of religious convictions of simplicity. Each has a different view on material resources, and each has significant implications for the religious, social, and political life of lay and renunciants as both involve the *dāna* process.

Poverty as deprivation prevents a person from full participation in the life of the community, and produces a state of dehumanization that severely limits progress along a spiritual path. Most fully analyzed in the Cakkavatti-Sīhanāda Sutta, poverty as deprivation results not only in social disintegration but also in the degradation of the human being: when resources are withheld from those in need, poverty ensues, and with poverty comes theft, with theft weapons, with weapons murder, with murder lying, and then the decline of lifespan and all pleasant appearance. As the cycle of violence spirals downward, the animal nature of humans overcomes their humanity until such time when a *cakkavatti* (universal ruler) appears and turns the world towards righteous action again.

Poverty, in Fenn's analysis of the *sutta,* is expressed on three levels. It is found, first, in an individual, personal destitution that causes stealing from and injuring others. This poverty so affects a person's consciousness that the person eventually loses most qualities of humanness and, in consequence, is removed from the proximate possibility of *nibbāna*. Poverty is expressed, second, in the moral deprivation of society. Here the king fails to take the lead in responding to social problems and, with others, shuts the poor out leaving them no redress. Abandoned by society, their situation worsens affecting the integrity of the larger social infra-structure. Poverty is expressed, third, in political leadership. While a king may be well-born, well-educated, and personally moral, he may be limited in knowing how to rule with benefit for the poor. Capable of individual acts of generosity, he isn't able to provide for all members of his community, particularly the most needy. As Fenn notes, it is here in the Cakkavatti Sīhanāda Sutta where some basic Buddhist notions of social justice are expressed, i.e., that "everyone should have sufficient resources to care for themselves and others, and to make religious life possible," and that "these values should be incorporated into the political system."[122]

The second notion of poverty identified by Fenn is one marked by voluntary simplicity and forbearance. It is the poverty of the Buddhist renunciant who rejects wealth and chooses a life of minimum material resources so as to enhance the possibilities for religious development. The voluntary poverty of renunciants belongs to the ethos of the Saṅgha community and, in this, Fenn argues, the Saṅgha represents an institutionalization of "communitas." Here, for Victor Turner, a common bond develops among people and, in this time of liminality, a state of being "betwixt-and-between" exists: after one has separated from an earlier life structure, but before one enters a new one. Liminality is differentiated from the structured and hierarchical periods on either side of it, and is the period of transition marked by the "experience of communitas... [as expressed in] a spontaneous, immediate, concrete relation between people who are, at once, recognized to be unique in their individual attributes and abilities and common in their humanity."[123]

Fenn suggests that the values of Buddhist renunciants as participants in the Saṅgha reflect those of "communitas" and, in the context of poverty and the social order, are clearly expressed in the Aggañña Sutta of the Dīgha Nikāya. Here the text argues that the values imbuing the social order are not sufficient for Buddhist perfection and that these values can only be reversed by the renunciant life. While the normative ideal of Buddhism is individualistic, texts like the Aggañña Sutta repeatedly stress a common humanity as the community open to all. Further, it emphasizes that membership in such a community "fosters relationships characterized by compassion." The case of the

Saṅgha, Fenn argues, represents an "intentional" community where members "are not joined by ties of kinship but by a common dedication to achieve liberation through a process of purification,"[124] a process that then gives rise to compassion. This process is thoroughly oriented toward a self-conscious abandonment of all but the most basic material supports and of all harmful mental states. It is concerning this voluntary poverty, as shaped by a structure that enhances communitas, that *dāna* now becomes significant.

In the Buddhist "spiritualization of giving," *dāna* responds to both types of poverty. In recognition that one outgrowth of the new wealth and of its consequent redrawing of social patterns around the householder may be the multiplying of impoverished persons at the margins, the doctrine of *dāna* calls for the redistribution of wealth and material resources such that there is a more equitable balance across the social spectrum. For householders and lay, this means the use of wealth well-won to support the needs of family, friends, and associates so that greater even-handedness appears in every strata of non-renunciant life. For householders and lay, it also means meeting the material needs of renunciants who, without this support, will certainly find themselves increasingly disenfranchised and subject to all the distractions of involuntary poverty's downward spiral. For renunciants, the doctrine of *dāna* reflects the middle way—while not to live lives of luxury, they are also not to be without sufficient resources to support their spiritual practice.

Using Turner's analysis, Fenn suggests that the Buddhist Saṅgha is an attempt "to institutionalize a permanent realm of liminality," to provide clear ground for "the anti-structural values of the renouncer."[125] Here the renouncers shun household pleasures and live lives of greater communal ownership of property. Renouncers, however, cannot live completely separate from wealth because they need a livelihood, and of that property a few resources, like food and robes, naturally come to be personalized. These caveats preclude the Saṅgha "from providing a complete alternative to structure," but what does happen, Fenn continues, is that the doctrine of *dāna* is used for purposes of communitas:

> *...the spiritualization of giving turns the receipt of gifts into a means by which the* saṅgha *exercises its mandate to assist others in their spiritual development. Further, through its receipt of* dāna, *moral teaching* (dhamma/kamma), *and views on kingship,* the saṅgha attempts to infuse the laity with the values of communitas that will encourage them to aspire to incorporate those values in their socio-political life.[126]

Thus, *dāna* becomes a way of redressing poverty as deprivation—materially, by encouraging equity through the redistribution of wealth and, spiritually, by encouraging the spread of values through the broad use of the donation contract. Moreover, *dāna* makes poverty as simplicity possible, by ensuring that those taking such vows are guaranteed a regular, minimally comfortable life-style.

Returning to the progressive and instructional role *dāna* plays in spiritual development, it's significant that the abandonment of material possessions by the lay is the foundation of the abandonment of other aspects of the self later on. Moreover, *dāna* is the most powerful point of fluidity between the fixed and liminal worlds of lay and renunciant for here the values of communitas are engendered in the larger arena of householder life. As Fenn notes: "Viewed through a Turnerian lens, it is by the ritualized exchange of gifts that the values of communitas pass into structure,"[127] primarily through the teaching of monks and nuns. Boulding's notion of an "exchange economy" then comes into play for householders as the *quid pro quo* possibilities of the exchange economy show all the ways in which 'the giver of good gains the good.'[128] The hard work of an exchange economy is evident throughout the canon. As noted above, teachings about *dāna* rest upon the acknowledgement that giving is often a hardship for the donors, but being party to the *dāna* exchange is hard work for renunciants as well, for as Katz notes:

> ...the notion of an arahant's being a *puññkkheta* does not mean a passive accepting of gifts from the laity. The role of *puññākkheta* is such that it entails a very active receiving; it provides strong motivation for the monk to progress spiritually in order to fulfill the *puññākkheta* role.[129]

The hard work of the *dāna* exchange pays off, however, for as the renunciant receives material resources and a chance, perhaps unwittingly, to redress (through teaching) personal and social poverty as deprivation, the householder receives merit, heaven, a good rebirth, and an entré into the values of communitas.

Boulding's grant economy, however, is also operative, for the Buddha contrasts the giver who gives to gain a reward with the giver who gives thinking only 'it is good to give.' [130] The grant economy, involving a one-way transfer of economic goods, is founded upon feelings of identification and benevolence between donors and recipients in such a way that there are built up between them "integrative structures and communities."[131] The great benefit of these, on one hand, is "an equilibrium in the distribution of resources"[132]—an "equipoise in the developing economy."[133] There is benefit, on the other hand, in the community itself in which the gift-worthiness of the renunciant serves to bind and guide all those with confidence.

The act of donation, then, is a process in which all are "in relation to" each other and, therefore, are defined by this relationship such that "a person is" what "a person does"—another way of looking at kamma. This relationship has elements of both exchange and granting, but is a relationship that intensely works the interplay between structure and anti-structure, thus allowing communitas to be more fluidly located.

ENDNOTES

1. D 3.231-32; M 3.24.
2. A 3.336.

3. Vin 3.181.
4. Vin 1.283.
5. Vin 3.250; D 2.88. Moreover, it is said that the brahmin householders in the town and countryside are especially inclined to give gifts to the Buddha because of his moral habit and wisdom (A 3.31).
6. *Kāmachanda, vyāpāda, thīnamiddha, uddhaccakukkucca, vicikicchā,* and to have cultivated moral habit, concentration, wisdom, and freedom through knowledge and vision *(sīla, samādhi, paññā, vimutti, vimuttiñāṇadassana;* A 1.161-62; see also A 5.198).
7. D 1.4; A 4.388.
8. D 3.46.
9. Gombrich, *Theravada Buddhism*, p. 95.
10. S 1.141-42.
11. A 1.132; 2.70.
12. A 4.45.
13. D 3.253-54; see D 3.105; A 3.279-282; 4.13-14; Thera no. 343.
14. D 3.255.
15. A 4.373.
16. As translated by Hare, *Gradual Sayings* 4:247n.
17. A 5.23; see also M 1.446-47.
18. *Arahā dakkhiṇeyyo 'mhi tevijjo amataddaso* (Thera nos. 296, 336).
19. *Arahā dakkhiṇeyyo 'mhi vippamutto nirūpadhi* (Thera no. 516).
20. *Isallaṃ khīṇasaṃyogaṃ tevijjaṃ maccuhāyinaṃ dakkhiṇeyyaṃ manussānaṃ puññakhettaṃ anuttaraṃ.*
21. *Namo te...yassa te āsavā khīṇā, dakkhiṇeyyo 'si mārisa.* Other monks like Subhūti are especially known as being worthy of gifts (A 1.24).
22. M 1.446; A 1.244, 284; 2.117, 171; 3.134, 161, 248, 279, 387; 4.113, 290-91; 5.67, 198; Thera. nos. 566, 1177, 1179. This same formula is descriptive of seven persons who in seeing impermanence in constituted things reach seven different levels of advancement (A 4.13-14, 146).
23. D 2.94; 3.5; M 1.37; 3.80; S 4.272; A 2.56, 183; 3.36; 4.407.
24. Amore, pp. 6-18.
25. Amore, p. 15.
26. Amore, p. 16.
27. Amore, p. 7.
28. D 3.217; A 4.41.
29. Amore, p. 25; see pp. 19-25.
30. RV 1.44.4; 1.58.6; 1.73.1; 1.127.8; 1.128.4; 1.186.3; 2.2.8; 2.4.1; 3.2.2; 3.3.8; 3.26.2; 4.1.20; 4.2.7; 4.40.5; 5.1.8, 9; 5.3.5; 5.4.5; 5.8.2; 5.18.1; 6.2.7; 6.4.2; 6.7.1; 6.15.1, 4, 6; 6.16.42; 7.3.5; 7.8.4; 7.9.3; 7.42.4; 8.19.8; 8.23.25; 8.44.1; 8.74.7; 8.103.10, 12; 10.1.5; 10.91.2; 10.92.1; 10.122.1; 10.124.3.

31. Amore, p. 33.
32. Heesterman, "*dákṣiṇā,*" pp. 243, 247.
33. Heesterman, "*dákṣiṇā,*" p. 244.
34. Heesterman, "*dákṣiṇā,*" p. 251.
35. Heesterman, "*dákṣiṇā,*" p. 255.
36. Little and Twiss, p. 70.
37. Little and Twiss, p. 71.
38. Gombrich, "Intention," p. 95.
39. S 1.98-100.
40. Sn no. 488: *dakkhiṇeyyehi* is used here in the instrumental. As McDermott notes (*Early Buddhist Concept,* p. 32): "While all such acts of charity have their result, the fruit they bear is in direct proportion to the worthiness of the recipient."
41. The Dakkhiṇāvibhaṅga Sutta (M 3.253-57), spoken on the occasion of Mahāpajāpatī's attempt to give robes to the Buddha rather than to the Saṅgha. The Kathāvatthu (549-552) notes that one sect, the Vetulyakas (= Mahāsuññatāvādins) hold that, because the Saṅgha in the metaphysical sense *is* the path and the fruits, it cannot accept or purify gifts. It (556-58) also notes that some sects, like the Uttarāpathakas, hold that the gift is sanctified only by the giver and not by the recipient.
42. A 2.44. As other texts do, the Vimānavatthu, in its many stories of the future rewards for donors of the gifts they give, makes clear throughout that the efficacy of a gift depends on *both* the thought or intent in which the action is performed *and* the worthiness of the field of merit to whom the gift is given.
43. *Tathāgato arahati pūraḷāsaṃ* (Sn nos. 467-479).
44. *Patigaṇhātu me Bhagavā, bhuñjatu me Bhagavā pūraḷāsaṃ* (Sn no. 479).
45. Sn nos. 481, 482, 486.
46. Therī no. 287.
47. *Juhāmi dakkhiṇeyyaggiṃ, namassāmi tathāgataṃ* (Thera no. 343).
48. Note especially the passing of the flame from candle to candle as an analogy for rebirth (M 3.245).
49. A 4.237-39.
50. Hare, *Gradual Savings* 4:162.
51. *Ye dakkhiṇeyyā idha jīvaloke // etesu dinnāni mahapphallāni // bījāni vuttāni yathā sukhette ti* (S 1.21). See the discussion of organic and agricultural imagery as it pertains to monks as fields of merit, in Collins, pp. 218-224.
52. S 5.378-380. In another version of the field image, descriptive here of the basic human condition as understood in Buddhism, the field is action, the seed is consciousness, and the rain is craving (A 1.223).
53. S 1.100.

54. *Puññābhisanda, kusalābhisanda* and *asaṅkheyya, appameyya puññakkhandha* (A 2.54-57).

55. McDermott, *Early Buddhist Concept,* p. 33; see also p. 71.

56. *Mahāpuñño 'si tvaṃ āvuso Upananda, bahuṃ te cīvaraṃ uppannan* (Vin 1.300; see also Vin 3.217-19). See Rājavaramuni, p. 40. Swearer (p. 3) makes this point as well, that monks who are recipients of large gifts are regarded as, because of this, especially worthy.

57. Amore, p. 52.

58. Here, then, emerges a clear sentiment that the "householders of Gotama's time [have]...the fortune to live in a time and place where such a merit-field [is]...available."Amore, p. 56.

59. Katz, pp. 186-87, 188.

60. Katz, pp. 185-88.

61. A 4.392-96.

62. M 1.236-37.

63. A 3.49-51.

64. Writers such as Caroline A. Foley, I.B. Horner, Nancy Auer Falk, Kajiyama Yuichi, Alan Sponberg, and Jonathan S. Walters discuss some of the women they encounter in the early texts in terms of the status of the *arahant.* See Mrs. Rhys Davids (Foley), *Psalms of the Sisters,* p. xxiv; Horner, *Man Perfected,* pp. 73, 97, 98, 105, 107-108, 109, 119, 121, 238-239; Falk, "Vanishing Nuns," p. 217; Falk, "Image of Women," p. 105; Yuichi, p. 53; Sponberg, pp. 6, 7, 8, 9; Walters, p. 377.

65. Findly, "Women and the *arahant* Issue."

66. Findly, "Women and the *arahant* Issue."

67. *Arahā dakkhiṇeyyo 'mhi* (Thera nos. 296, 336, 516).

68. E.g., having the triple knowledge, having annihilated the *āsavas,* being beyond death, and being without basis for rebirth (A. 4.374; 5.23).

69. RV 4.55.7.

70. See Findly, "Women and the *arahant* Issue."

71. See RV 5.79.10, 7.18.22.

72. Jamison, pp. 153-203; Ḇ 3.3.3.1, 3; 3.4.1.3, 6, 8.

73. D 1.144; 2.75, 266-267; see Vin 3.129; D 3.258; A 4.61-62, 236.

74. *Bhikkhu āhuneyyo hoti pāhuneyyo dakkhiṇeyyo añjali karaṇīyo anuttaram puññakkhettaṃ lokassa* (M 1.446; A 1.244, 284; 2.117, 171; 3.134, 161, 248, 279, 387; 4.113, 290-291; 5.67, 198). For the *sāvakasaṅgha* version, see D 2.94; 3.5; M 1.37; 3.80; S 4.272; A 2.56, 183; 3.36.

75. See M 3.253-257.

76. S 4.239.

77. Jamison, pp. 14-16, 32-36.

78. Vin 2.272; 1.294; 4.303.

79. S 1.21; 5.379; see also S 3.54-55.

80. Vin 4.227-230, 295; see A 4.278-279.

81. Vin 3.208; 4.175.

82. Falk, "Vanishing Nuns," p. 211; Lang, p. 79.

83. Knipe, "*Sapiṇḍīkaraṇa,*" p. 113; Tull, pp. 25-27.

84. See also AV 18.2.7, VS 40.15, ŚB 14.6.2.13.

85. CU 6.15.1-3; see also 4.3.1, 5.4-9. This doctrine, says Tull, is "an obvious reversal of the central Brāhmaṇic mythology of the cosmic man (Puruṣa, Prajāpati), according to which the cosmos arose from the body of a primeval anthropomorphic being" (Tull, p. 26; see also pp. 50-71) , first articulated in hymns like the Ṛg Vedic Puruṣa Sūkta (10.90) and later supported by sacrificial theologies of dismemberment applied to the cosmic man.

86. BĀU 1.4.6: *etāvad vā idaṃ sarvam annaṃ caivānnādaś ca;* MU 6.11: *paraṃ vā etad ātmano rūpam yad annam, annamayo hy ayam prāṇaḥ.* See also BĀU 1.5.1-23.

87. TU 2.2: *atho'nnenaiva jīvanti, athainadapi yanty antataḥ;* MU 6.10, 11, 12, 14.

88. BĀU 6.2.16; see also 5.10.1.

89. *Mahān aja ātmā, annādo vasu-dānaḥ* (BĀU 4.4.24; see Collins, pp. 54, 208-209).

90. Tambiah, "Ideology of Merit," p. 117.

91. Knipe, "*Sapiṇḍīkaraṇa,*" p. 117.

92. See RV 10.14.8; AV 18.2.26; 18.3.13, 22, 58; 18.4.51, 52; O'Flaherty 4n, 5. Parry suggests that, because *piṇḍa* belongs to the category of *kachchā* (more cooked or transformed food), *piṇḍa* actually represents food that "has a greater *transformative* potential" ("Death and Digestion," p. 625).

93. O'Flaherty, p. 3.

94. O'Flaherty, pp. 10-13; Knipe, "*Sapiṇḍīkaraṇa,*" pp. 112-117.

95. O'Flaherty, pp. 7-9, 12, 13. An Aṅguttara Nikāya passage (3.43-44) describes outright why parents desire a son: he that has been helped by his parents will in turn help them by keeping up traditions, by fulfilling his heritage, and by offering *peta* offerings when they are dead.

96. Skt. *gandharva* or, alternately, *gantavya* 'one who is ready to go.' See O'Flaherty, p. 13.

97. Saddhātissa, p. 334.

98. Horner, *Middle Length* 1:321n-322n, quoting the commentarial tradition.

99. Collins, p. 212; see also pp. 208-213.

100. M 1.265.

101. Kalupahana, p. 116.

102. Hoffman, *Rationality and Mind,* pp. 67-68.

103. Kalupahana, p. 118; Hoffman, *Rationality and Mind*, pp. 63-64.
104. Heesterman, *Inner Conflict*, p. 27; see also. p. 35. See Parry on priestly eating of foods offered on behalf of the deceased. "Death and Digestion," p. 620-624.
105. Tambiah, "Ideology of Merit," p. 97; see also p. 103.
106. Thera no. 20.
107. AV 18.2.27. The Khuddakapāṭha (6) draws an exact equation of departed ones and monks, and the Petavatthu (in the first story on fields) likens the field to the *arahant* and indicates that *petas* enjoy the produce from the field.
108. Knipe, *"Sapiṇḍīkaraṇa,"* pp. 116-17.
109. AV 18.3.53, 54.
110. A 2.54, 57; 3.51, 52; 4.245-46.
111. Heesterman, *Inner Conflict*, p. 32.
112. ŚB 4.3.4.6; 1.9.3.1; Tull, pp. 76-77, 79.
113. O'Flaherty, p. 12.
114. AV 18.2.4-5, 10; 18.3.42-46; 18.4.1, 10, 13, 22, 40, 65, 88.
115. BĀU 5.11.1.
116. Another version suggests the renunciant as a womb, a place where the *piṇḍa*-seed ripens as *gandhabba* in preparation for the next rebirth.
117. Collins, p. 219.
118. Collins, p. 222; see pp. 218-224.
119. KV 7.4.
120. Heesterman, *Inner Conflict*, pp. 34-41.
121. Fenn, "Two Notions of Poverty." The following is a brief recapitulation of some of Fenn's argument.
122. Fenn, pp. 105-108.
123. Fenn, p. 109.
124. Fenn, pp. 112-113.
125. Fenn, pp. 115, 117-119.
126. Fenn, p. 119. My italics.
127. Fenn, p. 116.
128. A 3.49; see also S 1.31-32; A 3.31-33.
129. Katz, pp. 186-187.
130. This giver is "no self-seeker, not bound up in the result, not seeking a reward, nor thinking 'I will enjoy the fruit after death' "(A 4.61).
131. Boulding, *Love and Fear*, pp. 1, 27.
132. Boulding, *Love and Fear*, p. 8.
133. Wagle, p. 156.

CHAPTER 6

Making, Using, and Transferring Merit

MAKING MERIT

The means of exchange in the donation transaction is *puñña* or 'merit.' In this "extensive cash economy,"[1] *puñña* is much like a form of money: work (giving a gift) produces "cash" (merit) that can be used to "buy" a final product (heaven, good rebirth, happiness). When the idea of merit, as derived from giving, is first introduced into the Buddhist setting, householders immediately understand its transactional effects. According to the Mahāvagga, at the time just after the Buddha's return to health, his physician Jīvaka engineers the substitution of a householder-given robe *(gahapaticīvara)* for the traditional rag robe, presumably for reasons of health and convenience. When the Buddha then formally allows the acceptance of householder-given robes by renunciants, the people are overjoyed saying, 'now, we will give gifts, we will make merit' *(idāni kho mayaṃ dānāni dassāma puññāni karissāma).*[2] Merit-making then becomes an important feature of householder religious life as the "*puñña*-generating" householder[3] becomes the agent of lay Buddhist ethics.[4] In defining the householder's life as *puñña*-generating, exchange is central: the householder gives 'something expecting something in return' *(yaṃ deti taṃ paccāsiṃsati).*[5]

Merit-Making and Dāna

The *puñña*-generating householder seems firmly planted in what Melford Spiro calls "kammatic" Buddhism, where a good rebirth is achieved through the acquisition of merit, rather than in "nibbanic" Buddhism, where there is the "type of action which...has no fruit"[6] and, ultimately, the cessation of rebirth.

Collins argues, however, that this distinction is not quite so easy to make, for the two systems are intricately interwoven. The *"existence of...enthusiastically self-interested merit-making is socially, psychologically, and indeed logically necessary as the raw material which is to be shaped by* anattā."[7] Indeed, merit-production is found in the monastery among spiritually young Buddhist renunciants, who have as their goal *nibbāna* in this life[8] and who make merit until that time. In fact, the experience of *nibbāna* changes the dynamics of kamma and, as an *arahant,* a renunciant still acts but cannot by definition, be accompanied by "the mental state necessary for *puñña*-making" and so is without the resultant accumulation.[9] For, whoever has no lust, says the Suttanipāta, has no accumulation of merit.[10] He who is completely cool is like a lamp without fuel that, oil-less and wick-less, cannot produce a light again or, alternately, like a palm-tree stump that, cut off at the root, cannot produce a shoot again.[11] Those not yet cooled or not yet barren, however, live in a realm of cause and effect where 'there is consequence, the fruit of good and bad actions.'[12]

By doctrine, some activities are specifically merit-producing and while three are normative—giving *(dāna),* moral habit *(sīla),* and mental cultivation *(bhāvanā)*[13]—alternative groupings are usually variations on giving. *Dāna* is, practically speaking, the most merit-making of all meritorious actions,[14] and McDermott argues that it is because of "the importance of alms for the continued survival of the community of monks, [that] the suttas [pay so]...much attention to *dāna* as a means of accumulating merit."[15] Horner concludes that the association of giving with merit-making is an express act of compassion by early renunciants "in allowing...[donors the] scope to give and thereby to acquire merit."[16] Although *dāna* is sequentially the first and most practically utilized activity of merit-making for householders, it is not necessarily the most efficacious. The Aṅguttara Nikāya, for example, lists the eight rebirths due to merit from *dāna* and, while these cover the same wide range as the rebirths due to merit from varying degrees of *dāna, sīla,* and *bhāvanā*, it is only merit from the highest degrees of all three activities combined that brings the very best rewards to the householder.[17]

Moral Causality and its Ritual Roots

Buddhist merit-making has its antecedents in the Vedic sacrificial system and particularly in what Collins translates as "the world of sacrificial merit." The terms *sukṛtāṃ loka* and *sukṛtasya loka* belong to a concept of ritual efficacy that keeps the ritual patron coming back and investing increased time, effort, and material resources in the sacrifice: *sukṛtāṃ loka* is the world or condition of those who have "earned the rewards of well-performed rites" *(sukṛt* 'well-doer'), while *sukṛtasya loka* is "the sphere of ritual and religious merit" *(sukṛta* 'well-done'). The theory is that "if the sacrifice [is]...performed correctly, the action [leaves]...a residue of merit, which though unseen must nevertheless produce, automatically, future benefits for the sacrificer."[18] As Heesterman notes, "Vedic...ritualism...deals with the invisible *(adṛṣṭa)*. The effect, the 'fruit' it promises to the faithful sacrificer, comes about in an invisible way, and the promised effect itself is often said to be the invisible, namely, heaven."[19] While in the Saṃhitās ritual action, and thus ritual merit, gives the patron access to both the world of the Pitaras (fathers, ancestors) and the world of the gods, in the Brāhmaṇas it is primarily the world of the gods that the patron can anticipate as his reward. Rebirth in this world is not permanent for, just as the sacrifice, and its "cosmic analogue" the sun, undergo repeated deaths over time, so also will even the greatest *sukṛt* 'well-doer;' 'death again and again' *(punarmṛtyu)* awaits the sacrificer in a sequence of death and new life that in time comes "to be seen as an inevitable return to the life on earth."[20]

The operative power of the ritual is what Collins calls a "magical automatism" that, using the analogies and correspondences structurally in place in the Vedic world,[21] effects the desired result mechanically. Because of the precision of the analogies and correspondences built into the Vedic understanding of the cosmic structure, a single correct performance *(sukṛta* 'well-done') of the ritual has powerful results: "for the sacrificer... building a space with bricks, bringing into being a sacred reality, and creating merit for the next life [are]...all accomplished, with equal facility, by one and the same action."[22] For the patron emerging into the next life, this automatic channel of effectiveness has its origins in the old Ṛg Vedic term *iṣṭāpūrta,* "filled or stored up sacrificial rites," offerings made to the gods and priests of the ritual that await the patron in heaven or in his next life.[23] Just as the offering of food means that there will be a store of food upon which to draw in future time, so proper performance *(sukṛta)* of the ritual means that there will be a store of merit for use by the person in lives to come.

Collins takes pains to point out, however, that while indeed there is a new person created directly out of the ritual, that "person created by sacrifice [is]...a *composite:"* just as the physical elements of the body return to the natural world upon death—the eye to the sun, the breath to the wind, and so forth—so upon rebirth there is a reaggregation of elements into a composite whole. Thus, the "person who exist[s]...in the *loka* obtained by sacrifice [is]...a composite creation...made up *(saṃskṛta)* during the ceremony, and...put together by the priest's verses from breath, mind, speech, and hearing." The Brāhmaṇical theme that the patron is 'constructed' *(saṃskrīyate)* into a being in the next world[24] is continued in the Upaniṣads where, explaining the sacrifice, the Adhvaryu priest is said to construct 'the person which is of the offering and is made of action.' [25] The Aitareya Upaniṣad describes the human person as being so *sukṛta* 'well-made' that the natural elements (fire, air, light, space, plants, moon, and so on) can enter the body and enliven it again, and the Taittirīya Upaniṣad calls that which is *sukṛta* 'well-made' the very essence of existence.[26]

While the Vedic and Upaniṣadic traditions come to view the human being as both the doer of actions and the enjoyer of the consequences,[27] the quality of those consequences, that is, of the next life of the composited person created out of the sacrifice, is not developed until attention is focused on the nature of karma. Collins calls this development "the ethicisation of a formerly magical, and morally neutral, eschatological scheme" and sees the shift as a way to move beyond black and white in understanding causality and into the many shades of gray. The success or failure of a ritual has always been not a question of degree, for example, but exceedingly clear cut. If performed precisely, and so "automatically efficacious," the result is attained;

if performed with a mistake, no result or even negative result pertains. In order to allow differentiation in terms of shades of quality, the concept of karma is generalized to cover all behavior, a trend Collins argues is in great measure the work of Buddhism: "the thorough ethicisation of the *karma* idea owed much to the teachings of Buddhism."[28] As sacrificial action is interiorized, such that "one's entire life [is]...a sacrificial performance,...every action [having]...the results which sacrificial performance" has, the focus turns to what might be the crux of the quality of the next life. The Bṛhadāraṇyaka Upaniṣad, where the traditional concept of karma first appears, then locates the root of these continued lives in a person's desire: attached to an object the self arrives at that in the next life, while without desire the self achieves freedom from the entire round of rebirths.[29] This focus on desire then appears in the Buddhist context as consciousness, the form kammic aggregates take as new life is conditioned by the old.

Early Buddhist Kamma

In Pali Buddhism, the kammic system is also rooted in an assumption of ongoing rebirths, a process known as *punabbhava* 'renewed existence' or "a series of lives taking place anywhere in the system...as a series of *attabhāva*"[30] or continued individual existences. And it is "the elimination of the effects of karma (kammakkhaya)" from these renewed existences that is the soteriological teaching of Buddhism.[31] Amid contemporary views,[32] early Buddhism charts a course that focuses on a theory of "moral causation"[33] in which action (kamma) of certain quality gives rise to fruit *(phala)* of certain quality.[34] While advanced renunciants are able to know the specific fruits of their kamma, i.e., what in the present is due to specific activities of the past,[35] most Buddhists simply understand their lives as playing out according to kamma. The understanding of this "playing out," however, is as "a theory of conditionality rather than [as] a doctrine of strict determinism;"[36] and, while a person can say of himself 'I go on according to kamma,' the focus is on the harvesting of fruit sown freely by the doer rather than on the working out of a fated pattern of experience.[37] Moral responsibility is the keynote of the doctrine, placing full accountability for choices made and for deeds done squarely on the shoulders of the individual doer.[38] Nevertheless, the precise working out of kamma is beyond both the manipulation and the understanding of the ordinary person for, although one freely chooses to sow whatever deeds are done, one cannot hurry up or slow down or in any way influence their accumulation or their maturation or their final ripening.[39] Kamma, thus, ripens within a system that has boundaries and limits and that works internally by its own laws[40] and, within this system action and result are mutually dependent for the "measuring-yard for the judgement of an action" is the result it brings about as ripened fruit.[41]

Kamma is classified as *kusala* 'wholesome' or 'skillful,' *akusala* 'unwholesome' or 'unskillful' and *avyākata* 'neither.'[42] *Kusala*-kamma, or kamma done with a *kusala* attitude, is motivated by *arāga, adosa,* and/or *amoha* and leads to *sukha* 'happiness'; *akusala*-kamma, or kamma done with an *akusala* attitude, is motivated by *rāga, dosa,* and/or *moha* and leads to *dukkha* 'suffering';[43] and *avyākata*-kamma leads to neither *sukha* or *dukkha,* with all of these categories being subject to further division.[44] Both *kusala*-kamma and *akusala*-kamma are divisions of *sahetuka*-kamma, action having a cause (that is, done with desire), whose "ultimate result...is pain," while *ahetuka*-kamma has no result at all, giving "neither pain nor pleasure."[45]

The working out of kamma is a system of causation set among other causal laws operating within nature. There are, for example, physical (inorganic) laws, biological (organic) laws or laws of heredity, psychological or mental laws, and laws of spiritual phenomena. Laws pertaining to social and moral acts and their consequences (kamma-*niyāma)* are like all the other sets of laws that describe patterns of events in nature in that they are not deterministic but "only probable and statistical:" that is, good deeds bring about good consequences while bad deeds bring about bad ones. Kammic laws, then, state "tendencies rather than inevitable consequences" and kamma is "only one of many factors conditioning the nature of experience."[46] Because of this Obeyesekere calls the kammic system "psychologically indeterminate:"

although "the individual knows that the good he does in his present lifetime will be rewarded in a future lifetime, he has no idea *how* his future will be related to his present existence."[47]

The effectiveness of kamma, as it is operative *(kiriya),* [48] is in an action's intention. In the Aṅguttara Nikāya the Buddha says: "Monks, I say that intention is action; in intending, one does deeds with the body, speech, or mind."[49] Conscious intention, though "a necessary condition of...[any] morally good, evil or mixed act" does not, however, "constitute the whole of it except when it happen[s]...to be a purely mental act." In kamma of body and speech, then, intention is necessary, but not sufficient, to the full constitution of the act and takes precedence in characterizing the resultant fruit.[50] The categories within intention that produce bad behavior are *rāga, dosa,* and *moha*, and *vītarāga, vītadosa,* and *vītamoha* that produce good behavior.

The round of rebirth is reflected in the doctrine of dependent origination where the cycle of life turns "continuously without any self as a causal agent or persisting subject of *karma*."[51] While ignorance and craving are understood as conditions of rebirth,[52] the driving force behind rebirth linkage is *(abhi-) saṃkhāra* that Collins defines as "a karmically forceful, 'constructive' act, which determine[s] a specific length of *saṃsāric* continuity."[53] When combined with consciousness, *abbisaṃkhāra-viññāna* or 'construction-consciousness' is the "condition...for the future occurrence of an appropriate form of consciousness, which [is]...itself the 'dependently originated' condition for psychophysical individuality ('name-and-form')."[54] Through the ongoing conditionality of this construction-consciousness, there is the "creation of continued life in time," and, as there is a "*gradual* lessening of the karmic construction of future life," the practitioner moves through the stages of stream-winner, once-returner, non-returner, and *arahant.* With the experience of *nibbāna* "constructive-consciousness," that is, the ability to create new kamma, comes to an end (though past kamma continues to ripen for the remainder of the renunciant's last life), and with the experience of *parinibbāna,* "constructed-consciousness" comes to an end. Thus, *abhisaṃkhāra-viññāna* is the consciousness that links rebirths, constructing time to be an accumulation of instances both as a medium for experiencing present reality and as constructed future experience.[55]

The ability to verify the doctrines of kamma and rebirth depends upon the extent of a person's mental cultivation. For most, the doctrines are a matter of *saddhā* 'confidence,' doctrines whose truthfulness and reliability depend upon one's trust in the Buddha and his teaching.[56] For others, however, it is a matter of one of the special knowledges that allow one, through retrocognition, for example, "to reveal *kamma* (action), *phala* (consequence), *punabbhava* (rebirth) in...[one's] own case" and through clairvoyance to reveal these same in others.[57] Householders, for the most part, are too inexperienced spiritually to verify the laws of moral cause and affect through their own insight; rather they have to have confidence that the teaching on this is reliable. Thus, when the Buddha speaks of *puñña,* his audience is primarily householders who are intensely interested in the fruit of action, especially in the workings of merit through *dāna,* and whose activities depend on the merit system's perpetuity for the realization of *saṃsāric* rewards. When the Buddha speaks of kamma, however, his audience is primarily advanced lay persons or renunciants whose interests are not in the accumulation of rewards within rebirth but the development of mental cultivation to bring the experience of rebirth to an end—by breaking the causal linkages of kamma itself. At Gombrich's suggestion, the convergence of these two types of religious concern may happen in this way: gradual "self"-perfection continues until the force of merit is enough to work for the "un-selfing" of *nibbāna,* and this is done by eventually turning one's attention to the underlying cause and production of merit within the kamma system. Thus, early discussions of *puñña* place householder goals decidedly within the realm of rebirth.

Persons wanting merit actively seek to do things productive of merit. [58] Many examples show that merit is acquired and accumulated,[59] produced[60] and obtained,[61] and held in store. These suggest that the best translation of *puñña* (with the various forms of *karoti* with which it often appears)[62] is not 'to do merit,' as Amore argues,[63] but rather the more traditional 'to make merit.' Using the "cash" analogy again, activities make merit, and merit, as a medium of exchange, is subsequently used to get other fruit.[64] Because it is a fruit of action (though intermediary), merit pertains only to the individual—'whatever merit I make, that fruit falls to me'[65]—and its production remains with the individual until the ignorant sensations of the experience of individuality subside.[66]

Puñña is the good result of good action. By doing such things as giving, taming oneself, restraining oneself, and speaking the truth, merit comes; 'from doing, from making someone else do, from that source where there is merit, there is the fruition of merit.'[67] Thus, both merit and what merit "buys" are the fruit of kammic action. *Puñña* is offset by bad results from bad actions, called variously *apuñña* 'demerit'[68] or *pāpa* 'evil,'[69] the result, for example, of deeds of violence, thievery, covetousness, and false speech. The pairs *puñña/apuñña* or *puñña/pāpa* correspond to the *kusala/akusala* 'wholesome/unwholesome' pair, such that a *kusala* 'wholesome' deed produces 'wholesomeness' or 'merit,'[70] while an *akusala* 'unwholesome' deed produces 'unwholesomeness' or 'demerit/evil.'[71] Early on, the correspondence of *puñña* and *kusala* is made fairly often, applying only to someone in an unfinished spiritual state. For, as Amore points out, the *arahant* is beyond *puñña*-making and therefore the Theravādins cannot apply *'kusala'* to his behavior because to call something *'kusala'* "would imply that it produced a result."[72]

Merit-Making in the Context of Dāna: The Intention or the Result?

Householders practising *dāna,* then, know that a person performing an action in body, speech, or mind performs something that carries quality and that, based on that quality, the action produces fruit or result. [73] This transaction has the mediating element of merit or demerit whose source is in the 'doing' or in the 'causing someone to do.' [74] Unwholesome action that produces demerit has its roots in the three negative categories of intention, while wholesome action that produces merit has its roots in the intention that strives to avoid these three elements.[75] It is intention, the necessary but not always sufficient element of efficacious action, that drives the result. Through intention,[76] action is *puññakiriya* 'merit generating' or *apuññakiriya* 'demerit generating.' And the merit thus generated by action then translates into—in the second part of the transaction—a result such as heaven or a good rebirth.[77] As "the karmic consequences"[78] give rise to the generation of reward, *puñña* is a transactional medium of exchange, accumulated not for its own sake but for the sake of translating into, through its expenditure, a desired reward for the householder consumer.

The standard early Buddhist position on the efficacy of action, then, is that it has its central location in intention or volition *(cetanā).*[79] This "ethic of intention"[80] emphasizes the meritoriousness of the mental state of the agent over other factors, like the contextual effect of the deed, in any given action. Since demeritorious *(akusala)* actions have their roots in greed, hatred, and confusion,[81] transforming one's consciousness by getting rid of these mental qualities positions oneself for the greater accumulation of merit. And since the first of these demeritorious roots is greed or craving it makes sense to modify one's behavior in the direction of *dāna,* whereby one's relation to the materials of the world is rethought; through *dāna,* a middle ground is sought between extreme avarice and extreme renunciation. Accumulation of wealth as an end goal is supplanted by accumulation of merit (acquired by giving away wealth through *dāna),* to be supplanted in time by greater wisdom. Wealth "well-won" and "well-used" is the first step in reorienting one's desires, and teachings on *dāna* then place the generous donations of householders squarely at the beginning of a process that will transform intention, increase the accumulation of beneficial merit, and set the course for the eventual final ripening of all kammic fruits.

How do passages suggesting there is more to the efficacy of *dāna* than just the mental state of the donor fit in? In one example, the defeated Jain Saccaka suggests that the merit from the meal the Licchavis prepare for the Buddha and the Saṅgha are for the happiness of the donors *(dāyakānaṃ sukhāya),* but the Buddha notes that the donors also receive whatever attaches to the recipient of the gift *(dakkhiṇeyyaṃ āgamma):* if the recipient has craving, hatred, or confusion (like Saccaka) then the donors will receive *that,* but if the recipient is without craving, hatred, or confusion (like the Buddha) then the donors will receive *that.*[82] Thus, the standard expectation for donors wanting merit is that:

> *bhikkhu āhuneyyo hoti pāhuneyyo*
> *dakkhiṇeyyo añjalikaraṇīyo*
> *anuttaraṃ puññakkhettaṃ lokassa*
>
> The monk be worthy of offerings, worthy of hospitality, worthy of gifts, worthy of salutation, the unsurpassed field of merit for the world.[83]

Here again, giving is effective because of both the confidence of the giver and the worthiness of the receiver. The positive approach of the Buddha's merit teaching develops the optimum benefits for each situation even further by suggesting that good merit accrues to the donor from whatever source is immediately available.

1. if the giver is moral in habit *(sīlavant),* but the receiver poor in moral habit *(dussīla)*—the gift is purified by the giver;[84]
2. if the giver is poor in moral habit, but the receiver moral in habit—the gift is purified by the receiver;
3. if both giver and receiver are poor in moral habit—the gift is purified by neither;
4. if both giver and receiver are moral in habit—the gift is purified by both and is a gift abundant in gain *(āmīsadāna vipula).*[85]

The Kathāvatthu (7.4) continues the case for efficacy by arguing that it stems as well-from the gift itself, stating that *dāna* is not only the mental state *(cetasika)* at the time of giving but the act of giving and *the actual gift itself.* The importance of the gift, the Theravādins argue, is that the Buddha declares that giving produces desirable results *(iṭṭhaphala),* and this necessarily implicates the actual gifts of robes, food, lodgings and medicines,[86] as well as the origins of the gift (i.e., that it comes from wealth well-won and that it constitutes a reasonable share of the donor's own stock of wealth). The Theravādins then argue against, however, the notion that merit to the donor increases with subsequent utility *(paribhogamaya)*[87]—i.e., that a really good gift keeps on giving—suggesting instead that what accrues to the donor is based on the state of circumstances at the time of the gift.

Of the activities that produce merit, *dāna* is certainly the only meritorious activity in which such great attention is given not only to the intention of the actor but to the object and the nature of the action as well. Donors are called especially *puññassa kovidā* 'skilled in merit,'[88] and *dāna* appears to occupy, with these additions, a peculiar place for the householder in the *puñña* system. Moreover, *dāna* is part of a progressive teaching. Ordinarily, it is the first step in a transformative sequence representing the onset of a person's reorientation towards the material world. *Dāna* begins the process of cutting off attachment to the riches of a newly wealthy environment and of increasing independence in spiritual progress. Perhaps it is proper, then, that *dāna,* particularly, in its transitional and pivotal location on the Buddhist way, pay heed 1) to continued need of the renunciant for material support through to his *parinibbāna,* as well as 2) to the relational nature of experience for the less spiritually advanced. These two elements will diminish in importance as the *kevala* 'solitary' tendency of the renunciant develops, and *dāna,* while it inaugurates this development still, however, looks "both ways" from the home life to the homeless and then back again.

Because *dāna,* of all householder activities, is so important to the material support and survival of the Saṅgha, special attention is given to the details of the efficacy of *dāna* and to the specific governing of *dānapuñña.* It is to the great benefit of the Saṅgha that Buddhist teachings emphasize the efficacy of giving to the worthiest of recipients so as to steer donors towards giving singularly to Buddhist renunciants. It is of equally great benefit to the Saṅgha to emphasize that even gifts from a meager store are merit-producing so as to promote the ideal that everyone can and (soteriologically) should do his or her part: that, no matter how small the gift, merit will accrue to the donor for his or her own future benefit. While it can be argued that the *dakkhiṇeyya* doctrine is a deliberate tampering of the *puñña* system to the particular advantage of the Buddhist Saṅgha, i.e., that this is in fact a great Buddhist con game, another view is to underscore the practicality of the community's wisdom in this instance. To allow intention alone to govern the efficacy of *dāna* would be to diffuse its benefits among all renunciant groups and thus to undermine the viability of the new Buddhist institution. As in many other things, however, the Buddha's flexibility and "situational" approach is to understand *dāna* as a peculiar activity in Buddhism that has to be treated in uncommon ways in order to allow it to provide for the other more considerable tasks of the religion.[89] There is, hence, an indulgence and accommodation in the tradition's attention to *dāna* that, perhaps is not entirely unselfconscious.

The development of a teaching on the making of merit is no accident in early Buddhism, nor is it accidental that it becomes so central to non-renunciant life. Although the *puñña* system has its origins in the Vedic sacrifice, whereby gifts are given to worthy (i.e., successful) officers of the ritual, and sacrificial action now is understood to have beneficial results later, merit-making finds its ideal correspondent in the life of the business community of the householder. Here, earned value takes precedence over assigned value, and merit rather than birth is the measure of worth; here, fair play in negotiated dealings and just adherence to a social contract prevail; here, investing now for future profit plays an important role in monitoring behavior; and here, individual effort is thought to give rise singularly to individual reward. Thapar argues that there are a number of reasons why Buddhism appeals to middle and lower level urban business groups—Buddhism's anti-caste implications, the lack of expenses in worship, and the use of local languages rather than Sanskrit,[90] being some. Not only, however, are there real material benefits to the Saṅgha from the economic resources of the newly enfranchised group, but the religious benefits to the givers of the resources are encoded in strikingly familiar economic terms. It is the new entrepreneurial economy that provides metaphors for householder soteriology[91] and, in understanding *puñña* as a means of exchange earned through giving and laid out for future reward, the householder, newly a significant player in the burgeoning consumerism of the Gangetic plain, becomes a consumer of Dhamma as well as a consumer of the merit promised by Dhamma.

USING MERIT

The rewards for giving are specifically enumerated in the canon. Having made merit, the householder can now use that merit to "buy" a pleasurable state of being for himself either here or after death in his next life. While there is some talk that the donor who gives gifts will have a long life[92] this time around, the greater attention is given to what will happen after the breaking up of the body in death when the person goes on to some new form of existence. Because wealth can't lengthen life and because wealth doesn't follow the person beyond death, the riches one gains as a householder can only be carried off by heirs at the time of the body's cremation, the person himself going on according to the laws of kamma as merit and demerit ripen.[93] Indirectly, however, wealth can bear great fruit for the owner: those who give with unhindered thoughts while living are assured of life after death in another world *(paraloka)* because of their good deeds.[94] Thus the 'results of merit' *(puññābhisanda),* and the 'results of wholesomeness' *(kusalābhisanda)*[95] are any number of pleasurable and beneficial forms of existence, for 'the giver of good things,' teaches the Buddha, 'gains the good'.[96]

> *Who gives the good shall gain the good; who gives the best shall best receive again; the choice, the choice receive; the chief, the chief place win. Who gives the best, the choice, the chief—that man has honour and long life where'er he rise.*[97]

Heaven

One of the most frequently named rewards of meritorious deeds is rebirth in 'another world' *(paraloka).*[98] This place is variously called *sagga* 'heaven,'[99] *sagga ṭhāna* 'heavenly place,'[100] *devaloka* 'world of the gods,'[101] *dibba ṭhāna* 'heavenly place,'[102] *siva loka* 'world of bliss,'[103] and *avyāpajjha sukha loka* 'a calm, happy world.'[104] The most common phrase used to refer to this most desired of all next existences is:

> *kāyassa bhedā parammaraṇā sugatiṃ*
> *saggaṃ lokaṃ upapajjati*[105]

> Upon the breakup of the body, after
> death, he is reborn in a good rebirth,
> in the heavenly world.

It is in this heavenly place where donors and generous patrons go as a result of giving,[106] just as it continues to be the exact same place where those who perform Vedic sacrifice or who are patrons of the sacrifice go at their deaths.[107] Those who make merit by giving find delight in this heaven,[108] for they are among the gods[109] and are protected by the gods,[110] and their actions here on earth are designated as 'leading to heaven' *(saggasaṃvattanika)*[111] and being 'heaven-ward.'[112] Although Gonda suggests that there is an "inherent vagueness"[113] in the term *loka,* and Collins that it does "not necessarily refer to a particular spatial location at all, but often simply to a state of happiness and stability,"[114] there is real concreteness to some of the Buddhist descriptions of this other world. One of the names for this next world is *tidiva* 'the three heavens'[115] or the Tāvatiṃsa heaven, the heaven of the thirty-three gods,[116] and there is a grove in this world called Nandana where the reborn are thought to be attended by nymphs and surrounded by celestial sense pleasures *(dibba kāma).*[117]

Good Rebirth

While there are said to be fourteen hundred thousand chief types of birth *(yoni)*[118] there are, in Buddhist tradition, five general courses *(gati)* or realms of existence for the rebirth of sentient beings: 1) the realm of the gods *(deva)* or heaven; 2) the realm of men *(manussa);* 3) the realm of ghosts/spirits *(peta);* 4) the realm of animals *(tiracchāna);* and 5) Niraya hell.[119] Only the first two of these rebirths, the human and the divine, are considered desirable rebirths *(sugati)* and the most desirable of all rebirths for the person who has accumulated much merit is that of heaven.[120] The good person (the *sappurisa,* ordinarily the donor to the Saṅgha) normally takes one of two rebirths, that of divine greatness or of human greatness;[121] and a beneficial rebirth among humans is often called a rebirth among people of good luck.[122]

Once again it is *dāna* whose rewards receive special treatment for, of all the meritorious activities that can be singled out as leading to good rebirths, it is primarily donation that is said to lead to rebirths that can be specifically identified. Both the Dīgha Nikāya and the Aṅguttara Nikāya give a list of eight rebirths due to *dāna.*

1. among wealthy nobles, brahmins, and householders who live among sense pleasures,
2. among the four royal gods who are long-lived, beautiful, and very happy,
3. among the Tāvatiṃsa gods,
4. among the Yāma gods,
5. among the Tusita gods,
6. among the Nimmānarati gods,
7. among the Paranimmitavasavattin gods,and
8. among the gods of Brahmā's retinue, who are long lived, beautiful, and very happy.[123]

The first of the "giving rebirths" emphasizes that wealth well-used begets more wealth, that is, if one is "properly" wealthy in one life one can become even more wealthy in the next. In addition, it supports the wealth-generating ethic of the householder that portrays this life favorably in the hopes, it can be argued, of encouraging householders to stay put as householders and to continue donating to the Saṅgha. The other seven rebirths are among the gods, all of whom have once been human beings and will some day be reborn as human beings again, thus continuing like all sentient beings in the round of rebirth and, more importantly, continuing to be in need of salvation. The gods of numbers two through eight belong to a category of gods called *upapatti,* that is, those gods who are born divine in a heavenly state, not *sammuti* gods who are conventional or public gods, such as kings and princes, or *visuddhi* gods who are gods by reason of their purity or spiritual attainment, such as an *arahant* or the Buddha.[124] Rebirth in any of these eight courses *(gatis)* is a matter of two conditions: first, of being moral in habit, by which, in this particular case, is meant living a life of proper *dāna* and, second, of fixing one's mind at the time of death upon the thought of the desired rebirth so that that thought becomes actualized: "[if] he fixes his mind on that thought, [if] he concentrates his attention on that thought, he will make that thought come to be."[125] It is in the Abhidhamma where details of the process of this deathbed activity and of the 'rebirth-linking consciousness' *(paṭisandhiviññāṇa)* are more fully worked out,[126] but it is clear already from these two Nikāya passages that care is taken early on, at least in terms of *dāna,* to pay attention to the connective aspects of merit exchange so that it is persuasive as a "religious technology" to its consumers. And, here, thinking a state of being into existence at the time of death is a plausible view of causation.

The Aṅguttara Nikāya goes on to discuss rebirths available to those practising all three of the specifically meritorious actions of *dāna, sīla,* and *bhāvanā.* He or she, for example, who only on a small scale creates a base of meritorious action using *dāna* and *sīla,* but not *bhāvanā,* will be reborn among people of bad luck, while he or she who creates such a base on a medium scale will be reborn among people of good luck. Those who create such a base on the highest scale, however, will be reborn among the gods of numbers two through eight.[127] No mention, however, is made in this passage of rebirths consequent to the meritorious action of *bhāvanā.* Although the early canon is clear that *bhāvanā* is merit-producing,[128] it may well be that it is not an immediately practical topic in teachings given to ordinary wealth-generating householders, and is, therefore, more seriously at issue in teachings given to those more advanced who are seeking the end of rebirth.

Teachings on the rewards of meritorious action often include, by contrast, negative passages that, in their tortuous details, are meant to scare householders away from doing unmeritorious deeds (or perhaps, better, towards doing meritorious ones, such as giving). While there is some discussion of the horrors of being born in the realm of the animals or even in that of the ghosts, the greatest horrors are reserved for existence in the Niraya hell. Reference to Niraya most often occurs with the phrase:

> *kāyassa bhedā paraṃ maraṇā*
> *apāyaṃ duggatiṃ vinipātaṃ*
> *nirayaṃ upapajjissati*
>
> Upon the breakup of the body, after death, he will be reborn in a sorrowful state, in a bad rebirth, in the downfall, the Niraya hell.[129]

Rebirth in the Niraya hell comes to those who are fools; who do evil deeds; who behave wrongly in body, speech, and thought; who do not pay their respects to their mothers or their fathers or the elders of their family or brahmins and recluses; who are lazy and negligent in their attention to the many sufferings of others, even when warned otherwise; who injure other creatures, take what isn't theirs, improperly enjoy the pleasures of the senses, speak falsely, covet goods, and who are filled with malevolent thoughts and wrong views.[130]

Descriptions of the Niraya hell found in the Majjhima Nikāya are fearsome. The anguish *(dukkha)* and distress *(domanassa)* experienced by a person pierced three hundred times with a spear is infinitesimally small compared to the anguish he will feel in the Niraya hell. In the Niraya, he will be subjected to the five-fold bondage: red-hot iron stakes will be driven through each hand and foot and through the middle of the chest. Then the guardians of the Niraya will plane him with adzes, turn him upside down and plane him with razors, tie him to a chariot and drive him over flaming hot grounds, push him up and down the sides of mountains covered with glowing and burning embers, and plunge him headfirst into a flaming cauldron where he will boil around and around. All these will produce severe, sharp pains over and over again, but with the end of this torture the evil doer will still not bring his evil deed to full ripening; this takes place in the Mahāniraya or Great Niraya hell (Avīci),[131] and in other subsequent hells, each more ghastly and tortuous than the preceding.[132]

These 'hells' are like purgatories, intermediate states of temporary suffering after death where the evil-doer goes for expiation and purification. Certainly, this term fits the canonical teaching for, because of his demerit, the evil-doer is said to ripen or 'cook' in Niraya for a long time,[133] in the company of similar others, until rebirth as a human again. Even so, that human birth is in one of five very humble families: a low caste family, a family of hunters, of bamboo plaiters, of chariot makers, or of scavengers of human refuse.[134] Born here, a person is ugly and deformed; without favor, he has trouble finding food, drink, clothes, lodgings, and other amenities.[135] The struggle to get back to a more favorable life is long and torturous but, just as a blind turtle who comes to the water's surface every hundred years might once in a long time be able to poke his neck through a yoke with one hole floating in the great ocean, so also might a fool who has gone to the Niraya hell be able to come back as a human again.[136] Though forever optimistic about the spiritual possibilities for sentient beings, Buddhist teaching here places low odds on the possibility of being reborn immediately in the course of humans or gods. While the chance is great of being reborn in a low rebirth, the chance is slim of being reborn in an auspicious course—as slim as the dust on the Buddha's finger tip is to the dust of the whole earth.[137] Thus, though the hells are not permanent, the stages out of them are long and ardurous.

The traditional teaching on the relationship between rebirths in the lower courses and one's spiritual advancement is that once a person attains the fruit of the *sotāpanna* stage, that is, becomes a stream-winner, he or she can't fall back into rebirth in the Niraya hell, in the realm of the animals, or in the realm of the ghosts. Once the five fears associated with the transgression of the first five moral habits[138] have been mastered, once the four possessions of the stream-winner are his or hers,[139] and once the adept has appropriated the noble law by insight, then he or she can be assured that the lower courses have perished forever as future possibilities: now the adept is sure of enlightenment as his or her destined goal.[140]

Happiness

A final reward for giving is happiness or worldly satisfaction here on earth. The Aṅguttara Nikāya notes that a gift given in confidence often results in more wealth, riches, and property,[141] and the appearance of such wealth is then accompanied by great honor.[142] The *sappurisa* who gives becomes dear and beloved to those who live in the countryside. He is loved by other good and wise people, has a good reputation spread abroad about him, is able to follow the householder path *(gihidhamma)* without fault, and dies without anxiety.[143] Moreover, the confident giver is rewarded with good looks, is handsome and has a great beauty of complexion,[144] and lives out a long life here or in whatever good rebirth comes to pass.[145]

Most significantly, however, giving leads to *sukha* 'happiness,'[146] or *uttama sukha* 'the ultimate happiness,'[147] here and now or in some future state.[148] The donor's gift is thought to have happiness as its fruit *(dinna sukhaphala),*[149] to be given 'seeking happiness' *(sukhesin),*[150] and to have 'happiness as its result' *(sukhavipāka).*[151] Developing the consumer theme of merit as a medium of exchange, a householder who gives the food, robes, medicines, or lodgings used by monks receives great merit as the 'food of happiness' *(sukhassāhāra).*[152] Thus, merit earned by the householder's work of giving is expended by him for the purpose of happiness, just as crops are grown in a fertile field and then eaten by the farmer as food for satisfaction. The exact nature of this *sukha* or 'happiness' is not altogether clear, but the Aṅguttara Nikāya makes some suggestions: happiness is what is 'pleasing', 'enjoyable', 'pleasant', and 'beneficial' within a person's proper experience of the sensual gratifications of the material world.[153] Moreover, the perfect experience of happiness *(sammā sukha)* is not only in making oneself happy and cheerful, but in making others so as well.[154]

Merit and Salvation

If merit-making through giving leads to heaven, a good rebirth, and happiness, can it also lead to more spiritually advanced goals such as *vipassanā* or *nibbāna?* A number of scholars have amended Spiro's "radical distinction" between "kammatic" and "nibbanic" Buddhism,[155] and Collins notes that, "as Spiro himself points out," these two should not "be seen as denoting two entirely separate systems of belief and practice. Rather, we might see these interpretative categories as representing two ends of a continuum."[156] McDermott argues for the "continuum" idea early on (with *sagga* at one end and *nibbāna* at the other) and uses, as textual support, material from the Khuddakapāṭha.[157] This passage argues that in addition to bringing the usual worldly benefits and protection, merit can also bring human excellence *(mānusikāsampatti),* the world of the gods *(devaloka),* and the excellence of extinction *(nibbānasampatti).* Under this latter, the text says that by this *(etena,* that is, by the treasure of merit) one gets "discriminations, liberations, perfections of disciples, enlightenment as a solitary, and the ground of Buddhahood."[158] Of these verses, McDermott remarks:

> *It is significant that the lone clear*
> *canonical expression of the view*
> *that* Nibbāna *is simply the reward*
> *for the most meritorious of* kamma
> *is to be found in the Khuddakapāṭha,*
> *for this text bears every mark of being*
> *a handbook composed for the use*
> *of the Buddhist laity.*[159]

Although McDermott continues by suggesting that this "idea found little support in the stricter monastic circles of canonical times,"[160] there are some earlier passages that encourage the view that householder giving brings one into a continuum that will culminate among those who have reached the highest point *(sammaggata).* Freed from greed, for example, the headman of the Saṃyutta Nikāya is taught, there comes the mental calm of righteousness *(dhammasamādhi)* and having reached this mental calm one abandons doubt.[161] Again, desiring merit *(puññakāma),* firmly set in wholesomeness *(kusale patiṭṭhita),* and cultivating the pathway to reach the deathless *(amata),* the person arrives at the mental calm of righteousness *(dhammasamādhi).*[162] Although teachings directed especially to householder listeners have to be careful not to promise overly much in terms of the final fruits of the Buddhist life, for fear that large scale householder renunciation will result in a loss of wealthy donors to the Saṅgha, there is some hint that the path of meritorious giving is the first step in the long discipline to final Buddhist freedom. The Mahāvagga is clear that the householder audience responds immediately to the promise of heaven, a good rebirth, and happiness, but it takes until the Khuddakapāṭha for the householder to see that the *dānapuñña* 'merits of giving' he or she has acquired early on might have other more considerable fruits as well.

It is suggested that early Buddhist teachings on merit have a social as well as a soteriological function, that the good behavior enjoined by the texts has larger sociological ramifications than as just simple codes for the householder. Amore argues, for example, that the material support of the monks and Saṅgha by donors builds character in them, spreads positive moral behavior among members of society at large, and promotes the development of a broad "social consensus concerning proper human conduct."[163] The specific stories of later texts like the Petavatthu and Vimānavatthu, in fact, serve these ends, he argues, for, in detailing the resultant destinies of persons with previous actions, the texts can better encourage good behavior in the present by pointing to what will certainly result in the future.[164]

In this light, the merit teachings of the canon draw from and in turn support the two occupations that serve as primary economic stockpiles for the Saṅgha: farming and trading. These two occupations, whose material resources are drawn off of to support the Saṅgha, are themselves encouraged to thrive through their use as metaphors for the merit-making and merit-using process. The concept of the worthy renunciant as 'field' has already been mentioned, but an important passage in the Suttanipāta takes the ploughing-sowing-reaping image of the farmer and applies it to the quest of the Buddha himself. Just as the farmer ploughs and sows (gives requisites) in the fertile field (to worthy renunciants) and then, when he has ploughed and sown, eats (goes to heaven, etc.), so also does the Buddha: the seed is confidence *(saddhā)*, the rain austerity *(tapas)*, the yoke and plough wisdom *(paññā)*, the pole modesty *(hiri)*, the yoke-tie mind *(manas)*, the goad mindfulness *(sati)*, the weeder truth *(sacca)*, and the beast of burden energy *(viriya)*. Having ploughed and sown, the Buddha's fruit is to reach the undying *(amatapphala)* and to be free from all suffering *(dukkha)*.[165] Thus, the transaction of sowing and reaping is a process paralled in three contexts: secular life, non-renunciant Buddhist life, and renunciant Buddhist life.[166]

Like farming, trading also provides a useful metaphor for the transactions of spiritual life. In the material examined so far, merit-making and merit-using are like a cash economy: merit (cash) is acquired through giving (work) that accumulates for the individual donor (worker); from this store (bank) merit can then be used (spent) to enjoy (buy) a future reward. While the early Nikāyas and Vinaya do not overtly use this image, the later Milindapañha does. In a section on the "city of righteousness," one street is described as housing the Buddha's bazaars. These bazaars sell flowers, fruits, medicines and all kinds of merchandise representing the many rewards available to the good man. To buy something one has to pay a price, that of kamma, making "*kamma*...the medium of exchange in the Buddha's bazaar."[167] The reference here, however, is only to good kamma (effective or positively producing work) rather than to bad kamma, as that which can be used from one's "purse" in a purchasing transaction. While McDermott's interest in this passage is the reference to buying final freedom *(nibbāna)* with kamma, there is an overt statement of what is only intimated in the earlier texts: that there is a convergence of the new urbanism, with its rapid growth of business and cash economies, and early Buddhist teachings on merit, that characterize *puñña* as a medium of exchange in the religious lives of the householders. As Gombrich notes, the "view of merit as spiritual cash," of "merit as a kind of spiritual money" to be invested in "a bank account, to be drawn on at will," is commonplace in later Pali literature,[168] while it is only a suggestion in earlier texts. But a strong suggestion it is, for to tap into the new wealth, early *dāna* teachings are providing from the start soteriological structures that are familiar to householders through their daily occupations. And, likewise, in order to find a suitable place in the prevailing religious panorama, householders are supporting from the start a soteriology that speaks more directly to them in their own language.[169]

TRANSFERRING MERIT

Studies on later periods of Buddhist merit-making describe in detail an aspect of the system that provides for the transfer of merit from one person who originally produces it to someone else as its beneficiary. This system, as noted by Gombrich, allows "one's good actions [to] build up a kind of spiritual bank account from which one [can]...make payments to others,"[170] and constitutes a mechanism featured centrally in modern forms of Buddhist practice. Obeyeskere finds in the Sri Lankan case that the living believe they can transfer their merit (Sinhalese: *pin)* "to the dead and thus enhance the salvation prospects of the latter."[171] And Tambiah cites the Thai belief that transfer "of merit by the living to the dead does not stop with mortuary rites but goes on long after death."[172] Normally, in the history of Buddhism, the idea of encouraging good merit in others is "associated with the belief in bodhisattvas, who do good not only for their own spiritual advance toward nirvana but also to alleviate the sufferings of others."[173] Mahāyāna inscriptions from donors, for example, routinely follow "the common Mahāyāna formula:" "This is the religious gift...(of, title & name)...what merit is here, may that, going to my parents first, be for the obtaining of supreme knowledge by all beings."[174] Although this formula appears in several different inscriptional variations throughout the South Asian sub-continent, the standard elements are the giving of a religious gift *(deyadharma),* the accruing of merit *(puṇya),* and the imperative *(bhavatu,* 'may this become') transfer of that merit to all beings.[175]

As Gombrich notes, however, the transfer of merit is an idea already "fully developed...in the Theravāda Buddhism of Ceylon"[176] as founded upon its roots. It is the general consensus "that the idea of the transfer of merit [is]...a late addition brought into the Pāli canon as a result of prior popular acceptance."[177] In the early texts, however, the concept of merit transference is "foreign" and "repugnant," and is "demonstrably inconsistent" with "canonical formulations."[178] These canonical formulations, the argument states, stress individual responsibility for individual actions, urging renunciants and non-renunciants alike to think of themselves as islands and as refuges unto themselves: be 'an island unto yourself, a refuge unto yourself,' taking 'no one else as a refuge' for you.[179] Kammic fruit accrues to the doer of the deed who sows it and to no one else: 'indeed, this evil deed is done by you; you alone will experience its ripening.'[180] Later texts echo this teaching and, in the Sādhīna Jātaka (#494), King Sādhīna refuses the offer of merit from the king of the gods in order to stay on in heaven after his own merit is exhausted, by saying: 'I do not want that which has been caused by the gift of another; my treasure is peculiarly mine, as are the merits from my own deeds.'[181] But by "the final closure of the Pāli Canon," Gombrich argues, an "entire evolution" has taken place and the stabilization of this evolution brings what is to be the "modern doctrine" fully into its fold.[182]

There are a number of canonical passages that teach the transfer of merit, and early ones suggest non-Buddhist origins for the doctrine—in particular, again, Vedic funeral practices, where the idea of the ritual transfer of merit by the living to the dead is clearly incorporated into Buddhist thought. In the Vedic case, a male relative gives the food of *piṇḍa* (rice cakes) and performs ritual actions so that the nourishment and ritual efficacy engendered by the performance go to benefit the dead ancestors. Here the Śrāddha mechanism at work allows the actions of one person to benefit another. B.C. Law is one of the earliest to suggest the origin of some Buddhist practices in the Śrāddha rites although, as O'Flaherty points out, there is "the stark chronological fact that the *śrāddha* [rite] first appears in Gṛhya Sūtras roughly contemporaneous with Buddhism, and that many Vedic doctrines continued to develop under Buddhist influence."[183] Canonical materials reflective of Vedic influence include, for example, the Aṅguttara Nikāya story of the brahmin Jāṇussoṇi where there is specific reference to the *saddha* ceremonies. Here brahmins give gifts *(dāna)* to *petas* who are related by blood, in order that the gift be beneficial to them and that they might enjoy it.

Transfer of merit by the living to the dead is found again in the Tirokuḍḍa Sutta of the Khuddakapāṭha in which human beings dedicate *(uddisati)* a gift for their *petas* saying, 'let this be for our relatives', whereupon those *petas* gain fortune.[184] In due course of time, the story continues, King Bimbisāra appears and, when once he hosts an alms meal but does not dedicate the gift to his relatives born as *petas* as they hope, the *petas* make a horrible screeching noise at his house during the night. Extremely frightened, Bimbisāra goes to the Buddha the next morning and asks what will become of him. Nothing, the Buddha replies, for if it happens that no one remembers to call the *petas* to a feast one particular time, it is due to the unfortunate ripening of some bad action of theirs in the past.[185] Such a story, however, besides interweaving the canonical notion of reaping what one sows oneself into the Śrāddha transfer of merit idea, also impresses upon a non-renunciant audience the practical horror of *petas* who go unfed.

The Aṅguttara Nikāya passage discussed by Gombrich raises issues about the exact beneficiaries of the gift. When Jāṇussoṇi asks the Buddha if the departed really benefit from the gift, the Buddha replies only if they are reborn as *petas* and, if the departed have not arrived in the region yet, the benefit will go to other relatives already there. Should there be no one there yet, there is never not a reward for the donor anyway *(dāyako pi anipphalo)*. As Gombrich points out, however, no reference is made in this passage to the merit of the act, rather, it is the gift itself that is "presumably" passed on "to them direct."[186] The main thrust of this passage is two-fold. First, it underscores the material importance of *dāna:* he or she who gives gifts to recluses and brahmins can be assured of a good rebirth.[187] Thus, the Buddha again couches soteriological teachings within the context of the ongoing living needs of the Saṅgha.

Second, it emphasizes the benefit that goes to the doer of the gift as well as to the receiver. In the classical statement of the

Pali transfer of merit doctrine, the Milindapañha, King Milinda poses, as the seventy-fourth dilemma, the question whether the dead derive any advantages from the gifts that are given for them or not. The Venerable Nāgasena replies that some don't, but that some do: those who do are those who have been reborn as *petas,* 'hungry ghosts,' and who are specifically known as *paradattūpajīvin* 'living on the gifts of others.' If for some reason, he continues, these *petas* cannot or do not take advantage of the merit transferred to them, then the advantage of the merit reverts back to the donor. Moreover, it is only a good deed that can be shared, not a bad one.[188]

A further development reflected in the canon is the dedication of merit from the giving relationship between a donor and a donee to a third party. In the Dīgha Nikāya, for example, the Buddha is said to tell householders who have just given him a meal that the wise man should feed the deserving renunciants of his local area and should then dedicate the merit of his gift to the deities who are living right there at the spot.[189] This is an important passage because it not only establishes the occurrence of the offering of merit from one's gift to the gods (a third party) already in the Nikāyas, but it is also an early passage that establishes *dāna,* to no one's surprise, as the original practice-context in which Buddhist ideas about transfer of merit are developed.[190]

Again, in the Aṅguttara Nikāya, the *deva* Mahārāja Vessavaṇa appears to Nanda's mother and tells her that when she feeds breakfast to the Saṅgha the next morning she should declare the gift to be his, not hers: 'you should announce the gift as mine, and it will be my gift of hospitality' *(mamaṃ dakkhiṇaṃ ādiseyyāsi, etañ ca me bhavissati ātitheyyaṃ).*[191] Of this passage McDermott says,

> *It is to be noted that the proposed gift of hospitality is not merely to be declared the gift of the deva. It is also his gift in that the idea for it originated with him. He planned the gift, and good intention bears good fruit. However, creatures in non-*

> *human form are not usually capable of doing meritorious deeds; thus Vessavana turned to Naṇḍa's mother to have her carry out the actual meal.*[192]

Moreover, when Nanda's mother actually says to Sāriputta, 'Sir, let the merit that is established in this gift be for the happiness of Mahārāja Vessavaṇa,'[193] the passage makes explicit that merit accruing from donation can be acquired by the person in whose name it is performed.[194]

The Vedic *śrauta* ritual is the clear precursor to this dedication of merit to a third party and provides, as the paradigm, dedication to a specific deity. As Staal notes, one of the basic elements of the early ritual is the *tyāga* 'giving over' (P. *cāga,* an alternate to *dāna),* the formula recited by the sacrificer-patron at the time of his oblation whereby he renounces the fruits of the ritual to the benefit of a god. The early sacrificer might say then, for example, 'this is for Agni, not for me.'[195]

As the cult of the *petas* continues to develop in the domestic environment at the time of early Buddhism, transfer of merit theory becomes more complex as well. The *petas,* the 'hungry ghosts' who are tormented by hunger and other related needs in canonical texts, are seen to inhabit a certain intermediate space. Their particular reasons for being reborn in this purgatorial region are given in a late collection of destiny stories known as the Petavatthu. While the Pettavatthu is governed by the traditional idea of individual responsibility for kammic action (each story being the particular history of what brought this *peta* to 'his present tormented condition'), it does allow for intervention into this suffering by those presently reborn as humans. Although gifts cannot be given directly to *petas* in this text, unlike in the Aṅguttara Nikāya story of the brahmin Jāṇussoṇi, "their suffering [can]...be alleviated through a gift to the saṅgha—or, indeed, to anyone worthy of such a gift."[196] In this way, early Buddhist practice reworks the Vedic Śrāddha rites: instead of giving food directly to the departed ghosts for their own enjoyment, for example, it is given to worthy recipients (i.e., Buddhist renunciants) and its merit dedicated to the *petas* for their spiritual benefit. The usual word for this process in the Petavatthu is *ādisati* 'dedicate' or, less frequently, *uddisati* 'allot,' already in the Dīgha and Aṅguttara Nikāyas (the former) and in the Khuddakapāṭha (the latter). While many translate *ādisati dakkhiṇam* as 'transfers merit,' McDermott argues instead for 'ascribes the gift.'

> *Strictly speaking, in the* Petavatthu *there is no actual transfer of merit from one account to another. Rather, what is happening is that the benefactor gives a gift to the saṅgha, for example, and declares the act of charity to be the peta's. Through being ascribed to the* peta, *the act of giving becomes his in actuality. Saying it is so, in this case makes it so.*[197]

Since the gift, then, is in fact the gift of the *petas,* the merit from it is also theirs.

The issue of how the *petas* actually benefit from the gift is taken up again in the Kathāvatthu (7.6). The controverted point states that, 'through what is given from here, they [the *petas]* are caused to be sustained by there.' While two sects, the Rājagiriyas and the Siddhatthikas, hold the view that the material gifts of robes, alms food, lodgings, and medicines (the four requisites of the renunciant community) are themselves enjoyed in the next life, the Theravādins counter by stating that such a view commits the followers of these groups to the further idea that 'one person is the agent for another, that one person experiences the happiness and suffering that is made by another, that one person is caused to experience the experience' of another—a position these sects deny.[198] The position of the Theravādins is then given: that 'the mind of the Petas might be favorably influenced but the material food cannot be enjoyed by them.'[199] The notion that it is the mind that is being influenced is crucial to the Theravādin view, as is the concomitant defining of the gifts in question as the four requisites of Buddhist renunciants.

With this reorientation, the doctrine serves to specify this giving as *dāna* to the Saṅgha—which is really what Theravādin discussion is all about. As Gombrich concludes here,

> *sensible Theravādin monks decided that food being visibly consumed by a monk could not possibly be eaten by someone else, so that, if people persisted in their habit of feeding dead relatives, the custom required reinterpretation. What the relatives are really getting is something else—merit.*[200]

It is the Theravādin position expressed in this Kathāvatthu passage that provides the key to the evolution of their idea of the transfer of merit. This evolution, first, separates enjoyment of the gift from enjoyment of the merit earned by the gift and, second, clarifies that it is the favorable influence made on someone else's mental state that is the main point.[201] The canonical framing of this process is in a doctrinal term associated with earning merit, *anumodanā* or *pattanumodanā.* This term, Malalasekera notes, is actually a means of 'rejoicing in' or having a 'joy of rapport,' with someone or something, whereby "the recipient of the transfer [becomes]...a participant of the original deed by associating himself with the deed done."[202] The original Pali use of *anumodati* is as 'to agree with,' 'to support,' or 'to thank,' a word applied from the beginning in the Nikāyas and Vinaya most often "as a technical term for the thanks uttered by a monk on being given alms."[203] Although the offering of merit to the gods is present in some of these texts, "the doctrine of *pattānumodana,* the acquisition of merit by anyone through empathizing in another's merit, [is]...not." The evolution of *anumodati* from 'thank' to 'empathize or rejoice in another's merit' happens, according to Gombrich in the following way. Monks tell the Buddhist donors at a funeral feast that their dead relatives are not getting food but merit instead, thus still allowing donors the satisfaction of giving something. The dead say 'thank you' but, since, canonically, merit cannot be given away the dead are in fact being allowed "to improve their minds by expressing sympathetic joy at your [the donor's] good action in feeding us."[204] In this way, then, the undoctrinal behavior of rituals for merit transference becomes rethought along doctrinal lines[205] and brought into harmony with traditional teachings.

The receipt of merit by several parties to a gifting transaction, then, is based in at least two processes. In the first, the field image, the donor sows kammic seeds (gifts) into the field (renunciant) and reaps the kammic fruit when ready.[206] While the process reflects the traditional individualized reap-what-you-sow transaction, the image does not preclude someone else harvesting a field the donor has sown. Second, the use of *anumodati*—meaning 'to appreciate,' 'to give one's mind thoroughly to,' and 'to benefit from'—helps explain how *petas* can get merit when monks and nuns eat, that is, that they acquire mental benefit from appreciating the nutritional gift that has been offered to another. Here the merit is "transferred" to third parties (i.e., to gods, *petas,* or others) who, through mental empathy, find benefit in a gifting relationship. By extension, the original *dāna* transaction might be interpreted as follows: a donor, through the process of *anumodati,* might appreciate a renunciant's satisfaction in a gift given over to him or her. The donor derives merit, in this explanation, from the changes, due to appreciation, in his or her own mental state. This explanation fits well with the field image, such that 'receives benefit from mentally' might correlate with 'harvesting.'

On the transfer of merit issue, then, three views are reflected in the canon. In the first, the strict Buddhist view, only formal elements of the Vedic heritage survive (in such names, for example, of the alms tour as *piṇḍapāta* and *piṇḍacāra),* with the focus instead on a carefully, narrowly, drawn kamma doctrine of own action bringing forth own fruit. In the spirit of the "be an island unto yourself" doctrine, the new Buddhist field image portrays the donor as reaping exactly as he sows when the seed of his gift is sown in the renunciant and he himself harvests the reward. In the second, the Vedic view, the mechanism of the ancestral rites is at work, such that one person's action benefits another. Here the male relative gives a rice cake *(piṇḍa)* and performs certain ritual actions such that the nourishment of the food as well as the merit of the effective ritual benefit the *peta (preta).* In the third, a developed Buddhist view, the benefit of a *dāna* act can be appreciated *(anumodati)* by a third party and, in this appreciation, can serve as a catalyst for mental transformation in that third party that amounts to acquisition of merit. While there is no doubt that these varieties of views are held contemporaneously by the tradition with only little attempt to integrate them, forcing an integration (rather than accepting the inconsistency) may do an injustice to the Dhamma of the time. For, as McDermott notes, the "presence in the canon of these...mutually contradictory positions may be taken as indicating that [several] views were prevalent among a significant number of Buddhists at the time the canon was compiled."[207]

ENDNOTES

1. Wagle, p. 28.
2. Vin 1.281.
3. Amore, pp. 30-32.
4. Amore, p. 1. In the stories about the two monks Sudinna and Raṭṭhapāla, for example, the families try to win their sons back to the householder life by clarifying the two religious life-styles available to them: either be a monk or, in throwing off monastic training and returning to secular life, 'enjoy riches and do meritorious things' *(bhoge bhuñjassu puññāni ca karohi)* (Vin 3.16-17; M 2.63-64).
5. A 4.239; see also A 3.49-51.
6. Katz, p. 174.
7. Collins, p. 152 (his italics).
8. Most discussion of renunciant merit-making is in the context of harmony or disharmony within the Saṅgha community: those monks dwelling without conflict, eyeing each other full of courtesy and affection 'produce merit' *(puññaṃ pasavanti)* (A 1.243; Vin 2.198, 205), while those who sow dissension in the Saṅgha and encourage hostility among peers 'produce demerit' *(kibbisaṃ pasavati; apuñña pasuta)* (A 5.75-76; Vin 2.193, 204).
9. Amore, p. 116.
10. Sn no. 953.

11. M 3.245-46.
12. *Sukaṭadukkaṭānaṃ kammānam phalaṃ vipāko* (S 4.352; M 1.402).
13. D 3.218; A 4.241-43, see Vin 1.281; M 1.405. Tambiah ("Ideology of Merit," pp. 69, 115) lists the six most meritorious activities in contemporary Thai Buddhism:
    1. Completely financing the building of a *wat*—this is the act *par excellence* that brings the most merit.
    2. Either becoming a monk oneself or having a son become a monk.
    3. Contributing money to the repair of a *wat* or making *kathin* gifts.
    4. Giving food daily to the monks.
    5. Observing every *wanphra.*
    6. Strictly observing the Five Precepts.
14. See Tambiah, "Ideology of Merit," pp. 103-104; A 2.54-56.
15. McDermott, *Early Buddhist Concept,* p. 32. The efficaciousness of giving, for example, makes a chief minister who provides a large meal for the Saṅgha in anger worry whether his act will thereby be detrimental to his spiritual state, reaping him poor rewards in the future (Vin 1.223). And the desire for merit *(puññakāma)* from giving so moves the housemistress Visākhā that she vows to give life-time gifts of requisites to the Saṅgha (Vin 1.294).
16. Horner, *Discipline* 5:275n.
17. A 4.239-243. According to the commentary, "a man...[can] not by gifts alone attain Brahmā's world, the possession of concentration and insight [is]...also needed" (Hare, *Gradual Sayings,* 4:164n).
18. Collins, p. 46.
19. Heesterman, *Broken World,* p. 77.
20. Collins, pp. 46-47.
21. See Smith's book on classifying the Vedic universe.
22. Collins, p. 54.
23. Or as Kane (2.2:843) notes, *iṣṭāpūrta* is "the cumulative spiritual result or merit due to a man's performance of sacrifices and charitable acts."
24. ŚB 11.2.6.13; AB 2.40.1-7.
25. *Aiṣṭikaṁ karmamayam ātmānam...saṃskaroti* (KBU 2.6; see also BĀU 6.4.6).
26. AB 1.2.3; TU 2.7.1.
27. Kalupahana, p. 125.
28. Collins, pp. 55-56.
29. Collins, pp. 57-58; BĀU 4.4.6.
30. Collins, p. 159.
31. Jayatilleke, "Doctrine of Karma," p. 320.

32. S 4.348-350.

33. Kalupahana, p. 131.

34. The doctrine of kamma-*phala* 'fruit of action' is evident in early teachings such as that given to Cunda the metalsmith who offers the Buddha his last meal. It is after eating Cunda's meal that the Buddha becomes sick unto death and, fearing that someone will stir up remorse in Cunda for what might appear to be an act that kills the Buddha, the Buddha sends Ānanda to tell Cunda that on the contrary, his act (kamma) will produce the great fruit *(phala)* of long life, good fortune and fame, and good rebirth (D 2.126-28, 135-36). Kamma, then, is understood as the basis of ongoing rebirths and, through the commission and accumulation of acts of body, speech, and mind (A 1.122-23), the individual experiences repeated births in a great variety of forms as fruits ripen over the course of time (D 3.147-179; M 2.105). The workings of the kammic system effects differences between people and is responsible for the great array of humanity spread out across the four *vaṇṇas* (D 3.93-98; see also CU 5.10.7). Early Buddhism enumerates thousands upon thousands of types of rebirth (including eight specific ones resulting from *dāna)* (A 4.239-241), hundreds and thousands of regions of rebirth not here on earth, hundreds of types of kamma, and a great variety of existences available for specific occupations (D 1.53-55; M 1.517-18).

35. D 1.137.

36. Kalupahana, p. 127.

37. *Ahami...yathākammaṃ gamissāmi* (M 2.71-74).

38. M 3.179-180.

39. "The ease and pain, measured out, as they are, with a measure, cannot be altered in the course of transmigration; there can be neither increase nor decrease thereof, neither excess nor deficiency. Just as when a ball of string is cast forth it will spread out just as far, and no farther, than it can unwind, just so both fools and wise alike, wandering in transmigration exactly for the allotted term, shall then, and only then, make an end of pain" (T. W. Rhys Davids, *Dialogues* 1:72-73; D 1.54; see also M. 1.518).

40. Kalupahana, p. 131; M 2.104-105. Some deemphasize the importance of the result of an action for *kammic* fruit. See Sizemore and Swearer, "Introduction," pp. 2-3.

41. Misra, p. 82.

42. Misra, p. 85.

43. M 1.401-402.

44. A 5.265-6.

45. Misra, p. 85.

46. Jayatilleke, "Doctrine of Karma," pp. 318-19.

47. Obeyeskere, "Religious Symbolism," p. 21.

48. M 1.405-408, 483; 2.167.

49. *Cetanāhaṃ bhikkhave kammaṃ vadāmi; cetayitvā kammaṃ karoti kāyena vācāya manasā* (A 3.415). The designation of kamma as intentional or volitional action makes evident what Kalupahana calls "the Buddha's emphasis on the psychological aspect of behavior" (Kalupahana, p. 126).

50. Jayatilleke, "Doctrine of Karma," p. 315; see M 3.178-79.

51. Collins, p. 204; see D 2.55-71.

52. Saddhātissa, p. 336.

53. Collins, p. 205.

54. Collins, p. 205.

55. Collins, p. 205-208.

56. Jayatilleke, *Knowledge,* p. 467.

57. Hoffman, *Rationality and Mind,* p. 93; see Kalupahana, pp. 129-130. The Buddha is said to have attained such "awareness of the nature of the operations of karma" at the time of his enlightenment, and others of his disciples to have verified these operations personally as well (Jayatilleke, "Doctrine of Karma," pp. 317-18; see M 1.22-23). Using the faculty of the 'divine eye' or 'devasight' *(dibbacakkhu),* for example, disciples like Sāriputta and Moggallāna are able to train "their minds so as to trace their past lives" (Saddhātissa, pp. 336-37) as well as the past and future lives of others. Such knowledge then leads to the destruction of ignorance and to freedom from rebirth (M 1.183; S 2.156; A 1.23, 25).

58. Examples include the brahmin of the Suttanipāta who 'looking for merit' is urged to sacrifice (Sn nos. 463, 464; see also S 1.167), or the housemistress Visākhā who 'desirous of merit' seeks to give ever greater gifts to the Saṅgha (Vin 1.294; see also S 5.462). Merit is measurable in 'heaps' (S 5.145-46, 186-87) and 'floods' (S 5.391-92; A 2.54-57; 3.51-53; 4.245-47), or is immeasurable like hundreds and thousands of pailfuls of water: 'Truly, the great mass of merit...[is] counted uncountable, immeasurable' *(atha kho asaṃkheyyo appameyyo, mahāpuññakkhandho tveva saṃkhaṃ gacchati.* A 3.337).

59. S 1.92.

60. A 2.3.

61. S 4.349.

62. Vin 1.281; S 1.58, 142; 4.331-37.

63. Amore, abstract.

64. A 2.63. Productive merit, thus, effectively translates into certain results: givers of robes get merit in order to get future reward (Vin 1.281); a builder of lodgings builds lodgings in order to get merit in order to get heaven (Vin 2.147); and, when there is merit in giving for donors, that merit is often for their happiness (M 1.236).

65. D 2.266-68.
66. A 3.412.
67. M 1.404; see 1.404-406.
68. M 1.371; A 3.412.
69. D 3.90-94; M 1.404-405; S 1.74.
70. S 1.59; 5.145-46, 186-87; A 3.51-53.
71. M 1.402; S 5.145-46.
72. Amore, p. 117.
73. E.g., *atthi sukata-dukkatānaṃ kammānaṃ phalaṃ vipāko,* 'there is fruit, the result, of good and bad actions' (D 1.27, 58; M 3.72; see also D 3.160).
74. *Karato kārayato* (M 1.403-406).
75. That is, in greed (here, *lobha,* but often 'craving,' *rāga),* hatred *(dosa)* or confusion *(moha)* (A 1.201-205).
76. A 3.415.
77. *Puññavipāka,* 'result of merit' (S 1.59).
78. Little and Twiss, p. 84.
79. Kalupahana, pp. 126-27; Misra, pp. 81, 84; Jayatilleke, "Doctrine of Karma," pp. 314-16; Amore, p. 116.
80. Gombrich, "Intention," p. 92.
81. A 1.201-205.
82. M 1.236-37.
83. That the gift-worthiness of the recipient is a central part of the teachings on *dāna* has already been made clear: anyone seeking merit will obtain his aim precisely *because of* the worthiness of the recipients of the gift (Sn nos. 488, 489, 509). Gifts given to those, for example, who wrongly expound the teaching and who wrongly follow the discipline produce much demerit, while gifts to those properly expounding the teaching and properly following the discipline produce much merit. Likewise, in the former case, the greatest measure *(mattā)* of the gift is to be calculated from the giver, while in the latter case it is to be calculated from the receiver (A 1.33-35).
84. The Aṅguttara Nikāya gives a number of cases showing how the commission of the same deed brings about different fruits based on the particular nature of the person who commits the deed (A 1.249-253).
85. M 3.257. The Theravādin position here is confirmed and expanded in the Kathāvatthu (17.11), and argues the position that a gift is purified by both the giver and receiver, based on the 'merit field' formula (KV 556-57).
86. KV 339-343.
87. KV 343-47.

88. A 2.44.

89. As Kalupahana (p. 128) notes, the "Buddha gave different explanations for different problems" and exhibits a "reluctance to posit an overall theory of motivation that might create confusion by elevating an answer to a limited question to the status of a general postulate."

90. Thapar, pp. 67-69.

91. The new entrepreneurial economy provides metaphors for the renunciant community as well, as when the monk is enjoined to be like the shopkeeper in being clear-sighted, supremely clever, and confidence-inspiring in order to attain greatness and an increase in profitable states *(vepullattā...kusalesu dhammesu)*. For shopkeepers the latter phrase is, *vepullattā...bhogesu* "an increase in wealth" (A 1.116-18).

92. A 3.42.

93. M 2.73.

94. A 3.41.

95. A 3.51-53; 4.245-47.

96. A 3.49-51; 2.34-35.

97. After Hare, *Gradual Sayings* 3:42.

98. M 1.401-404; S 1.32; 4.352; A 3.41.

99. Vin 2.147; S 1.23, 33; A 3.40, 46-48.

100. S 1.32.

101. A 2.59.

102. S 1.21.

103. A 4.245.

104. A 4.244.

105. Vin 1.228; M 1.404, 407, 409-410; 2.150; 3.178; S 1.94-95; 4.312-14, 353; 5.342, 363; A 3.39-42.

106. Heavenly place *(sugati, sagga loka)*; donors *(dāyaka)*; generous patrons *(dānapati)*; and result of giving *(dānaphala)* (A 3.39).

107. D 1.143. *Svarga*, the Vedic heaven that becomes a stage of growth for the individual in the Upaniṣads, is offered as a reward for conformity in the performance of the ritual. See Chāndogya Upaniṣad 4.17.1-10 for a description of priestly correction of ritual mistakes.

108. A 3.48.

109. A 3.40.

110. A 3.47.

111. D 1.51; A 2.54, 56, 68; 3.46, 51-52; 4.245-47.

112. D 1.51; A 2.54, 56, 68; 3.46, 51-52; 4.245-47.

113. Gonda, *Loka*, p. 110.

114. Collins, p. 45.

115. D 2.167, 272; S 1.96; A 3.40.

116. D 2.209, 211, 221, 227; M 1.252; 2.78; 3.100; A 3.287; 4.396.

117. S 5.342; A 3.40.

118. S 3.211.

119. S 5.474-77; D 3.264-65; see the discussion in McDermott, "Karma and Rebirth," pp. 172-74.

120. D 3.155, 157; M 1.404, 407, 409-410; 2.150; 3.178; S 1.94-95; 4.312-314, 353; 5.342, 363; A 3.39-42, 93.

121. M 3.24.

122. A 4.241.

123. D 3.258-260; A 4.239-241.

124. Rhys Davids and Stede, p. 329.

125. D 3.258; A 4.239.

126. See Saddhātissa, pp. 334-36. As Collins (pp. 45-46) notes, the 'world of the gods' *(devaloka)* and the 'world of the fathers' *(pitṛloka)* are often indistinguishable in the Saṃhitās but in the Brāhmaṇas are increasingly separate. Along with this goes the undermining of the status of *deva:* "Just as in the *Brāhmaṇas* the status of the gods falls, and they become less and less transcendent of mankind (and especially of the Brahmins), but dependent, like them, on the sacrifice, so too the goal of man's ritual aspirations rises, to become that of equalling the gods in status."

127. A 4.241-43.

128. D 3.218.

129. M 1.403, 406, 408, 409; M 2.149, 150; M 3.165, 179, 182-87, 212-15; S 1.94-96; 4.313-14, 317-320, 342; 5.342, 362.

130. M 3.165, 168, 170, 179-182, 209-215.

131. M 3.166-67; 182-83; A 1.141-42. Avīci is where Devadatta is said to have spent an eon after his offense of *saṅghabheda* 'schism in the community' (Vin 2.201-202).

132. "Four-cornered and with four gates, it is divided into equal portions, encircled by an iron wall, with a roof of iron above; its incandescent floor is made of glowing iron; all round it stands a hundred *yojanas* square" (Horner, *Middle Length* 3:213, 227). In the Great Niraya, huge flames are hurled from wall to wall continuously back and forth, and from below above and from above below. Occasionally, one of the gateways on one of the sides will open and the evil-doer will rush towards it flaming and burning and covered with smoke, and although he runs far he will still not reach it, but the gate will nevertheless remain open for him. Should he somehow reach the gate and issue forth out of it he will enter the adjacent Gūthaniraya or 'great excrement' hell where he will turn into one of the creatures with skin cut away, with flesh cut to the

bone, and with bones eaten down to the marrow. Falling into the Kukkuḷaniraya or 'hot ash' hell next door, he will continue to feel severe, sharp pains over and over again until he then falls into the Simbalavana or 'grove of silk-cotton trees' where he will climb trees up and down continuously and be burned by their scalding hot prickles.

Next door, he will fall into the Asipattavana or 'grove of sword-leaved trees' where the sharp-edged leaves will cut him all over his body as the wind blows incessantly, and next door yet again he will fall into the Khārodakānadī the 'river of potash' poison that will burn him as he is forced up and down the channel by the current. Finally, the guardians of the Niraya hell will fish him out with a fish hook and, setting him on the ground, will ask him what he wants; if he is hungry they will thrust a blazing, burning iron spike, and then a glowing hot copper pellet, down his throat so that all his inside organs will burst into flame until the fire passes out his bowels and intestines—a torture inflicted, likewise, if the evil-doer is thirsty. Should the evil-doer, however, wish to be reborn as a human and, in overcoming his lazy negligence and in becoming a *sappurisa,* to wait upon the Buddha and to hear the Dhamma, he can do so passing beyond, but not necessarily finally beyond, all such anguish *(dukkha)* of the hells (M 3.183-87).

There are other hells as well. Mahāpariḷāha or the 'great pain' hell is a place where all that the evil-doer sees or hears or tastes or smells or feels, he senses not as pleasant and attractive but as unpleasant and repellant (S 5.450-52). Paduma or the red and white 'lotus' hell is a place where the evil-doer goes because of his hardening of heart against renunciant worthies, and where the measure of life can be up to hundreds of thousands of years. The measure of life in the Paduma hell is said to be twenty times that in the Puṇḍarīka hell, which is twenty times that in the Uppalaka hell, which is twenty times that in the Sogandhika hell, which is twenty times that in the Kumuda hell, which is twenty times that in the Aṭaṭa hell, which is twenty times that in the Ahaha hell, which is twenty times that in the Ababa hell, which is twenty times that in the Nirabbuda hell, which is twenty times that of the Abbuda hell. And the measure of a life in the Abbuda hell is calculated as follows: a cartload of twenty measures of seed is emptied one seed per century; the cart will be fully empty before the Abbuda life is over (A 5.172-74; S 1.149-153; Sn pp. 123-26).

133. A 5.75-76.

134. M 3.169; 2.152, 183; Vin 4.2.6; S 1.93; A 1.107; 2.85.

135. M 3.169-170.

136. S 5.455-57.

137. S 5.474-77.

138. That is, the moral habits (=the five precepts) of not taking life, not violating sense-desires, not giving false speech, not stealing, and not indulging in strong drink. S 2.68-69; 5.375-380.

139. That is, unwavering devotion *(pasāda)* to the Buddha, the Dhamma, and the Saṅgha, and to the moral habits *(sīla)* of the noble (S 2.69-70; 5.362-64, 375-380).

140. S 2.68-70; 5.375-380, 396-97, 403; A 2.238.

141. *Aḍḍho ca hoti mahaddhano mahābhogo* (A 3.172).

142. A 3.42, 47-48, 51-52.

143. D 2.86; A 3.41.

144. A 3.172.

145. A 3.42, 47-48, 51-52.

146. D 3.157; S 1.42; S 4.353; S 5.391-92, 399-402; A 3.42, 47, 51.

147. D 3.155.

148. S 1.142.

149. S 1.32.

150. A 3.40.

151. D 1.51; A 2.54, 56, 68; 3.46, 51-52; 4.245-47. Whenever householders such as the Licchavis give a great feast to the Buddha and the Saṅgha, the merit that accompanies the meal is 'for the happiness of the donors' *(dāyakānaṃ sukhāya)* (M 1.236).

152. A 2.54, 56; 3.51-52; 4.245-47.

153. A 2.54-57; 4.245-47.

154. A 2.67.

155. Katz (p. 58; see also pp. 173-180), for example, says that "while useful for some scholarly distinctions, [it] can become dysfunctional if pushed too far in one's attempts to understand the Buddhist world."

156. Collins, p. 153; 16-17, 150-53; see Rājavaramuni's chart, p. 51.

157. Kh 216-231, the discourse on the treasure-store *(nidhikaṇḍa);* McDermott, "Nibbāna," pp. 344-45.

158. *Paṭisambhidā vimokkhā ca yā ca sāvakapāramī paccekabodhi buddhabhūmi: sabbam etena labbhati* (Kh 229).

159. McDermott, "Nibbāna," p. 345.

160. McDermott, "Nibbāna," p. 346.

161. S 4.352-53.

162. S 5.402.

163. Amore, p. 53.

164. Amore, pp. 61-82; see McDermott, *Buddhist Concept of Kamma,* p. 12. In the Vimānavatthu, in fact, where the rebirths of virtuous lay are recounted, about three-fourths of the stories describe the wondrous rebirths of those practicing *dāna,* and over half of those involve donors who are women.

165. Sn pp. 13-14.

166. See Collins, p. 152.

167. McDermott, "Nibbāna," p. 346; see Rhys Davids, *Milinda,* 2:208-243.

168. Gombrich, "Merit Transference," pp. 216-17.

169. The continued appropriateness of this economic metaphor is reflected, moreover, in Thai villages today, where "one's fund of merit accumulated in this life" is fully called upon, and the "credit mechanism" of a gift and its meritorious return is scrupulously monitored (Tambiah, "Ideology of Merit," pp. 49, 117).

170. Gombrich, "Merit Transference," p. 204.

171. Obeyeskere, "Theodicy," pp. 25-26; Gombrich, "Merit Transference," pp. 208-209.

172. Tambiah, "Ideology of Merit," p. 98.

173. Gombrich, "Merit Transference," p. 204.

174. Schopen, p. 5: *deyadharmmo 'yaṃ...* (of, title & name)...*yad atra puṇyaṃ tad bhavatu mātāpitṛpūrvvaṅgamaṃ kṛtvā sakalasatvānāṃ anuttarajñānāvāptaye.*

175. Schopen (pp. 7-8) cites corroborating textual passages from the *Aṣṭasāhasrikā Prajñāpāramitā,* the *Bhadracaripraṇidhāna,* and the *Bodhisattvabhūmi,* for example, which describes the transference as *pariṇāmayati, nāmayati,* 'he turns (merit) over to.'

176. Gombrich, "Merit Transference," p. 204; see Schopen, p. 7.

177. McDermott, *Early Buddhist Concept,* p. 44.

178. O'Flaherty, pp. xvii, xv.

179. *Attadīpa, attasaraṇa, anaññasaraṇa* (D 2.100; S 3.42-43).

180. *Tayā v'etaṃ pāpaṃ kammaṃ kataṃ; tvañ ñeva etassa vipākaṃ paṭisaṃvedissasi* (M 3.180)

181. J 4:358. *Na cāham etaṃ icchāmi yam parato dānapaccayā, sayaṃkatāni puññāni tam me āveṇiyaṃ dhana.*

182. Gombrich, "Merit Transference," p. 218.

183. O'Flaherty, pp. xv, xviii.

184. Kh 203. See Kh 213: 'giving given here can serve the ghosts of departed kin.'

185. Kh 201-216. See Malalasekera, "Transference of Merit," pp. 86-87; Gombrich, "Merit Transference," pp. 209-210, 213; McDermott, "Karma and Rebirth," p. 191.

186. Gombrich, "Merit Transference," pp. 210-11.

187. A 5.269-273.

188. MP 294-96. See Malalasekera, p. 89; Gombrich, "Merit Transference," p. 205; McDermott, "Group Karma," p. 70.

189. D 2.88.

190. Gombrich, "Merit Transference," pp. 207, 214. McDermott discusses this Mahāparinibbāna *Sutta* passage at length and determines that it is relatively authentic to the sutta, that "is not a unified work, but rather is composed of elements belonging to various strata of the tradition." The passage in question that seems not to fit well with the *arahant* ideal "may have been too well-known and too popular either to have been modified or omitted." McDermott, *Early Buddhist Concept,* pp. 41-45.

191. A 4.64.

192. McDermott, *Early Buddhist Concept,* p. 41.

193. A 4.65.

194. McDermott, *Early Buddhist Concept,* p. 41.

195. As quoted in O'Flaherty, p. 12. Heesterman notes here the strong aversion of the priest to accepting gifts directly, as a way of safeguarding his purity. This aversion then results in his "turning away" from gifts and assigning them to various deities. Heesterman, *Inner Conflict,* pp. 35, 37. Amore notes that the "motif of transfer" can also be found in the Mahābhārata:

    Tejas (vital power) could be transferred from one god to another, taken away from a god or man, and lost due to suffering a curse. *Tapas,* meaning the power generated by austerities, could make a curse effective, be transferred to others, and be lost by anger. The power of fulfilling *dharma* also could be transferred, and one-sixth of his subjects' *puṇya* could be transferred to the king. [Minoru] Hara refers to all of these powers collectively as 'merit.'

196. McDermott, *Early Buddhist Concept,* p. 37. The Petavatthu makes very clear that the transfer or ascription of merit is a transaction associated primarily with *dāna* and not with some other kind of lay Buddhist behavior.

197. McDermott, *Early Buddhist Concept,* p. 38.

198. KV 347-49.

199. Gombrich, "Merit Transference," p. 213.

200. Gombrich, "Merit Transference," p. 214.

201. Gombrich, "Merit Transference," pp. 216, 213.

202. Malalasekera, "Transference of Merit," p. 86; Collins, p. 153; Schopen, p. 7.

203. Gombrich, "Merit Transference," p. 206; see Vin 2.212.

204. Gombrich, "Merit Transference," pp. 206-207, 214-15. See A 3.194.

205. Gombrich, "Merit Transference," pp. 204, 215.

206. Although the field image admits no re-gendering it does, however, allow for exploration of the idea of transfer of merit. In the Petavatthu, in

particular, where Vedic notions of the dead reaping benefit from the livings' gifts become conflated with Buddhist *dāna* notions of the donor reaping benefit from his own gifts to the renunciant, not only do living donors and *petas* of the dead become beneficiaries of gifts to renunciants, but gifts given by one donor can be credited to another. Thus, as causal linkages are newly explored, they are so in contexts where gender is not a significant marker.

Although their and others' stories portray not only the renunciants' cultivation of donor good will on the alms tour through silence, patience, and humility, they also portray the donors' authentically personal service to the gone forth through the bathing and washing, the sewing by hand, and the dish cleaning. Moreover, and most importantly, their stories confirm the conclusion that, as an ideal, gender does not matter. Although women donors and male renunciants predominate in early stories, the frequency of the layman himself at the household door giving alms, and the inclusion of nuns as recipients of householder largesse, indicate an overall preferred gender inclusiveness within the *dāna* process (Pv I, 3-4).

The alternate version offered by the Petavatthu suggests that the *arahants* are the fields, the donors are the farmers, the gifts are the seeds, and the fruits produced by the *arahants*/fields are enjoyed by both the givers and the *petas.* While this syncretic version allows for the givers and the *petas* both to be beneficiaries of the ritual action, it puts at odds the notion that renunciants themselves are like unto the dead.

207. McDermott, *Early Buddhist Concept,* p. 98.

CHAPTER 7

Renunciation and Property

If material property and wealth are at the center of the various relationships that grow out of the emergence of early Buddhism, then the understanding and disposition of that property coming into the Saṅgha is important as well. Interpretations of the renunciant relationship to property vary. Olivelle suggests, for example, that there is "common ownership of property" with individuals having "only the right of use...[over this] commonly owned property,"[1] while Wijayaratna suggests that "lodgings and furniture belong...to the Community,...[but] clothes belong...to those who...[wear] them."[2] Most views concerning property rights of Buddhist monks and nuns have two things in common. First, there is a recognition of something called "ownership" of property and, second, a recognition that this ownership extends over a wide range of items, and includes two important sets of variables: individual renunciant versus Saṅgha ownership, and differences in the degree of ownership depending upon the item in question.

ON PROPERTY

Any discussion of property among those gone forth is set against an ideal enjoined upon many groups of the time, that of renunciation. Just as the Vedic *saṃnyāsin* is to live without a fire, without a house, without pleasures, and without protection, not possessing any store of property, and just as the Jain ascetic like other wanderers vows to forsake a home and all property,[3] so the Buddhist renunciant is defined by what is given up at ordination.

> *...at the time of his entry into the*
> *Order...[the renunciant] renounced*

> *his claim to all personal and private possessions, and...henceforth...regarded anything he used as communal property, lent to him for his needs....[All] tendency towards acquisition had to be suppressed in the monks, all inclination to regard objects in the light of possible possessions to be checked....The Buddhist* bhikkhu *has to renounce his worldly possessions before he is ordained, and after his ordination he should own no private property, but should regard his bowl and robe and other requisites as being the communal property of the Order, lent to him for his use.*[4]

The emphasis on "non-possession" in Horner's description is important as a description of proper attitude. As Schumacher notes, "Buddhism is...in no way antagonistic to physical well-being. It is not wealth that stands in the way of liberation but attachment to wealth; not the enjoyment of pleasurable things but the craving for them."[5] Although attachment to material goods is eschewed, as is most kinds of work[6] and any kind of involvement in business dealings,[7] the use, disposal, and care of some material objects is not. As Rājavaramuni notes, poverty is "never encouraged even for monks,"[8] only the abandonment of greed and acquisitiveness. In this way, the ideal of non-possession becomes a way of life reflected in Vinaya rules but as a way of life it is, most importantly, a reflection of a certain mental state.

The Buddhist understanding of the renunciant relationship to property begins with the original formulation of the four *nissayas* or resources. Here, the emphasis on non-possessiveness towards these goods is reflected in the discussion of the resources as the original category for taking material goods into renunciants' lives: that is, that renunciants are to live depending on four types of things found in their environs.[9] When found, these items are owned by no one, but are present in nature available for whomever discovers a use in them.[10]

John Locke's view of property supports this delineation of the four resources. Originally, he argues, human beings hold the world in common, this being what he calls "the state of nature." Property arises when an individual appropriates something from the common, without necessarily getting the consent of others, and applies his labor to it.

> *Whatsoever then he removes out of the state that nature has provided and left it in, he has mixed his labor with, and joined to it something that is his own, and thereby makes it his property.*[11]

In the Buddhist case, the very act of picking up, of gathering, of appropriating in any way—whether the object be food scrap, cloth rags, or cow urine—is an act of labor that makes the found object the property of the renunciant. "The original owner...[is] the one who mixe[s] his (or her) labor with the previously unowned thing, and by commingling labor to the thing, establishe[s] ownership in it."[12] This might be called ownership through the "mixing-of-labor." That the *nissayas* fall under such a rubric is clear, for example, from the renunciant responsibility of sewing together the pieces of rags found on scrap heaps in order to make a robe from them. In this way, the Lockian view describes the early renunciant as having a rudimentary form of ownership.[13]

Out of the "mixing-of-labor" model as reflected in Pali texts, property comes to be not just a thing or things but rather *a bundle of rights and responsibilities.* Property becomes a relational concept between a person and a thing describing what a person can or cannot do with that thing as it affects other people.[14] As ordinarily understood, the elements associated with property include the following: 1) the right to determine how a thing is going to be used, in particular as that use may have an impact on others; 2) the right to dispose of an object, such as by giving away, selling, or bequeathing; and 3) the responsibility to care for and maintain all things that one has rights to.

When there is a shift from resources to requisites, that is, from found items to given items, ownership through donation involves ownership that is "transferred" from donor to donee—a transaction Kane argues is the real process of *dāna.*[15] In Buddhist *dāna,* where there is the act of giving and then of accepting a requisite that is donated, a transfer of ownership is suggested. Renunciants may then additionally compound that ownership by applying their own labor to the donated item. In this way, a thing becomes "more propertied" because effort is put into it, and effort is put into it because the object already represents a bundle of rights and responsibilities for the laborer.[16] Thus, the making of *kaṭhina* cloth into a robe, the washing of a bowl, and the sweeping of a *vihāra,* for example, are all acts further establishing ownership because this labor reflects the rights and responsibilities that are already present through transfer. And, in the particular case of the robe, cutting new *kaṭhina* cloth into pieces and then sewing it up again into whole cloth for a robe is not only (or necessarily), as Wijayaratna suggests, "to reduce the original value of the cloth to a minimum" and to destroy its "commercial value before using" it,[17] thereby approximating the original custom of sewing together rag pieces into a robe. Rather, the process investing renunciant labor in the cloth also further establishes the robe as the renunciant's property.

Another understanding of the process of ownership is the "clear-act principle" in which the act of possession involves making a linguistic statement. A verbal act before an audience, made as a thing is claimed effects the consent of that audience to the new ownership; it also establishes the rights and responsibilities of ownership firmly with the new person.[18] Such a speech act is found, for example, in the Buddhist ordination where the ordinand, after choosing a preceptor, is instructed: "This is a bowl for you, this an outer-robe, this an upper-robe, this an inner-robe; go and stand in that place."[19] Here, as part of entrance into the life of a Buddhist renunciant, the ordained is charged with the two essential material elements of that life (a bowl and three robes) in an act effected in public: that is, 1) before the Saṅgha, 2) through the "verbal- claim" to property, 3) officiated by someone properly agreed upon by the Saṅgha, and 4) to which the ordained consents with silence. While the claim-taking to property appears to be a passive affair with the choice of the objects left to others and the act of claiming confirmed only in the silence of the new renunciant, two themes central to property amongst renunciants are made clear here: first, the acceptance of things as given, per the Majjhima Nikāya passage above and, second, the preeminence of Saṅgha disposal rights over those of the individual renunciant.

The verbal component of the act of possession is also seen at the time of the distribution of *kaṭhina* cloth for making into robes. The formula given in the Mahāvagga is as follows:

> *This material for* kaṭhina *cloth has accrued to the Saṅgha. The Saṅgha gives this material for* kaṭhina *cloth to the monk named such and so for the making of* kaṭhina *cloth.*[20]

After transfer of ownership from donor to Saṅgha, and from Saṅgha to renunciant, the renunciant reaffirms ownership rights by investing labor in the cloth through making it into a robe. The verbal formula used in distributing cloth cannot, then, be more explicit, for the renunciant is designated by name *(itthannāma)* in the act of disposal.

There is some speculation as to why the category of *nissayas* originally gives way to that of the *parikkhāras* as a more appropriate category "for a stable and permanent life-style."[21] Perhaps there is a need to integrate householders as householders more fully into the emergent Buddhist life. Or, perhaps, there is a fear that members of the Buddhist community will soon run out of resources, making it a question of resource management for renunciants and non-renunciants alike. Or, perhaps, there is the fear that in relying only on the four *nissayas*, a renunciant might inadvertently avail him or herself of an item in the surrounding environment that actually belongs to someone else, such as a king who owns an unpopulated forest or an ordinary householder who has carelessly left something out of doors. This last concern, that might bring to bear charges of stealing, leads to prohibitions against renunciants taking what has not actually been given.[22] And it is perhaps this susceptibility to accusations of theft, as occasioned by the early life-style of the *nissayas*, that compels not only the shift from the *nissayas* to the *parikkhāras* but the designation of stealing as the second of the *pārājika* offenses (resulting in expulsion from the Saṅgha) as well.

In large part, the Vinaya is a compilation of rules about the use, disposal, and care of the four *parikkhāras*, and for this reason it is inaccurate to argue that a strict rule of non-possession is at work here. Since, for the Saṅgha and its individual renunciants, the main question focuses on how to live in community with respect to the goods coming in, it is precisely this question of determining exactly what mandates for use, disposal, and care the Saṅgha and the monk or nun have that constitute Vinaya discussion. Thus, although some rights and responsibilities normal for householders are absent in the life of the gone forth, issues such as distribution, exchange, hoarding, and forfeiture are major topics of adjudication. And this is indication enough that receiving goods into the community is clearly understood as bringing with it certain rights and responsibilities of property. The shift from *nissayas* to *parikkhāras*, then, as evidenced by the sheer volume of Vinaya discussion on the latter, may happen because it makes it easier to manage property—that is, to manage rights and responsibilities—by specifying exactly what, when, how, and through whom goods can be given to and taken in by the community.

The limitation on rights vis-à-vis property in the Saṅgha is governed by the middle way: on the one hand, by the fact of renunciation and, on the other, by the need for minimum levels of comfort. Renunciant status is given by the condition that the monk or nun goes forth from home into the homeless life[23] and, in doing so, eschews the work, the comforts, and the attachments of the householder life. The maintenance of this extreme for renunciants—this living opposed to the householder—is reaffirmed whenever there is renunciant lapse. When donors become critical of renunciant life-style, it often has to do with attachment; the renunciant under scrutiny is described as *gihikāmabhogin* 'enjoying sensual pleasures like a householder,'[24] his offense examined, and a rectification set down. The donor criterion for criticism, then, is renunciant *violation* of the oppositional relationship between renunciant and householder life-styles, and *upholding* this antipodal vision is, then, grounds for donor support for the Saṅgha.[25]

Expressive of the tension between the householder and the renunciant position is the degree of adherence to the ideal of non-possessiveness. Any appearance that a renunciant might be attached to material goods is a sign that he or she has slipped from "using possessions" into a "possessive" mentality. The expectation of renunciants is that they live a personal life of moderation[26] (as modest,[27] contented, conscientious, and scrupulous renunciants focused on progress along the Buddhist way[28]), that they be separated from donors by the curtailment of their desires, and that they work to maintain the goodwill of the donors for their continued material survival. It is expected as well that the renunciants will, among themselves, live a friendly and harmonious life, ritually set aright by the yearly *Pavāraṇa* ceremony,[29] and that such a life will be expressed materially in the equitable sharing and use of goods and services.

This threshold of non-possessiveness marks one boundary of the middle way, with the other boundary falling at what Misra calls an "easy maintenance of life."[30] In order, optimally, to facilitate spiritual growth, Buddhist tradition insists on a life-style of moderation and balance, that has its central stay in the maintenance of a minimum level of comfort. Emphasizing simplicity in the early Buddhist standard of living, Schumacher notes that "the aim should be to obtain the maximum of well-being with the minimum of consumption."[31] Thus, while householders have a greater number of rights of use and disposal over, as well as responsibilities of care for the goods in their lives, Buddhist renunciants still have some of these rights—the threshold dividing the two being determined by the way property helps to define the concept of person in each case.

Within the middle way, then, some property is allowable, and it is allowable precisely because it serves as a means in facilitating a renunciant to do things useful to his or her Buddhist quest. According to Margaret Jane Radin's account, property is necessary for the development of the person. A person's identity and well-being depends upon having property, such that that person flourishes only in relation to the rights he or she enjoys vis-à-vis the goods in his or her life.[32]

> *The premise underlying the personhood perspective is that to achieve proper self-development—to be a* person—*an individual needs some control over resources in the external environment. The necessary assurances of control take the form of property rights.*[33]

This view focuses on the embodiment of a person or the self-constitution of a person in things, that is, that a person "should be accorded broad liberty with respect to control over 'things' because liberty" is associated with "the idea of the self-being intimately bound up with things in the external world."[34] In applying this to the Buddhist renunciant, personhood is tied, first, to the *absence* of a whole gamut of things from his or her immediate experience and, second, to a range of limitations placed upon his or her rights and responsibilities with regard to those things that *are* in immediate experience. Says Schumacher, "the Buddhist...[sees] the essence of civilization not in a multiplication of wants but in the purification of human characters,"[35] with that purification stemming from an on-going and necessary minimizing of rights and responsibilities over the property that the canon allows to be at hand. When Buddhist renunciants have recourse to the four *nissayas,* then, and subsequently to the four *parikkhāras,* they do not have external signs to demarcate internal changes alone. In addition, the four resources/requisites have crucial roles in the Buddhist life such that the renunciant's on-going relation to each material item within the communal parameters of the Saṅgha is a critical instrument in his or her progress towards *nibbāna.*

PROPERTY AND THE SAṄGHA

Saṅgha rights to and responsibilites for property are mandates held by the renunciants as they form a community. The term *saṅgha (sam han,* 'to collect, assemble, associate') is current in northern India prior to the time it comes into use by Buddhists to describe their community.[36] Like *gaṇa,* it means "in a socio-political sense, a type of group life, [while] in the community of 'wanderers'" it means a sect; and, while *gaṇa* is "appropriated by the followers of Nigaṇṭha Nāṭaputta," *saṅgha* is appropriated by followers of the Sakyamuni.[37] As an associational group of renunciant Buddhists, the Saṅgha includes those committed to a common viewpoint and practice, and to a cooperative life-style. It supplants, Horner argues, an earlier understanding of an assembly or a company of monks, the *bhikkhuparisā,* that may belong "to those earlier days before Gotama's followers... [are] fully organised into a saṅgha."[38]

Gotama's original idea is that the Saṅgha be one unitary body, incorporating renunciants from all geographical areas into a single community. This community ideal called, for example, the 'Saṅgha of the Four Quarters,' [39] is soon supplemented by practical distinctions that grow up between local and regional communities. That is, the Vinaya comes to demarcate the Saṅgha of Jetavana, the Saṅgha of Sāvatthi, and so forth, as distinct self-governing communities.

> *Evidently, the Saṅgha of the Four Quarters was splitting up in actual practice and* āvāsas *and* ārāmas *were becoming units of Saṅgha life. Yet, the old idea of the Saṅgha of the Four Quarters persisted and an* āvāsa *or an* ārāma *could not therefore be reserved for any particular company of monks.*

S. Dutt concludes that each local Saṅgha comes to be understood as a single unit within the larger unitary community.[40] Each chapter or community functions in the manner of a corporate body through the institution of the *saṅgha*-kamma, that is, a formal act or ceremony, and is defined by a *sīmā* or boundary in the following way: a complete local Saṅgha is one in which its constituents 1) belong to the same communion *(samānasaṃvāsaka),* that is, undertake one and the same work *(ekakamma),* one and the same rule *(ekuddesa),* and equal training *(samsikkhā),* and 2) belong to the same bounded area *(samānasīmāya).*[41] The boundary is established through a sequence of natural markers—viz., a hillside, a rock or rocks, a tree or trees, a road, a river or other body of water—and then announced by an experienced and competent monk to the rest of the community. Within its boundaries, Saṅgha members carry out the same communion and a single Uposatha observance.[42] Renunciants belonging to the same Saṅgha are all those who participate in the fortnightly Uposatha together, that is, all those within the same *sīmā* who depend on the same towns and villages for the donation of requisites.[43]

At the beginning of the Mahāparinibbāna Sutta, Gotama outlines seven conditions of joint public life that make the tribal republic of Vajjians prosperous. He then enjoins a parallel seven conditions upon the communal life of Buddhist renunciants, the first four of which are the same as for the secular Vajjian community: the renunciants will assemble regularly and be committed to a complete assembly on each occasion; they will assemble in union, rise in union, and carry out the actions of the Saṅgha in union; they will not establish more precedents, nor will they repeal any precedents already established, thus acting according to the rules of training already in place; and they will honor, esteem, revere, and worship those elder monks of long-standing who have been ordained for a long time and intently consider their words.[44] In discussing these directives, Bhagvat calls Gotama "a shrewd and quickeyed politician who pick[s]...up the best out of the controlling and progressive forces of active life and applie[s]...them to his system."[45] Many others, moreover, make much of the fact that Gotama not only sees parallels between what he envisions for the structure and governance of Saṅgha life and that of tribal republics, but that he urges the renunciant community to pattern itself organizationally after these republics as well.[46]

Whatever the organizing model most appealing to the early Buddhist community, there are several principles that pattern the arrangement of goods and services within the Saṅgha. First, governance is a matter of being in community and of regular and complete joint convening. Second, harmonious concord among all members is necessary for making and carrying out acts of the community. And, third, those members with the wisdom and experience of longevity within the community are to be taken particularly seriously in matters of honor and reverence and their words paid heed to intently. If to this is added the sentiment recorded a few passages later in the Dīgha Nikāya, that members of the community adhere to the principle of impartial distribution and of sharing in common,[47] then a general pattern of life as governed fundamentally by its being economically egalitarian becomes evident.

In his essay on Buddhist economic ethics, Ronald Green wonders "what principles of economic distribution would be selected by a society whose members [have]...been reduced to the barest and most rudimentary situation of moral choice." He concludes "that the only principle likely to receive the assent of all in this situation is something like a rule of equal distribution." [48] It is precisely this rule, of collective sharing and of the equitable use of goods and services, that becomes the material basis for community in the canon. A Dīgha Nikāya passage formulates the process for life in the Saṅgha community:

> *...they shall divide impartially and share jointly with their virtuous religious colleagues all those just goods received according to the Dhamma, even down to the contents of the alms bowl...*[49]

This focus on equity in Saṅgha administration of goods parallels that prescribed by the Artha Śāstra for guilds of workmen and for those doing cooperative work, that is, that they should divide their earnings among themselves or as previously agreed upon.[50] Since, for early Buddhists, life in affiliation with a community is, in a manner like the Artha Śāstra groups above, the norm (even with portions of the year spent on the road), the issue of main concern is how to make equitability work. The concern is, first, to ensure the rightful access of all to material goods as these goods become available for renunciant life and, second, to adjudicate conflicts along principles of fairness and impartiality in light of the peculiar circumstances and individual temperaments that may threaten the material stability of communal life.

Gotama and the early leadership of the Saṅgha are concerned that the principle of equitability not conflict with the limited recognition of individuality practiced in the Saṅgha context. While individual monks and nuns can be distinguished for prominence in spiritual gifts and accomplishments resulting from their interior quests,[51] for example, their individuality is minimized by their common shaving of the head, by their wearing of identical yellow robes, by their conforming silence and modest behavior and, to the point here, by their equitable sharing in the goods and properties accruing to the community. Gotama does respond to individual lapses, to individual special needs, and to unique circumstances beyond the individual's control, and this he does on a case-by-case basis, producing, in the full, a system covering an inclusive array of most of the possibilities arising in the early Saṅgha life. In these cases, while the principle of equitable use is maintained, individual needs are accounted for—a policy consistent with Gotama's general openness to the flexibility and compromise needed in changing circumstances. This model, applied to property, corresponds to what Radin calls the communitarian model, that holds "that changing conceptions of property reflect and shape the changing nature of persons and communities."[52]

Organizational support for the equitable use and communal sharing of goods and services is rooted in two features of the non-monarchical political patterns of the day: the lack of a central authority and the commitment to democratic procedures.[53] The implications of Gotama's refusal to name a successor, someone who will be *satthar* 'master' after him, are clear in his deathbed instructions to Ānanda: 'the Teaching and the Discipline, Ānanda, that are set forth and ordained by me for you, these are to be your master at my passing.'[54] In the post-Gotama era, then, all Saṅgha members are to stand in equal relationship to the collective body, using the teachings as their spiritual guide and the disciplinary standard as their practice guide.

As a self-governing body that uses the Vinaya as its charter or constitution, the Saṅgha makes laws for itself whose authority emanates not from some central figure but out of whatever agreement is arrived at by its members.[55] S. Dutt suggests that in India at this time diverse types of aggregated units of society exist, and each is "regarded as subject to its own conventional system of law" called *samaya.* It is "the king's constitutional duty to see that none of them suffered from internal or external disruption and that the established system of conventional law of each [is]...not transgressed," such a disruption being called a *bheda.* The Saṅgha is one such unit, "an 'association group' functioning under a system of law of its own,"[56] and, thus, it is by virtue of its possession of the Vinaya, that is, says Horner, "a very complete system...[a] whole method of conducting Buddhist monasticism,"[57] that the Saṅgha enjoys some independence in society. Within the Saṅgha, the legal functions are carried out through specific corporate acts, *saṅghakamma,* that are formally discharged by renunciants in their official capacity and that carry decisive juridical authority.[58]

A second feature of Saṅgha life paralleling contemporary non-monarchical political patterns is a process of joint deliberation, in which each group member is considered equal, in which the majority rules, and in which there is a rejection of purely personal claims.[59] This democratic character of early Buddhist monasticism is reflected in decisions made by 'a collective agreement of the monks' *(bhikkhusammuti).* Gotama rules, for example, that all legal questions are to be adjudicated by a decision of the majority, and that the use of secret ballots is, in most cases, the best method for casting and counting votes.[60] The democratic principle of individual equality is evident as well in the devaluation of past caste background once an individual is a member of the Saṅgha: just as individual rivers lose their individuality at the time they merge into the great ocean, so also do members of each of the four castes lose theirs once ordained into the life of the gone forth.[61] To ensure that this loss of individuality is protected in the equitable allocation of goods and services, then, the Saṅgha provides, through the silent collective agreement of its members, for the appointment of certain officers who will be immune to the distractions of favoritism and who will work for the benefit of each member disinterestedly.[62]

Given these characteristics of governance, then, how does the Saṅgha function as an economic institution? Olivelle suggests that the "common ownership of property" with individuals having "only the right of use...[over this] commonly owned property,"[63] is one way of understanding the system. S. Dutt calls it a "tribal communism,"[64] a designation that pinpoints the thrust of the early vision, as having goods managed in common and being equitably available even in cases of special need. Again, as Radin notes of the communitarian model, changing patterns of people and community are symbiotically related to changing conceptions of property.[65] The early vision eschews, however, any sense of "Saṅgha Inc.," any sense that, at least in terms of goods and property, the whole might be greater than the sum of the parts. While goods such as robes are 'presented and given over to the Saṅgha,' [66] this gloss on *saṅghika* as 'belonging or connected to the Saṅgha'[67] focuses on the Saṅgha's management and disposal duties only insofar as the Saṅgha represents its members when in community, but not as an entity separable from them. While scholars like Bhagvat[68] and Wijayaratna[69] discuss property in terms of what the Saṅgha owns versus what individual renunciants own, a better understanding is to see the issue as *a sliding scale of rights and responsibilities:* a renunciant has more rights and responsibilities as a voting member of the Saṅgha than on his or her own, and more rights over a robe than over a *vihāra,* for which, however, he has some responsibilities.

The sliding scale of rights as the operative principle of property is founded on both the Saṅgha and the individual renunciant being designated *dakkhiṇeyya* 'worthy of a gift.' To be worthy of a gift, moreover, means that each has the right to receive a gift. In texts such as the Dakkhiṇāvibhaṅga Sutta, the merit of a gift is distinguished according to its recipient and while there is a gradation of Saṅgha recipients there is also a gradation of individual renunciant recipients.[70] Texts like this, then, do not make the same kind of radical distinction between the community and the individual vis-à-vis property as some modern scholars do, because the issue in Pali texts is not who has rights to receive, dispose, and care for and who doesn't, but in what cases there are more rights and responsibilities and in what cases less.

In Dīgha Nikāya 2.80 again, the decision about rights and responsibilities is based on determining in what manner the critical terms, *appaṭivibhattabhogī* 'adherents of impartial distribution' and *sādhāraṇabhogī* 'adherents of common sharing,' can be made most operative. Accordingly, it is decided early on to locate the bulk of the authority on impartial distribution and common sharing in the wisdom of individuals as they constitute a collective, that is, in the Saṅgha. The idea of communal ownership suggested by Olivelle, then, is really an avowal of communal management and disposition. When goods are said to have 'arisen for or accrued to' *(uppanna)* the Saṅgha (either as found in nature or as given by donors), this indicates that they are now *saṅghika* 'connected to the Saṅgha.' And they are connected to the Saṅgha precisely for that body's cooperative adjudication concerning their proper (i.e., fair and equitable) dispersement among its individual members, and not for anything other.

PROPERTY AND THE INDIVIDUAL RENUNCIANT

In this way, then, the Vinaya is concerned, generally, with how to apportion goods as they come in and, specifically, with where the highest authority for apportioning rights and responsibilities is located. Since, parallel to the Vajjians, the highest authority is soon determined to be the collective decision of the majority, the remaining determinations to be made are what use and disposal rights and what responsibilities, if any, are left for the individual renunciant.

The granting of some minimal disposal rights to individual renunciants over items they use is based on their ability, parallel to the Saṅgha's, to receive gifts. Being *dakkhiṇeyya* 'worthy of gifts,' then, is the foundation of the individual renunciant's rights and responsibilities of property. Like the Saṅgha, individual renunciants can receive items falling into any of the four categories of requisites, excluding gold and silver.[71] Like various types of Saṅgha groupings, individuals are graded according to the amount of merit that accrues to the donor who gives to them.[72] This point is important because it underscores once again that the Saṅgha and the individual renunciant are subject to the same rights and responsibilities one with the other; the Vinaya has not ruled that one can receive goods and the other not, that one has disposal rights and the other not. That both the Saṅgha and the individual renunciant are deemed *dakkhiṇeyya* means that both are understood to be able to use these gifts once the gifts have been accrued.

The relationship between a person and property is understood consistently. This relationship is exemplified by that intended between the food given by donors and the renunciants who receive it, i.e., that the food is *paribhoga* 'material for use or enjoyment.'[73] This term is used, for example, in connection with the mangoes Gotama allows the renunciant to have—i.e., he or she *paribhuñjati* 'enjoys, makes use of' the mangoes.[74] These same terms, moreover, are applied to deer who happen upon a field of farm crops and eat ('use') them as food,[75] and to the renunciants who 'use' and 'enjoy' the other of the four requisites *(parikkhāra)* that they happen to receive from donors.[76] Thus, the passages containing *paribhoga/paribhuñjati* confirm, first, that the renunciant's relationship to the material goods in the Buddhist life is the same whether the materials are found in the environs (as *nissayas)* or are given by donors (as *parikkhāras);* second, that the relationship between renunciant and object is one of use and enjoyment, a relationship that entails some rights and responsibilities, thus making it property; and, third, that the relationship to the goods is the same whether it's one renunciant or a group of renunciants who uses them.

Having received goods to use and enjoy, the renunciant can then dispose of them, i.e., give them away, under certain limited circumstances. Although food from the alms tour can be brought back on behalf of another renunciant (ordinarily one who is sick or who is in solitary practice), food is generally not to be given away, as such an action is thought to be an insult to the particular donor who gives it.[77] Renunciants do, however, have somewhat greater jurisdiction over the disposal of robes in their use.[78] Renunciants can exchange robes within the community[79] and can give away robes to elderly parents, but cannot, then, take back in anger a robe that has been legitimately handed over to another renunciant.[80]

As seen previously, use of goods and services by the individual renunciant has to be equitable, and the sound judgment of the collective is granted considerable oversight in communal sharing. The subordination of the individual to the Saṅgha in matters of material goods[81] ensures fair and balanced accessibility, and is crucial for the development of higher mental disciplines. When a renunciant dies, for example, no bequeathing is allowed and, as in the practice of escheat (where, on the death of its owner, property reverts back to the state), items used by the deceased revert back to the Saṅgha that often reassigns them to those renunciants who have attended the deceased in his or her previous illness.[82]

Equitable use also means that if one renunciant's need are made known to a donor, the renunciant can't then change his or her mind part way through the transaction.[83] Not only will this infringe on donor goodwill, but it also gives tremendous play to renunciant preferences. Likewise, an individual renunciant is not allowed to divert goods or benefits already connected to the Saṅgha to himself; such goods will eventually be appropriately distributed, and renunciants cannot on their own or in smaller groups intervene in the process.[84] In general, a type of honor code is at work among renunciants who watch each other's behavior and work to help others, and who are individually responsible for knowing the rules of training as well as the seasonal variations of renunciant life. In this way, collective adjudication in matters of material life-style is ultimately only a check on individual development when interior discipline is not sufficient.

Robes

Particular rights of disposal are also governed by what is being disposed of. Robes occupy one end of the spectrum, for not only do some think that they are the most personal and private of all articles used by individual renunciants, but that if anything can be considered a "possession" it is the robe.[85] Says Wijayaratna:

> *Monks' lodgings and furniture belonged to the Community, but clothes belonged to those who wore them....the robes worn by each monk are regarded as his personal property.*[86]

Wijayaratna also notes that, as donors increasingly give robes to the Saṅgha, it becomes "necessary to establish rules about communal ownership of them," a trend that complements, he argues, the shift away from giving to individual renunciants and towards giving to the community as a whole.[87] Thus, while early on, more rights of use and disposal are granted to individual renunciants over robes than over any other requisite, these rights are increasingly subsumed under collective adjudication as Saṅgha membership grows and, perhaps, as abuses proliferate.

Rights of use over robes begin at the time the renunciant enters the Saṅgha. Initial appropriation of the three assigned robes takes place at the ordination, when a "verbal-claim" act is used to effect possession by each individual renunciant. Thus, being invited to choose a teacher *(upajjhāya),* the initiate is then shown the items with the words, 'this is a bowl for you, this an outer-robe, this an upper robe, this an inner robe; go and stand in that place.'[88] It is clear from this, and from many other canonical statements about the three robes, that they are meant for the exclusive use of the renunciant, that is, robes are given out individually from the beginning and are meant to be used only by the individual they are given to. Thus, a robe used for ordination cannot be lent but must be used solely and lastingly by the person to whom it is charged.[89] In fact, a new robe is marked with a small smudge in dark green, brown, or black so as to indicate the individual who is its singular proprietor.[90]

Again, when *kaṭhina* cloth is donated to the Saṅgha it is given over to an experienced and competent renunciant responsible for the making into robes.[91] The Mahāvagga is explicit that the sewing up of *kaṭhina* cloth *(kaṭhinadussa)* into *kaṭhina* robes *(kaṭhinacīvara)* is to be discharged by an individual, all in the course of one day: the *kaṭhina* cloth does not become made 'except that the spreading (or making) be fixed by an individual' *(aññatra puggalassa atthāra)*.[92]

> *It seems that each monk must make up the* kaṭhina *cloth distributed to him by the Order, and not rely upon the Order or a group to do so for him.*[93]

As giving to renunciants for individual use occurs in increasingly complex settings, rules to govern these settings proliferate. Individual renunciants, for example, can make specific requests for robes to non-relative householders only under certain conditions, e.g., when one of his or her robes has been stolen or destroyed.[94] When a non-relative householder offers robe material to an individual monk, the most material that can be accepted is enough to make an inner and an upper robe,[95] and a renunciant cannot request a robe from a householder while offering ordination to that householder in return.[96] In general, when accepting robe material from householders, individual renunciants are not permitted to make suggestions or demands, or to detail any special preferences about materials; likewise, the transaction is to remain simple, with the renunciant abstaining from bargaining, negotiating, or improperly involving other parties.[97]

The other aspect of rights of use, in addition to rules about accrual, are rights about proper wearing of robes. These rights of wear are, in fact, much more like responsibilities, for the Saṅgha carefully adjudicates the public presentation of monks and nuns. Robes are, for example, to be three in number for monks, five for nuns, of regulation ocher color, and cut into patches and sewn properly. While not all three have to be worn in private, all three have to be worn in public when the renunciant goes out on alms tour. The robes need to be worn modestly, covering all three lines or folds on the skin of the abdomen, and they are to be wrapped not too loosely and not too tightly around the body. The cloth of the outer robe can also be folded up and used as a mat for sitting on, but is not in general used as an all-purpose covering, such as for sleeping. The right of use for robes, then, is that, within the parameters of Saṅgha dictates about what constitutes use, agency of use is preminently individual.

Rights of disposal are held by both the Saṅgha and the individual renunciants. While individual renunciants are allowed to accept robes from householders, it is up to the collective judgment of the Saṅgha to ensure proper allotment throughout. At the time of the giving of the *kaṭhina* cloth, for example, it is an experienced and competent renunciant, designated by the community, who is to distribute the robe material connected to the Saṅgha *(saṅghika)* to each individual renunciant. And, in each instance of apportioning, the community is asked for its assent. Individual renunciants are allowed to accept robes in exchange and to give robes in exchange, but only among five classes of people: monks *(bhikkhu),* nuns *(bhikkhunī),* female probationers *(sikkhamānā),* male novices *(sāmaṇera),* and female novices *(sāmaṇerī).*[98]

Outright gifts of robes, like exchanges of robes, are monitored so as not to change unduly the balance of equity within the Saṅgha. While the Saṅgha is ordinarily thought to be the dispenser of robes, individual disposal by gift can take place in a number of cases. A renunciant, for example, can assign to another, whose own robe is old or worn out, an extra robe that has accrued to him or her.[99] A monk can give a robe to a nun who is a relation,[100] and a renunciant can assign a robe to one of the five classes of people mentioned above, but having assigned it cannot then make use of it him or herself,[101] nor tear it back in anger.[102] A renunciant can give robe-material to needy parents[103] but not to other householders or to wanderers, male or female.[104] A renunciant can give robe material on trust to another renunciant to then deliver it to a third.[105] And a renunciant can give another renunciant rag material from the cemetery only if the receiving renunciant has stayed in wait at the cemetery boundary.[106] In these ways, then, an individual renunciant has not only the right of use over his or her robes, but certain rights of disposal as well.

Forfeiture of a robe or robes back to the Saṅgha is, in general, the mechanism for ensuring the precision of the three robe rule for each renunciant.[107] Forfeiture takes place when *kaṭhina* cloth is distributed at the wrong time,[108] when a renunciant leaves the Saṅgha or pretends some other status than what he or she has, or when a renunciant dies.[109] In the case of a renunciant who dies, the robes and bowl are normally given to the renunciant who tends the deceased while sick. This allocation takes place, however, only through the adjudication of the Saṅgha. Says Gotama: 'I allow you, monks, to give the three robes and the bowl to the tenders of the sick through the Saṅgha.' Because the allocation is an official act of the Saṅgha (i.e., done through the Saṅgha, *saṅghena)*, consent to it (i.e., the Saṅgha is pleased, *khamati)* is registered by the community's silence.[110] In this way, a renunciant cannot bequeath his or her robes and bowl to another after death, but has to give that right over to the good judgment of the collective community.

Finally, in addition to many of the rights of use and disposal, individual renunciants also have responsibilities of care and maintenance over their robes. Beginning with the charge for each to work the *kaṭhina* cloth into new robes—by washing, dyeing, and sewing[111]—there are two regular maintenance chores renunciants have. First, renunciants have to clean their robes regularly[112] and, second, they are responsible for sewing and darning any hole, tear, or broken seam. Through use and disposal, as well as of maintenance, robes then have value as individual property of the renunciant.

Food and Medicine

Rights and responsibilites for food and bowls compliment, but don't necessarily parallel, those for robes. As in the case of the robe, a bowl is a necessary provision at the time of ordination: it can't be lent but has to be at hand for the exclusive and lasting use of the individual and, in the act of possession by "verbal-claim," is shown to the ordinand just after he or she chooses a preceptor.[113] General rules for bowls are as follows: an extra bowl or a store of bowls can't be kept by an individual renunciant, as this constitutes hoarding,[114] but a renunciant can beg for a new bowl when the old one becomes broken (with five mends or more) or destroyed.[115]

Horner suggests that bowls are "regarded at some time as more especially communal property than...robes,"[116] that is, are items over which individual renunciants have fewer rights and the Saṅgha has more. In Nissaggiya 21, for example, an extra bowl kept longer than ten days has to be forfeited back to the Saṅgha.[117] And in Nissaggiya 22, a new bowl gotten in the place of an old one mended in less than five places is forfeited back to the company of monks where it is "put at the disposal of the Order."[118] It is then passed through the Saṅgha membership, senior to junior, for each to choose the bowl now in use or the new one being offered.[119] Both these discussions put emphasis not on correcting the attachment felt by the renunciant to an extra or new bowl, but on realigning the offending renunciant's action of independence within the more binding adjudication of the community. In both cases, the Saṅgha's general preeminence in the management and disposal of property is reaffirmed. Finally, like a renunciant's three robes, the bowl of a deceased is ordinarily disposed of at death by being handed over to the one ministering the deceased's final illness.[120] Again, this allocation is not a legal disposal until it's arbitrated through the Saṅgha.

Turning to food apportionment on the alms tour, the general principles are that individual renunciants are to receive food equally and only as donors are willing to give to them. Moreover, they are to eat only what is given and not to overeat.[121] Renunciants are not to ask specifically for certain food for themselves[122] and extra food can be taken and given over to another only in certain exceptional cases, so long as that person really exists[123] and so long as the original donors of the food are not insulted. The Cullavagga is very explicit in responding to donors who become concerned about monks giving away food. Such donors may say in criticism, for example: 'How does it come to be that the revered ones give to someone else what is given to them for their own enjoyment? [It is as if to say by this act that] we donors do not know how to give gifts.'[124]

Worry over maintaining donor goodwill, then, necessitates the monitoring of renunciants' disposal rights over food and, while Gotama does in time rule that monks can offer from a store of food to nuns and vice versa,[125] the giving of thanks *(anumodati)* in the refectory,[126] for example, becomes one way of averting donor ill-will and keeping the channels of donation amicably open. Such close monitoring over food gifts made by renunciants is found in the extreme case of the nun Thullanandā, on whose action the prohibition against giving solid and soft food to householders such as actors, dancers, acrobats, conjurors, and drummers, as well as to wanderers is based.[127]

In the particular case of foods used as medicines, it is ruled that a renunciant (here again, the nun Thullanandā) can't request one kind of medicine and then, once the transaction is begun, change her mind and request something different.[128] Moreover, medicine can be kept in store for only up to seven days,[129] a rule that may derive as much from the possibility of spoilage as from renunciant greed. In general, use and disposal of medicinal foods is oriented both to preserving donor goodwill and to preventing undue dependence on these delectable and highly perishable edibles.

The need to ensure equitable access to alms food by all members of the Saṅgha is addressed, among other places, in the rules for renunciants coming in to a residence. Among the questions such a monk is to ask on his arrival is about places to walk, and not to walk, for alms—one of a series of agreements discussed and entered upon by the whole Saṅgha.[130] Such a rule functions in two ways: not only does it ensure equal access to food sources for all renunciants in a given locale, but it establishes clear community adjudication over such issues.

Another ruling by Gotama, however, seems to provide for some flexibility of "equal access" when cases of food are involved. When, for example, some incoming monks divide up mangoes that are the Saṅgha's—apparently without thought to the established procedures of the resident monks—Gotama rules that there is no offence because the action is done 'for the sake of food' *(paribhogatthāya).*[131] While this term appears most often in discussing a renunciant's relation to food, it is applied, in fact, to all four of the *parikkhāras*.[132] There seems, moreover, to be reference here to the *nissaya* mode: all foods to which Gotama refers in this ruling (fruits of the mango, apple, bread-fruit, jackfruit, palm, and cucumber trees, as well as sugarcane) are uncooked products available directly from plants to eaters. Though all the plants in the ruling are *saṅghassa* 'of the Saṅgha,' they are, as plants, more susceptible to the "found in nature" category of the *nissaya* directives than to the "things explicitly given by a donor" category of *parikkhāra* directives. Gotama, then, may be either 1) recalling and thus preserving *nissaya* sentiment, a sentiment underscoring the freedom of renunciant life, or 2) suggesting ties to other rulings Gotama makes about found fruit, rulings that raise questions about what to do when there is no donor.[133] In either case, however, this particular example has as one intent, at least, the highlighting of the Saṅgha's rights over individual rights in the provision of food for renunciants.

Renunciant neutrality toward food is called into question by the custom of individual monks and nuns becoming 'regular or constant diners' *(dhuvabhattika)*,[134] 'continual diners' *(niccabhattika)*,[135] and 'frequenters of the [same] family' *(kulūpaka)*.[136] The individual families in turn are called families 'who minister unto, or who are supportive of' *(upaṭṭhākakula)*, a particular renunciant.[137] The term *upaṭṭhāka* is perhaps most well-known in its application to Ānanda, and this points up, first, an individual exclusivity in the *upaṭṭhāka* relationship and, second, the almost devotional nature of the service given to the renunciant. This application also suggests the cautionary note needed in approaching such a singular relationship, as reflected perhaps in the many issues surrounding the great attachment and emotionality that ensue Ānanda's attendance upon the Buddha. Gotama, in fact, notes this while preaching at Kusināra once, when he describes the significant danger to the renunciant posed by his taking pleasure in the good service from a particular householder and his subsequent desire to want more of the same in the future. Much better off, Gotama argues, is the renunciant who remains vigilant over his own senses and does not form such family-oriented longings for food.[138]

Another important example is the invited group meal *(gaṇabhojana)* where, more than in the alms tour, the supervisory role of the Saṅgha in allocating accessibility to certain meals is significant. Normally, an invitation for a group meal is issued to the Saṅgha as a whole and the Saṅgha then decides who is to go. Not only is it the Saṅgha who is invited, but the Saṅgha for whom meals are prepared by the donor so early on the day of the meal, and the Saṅgha to whom the meal is served by the donor's own hand. Two aspects of *gaṇabhojana* etiquette, in particular, are important here in the understanding of the meal as property: the silent assent to the invitation, and the hand leaving the bowl at the conclusion of the meal. First, while silence is the traditional mode of assent in Saṅgha procedures, it also underscores the Buddhist posture of willingness to make use of whatever is available: "whatever accrues to our use, we will use," the Saṅgha might say. Silent assent also serves as a "negative verbal-claim" to ownership in the property that is the meal. Just as the decided lack of verbal formula on the alms tour is an act of possession over the food put in the bowl, so the assent that is silence resounds firmly as a share-taking in the group meal. Second, the hand leaving the bowl is a sign to the donor that the renunciant is finished with the meal. In ownership terms, however, if investment of labor in an object is an act of possession, stopping that investment of labor signifies the opposite, that is, "dispossession." The lifting of the hand, then, not only closes the meal but gives up renunciant claim on both the food and the event.

Despite the individuality of these ritual signs, however, the *gaṇabhojana* process remains focused on Saṅgha agency. This agency deters the development of a donor's exclusive relation to an individual renunciant, allows the individual renunciant to retain a measure of anonymity vis-à-vis the donor, maintains the subordinate status of the renunciant to the Saṅgha, and in general fosters the non-possessiveness and loss of self-centeredness necessary to spiritual maturity.[139]

Because of its nature, then, food generates only a little concern over the range of rights of its use and disposal—and therefore over the degree to which it might constitute property—and much more over the immediate behavioral etiquette of acquisition, consumption, and closure activities. While the alms bowl is a more permanent item in a renunciant's life and, therefore, is subject to more specific rules of use, disposal, and care with Saṅgha adjudication at the center, the individual daily allotment of food provides, in its temporariness, a greater focus for issues of the development of mindfulness and of ongoing donor goodwill. The most basic of all the *parikkhāras,* and the one perhaps that more than any other keeps its closeness to the original *nissaya* concept, food is the one requisite that continually draws the renunciant away from possibilities of possessiveness and into uses of mental discipline that more immediately foster the proper Buddhist life. Unlike robes and lodgings that plunge the renunciant into detailed questions of who has what rights over which items, food, because it doesn't last and because its procurement needs to be attended to every day, deflects many of the usual questions about lasting property.

Lodgings

If many of the rights over robes fall to the individual renunciant, most of the rights over dwelling places fall to the Saṅgha. As, over the years, more and more land, buildings, furniture and other material items accrue to the renunciant life, it might be asked, as Wijayaratna does, "who own[s] all these goods?" "One might think that the Buddha and his disciples...[have] renounced everything and embraced the religious life, only to start living in a new house called 'a monastery.'"[140] The very first discussion of lodgings, however, makes clear that almost all issues of use and disposal concerning lodgings are not up to the individual renunciant but are matters of Saṅgha adjudication. When the great merchant of Rājagaha gives the first lodgings—sixty little *vihāras* built in one day—he gives them for the use of the Saṅgha of the Four Quarters in the present and in the future.[141] Monasteries and furniture are thus not ever "the private property of Buddhist monks and nuns,"[142] though there are issues of caregiving labor devolving on these items that give renunciants a very minimum of temporary investment.

For the most part, lodgings are described throughout the

Vinaya as *saṅghika* 'affiliated with, connected to the Saṅgha:'[143] *saṃghika vihāra,*[144] *saṃghassa pāsāda,*[145] etc. Even in cases where donors are said to give buildings to individual renunciants, such as the presentation by Dasama of Aṭṭhaka of an expensive dwelling to the monk Ānanda, all rights over these buildings are supervised by the Saṅgha.[146] An excellent example of the Saṅgha-centeredness of the gift of lodging is the case of Udena, for whom personally the brahmin Ghoṭamukha wants to build a *vihāra.* Udena tells Ghoṭamukha that he himself cannot accept a *vihāra,* and that the better alternative is for the donor to build an assembly hall for the Saṅgha.[147] Moreover, not only are the lodgings themselves *saṅghika* 'of the Saṅgha,' but all the furnishings inside are as well: couches, chairs, mattresses, stools, carpets, bedcovers, blankets, groundcloths, and mats.[148] The Saṅgha rules on all the possible uses of these articles and, in doing so, has utmost consideration for making sure renunciant behavior doesn't resemble that of 'householders who enjoy the pleasures of the senses' *(gihin kāmabhogin).*[149]

The Saṅgha is not only the main adjudicator of use and disposal issues concerning lodgings, but is the final arbiter on the finding, inspecting, approving, marking, clearing, and working of a building site as well.[150] The actual building of individual dwellings, though supervised and overseen by the Saṅgha, however, is allowed to be done by individual renunciants.[151] Buddhist renunciants are given clear direction about how to build huts for their own use themselves, even if there is no benefactor.[152] Even so, the Saṅgha supervises the inspection, clearing, measuring, marking, and working of the site, and any infraction of this process is responded to immediately.[153] Similar Saṅgha oversight is present for the building of larger *vihāras* that do have benefactors.[154] In order not to overtax the efforts or finances of donors, repairs to Saṅgha buildings are managed by a renunciant appointed by the community to this position permanently. Detailed discussions on the building parts needing repair, the nature of the disrepair, and the reasons for the disrepair are given in the Vinaya, but it is clear throughout that the buildings are always considered *saṅghika* (that is, that *saṃgho sāmī* 'the Saṅgha is the owner' of them) and that their ongoing upkeep is crucial so as not to cause problems within and for the Saṅgha .[155]

Much care is given to allotting individual accommodations in communal lodgings. There is, for example, an assigner of lodgings chosen by the Saṅgha to parcel out places for those of the same community. The most famous of the early assigners is Dabba the Mallian and, although controversial, Dabba is recorded as carrying out his job with finicky exactness, mindful of individual needs, and clear in each case about the details of the renunciant's agreement with the community.[156] In general, a renunciant is to give up the dwelling when setting out on alms tour,[157] but the Cullavagga notes that the assigner of lodgings can make a "reservation" for an individual renunciant at the end of one rain retreat 'with reference to the next rains-residence.'[158] Proper assignment of accommodations is a regular feature of Saṅgha life, and instructions to renunciants coming into a residence, for example, have details about how to ask about lodgings—e.g., 'What lodging pertains to me?'[159]

If a dwelling place assigned to a renunciant is unoccupied, care of the space is required. Even though the final disposal rights remain with the Saṅgha as a whole, the investment of labor in the cleanliness and usability of the room is a clear act of possession for the renunciant under the agreement with the community.[160] Renunciants are not to walk in lodgings with wet or dirty feet or with sandals on; they are not to spit on the ground or to scratch the ground unduly by moving furniture around; and they are not to lean against the walls and spoil its color.[161] Incoming monks are to beat the dirt out of their sandals when entering, to clear their assigned dwelling spaces of soiled items or extra furniture, to position the couch, bed, chair, or spittoon, for example, so as not to rub the walls or knock the door or posts, to wipe the floor and windows free of dirt and cobwebs, and to dry any damp items outside in the sun before using them.[162] Thus, the rules for the proper care and use of items entrusted to a renunciant within a dwelling have an emphasis on respect for the immediate environment and its continuous cleanliness. The general rubric for a renunciant is: 'In whatever dwelling place he stays, if that dwelling place becomes dirty, he is to clean it if he is able.'[163] Moving furniture, wiping, washing, shaking, beating, sweeping, and drying, then, are all part of the renunciant's daily domestic efforts to keep dust and dirt at bay—with the care and cleaning of the bathroom occupying unusually ample space in the Cullavagga.[164]

Co-residents of a dwelling are governed by close attention to their conduct, with the foremost rule being that incoming renunciants accommodate themselves to already resident renunciants—unless the incoming renunciants outnumber the residents. Incoming renunciants are taught to look and listen for signs of residence, and vice versa, and both are to take care to follow the rules of common Uposatha observance for those belonging to the same communion.[165] Equitable allocation of space and equitable treatment of one another with regard to whatever established priorities of residents (e.g., preceptor/pupil, incoming/resident) there are, then, are all adjudicated under the supervision of the wisdom of the collective.

SAṄGHA STRUCTURES FOR HANDLING PROPERTY

In order to handle all the items accruing to the Saṅgha, an internal structure develops for dividing up the labor of receiving, storing, and apportioning property. Such division of labor can be found in other areas of monastic life also, in particular in the guidance of spiritual development, with designations such as the *sāmaṇerapesaka* 'superintendent of novices'[166] and the *bhikkhunovādaka* 'exhorter of nuns,'[167] as well as the *salākagāhāpaka* 'issuer of voting tickets' who presides during communal decision-making.[168] Because there is no central authority (the locus of legitimation being deposited in the Dhamma and Vinaya as the norm for the self-governing community),[169] "all...members...[stand] in relation to the collective body on a footing of perfect equality."[170] As the community grows, and as properties accrue with even more complex use and disposal rights, this equality means that, by democratic process, work can be given to community members in, if not an equitable division of labor, at least an agreed upon one. Thus, comparable to distributions found in Western monastic systems[171] and to allocations of government duties found in the Artha Śāstra,[172] the

Buddhist Saṅgha provides for the designation of a few of its members to oversee the use and disposal of the four requisites.

As Horner notes, appointments "of officials...[are] not of one officer for the whole *saṃgha,* but of an officer for any of those lesser sections of it that, dwelling within one boundary or residence, [are]...also called *saṃgha.*"[173] Although seniority is a "fundamental yardstick in grants of privileges,"[174] it is also clear that in things pertaining to Saṅgha governance seniority is not the primary marker of privilege.[175] Rather, in the democratic allotment of jobs, whether temporary or permanent, a specific task is to go to the renunciant who is deemed *vyatta* 'experienced' and *paṭibala* 'competent'[176] by the common assent of fellows. Often, as in the case of the *salākagāhāpaka,* a candidate for the office has to fulfill five qualifications that bear on his or her character.[177] The appointment of the officer is then made by an act of agreement among members of the community, and his or her actions are subsequently considered to be done on behalf of the Saṅgha.

Food Officers

In the course of time, a great number of Saṅgha officials are designated in connection with food. The *pattagāhāpaka* or 'assigner of bowls' is needed temporarily whenever there is a commission of a specific bowl-related offense. He is chosen by agreement of the Saṅgha on the basis of five qualities: being unswayable through partiality, hatred, stupidity, or fear, and being knowledgeable of what is taken and what not. His job, for example, is to hold the new bowl, just confiscated from an offending monk who has acquired it in the place of another that is mended in less than five places, and to offer it to the senior elder who can exchange it for his own and then offer the rejected bowl on to a second. The *pattagāhāpaka* then supervises this passing of bowls on down to the junior-most member of the Saṅgha,[178] with the offending monk being last in line.

Probably, the most important official for food is the *bhattuddesaka* or 'supervisor of food distribution, supervisor of meals.' Like the assigner of bowls, the *bhattuddesaka* is chosen by Saṅgha agreement on the basis of being unswayable through partiality, hatred, stupidity, or fear, and being knowledgeable about what is issued and what not.[179] The role of this official seems to become important at a time when renunciants receive food not only from alms touring, but from meals to which they have been invited by householders; thus, it is an office "unlikely...[to be] formed during the earliest days of the Sakyan venture."[180] Several types of meals are noted in the Vinaya and the job of the *bhattuddesaka* is "to conduct the selection of monks"[181]—"to choose which monks to send to which house"[182] for meals when the whole Saṅgha cannot go, a job he does by issuing individual tickets.

The most famous early example of a *bhattuddesaka* is Dabba the Mallian who, having fully attained his spiritual goals, wants to give service to the Saṅgha and asks to be an assigner of lodgings and an issuer of meals. Gotama agrees to the idea and takes it to the Saṅgha, which, in the course of time, consents to the double designation by due process.[183] Dabba's tenure as *bhattuddesaka* is somewhat difficult, however. It happens, once, that there are followers of Mettiya and Bhummajaka, who are just ordained and of little merit. A householder, known for giving out good food, decides to give poorer quality food upon discovering that these monks are coming to eat at the house the next day. Eating the food, the monks are disappointed and decide that Dabba has set the householder against them. They persuade the nun Mettiyā to raise false charges of assault against Dabba, but Dabba's defense is accepted, he is declared innocent, and the charges are dismissed. When the nun is about to be expelled, the offending monks confess to conspiracy and defamation, and are found guilty of a *saṅghādisesa* 'formal meeting' offense.[184] These same monks levy another charge against Dabba, but again the monks are found to be at fault and are charged with a *pācittiya* 'expiation' offense.[185] In a third incident, monks following Mettiya and Bhummajaka persuade the Licchavi layman Vaḍḍha to accuse Dabba falsely of molesting his wife. When the charge is once again deemed false, Vaḍḍha receives a 'non-eating with the Saṅgha ban,' a condition that is signified by the householder's bowl being turned upside down.[186]

A variation on the *bhattuddesaka* office is the peculiar one "held" by the monk Sudhamma at the household of Citta Macchikāsaṇḍa. A resident there, Sudhamma presides over Citta's invitations to groups or individuals for meals at the donor's house. One day, Citta asks a group of high ranking monks to a meal before asking Sudhamma's permission. Sudhamma is insulted and complains the next day that Citta's meal is lacking in one item. After an exchange of words with Citta, Sudhamma approaches Gotama who then rebukes the monk for his abusive behavior to the donor. To bring things to a close and to ensure Citta's continued support, Gotama authorizes *an act of reconciliation* during which the householder's forgiveness is asked.[187] This unusual part of the assigner-of-meals office reflects both the individualizing tendencies of some donor-renunciant relationships, as well as the early community's need to curb such tendencies and to retain communal jurisdiction over issues of food disposal.

Other food officials are designated as well. The texts note a *yāgubhājaka* or 'distributor of rice-gruel,'[188] a *phalabhājaka* or 'distributor of fruit,'[189] and a *khajjakabhājaka* or 'distributor of solid food.'[190] It is not clear under what circumstances these officials are needed, but their appointment is probably temporary and is conditioned by the circumstances of certain foods becoming available.

Although the Suttavibhaṅga reports a strong early consensus on the part of donor householders against the storing and hoarding of foods and medicines by renunciants,[191] the vicissitudes of scarce and abundant periods of food-stuff make the storage of food a continuing issue. The office of the *bhaṇḍāgārika* or 'keeper of the stores' may be primarily for stores of robes,[192] but the Cullavagga does indicate that in time stores of food are allowed that can be made available from monks to nuns and vice versa.[193] Terms for a storehouse or a warehouse appear in the texts— *kappiyakuṭī* 'store hut' and *kappiyabhūmi* 'store ground'—and Misra assumes that these are places where food is stored.[194] Such storehouses are built outside the residence 'at its extremity *(paccantima),*'[195] and this leads Olivelle to conclude:

> *As storage of raw food went against established rules, this provision to have the storehouse outside the monastery, in an ox-stall* (goṇisādika), *or in a building belonging to a layman, may have been one way of getting round the law.*[196]

In spite of what may be an increasing official classification of monastic work vis-à-vis food, a passage in the Majjhima Nikāya is testament to the informality and situational nature of daily food etiquette. During questioning by Gotama, one day, the monk Anuruddha tells him of how he and his colleagues divide the labor for a meal:

> *...whoever of us returns first from (going to) a village for almsfood makes ready a seat, sets out water for drinking and water for washing (the feet), and sets out a refuse-bowl. Whoever returns last from (going to) a village for almsfood, if there are the remains of a meal and if he so desires, he eats them; if he does not desire to do so, he throws them out where there are no crops, or he drops them into water where there are no living creatures.*[197]

Relying on the first to make ready and the last to clean up, renunciants work together in silence, communicating by means of hand movements and hand signals, and breaking the silence only once every five days for an evening discussion of Dhamma.[198] In this way, judicious division of work among co-commensals can exist side by side with the more formal, democratic appointment of officials as it develops over time.

Robes Officers

As Misra notes, in "order to cope with the increased complexities of the Saṅgha-life in regard to the proper arrangement of the *cīvaras,* several office-bearers...[are] appointed."[199] The *cīvarapaṭiggāhaka* 'receiver of robe material' is agreed upon by the consent of the Saṅgha as being a person of all five qualities—unswayable through partiality, hatred, stupidity, and fear, and knowing what is taken and what not—and is the one who receives robe material given by donors who come to the monastery. This office is needed to prevent donors, coming with robe material, from leaving with the gifts still in hand because they have not been met at the entrance by an appropriate person.[200]

In order to keep the robe material from getting lost, Gotama allows the appointment of a *cīvaranidāhaka* 'keeper of robe material,' to be, again, a person of the five designated qualities and agreed upon by the consent of the Saṅgha.[201] Until this point, the robe-material has been stored in a shed and at the root or in the hollow of a tree where, unfortunately, it is preyed upon by rats and ants. In order to store the material properly, Gotama allows a storeroom *(bhaṇḍāgāra),* that can be in a variety of places—a dwelling, a curved house, a long house, a mansion, or a cave. Like the officers, the designation of this storeroom is agreed upon by the consent of the Saṅgha,[202] and it is into this storeroom that the keeper of robe material deposits the gifts.

Concern about robe material remaining unguarded, however, leads to the appointment of a *bhaṇḍāgārika* or 'guardian of the storeroom' through the regular process of having the five qualities and being agreed upon by the consent of the Saṅgha.[203] This officer's job, according to the commentary, is to guard the robe-material against pests and against excessively hot or cold weather, so that from this store one, two, or three robe-sets can be given out to renunciants in need. Finally, a *cīvarabhājaka* or 'distributor of robe-material' is allowed, by the usual process of having the five qualities and being agreed upon by consent of the Saṅgha, in order to complete the process of receiving, keeping, guarding, and distributing the material. This officer is 1) to make sure that piles of robe material do not become too massive, and 2) to oversee the material's orderly examination, measurement, equal allocation, and distribution to designated groups of renunciants. The process of giving out robe material is done not by the order of the renunciant's coming in or by their seniority, but by the casting of lots made of *kusa* grass.[204]

Lodgings Officers

The most important officer relating to lodgings is the one appointed to assign lodgings to individual renunciants. Two terms for this person are used in the early canon: the *senāsanapaññāpaka* and the *senāsanagāhāpaka.* The *senāsanapaññāpaka* 'assigns lodgings in the same place for monks of the same company.'[205] Those who know the *suttantas,* for example, are assigned lodgings in the same place so that they can chant the *suttantas* together; those expert in the discipline *(vinayadhara)* are lodged in the same place so that they can decide Vinaya questions together; and those who speak on the teachings *(dhammakathika)* are lodged in the same place for their own mutual discussions. Dabba also assigns lodgings together for those engaged in meditative practices *(jhāyin),* for those who speak 'animal or low talk' *(tiracchānakathika)* for those athletic ones 'devoted to bodily vigor' *(kāyadaḷhībahula),* and for those who come in late *(vikāla).* For those who come in late, Dabba assigns lodgings by the light of his own internal production of heat *(tejodhātu),* and it happens that renunciants come in late precisely, and only, to see the physical manifestations of Dabba's psychic powers *(iddhipāṭihāriya).* Dabba points to the dwelling assigned to the renunciant—a cave, rock, hill, grove, or park—with a finger glowing with heat before returning to his own dwelling place for the night.[206]

The other term for the assigner of lodgings is *senāsanagāhāpaka* and it is an alternate and perhaps slightly later term than *senāsanapaññāpaka.* Under both rubrics, the assigner of lodgings is to be endowed with the five qualities, and is to be agreed upon by the silent consent of the Saṅgha.[207] As *senāsanagāhāpaka,* the assigner of lodgings is to count both the renunciants and the sleeping places and to assign each accordingly.[208] Assignments are to be made only for those belonging within the monastic boundary, and assignments of lodgings for the rain retreat can be made only at three times: at the two times for entering the rain retreat (i.e., the day after the full moon of Āsāḷhī and a month after the full moon of Āsāḷhī) and on the day following Pavāraṇā when lodgings can be "reserved" for the next rain retreat.[209]

Additional officers for lodgings include the *āsanapaññāpaka* or 'assigner of seats' whose job it is to appoint seats for the elders who sit down for the recitation of the Pāṭimokkha. As with the other officers, the *āsanapaññāpaka* is agreed upon by consent of the Saṅgha and, if the case of Ajita in the Cullavagga is the norm, this office goes to the one who is also the reciter of the Pāṭimokkha at the time.[210] Another officer, the *navakammika* or 'overseer of new building' is in charge of supervising both the repairs made to old buildings and the building of new.[211] This officer is appointed by consent of the Saṅgha,[212] is in office for the duration of his or her life time, and, according to the Cullavagga account, is given full charge of the upkeep of dwelling places so as not to let the Saṅgha suffer.[213] Finally, as perhaps a later development, there is an officer in-charge of the monastery attendants, the *ārāmikapesaka*. The *ārāmika* or 'monastery attendent' is a non-renunciant who is given over to the service of the monastery by a wealthy donor and who lives with other attendants and their families in a separate village.[214] The supervisor of these attendants, the *ārāmikapesaka,* however, is a renunciant, agreed upon as usual by the silent consent of the Saṅgha, and having the charge of ensuring that the attendants' work is done properly.[215]

In these ways, the materials accruing to the Saṅgha are by and large the property of the community. In keeping with the spirit, at least, of the non-possession ideal for individual renunciants, and with the general opposition to householder culture of taking pleasure in objects of the senses, Saṅgha governance reserves for the adjudication of the community as a whole most decisions about the use, disposal, and care of the four requisites. Moreover, Saṅgha structure adapts in time to the need for fair and equitable oversight over the distribution of requisites and, for this, institutes a series of officers who will act on behalf of the Saṅgha and be above any criticism of favoritism.[216] Individuals cannot, in general, hoard, sell, or bequeath; they can exchange or give (robes) only among designated, mostly internal, groups; and they cannot interfere with the appropriate use of goods and services by others of the community.

Renunciants need the four requisites for survival, however. If property is as Munzer notes "relations among persons with respect to things,"[217] then the renunciant's relationship with the community involves approved acts of individual possession, of both the "verbal-claim" and the "mixing-of-labor" type. The bowl is verbally designated as being for the renunciant at the time of ordination, and is to be cared for daily by the renunciant throughout his career; food is acquired through the ritualized silence and highly disciplined process of the *piṇḍapāta/piṇḍacāra;* the three robes are verbally designated as being for the renunciant at the time of ordination and are made the renunciants' own through acts of sewing, marking, and washing; and lodgings are temporarily owned by the renunciant through acts of care and cleaning.

It is appropriate to say here, then, that property does have a role in the developing personhood of the renunciant and in the process of Buddhist self-integration.[218] If the householder donor is characterized by the proper acquisition and use of wealth, then so is the renunciant: while the householder donor uses and disposes of wealth under the influence of attachment, the renunciant does so with non-attachment, in ways that encourage the loss of individuality and egoism and that foster equitable sharing within the community.[219] A renunciant's growth is thus growth necessarily vis-à-vis property, for there is no time prior to *parinibbāna* when a relationship with material things does not exist.

ENDNOTES

1. Olivelle, *Origin*, p. 60; see also Bhagvat, pp. 155-157.
2. Wijayaratna, p. 48.
3. ĀpDS 2.9.10; GDS 3.11; VDS 10.6, 27; ōS 2.7.1.
4. Horner, *Discipline* 1:xxi, xxii, xlvii.
5. Schumacher, p. 54.
6. Horner, *Discipline* 1:xlvi-xlvii.
7. D 2.77-78. Schopen shows that not only, in slightly later times, do monks have and use private wealth, but that they are active donors, (giving gifts from their own wealth), buy and sell, and continue to inherit family

property even after their going forth. Schopen, "Death and Division of Property," pp. 482-483; "Monastic Law Meets the Real World," pp. 105 107, 108-109, 115, 123.

8. Rājavaramuni, p. 40.
9. Vin 1.58. A good discussion of what in the jungle is thought to be "owned" by the local ruler and what not (and therefore available for "finding") occurs in Vin 3.44.
10. Munzer, pp. 74, 267. As Wheeler (p. 172) notes: "A person can without violating rights do as he wishes with what is unclaimed or discarded."
11. Locke, p. 17; Tully, p. 159.
12. Rose, p. 11; see Munzer, pp. 58, 67, 75, 131.
13. Locke, p. 18; Tully, p. 160.
14. Tully, p. 164; Munzer, pp. 17, 23.
15. Kane (2.2:841) understands the traditional definition of *dāna* to be as follows: the cessation of one's ownership over something with the concomitant acceptance of another's ownership over the same thing.
16. Rose, pp. 54, 56.
17. Wijayaratna, p. 36.
18. Rose, pp. 12-14.
19. *Ayan te patto, ayaṃ saṃghāti, ayaṃ uttarāsaṅgo, ayaṃ antaravāsako, gaccha amumhi okāse tiṭṭhāhi* (Vin 2.94).
20. *Idaṃ saṃghassa kaṭhinadussaṃ uppannaṃ. saṃgho imaṃ kaṭhinadussaṃ itthannāmassa bhikkhuno deti kaṭhinaṃ attharituṃ* (Vin 1.254).
21. Zysk, p. 40; Vin 4.122.
22. Vin 3.45-46.
23. *Agārasmā anagāriyaṃ pabbajati* (D 1.18, etc.).
24. E.g., Vin 4.169, 185; Vin 1.192, 194; Vin 2.107-108.
25. "Those who had gone forth into homelessness were to withstand all temptation and ambition offered by life 'in the world,' they were to be beyond the reach of its quarrels, loves and hatreds. For, if they continued to behave as those who had not gone forth, their supporters would fall away, the non-believers would think but little of them, and the believers would not increase in number" (Horner, *Discipline* I:xxiii).
26. Vin 4.167, 178.
27. Vin 4.167, 213, 235; Vin 1.193; Vin 2.1.
28. Vin 4.213, 236.
29. Vin 1.159-178.
30. Misra, p. 97.
31. "Buddhist economics is the systematic study of how to attain given ends with the minimum means" (Schumacher, pp. 54-55).

32. Radin, pp. 957-961; see also Munzer, pp. 85, 137. On an account of the Hegelian view, see Munzer, pp. 57-68, 75.

33. Radin, p. 957.

34. Radin, pp. 960-961.

35. Schumacher, p. 52.

36. Bhagvat, pp. 124-26; S. Dutt, *Monks and Monasteries*, pp. 49-51.

37. S. Dutt, *Monks and Monasteries*, p. 50. Although its use outside the Buddhist context is reflected in an Artha Śāstra passage concerning guilds, once adopted by the Buddhists, *saṅgha* is "so fixed that it rarely convey[s]...any other idea than the Buddhist community of monks and nuns" (Artha 3.14.8; see Bhagvat, pp. 125-26).

38. Horner, *Discipline* 2.xvi. While S. Dutt contrasts the Saṅgha as the body of persons making up the association with the Saṅgha as the bond of association that ties that body together (S. Dutt, *Monks and Monasteries*, p. 20), and Prebisch distinguishes the *āryasaṅgha* or 'spiritual elite' from the *saṃvṛtisaṅgha* or the ecclesiastical or monastic unit (Prebisch, *Monastic Discipline*, p. 3), the term is used here only to describe the latter, that is, the corporate body/bodies of monks and nuns whose members act together in a cooperative life.

39. *Cātuddisa saṅgha* or *cātuddisa bhikkhu saṅgha* (Vin 1.305; Vin 2.147, 164).

40. S. Dutt, *Monks and Monasteries*, pp. 56, 82-84.

41. Vin 3.28, 47, 74, 92; 4.154; Vin 1.321.

42. Vin 1.106.

43. M 3.60.

44. I.e., the fathers of the Saṅgha, the leaders of the Saṅgha (S 2.73-74, 76-77). On the modeling of the Saṅgha on the political system of the *gaṇa-saṅghas*, see Chakravarti, pp. 55-58.

45. Bhagvat, p. 148.

46. E.g., Bhagvat, pp. 126-27; Misra, pp. 205-210; Warder, p. 38; S. Dutt, *Monks and Monasteries* pp. 85-87.

47. D 2.80.

48. Green says "a rule of equal distribution of scarce vital resources...is the fundamental rule of choice in the most rudimentary situation of distributive conflict... Equality of possession or equal access to goods needs no justification because it follows directly from the requirement of free consent by all" (Green, p. 218-220). See Munzer, pp. 191-93.

49. *Te lābhā dhammikā dhamma-laddhā antamaso patta-pariyāpanna-mattaṃ pi tathārūpehi lābhehi appaṭivibhatta-bhogī bhavissanti sīlavantehi sabrahmacārīhi sādhāraṇa-bhogī* (D 2.80).

50. Artha 3.14.18. On communal ownership of land during the early Buddhist period, see Chakravarti, pp. 87-89. Other scholars, like Misra, find some consensus that individual ownership of land is becoming customary among householders during this period. Misra, pp. 242-243.

51. A 1.23-26.
52. Radin, p. 958.
53. See Chakravarti, pp. 10-12.
54. D 2.154; Sn no. 556.
55. Misra, pp. 108-110; S. Dutt, *Monks and Monasteries,* p. 75.
56. S. Dutt, *Monks and Monasteries,* p. 80; see pp. 81-82, 92.
57. Horner, *Discipline* 5:xii-xiii.
58. S. Dutt, *Monks and Monasteries,* pp. 84-91; Horner, *Discipline* 2:xiv.
59. S. Dutt, *Monks and Monasteries,* p. 87; Bhagvat, p. 121.
60. Vin 3.199, 229; Vin 2.85, 97-99, 199; Horner, *Discipline* 2:xviii; 5:viii, xix.
61. Vin 2.239; see Bhagvat, pp. 128-29.
62. Bhagvat, p. 148.
63. Olivelle, *Origin,* p. 60.
64. S. Dutt, *Monks and Monasteries,* pp. 86-87.
65. Radin, p. 958.
66. *Saṃghassa dinnaṃ...pariccattaṃ* (Vin 3.266).
67. Vin 4.40, 43, 45-46.
68. Bhagvat, pp. 155-57.
69. Wijayaratna, p. 48.
70. M 3.253-57.
71. Vin 3.237; Vin 1.245.
72. M 3.253-57; see also Vin 1.236-37.
73. Vin 2.269-270.
74. Vin 2.109.
75. M 1.153.
76. A 2.54.
77. 'Monks, food given for your own enjoyment is not then to be given away (Vin 2.269-270).
78. Says Horner: "a monk had power to dispose of a robe in his possession, either by exchange or assignment, a point which wars against the view that the Order is the owner of the robes, even after they had been allotted or assigned to individual monks" (Horner, *Discipline* 2:xxxii).
79. Wijayaratna, pp. 48-49.
80. Vin 3.254-55.
81. Bhagvat, pp. 128, 155.
82. Vin 1.304-305.
83. Vin 4.248-254.

84. Vin 3.265-66; 4.155-57.
85. Gombrich, *Theravada Buddhism*, p. 99.
86. Wijayaratna, p. 48.
87. Wijayaratna, pp. 49-50.
88. Vin 1.94.
89. Vin 1.90. Although some monks like Upananda are known to be especially skilled in robe-making *(cīvarakamma)* (Vin 3.240), the *kaṭhina* process in all detail (Vin 2.115-17; Vin 1.253-54) is enjoined upon the individuals in the community.
90. Vin 4.120-21.
91. Vin 4.245-46, 284-285; Vin 1.196-98. A renunciant cannot, however, accept robe materials from more than one community (Vin 1.300-301).
92. Vin 1.255; M 3.124-26. There are recorded instances, however, of renunciants making robes for another, e.g., for the Buddha (M 1.437-39).
93. Horner, *Discipline* 4:356n. Moreover, it is the individual—*puggalassa deti*—who receives robe material as one of the eight channels of giving (Vin 1.309). The Buddha lays out fourteen different levels of individuals who can receive offerings, graded from Tathāgata on down to an animal. Like gifts to the Saṅgha, gifts to individuals who have reached at least the fruit of the *sotāpatti* stage yield an immeasurable return and, in the Vinaya, are given a clear endorsement in the donation process (Vin 1.253-57). Interestingly, of all the individual monks noted as receiving robes (e.g., Vin 3.213-19, 260-62), the one personally receiving the most is the monk Ānanda, the private attendant of the Buddha and a charismatic facilitator of lay-renunciant relations. This monk is often abused for his disciplinary lapses—including the acceptance of these several large hoards of robes.
94. Vin 3.210-13.
95. Vin 3.213-15.
96. Vin 4.332.
97. Wijayaratna, p. 47.
98. Vin 3.209; 2.59-60; see Wijayaratna, pp. 80-81.
99. Vin 1.287-89; Vin 3.195-97; Wijayaratna, p. 48.
100. Vin 4.59-60.
101. Vin 4.121-22.
102. Vin 3.254-55.
103. Vin 1.297-98.
104. Vin 4.285.
105. Vin 1.308-309.
106. Vin 1.282-83. Such rags are only allowed to be taken if the body in question has decomposed (Vin 3.58).

107. Vin 3.195-97.
108. Vin 4.245-46.
109. Vin 1.306-308.
110. Vin 1.303-305. Schopen notes a section of the Mūlasarvāstivāda Vinaya in which one monk promises his possessions to another "monk on the condition that the second monk will take care of the first in his final illness." "Monastic Law Meets the Real World," p. 109.
111. Vin 3.240-41; Vin 2.115-17; Vin 1.254, 300-301.
112. Vin 3.205-207.
113. Vin 1.90-91, 93-95.
114. Vin 3.242-44; 4.243-45.
115. Vin 3.244-48.
116. Horner, *Discipline* 2:xv.
117. Vin 3.242-44.
118. Horner, *Discipline* 2:123n.
119. Vin 3.244-48.
120. Vin 1.303-305.
121. Vin 2.212-15; Vin 4.89-90, 92-94.
122. Vin 4.193.
123. Vin 3.59.
124. Vin 2.269-270.
125. Vin 2.270.
126. Vin 2.212.
127. Vin 4.302-303; see Vin 4.285-86.
128. Vin 4.248-250.
129. Vin 3.251; Vin 1.209.
130. Vin 2.208.
131. Vin 3.65.
132. E.g., *cīvaraṃ paribhuñji...piṇḍapātaṃ paribhuñji...senāsanaṃ paribhuñji...gilānapaccayabhesajja-parikkhāraṃ paribhuñi* (Vin 4.30).
133. Vin 1.212, 215.
134. Vin 2.15.
135. Vin 3.237; 4.66.
136. Vin 4.67, 180.
137. Often named in this more enduring of *dāna* relationships are the monks Ajjuka, Upananda, Pilindavaccha, and Sudhamma, the nun Thullanandā, and the donor Citta, and this peculiar relationship of renunciant to donor is often one of adviser, monastic liaison, or spiritual mentor to members of the family (Vin 3.61, 66, 67, 155; 4.98).

138. A 1.274-75.
139. E.g., Vin 4.155-57; Vin 2.154-59; Vin 1.237-38.
140. Wijayaratna, pp. 25-26.
141. *Āgatānāgatassa cātuddisassa saṃghassa* (Vin 2.147).
142. Wijayaratna, p. 26.
143. E.g., Vin 2.162, 164, 170, 171.
144. Vin 2.166; Vin 1.139, 141; Vin 4.41-42, 43, 44-45, 46.
145. Vin 2.169; Vin 1.139.
146. M 1.353.
147. M 2.163.
148. Vin 4.39-40; Vin 2.149-50, 170, 174.
149. Vin 2.149.
150. Vin 3.149-155.
151. Vin 2.278.
152. Unlike in the case of Jain renunciants, for whom there is substantial ruling about the need to beg from donors for a domicile (ĀS 2.7.1.1-6; 2.7.2.1-15).
153. This is so in order to ensure that there is no injury to living creatures, and that there is provision for open space around the building (Vin 3.148-155).
154. Vin 3.155-57.
155. *Saṃghabhedaka* (Vin 2.159-160, 172-74).
156. *Saṃghassa saṇṭhāna* (Vin 3.158-160; Vin 2.73-80, 166-67).
157. Vin 4.304-305.
158. Vin 2.167.
159. Vin 2.208.
160. *Saṃghassa katikasaṇṭhāna* (Vin 2.208, 210-211).
161. Vin 2.174-75.
162. Vin 2.208-211.
163. Vin 2.218.
164. Vin 2.217-226.
165. *Samānasaṃvāsaka* (Vin 1.132-34). Among instructions for co-residence are that a renunciant cannot be thrown out of a *saṅghika* dwelling in anger (Vin 4.44-45, 292-93), a preceptor is required to conduct himself properly with regard to the pupil sharing his cell (Vin 2.227-231), and monks and nuns are each given access to any food of the other that has been stored in abundance (Vin 2.269-270).
166. Vin 2.177; A 3.275.
167. Vin 4.50; see M 3.270-77.
168. Vin 2.84.

169. Misra, p. 109.
170. S. Dutt, *Monks and Monasteries,* p. 75.
171. Horner, *Discipline* 1:xlviii.
172. Artha, book 2.
173. Horner, *Discipline* 2:xvii.
174. As seen in Gotama's affirmation of honor due to elder monks in the Mahāparinibbāna Sutta and in such practices as reserving the best seat, water, and alms according to seniority (Misra, p. 127).
175. Vin 2.162.
176. E.g., Vin 1.109, 254.
177. Vin 2.84.
178. Vin 3.246-47; Vin 2.177; A 3.275; Bhagvat, p. 154; Horner, *Discipline* 2:xvii-xviii.
179. Vin 2.175-76.
180. Horner, *Discipline* 2:xxxvii.
181. *Saṅghabhatta,* a meal for the whole Saṅgha; *uddesabhatta,* a meal by invitation; *salākābhatta,* a meal for those selected ones with tickets; *pakkhika,* a fortnightly meal at the waxing or waning of the moon; *uposathika,* a meal on the Uposatha day; and *pāṭipadika,* a meal on the first day of the fortnight. See Misra, p. 126.
182. Wijayaratna, p. 64.
183. Vin 3.158-59; Vin 2.74-75.
184. Vin 3.160-170; Vin 2.76-80.
185. Vin 4.37-39.
186. *Asaṃbhogaṃ saṃghena karotu* (Vin 2.124-27).
187. Vin 2.15-18.
188. Vin 2.176; Vin 4.38, 155; A 3.275.
189. Vin 2.176; Vin 4.38, 155; A 3.275.
190. Vin 2.176; Vin 4.38, 155; A 3.275.
191. Vin 3.250-51; 4.86-87.
192. Vin 1.284-85; Vin 2.176.
193. Vin 2.269-270.
194. Misra, p. 126; see Wijayaratna, pp. 64-65.
195. Vin 1.238-240.
196. Olivelle, *Origins,* p. 61; see also S. Dutt, *Monks and Monasteries,* pp. 58-59.
197. Horner, trans., *Middle Length Sayings* 3:201.
198. M 3.157.
199. Misra, p. 125.

200. Vin 1.283; Vin 2.176; A 3.274.

201. Vin 1.283-284.

202. Vin 1.284.

203. Vin 1.284-85; Vin 2.176; A 3.274.

204. Vin 1.285, 299-300; Vin 2.176; A 3.275. Two other officers of the Saṅgha pertain here as well. The *sāṭiyagāhāpaka* or 'receiver of undergarments' and the *appamattakavissajjaka* or 'disposor of trifles' are, like the other officers, to be of the five designated qualities and to be appointed by the consent of the Saṅgha. While the former's duties are clear, the latter is in charge of such things as needles, scissors, sandals, waistbands, bindings, and certain designated foodstuff (Vin 2.177; A 3.275).

205. The term *senāsanapaññāpaka* or 'assigner of lodgings' is used in the context of Dabba the Mallian who, as noted above, completes his spiritual training and wants to serve the Saṅgha in some way. The result of his conversations with Gotama is that he becomes the *bhattuddesaka* or 'assigner of meals' and the 'assigner of lodgings' by silent agreement of the Saṅgha.

206. Vin 2.74-76; Vin 3.158-160; 4.37-39.

207. Of being unswayable through partiality, hatred, stupidity, and fear, and knowing what is assigned and what not (Vin 2.166-67, 176).

208. If sleeping places are left over, he is to assign by dwelling place, if dwelling places are left over he is to assign by cell, and if cells are left over he can assign additional shares.

209. Vin 1.137; Vin 2.166-67.

210. Vin 2.305; see also Vin 2.160-63.

211. Vin 2.15; Vin 4.211; see also Vin 2.119, 159-160; Vin 3.81.

212. Vin 4.211.

213. Vin 2.172-74.

214. Vin 3.248-252; Vin 1.206-209; see Gombrich, *Theravada Buddhism,* p. 102, and Schopen, "Death and Division of Property," p. 476.

215. Vin 2.177; A 3.275.

216. Horner, *Discipline* 2:xxxvii.

217. Munzer, p. 17.

218. Munzer, p. 85.

219. See the discussion in Ornatowski, p. 201.

CHAPTER 8

Monastic Strategies for Encouraging *Dāna*: Curbing Misbehavior and Generating Goodwill

The care the early Buddhist community takes in formulating an internal understanding of rights to use and disposal of property is a function not only of its philosophical integrity but also of its donor proximity. The expanded number of people in need of things, and the transformed context in which those needs can be met, put renunciants on notice that donation of the four *parikkhāras* is not preordained by hospitality duties impinging upon the donor, but is a result of a donor's free and open choice based on his or her sympathy and goodwill. The shift in obligation, from the donor to the renunciant, means not only that the renunciant has to win over the donor initially but that he or she has to keep on winning over the donor for the duration.

To this end, then, several strategies are devised in order to capture donors' attention within the marketplace of current young religious movements, and to bind their attention to this particular movement for the long term. The most important of these strategies is the development of a doctrinal soteriology for householders that deals with proper acquisition and use of wealth and that provides a clear status-producing system of merit for those who give to the Saṅgha. Two other strategies, however, are more clearly oriented toward the day-to-day interaction of householder and renunciant, an interaction shaped so as to bring the householder firmly into Buddhism: first, the serious hearing given to householder complaints about renunciant appearance and behavior that gives householders a role in shaping the external signs of renunciant practice; and, second, a developed sensitivity to householder expectations of renunciant practice that attracts their attention to the young institution and that maintains their goodwill and confident sympathies towards it.

CURBING MISBEHAVIOR: THE GUIDING HAND OF THE BUDDHIST DONOR

From early on, serious hearing is given to householder complaints. Donor opinion is crucial and, increasingly, householders of all backgrounds are made to feel comfortable in appraising renunciant life critically and in shaping it to suit their expectations. Narratives show that monks' and nuns' behavior becomes "misbehavior" at points when donors object to something that doesn't fit their notions about how to live in a way that expresses otherworldliness. To be sure, the behavioral appearance of the renunciant is a function of constraints set by the Buddha and renunciants themselves, but it is also often a function of the complex reciprocal relationship the Saṅgha has with a partisan and highly judgmental world outside. The guiding hand of the Buddhist donor is allowed to reshape behavior in whatever way suitable, so long, from the Buddha's point of view, as it is in conformity with living by the middle way. While the early Vinaya reflects many of the ways 'the people' *(manussā)* encourage the renunciants to set their own straight and narrow, donor intervention derives from their sense of having a stake in the young Buddhist institution. The posture encouraged by the early community, then, is of an institution that is not isolationist but wholly involved in discussion with its donors.[1]

Vinaya rules appear on "the surface...[to be] not much more than an attempt to restrain unsuitable behavior," but they can result, as Horner points out, in "the kind of positive conduct to be pursued by the monk who wishes his life to be externally blameless."[2] Normally, a canonical rule has a narrative setting[3] that describes a specific occasion thought to give rise to the rule. The stock formula of the narrative most often focuses on the improper conduct of a renunciant, report of it to the Buddha, and the Buddha's adjudication, often involving some kind of punishment.[4] Thus, a rule is framed when

> *someone, lay-followers or the more dependable monks and nuns, has seen, heard or suspected a mode of behavior which seemed to them unfitting in a member of one of Gotama's Orders. Each rule is, therefore, very possibly the direct result of some actual event, and is not made with merely hypothetical cases of wrong-doing in mind.*[5]

Whether the preserved narrative setting is in fact a reliable report of the origin of the rule or not,[6] the bulk of these settings make clear that the Pali tradition reflected in these narratives places the initial impetus for many Vinaya rules in what Bhagvat calls the "wagging tongue of the public."[7] Judging by its frequency, public opinion plays a considerable role as one of several catalysts in initiating the formulation of a new rule. Says Bhagvat:

> *...the public tongue is always an efficatious reformer...[the] rules made on account of public comment are innumerable...[the] slightest mishap or shortcoming of the Bhikkhus did not escape public detection, and consequently their scornful remarks thereon.*[8]

Because it is important that Buddhist renunciants not look nor act like householders, the continued nudging by donors like Bimbisāra, Jīvaka, Meṇḍaka, Visākhā, and Anāthapiṇḍaka is indispensable in the shaping of early codes of behavior.[9] Thus, "the success of the Early Buddhist experiment in monasticism must be in great part attributed to the wisdom of constantly considering the susceptibilities and criticisms of the laity."[10]

The Householder Complainants

Because isolation "from society...[is] never the cue of Buddhist monachism,"[11] the role of non-renunciant sympathizers of early

Buddhism in shaping the appearance and behavior of renunciants is significant. To be sure, criticism of (or attention to) an offense is often initiated within the community itself: by the offending renunciant,[12] by Gotama,[13] or by other monks and nuns. 'Modest' *(appiccha)* monks and nuns, in fact, are the group most often cited as observing aberrant practice in one of their fellows and as reporting their observations for adjudication.[14] Other monastic critics include monks who are elders *(therā bhikkhū),*[15] groups of several monks *(sambahulā bhikkhū),*[16] and female probationers *(sikkhamānā),*[17] and in many cases "these various classes of critics put forward their complaints because they personally...[have] been in some way adversely affected by the monks' behavior."[18]

Non-renunciants of all kinds play a role as well. Although the texts don't discuss the unsuccessful attempts by donors to mold renunciant behavior, the breadth of the successful attempts is indicative of consistent Buddhist attention to donor watchfulness. Lay men and women keep a sharp eye out for what they see to be unacceptable deviations in monastic life and actively move to correct them by encouraging the adjudication of Saṅgha leadership in all cases.[19] Gotama, in fact, teaches that lay followers, if they want, can express disapproval of a monk who exhibits qualities that may bring material loss, physical or mental harm, or group disharmony to householders themselves.[20] Lay-followers like Visākhā are especially vigilant in pointing out "unsuitable behavior" in renunciants and, as Horner notes, Visākhā is a particularly "trustworthy woman lay-follower... instrumental in bringing to all reliable women lay-followers the responsibility of procuring investigation into a monk's conduct, if she...[sees] him sitting secluded with a woman."[21] Horner wisely, however, cautions against reading into these passages "a somewhat misleading notion of the amount of association between the monks and lay people."[22]

The general role of the householder in relation to monastic practice is important. In the Cullavagga account of the First Council, Mahā Kassapa says:

> *there are rules of training for us*
> *[renunciants] that affect house-*

> *holders and that householders know concerning us, [whereby they know]: "this is certainly allowable for Sakyaputtiya religious, this is certainly not allowable."*[23]

According to the text, after Gotama's death, the community decides against tampering with rulings made previously and, in so doing, confirms the culture reflected in Vinaya and Nikāya texts that allows householders to pass judgment on the appearance and behavior of Buddhist renunciants. This culture recognizes not only that renunciant behavior directly affects the lives of householders but also that it encourages or hinders their proclivity to donate requisites to the community.

The public from whom Gotama recognizes complaints made against renunciants covers a wide range of people—from poor workmen[24] and prostitutes[25] to kings.[26] In the narrative surrounding the rules, however, public opinion is generally designated by the term *manussā* 'people' or 'folk.'[27] In many places, it is the *manussā* 'people' who, like the 'modest monk,' see aberrant monastic practice and whose complaints bring new rules and rectifications. One of the standard formulas for introducing the complaint is that 'people become vexed, annoyed, and angry, saying "How can these religious, these Sakyaputtiyas,"' commit this offense? [28] Sometimes, the people laugh at the renunciants, as when they see a monk hiding sheep's wool under his robe;[29] sometimes they are personally affected by a renunciant's deviant behavior;[30] but most often they complain because they want the institution they give to to be deserving. The people *(manussā)* are confident about bringing their complaints of aberrant behavior to the Saṅgha because of their substantial patronage of monastic life: using the "merit-field formula," the people want to support only those religious renunciants who are worthy and they want to make sure, through their complaints, that those they do support are in fact worthy.

The basis for listening to the *manussā* is the Buddhist posture that it is a religion *bāhujañña* 'belonging to the people,'[31] that the spread of Buddhism is to take place through the preaching for the good of the many.[32] For this reason, the words and actions of the renunciant have to be *bahujanakantā* 'enjoyable to the many folk' and *bahujanamanāpā* 'pleasing to the many folk.'[33] Although the folk noted here may include the *puthujjanā* 'the ordinary people,' a term signifying those with unformed or uninformed views but who are open to hearing the Dhamma,[34] those who at the moment know little of the Dhamma are less likely to initiate change in monastic practice. Rather it is the *manussā* who ordinarily bring aberrant practices to the attention of Gotama and the Saṅgha elders, for they are characterized as responsible and informed reporters, whose views are considered significant in shaping the visible practice of monks and nuns. While the *manussā* have no role in classifying the type of legal situation involved,[35] nor in actually promulgating monastic law,[36] their role, when appropriate, is to initiate the process, and their matters of concern are listened to when they pass on reliable reports. Thus, because early Buddhism is committed to preaching among peoples, it is also committed to being molded by them.

The Nature of the Misbehavior

In a teaching preserved in the Aṅguttara Nikāya, Gotama warns monks that lay followers can express their disapproval of a renunciant based on any one of eight grounds.[37] Although some of these grounds relate directly to the householders' status as donors, for whom loss of property and community fragmentation through renunciant actions will almost certainly result in the falling away of that donor from the Buddhist community,[38] others relate more specifically to perceived problems within the renunciants' spirituality. Un-Dhammic behavior, behavior that suggests ignorance of or hostility to the young Buddhist tradition, is a common ground of criticism and, in its most extreme, is described as 'unscrupulous' and 'evil', 'violent' and 'rough:' a behavior marked thoroughly by 'bad habit.'[39] Householders are exacting and meticulous in their observance of monastic practice and the details of their criticism are revealing, both in the degree to which renunciants take liberties in their practice and in the degree to which householders monitor monastic life.

(A) Food

Complaints by the people cover a wide range of renunciant eating. The *manussā* see, for example, that the renunciant's bowls are made out of material too luxurious for non-householders, e.g., gold, silver, pearl, crystal, bronze, glass, tin, lead, and copper, and their complaints result in a rule allowing bowls to be made only of iron and clay. When the people complain about the materials and ornamentation used for bowl-rests, there is a ruling that allows only tin and lead, and no carving on the surface. Likewise, when *manussā* complain about the sloppy care of the bowls they see, new rules emerge again, e.g., full drying before putting away, using a prop to steady the bowl, and using a bowl bag with strap for storage.[40]

Complaints by the people about renunciant behavior during food distribution and afterwards abound: about the greedy positioning of bowls for alms, about special requests for savory dishes, and about the great noise made in the refectory. These specific charges result in new practices supervised under the guidance of a preceptor.[41] On the basis of *manussā* complaint, nuns are rebuked for taking medicinal ghee as food as well as other comestibles normally reserved for times of illness, because they like the pleasure such things bring.[42] On the basis of a layman's report, the nun Thullanandā is rebuked for asking for medicinal ghee and then changing her mind for medicinal oil.[43] And on the basis of the peoples' complaint that the renunciants don't give thanks in the refectory, Gotama encourages giving such thanks and has it take place under the leadership of an elder.[44] Misra suggests that the concern of Saṅgha leaders is to distinguish Buddhism from other movements by having some clear, singular features and that, to that end, they work to avoid confusion among or 'condemnation by the people'[45] in making new rules.

(B) Robes

Popular opinion is often heeded as well in the manner of dress perhaps, as Misra suggests, for the purpose of developing distinctive features for the young movement among its competitors. When people complain about monks wearing woollen clothes with fleece on the outside, saying the renunciants are like householders who enjoy the pleasures of their senses, Gotama forbids the practice.[46] When people complain that a monk's inner robe falls down once while on alms tour, Gotama allows a waistband of exacting detail with a buckle of unprecious materials.[47] When Ānanda's lightweight robes blow about and Gotama allows a block for tying, the peoples' complaints result in this block's not being made of gold or silver.[48] Popular criticism of luxurious waistbands is especially strong in the case of nuns' wear, and Gotama is detailed in his responses to *manussā* complaints of *bhikkhunī* use of leather, fancy weaves, and fringes.[49] When the people complain that monks and nuns are wearing robes of many colors—of all dark green, all yellow, all red, all crimson, all black, all brownish-yellow, all reddish yellow—and robes with fancy borders, Gotama rules against the divergent practices.[50]

Peoples' complaints instigate new rules about the proper use of small knives for sewing robe material,[51] about the prohibition of renunciant use of householder clothes,[52] about a nun's use of a petticoat and a bodice,[53] and about the frequency of getting a new rug.[54] In general, Gotama is exceedingly attuned to what it means for renunciants to be 'wrongly dressed, wrongly clothed, and wrongly attired.'[55] Such indiscretions, usually involving lack of moderation, are not only not conducive to spiritual development, but are also signs to potential donors of renunciant corruption, rendering such a renunciant no longer a 'good channel for gifts' *(dānapatha)* to the Saṅgha.[56]

(C) Appearance

The general appearance of renunciants is scrutinized as well. The treatment of bodily hair is especially significant, and *manussā* complaints about long hair on the head, hair luxuriously combed and hair smoothed with oil are met with rules prohibiting hair longer than two months growth or two fingerbreadths in length and hair smoothed with a comb or oil.[57] Popular opinion results in the norm of shaving the head with a razor rather than with scissors, although scissors can be used if necessary when the renunciant is ill. Monks are supposed to be clean-shaven, and the peoples' complaint about the growing and shaping of beards results in rules prohibiting this, as well as the shaping of other hair on the body. The removal of all-over bodily hair, however, is prohibited through *manussā* complaint (except in the case of illness), as is growing nostril hair long and plucking out gray hair.[58] Based on the complaint of prostitutes who happen to be bathing together with some of the nuns in a river once, Gotama rules that nuns should not let the hair under their arm pits or the hair on their private parts remain unshaven.[59]

When the people complain about monks having long fingernails, Gotama rules that fingernails be cut down to the measure of the finger end, and when the people complain about polish on the twenty finger and toe nails, Gotama rules against it, allowing only the cleaning of nails.[60] *Manussā* complaints result in permission to use an ear cleaner but only if it is made of a natural substances listed in the rule, and not of gold or silver.[61] When the people complain about the use of a mirror or water bowl to see one's reflection, Gotama rules against it except in cases of illness.[62] When the people see monks and nuns adorning their bodies with ornaments around the neck, waist, arms, wrists, fingers, and ears, they complain and Gotama rules against it.[63] When they see monks and nuns putting pastes, powders, and decorative ointments on their faces and limbs, they complain and Gotama rules against it, except in cases of illness.[64] When they see nuns using perfumes, paints, scented baths, and massaging ointments, the people complain and Gotama rules against it, except in case of illness.[65] Again, under scrutiny from the people, Gotama rules more specifically about the use of foot-scrubbers, fans, sandals, and sunshades[66] and, when the *manussā* complain, Gotama forbids riding in a vehicle, except during illness.[67] Many of these complaints by the people arise because they see monks and nuns who, in appearance, look as if they're householders enjoying the pleasures of the senses. Clearly, for these potential donors, such a significant internal act as going forth must hold to the standard that brings with it visible and distinct external changes as well.

(D) Behavior

Open to scrutiny also are the way these external changes shape renunciant behavior. Luxurious treatment of the body is especially odious, and when the *manussā* see renunciants rubbing their bodies against trees and posts, walls and boards, and beads and scrubbers while bathing, they complain that the behavior is too much like that of boxers, wrestlers, and village youth, and Gotama rules accordingly.[68] When they see nuns bathing with chunam and scented clay, the people complain and Gotama rules that only the red powder of rice husks and ordinary clay can be used. When nuns bathe with great noise, in a massaging current, and at the wrong place in the river, the *manussā* complain and Gotama rules accordingly.[69] When nuns are seen massaging their loins, arms, hands, calves, feet, and faces with cow bones, and having others massage them with ointment, the people complain and Gotama rules accordingly.[70] When monks are seen sleeping on beds scattered with flowers, leaning against ornamental cushions, and sharing dishes, couches, and coverings with each other, the *manussā* complain and Gotama rules accordingly.[71]

At the peoples' instigation, Gotama rules against travel in a vehicle, except in cases of illness, against making stores of copper and bronze goods, and against keeping a cut open to the air.[72] Listening to *manussā* complaint, he rules on carrying poles, climbing trees, and responding to forest fires.[73] Gotama acknowledges public criticism in the matter of sneezing: after some discussion and *manussā* complaint, he rules that when householders say 'May you live (long), sirs' *(jīvatha bhante)* to renunciants who sneeze, the renunciants must respond with 'may you live for a long time!' *(ciraṃ jīva)*. This is needed as a concession to householder attachment to lucky signs *(gihī...maṅgalikā)*—a significant capitulation to potential donors,[74] as renunciants normally avoid popular superstitions.

Finally, and perhaps surprisingly, *manussā* complaint is heard in the matter of internal Saṅgha ritual. Popular opinion is decisive in Gotama's decision in favor of entering the rain retreat in a caravan or in a boat, but not in a hollow tree, in the forks of trees, in the open air, without lodgings, in a charnel house, under a sunshade, or in a water jar. Upon the complaint of the lay woman donor Visākhā, for example, Gotama rules against a former practice and in favor of letting people go forth into the homeless life during the season of the rains.[75] Whether this intrusion into more internal matters is a function of Visākhā's high status as a donor or not is unclear, but it does indicate the clear weight given to householder guidance when that householder is in a good position to pay monastic bills.

(E) Lodging

The stories from the Vinaya reflect the importance of *manussā* criticism in practice concerning lodging. In the category of stealing is the story of the monk Dhaniya who, over the course of time, builds several lodgings for himself. At one point, he goes to a lumber yard to get wood and when the overseer repeatedly tells him he can't have any, Dhaniya responds by saying that the wood is a gift to him from the king. The overseer knows better and is surprised at the lie, but nevertheless allows the monk to take the wood. When the chief minister of Magadha intervenes, however, he checks with the king and, discovering the truth, has Dhaniya brought to court; Dhaniya, however, gets only a warning. Hearing this, the *manussā* are outraged and, when they complain, Gotama rules against the offending monk.[76]

Another story illustrates popular disapproval of theft by renunciants. As an example of one of the five great thieves, the Vinaya tells of a certain depraved monk *(pāpabhikkhu)* who favors and cajoles householders in order to receive possessions and requisites for the Saṅgha. These items range from building sites to buildings to furnishings to utensils, and many of them are luxury items. This type of renunciant is called the fourth great thief and, though the text doesn't specifically cite donor complaint, donor complaint is certainly implied in the narrative teachings against such behavior.[77]

In a third example, a group of monks are having huts built with no benefactor *(assāmikāyo),* and thus have to rely on much begging *(yācanabahulā)* and much hinting *(viññattibahulā)* in order to get what they need for building. People soon become annoyed with the monks' behavior and, to avoid requests, run away and hide behind closed doors. Although the *manussā* make no direct complaint to Gotama or to other monks, Mahā Kassapa happens to see the would-be donors fleeing and, having himself tried to get alms food, asks his colleagues why alms food is in such short supply. Hearing of the annoying monks' greedy behavior, Mahā Kassapa tells Gotama who convenes the offending group and rules accordingly.[78] Although the eventual ruling focuses on correcting the regulations for building the hut *(kuṭī),* the teaching leading up to the ruling emphasizes householder criticism of over-zealous and intrusive begging.

Finally, another story describes the clearing of a site, to be used for the building of a *vihāra,* by the monk Channa. In making the area ready for the building, Channa cuts down a tree that serves as a shrine for people in the surrounding area, angering local citizens. *Manussā* criticism focuses not only on the loss of a religious spot but also on the deprivation of life to the tree, a one-facultied *(ekindriya)* living being. When the people complain, modest monks hear them and tell Gotama who then questions Channa. Although Gotama's ruling highlights the problems of *hiṃsā* in the event, the original story places emphasis on not upsetting potential donors.[79]

While some might see these complaints as trifling, it is actually a matter of perspective. In later Buddhist views, whether a monk wears an earring or not may not have anything to do with his inner state, but the early tradition understands that a monk's choosing to wear something like an earring signifies his continuing attachment to pleasurable things. The early disciplinary view, then, believes that externals do matter; more than that, they are one of the clear verifiable markers for attesting to internal spiritual state. That donors can then toy with these externals is a remarkable testament to early Buddhism's flexibility. On issues of Dhamma, however, the evidence for donor intrusion is less obvious. While it is true that there are no overt cases of a lay person objecting to a basic Buddhist doctrine and the Buddha responding by changing that doctrine, many of the teachings are given in the form of dialogues with householders, whose comments and questions during the course of any given discourse probably push the evolution of Buddhist teaching in certain, perhaps unforeseen, directions. It may be, then, that donor influence works indirectly as well as directly in formatively shaping the young movement.

GENERATING GOODWILL: THE STRATEGIC POSITIONING OF THE BUDDHIST RENUNCIANT

Misra points out that what the "Buddha want[s...is] to harbour such a relationship between the Saṅgha and society...[that] there be no room for either of the two to be a hindrance in the smooth working of the other."[80] Thus, the conviction that on no account is the donor to be displeasured[81] is matched by an even stronger conviction that maintaining the goodwill of the householder is a central aspect of any renunciant's approach for material needs. Maintaining the goodwill of the donor is done in many ways, but uppermost is keeping the avenues of communication open so that householders' resources are not drained, their food not refused thus "wounding their spirit of generosity," and they and their families not ever kept waiting.[82] The hope for this goodwill is expressed in the monk Sāriputta's solicitous concern when the generous donor Anāthapiṇḍika becomes ill, a concern founded also in a genuine compassion for another's vulnerability to impermanence: 'So, householder, you are holding up? You are maintaining well? Your pains do not return? There is no return (of the pains) and there is no sign of worsening?'[83] Anāthapiṇḍika is, of course, sick unto death, but Sāriputta's vigilance over his condition reflects a clear sympathy for the patron as an individual.

The openness of communication that spawns what may seem to be excessive solicitation of the donors also spawns a certain presumptuousness towards them on the part of the Saṅgha. A story in the Aṅguttara Nikāya describes an encounter between Gotama and a householder wood-seller in which Gotama acknowledges the difficulty of acquiring goods and of living the householder life, but nevertheless goes on to request that this man and his family give alms: 'Come on, householder, give gifts to the Saṅgha.'[84] The forthrightness of the narrative's depiction of Gotama's request for alms reflects not only the Saṅgha's clear need, but also the perceived power of a direct pitch when made by the master himself. It does not reflect, however, the customary renunciant stance of humility, silence, and passivity that is normal in receiving gifts from donors and may be, though surprisingly, something only one of Gotama's stature can do.

Other members of the Saṅgha are said to make the pitch also, however. The brahmin Ghoṭamukha, having discoursed with the monk Udena, decides to become a layman and to give Udena part of the regular donations given him by the king of Aṅga. When Udena refuses, saying that renunciants are not allowed to accept gold or silver, Ghoṭamukha decides to have a *vihāra* built for Udena to which Udena replies that, if the brahmin is really going to do this, he should instead build an assembly hall *(upaṭṭhānasāla)* for the Saṅgha in Pāṭaliputta.[85] This story is normative in that it upholds the prohibition of renunciants receiving gold or silver and that it underscores the jurisdiction of the Saṅgha as a whole over properties that are lodgings. What is significant here, however, is that Udena willingly enters into negotiations with a donor, that they both recognize his stance as an active petitioner, and that they settle on an object of donation that is mutually acceptable to both parties. This kind of active and mutually reciprocal negotiation is hard to carry out when the force of the disciplinary rules is directed, as it can only be, at the renunciants and when the tool of choice for bringing in donors is mainly the exhortatory power of preaching.

There is at least one practice recorded in the Vinaya, however, in which the Saṅgha can actually rule against a householder donor. Having snubbed the Licchavi Vaḍḍha, a layman, for being indifferent to their complaints against Dabba the Mallian, the monks Mettiya and Bhummajaka are able to persuade him to falsely accuse the monk of seducing the householder's wife. After questioning Dabba and confirming that he's innocent, Gotama turns to Vaḍḍha and pronounces the sentence, 'let the Saṅgha turn the bowl of the Licchavi Vaḍḍha over,' a sentence that prohibits him from eating with the Saṅgha.[86] Although Vaḍḍha later repents and has his sentence removed, and even later enters the Saṅgha and becomes the *arahant* Vaḍḍhamāna Thera,[87] this incident is illustrative of one way the Saṅgha can adjudicate against a layman gone astray. The *saṃgho...pattaṃ nikkujjatu* ruling is imposed on lay followers when any one of eight conditions prevail; should the lay follower then set his or her misbehavior aright, the ruling is revoked.[88] On the whole, however, it is renunciant behavior towards householders that holds the attention of early texts and, in particular, the way in which this behavior can secure donor allegiance for the ongoing support of the Saṅgha

Renunciant Etiquette to Attract Donors

The most powerful lure for any supporter of the Saṅgha is the simple, pure presence of the renunciant in society. The clear spiritual attunement of his or her person, and the disciplined posture of his or her mental well-being, function to draw devotional and material commitment to the young tradition. As Gombrich points out, donors give when the renunciants are authentically perceived as not interested in material gifts:

> *The more a monk demonstrates his indifference to worldly comforts, the more he impresses the laity and comes to be regarded as worthy of their material support. Indifference to comforts thus causes them to be provided.*[89]

The importance of appropriate etiquette and of "decent, polite behavior" shown to householders is paramount, and it is of no small significance that of the seventy-five *sekhiyā dhammā*, rules for training, the first fifty-six focus on the way monks and nuns are to comport themselves when moving among houses for almsfood. These rules are critical because, as Horner notes,

> *...when in its infancy early Buddhism is groping its way, seeking to attract adherents in a very critical world which has a big choice of teachings and opinions before it, when it is in fact competing with other sects, it is necessary for it to do all in its power to make itself acceptable and to arrange its external features in such a way as not to jeopardise any chances of a fair hearing for its message.*[90]

The importance of renunciant etiquette toward potential donors rests on the oft-noted fact that renunciants are dependent upon householders for their material sustenance. Living in dependence upon *(upanissāya)* a certain region of fields and villages[91] means that renunciants have to develop a way of being in the world that places a premium on the social expression of impartiality and selfless humility.[92] Since it is true that a renunciant does not go forth for the sake of robes, almsfood, lodging, or medicine, a meditation to cultivate an ongoing awareness of such a stance is developed.[93] Keeping in mind that 'I have not gone forth from home into the homeless life for the sake of....' any of the four requisites, a renunciant is, then, to be neutral and even-minded toward the materials that may come his or her way.

Following Gotama, the renunciant lives 'forsaking the taking of what has not been given, abstaining from taking what has not been given...taking only what has been given, waiting for gifts to come.'[94] He or she sees that gifts are given to him or her in the same manner that they are given to all renunciants, with no favoritism intended.[95] The manner of acquisition of gifts by renunciants is, interestingly, described in similar fashion to that of the acquisition of wealth by householders: 'righteous possessions obtained rightly' *(lābhā dhammikā dhammaladdhā),* a parallel that emphasizes that, in both these cases (the householder and the renunciant) relationship to property appropriate to one's place is crucial for the development of the person. Proper relationship to property is then extended, moreover, to the whole Saṅgha for the impartiality of the giving is to be reflected in the impartiality of the renunciant's sharing with his fellows in the progressive life of community.[96]

The impartiality and selfless humility that are the foundations of a renunciant's approach to receiving gifts are developed in a detailed training in mindfulness.[97] Among the applications of mindfulness discussed in the Satipaṭṭhāna Sutta, is a pattern of acting in contemplation *(paccavekkhati)* while, for example, one sets out on tour or returns from tour, while one carries his or her robes and bowl, and while one eats and drinks—all of which bring about a dispassionate consciousness of the body not only within the framework of conditional arising but also within the framework of day-to-day material interdependency.[98]

This aspect of *satipaṭṭhāna* 'intent contemplation' is further developed in the Piṇḍapātapārisuddhi Sutta in which Sāriputta is instructed in the specific disciplines of mindfulness important for moving through each part of the alms tour: while entering a village, walking through a village, or leaving a village, for example, a renunciant should be fully conscious of the states of his pleasure or aversion and work to overcome them, of the role of each of the senses in those states, and of the mental reactions to information brought in by those senses. By fully mastering mindfulness of the self in the many ways directed by the *sutta,* the renunciant proceeds through the alms tour completely calmed,[99] a posture certainly noticeable to the potential donor.

Mindfulness in eating is also a focus of mental culture, and the cultivation of eating almsfood attentively is a practice appreciated by onlookers. Attentive eating is not only a sign of spiritual mastery, but also of mature respect for those in the vicinity, and is so important that it is listed in the rules of training.[100] Attentive eating is detailed in the Vinaya, primarily by what it is not,[101] and, while some of the bans, such as that against throwing the bowl-cleaning water containing lumps of rice out among the houses, are clearly made conscious of donor sensibilities, all eating rules are for the further development of a renunciant's mental state.[102] This mature mental state is then reflected in the mindful way a renunciant receives a gift, that is, out of compassion *(anukampaṃ)*:[103] compassion for the merit needs of the donor, compassion for how this gift might deplete the donor's stores, and compassion for the interdependence of all beings.

The appeal of a renunciant for a potential donor is no doubt influenced by the spiritual qualities perceived to be present in the person needing gifts—qualities grounded in a renunciant's degree of mindfulness. It is also influenced by a quality of comportment, a type of social behavior, a degree of polite etiquette, that the renunciant shows to others and especially to donors that is thought itself to be a function of that mindfulness.[104]

Governing all etiquette is the expectation that renunciant acceptance of gifts be done in moderation *(matta),*[105] with the acknowledgement that some gifts are necessary but that gifts in the extreme are highly inappropriate. The grounding of renunciant etiquette in moderation is perhaps most evident in eating *(bhojane)* and, when donors are mindful that food is not taken for pleasure or indulgence but in order to support the body along minimal levels of comfort so as to maximize spiritual fruition, they see this moderation as both essential to renunciant life and manageable for their own pocketbooks.[106] Grounded in moderation, then, the etiquette of eating is a highly monitored activity.

The attractiveness of a renunciant who knows how to comport him or herself within society is nowhere more evident than in the classic discussion of how a monk should walk among houses for alms. The incident that gives rise to the teaching takes place at a time when many monks walk around improperly dressed and with improper self-control. It seems that a certain monk appears at the door of a certain house where the housemistress happens to be sleeping naked on her back. The housemistress's husband, seeing the monk, cries out and accuses him of seducing his wife, but when the wife wakes up she proclaims the monk's innocence. Gotama, in spite of the positive verdict for the monk, wants nevertheless to prevent such an incident from happening again and rules strictly on the etiquette of the alms tour: proper dressing in three robes; composed and mindful walking house to house; with eyes focused a plough's length ahead; silent waiting at the door for food; watchfulness for signs that the housemistress is willing to give; signs of her rising from a seat, wiping of a spoon, or setting out of a dish; downcast eyes by the renunciant during the apportioning of food; the covering of the filled bowl with the outer cloak; and the renunciant's careful turning away.[107] With this closely orchestrated sequence of behaviors at the household door, not only is the renunciant able to test the sympathy and goodwill of the potential donor and her willingness to give, but the donor can likewise test the merit of the recipient by his or her awareness of and sensitivity to issues of donor concern.

Finally, the attractiveness of a renunciant or a group of

renunciants can be undermined by perceived confusion or breach in etiquette. The Anaṅgana Sutta, for example, describes the ways in which blemishes might appear in either attitude or conduct: disagreements about which monk will go in front of which other in the processional walking for almsfood; concern that some other renunciant has worked to get the best seat, the best water, or the best almsfood in the refectory; worry about who has or hasn't given thanks for food in the refectory; and jealousy that some other renunciant is receiving finer robes, food, lodgings, or medicine than one.[108] Although donors may not be able to witness all such grumblings first-hand, information about unbalanced, fraudulent, or immodest behavior certainly reaches them and certainly falls, it seems, on disappointed ears. Preventing such disappointment and attracting donors to the cause, then, is a function of appropriately expressing the Buddhist vision in moderate and balanced social formalities.

Maintaining the Goodwill of the Donor

Saṅgha members' ability to attract donor support by their calm, dispassionate demeanor and authentic spirituality is coupled with a focus on maintaining and enhancing the donors' goodwill. The goodwill of the householder is crucial to the ongoing maintenance of Saṅgha life and renunciants practice care and understanding in their mild encouragements to give, encouragements embedded primarily in their teachings on the use of wealth. The reciprocity of the goodwill relationship that grows up between renunciant and householder is predicated on the hope that all the benefactors will be as forthright and diligent in their offerings as the householder Citta is when he tells the monk Mahaka 'I will work eagerly' *(aham...ussukkaṃ karissāmi...)* to provide materials for all monastic needs.[109] Regardless of whether all benefactors are as openhanded as Citta, however, renunciants are continually mindful of certain issues in donor relations: to refrain from openly demanding gifts, to be aware at all times that giving gifts can be a hardship for donors, to praise donors often, to be exceptionally considerate in taking leave of donors after gifts are given, and to acknowledge the difficulties of giving when resources are scarce.

Although monks and nuns can publicly teach the virtues of wise giving and of the proper bestowal of resources on deserving fields of merit, they are prohibited from demanding gifts outright from donors. In times, for example, when no benefactor comes forth to offer food or robes, renunciants are strictly forbidden from aggressive begging or from hinting to householders for gifts.[110] Not only is the beggar disliked, but the potential donor who might decide not to give when such demanding takes place is put in the position of being looked down upon as well,[111] a position not too conducive to generating or maintaining donor goodwill. Moreover, in the hopes of not appearing too eager to receive gifts, renunciants can seek advice from donors about distributing what they have offered within the Saṅgha.[112]

Maintaining the goodwill of the donor also rests on the acknowledgement that giving can be a hardship. Renunciants are reminded that it is difficult for householders to collect and protect possessions, and that they are fools to hint or ask for things that are accumulated through extraordinary effort.[113] Moreover, the householder life is troubled: full of hindrances and bound to a dusty or obscured path[114] and attached to the enjoyment of the senses and distracted by children[115]—not at all like the free and illumined life of the renunciant.[116] Expecting great things from householders, even for good reasons, then, is not always possible or appropriate.

Praising the benefactor for his or her efforts on behalf of renunciants is another practice for developing donor goodwill. Gotama, for example, thanks *(anumodi)* the great merchant of Rājagaha for the building of sixty dwellings and, in his concluding teaching, says: 'The gift of a *vihāra* to the Saṅgha is praised by the Buddha as being the chief (of all gifts). A wise man, therefore, concerned for his own interests, should have pleasing *vihāras* built for the benefit of those who have heard much.'[117] In this way, thanking and praising a donor is linked with the teaching that such gifts are in the spiritual best interest of a donor. The opposite of one who praises a donor, however, is one who brings a donor family into disrepute and one by whom donor families are corrupted, and while renunciants are encouraged to be the former they are clearly prohibited from being the latter. Bringing a donor family into disrepute occurs when a renunciant's deviant behavior reflects negatively on a donor,[118] particularly in the householder environment, and this process directly undermines any goodwill already developed between the parties.

Taking considerate leave of a donor is also important for keeping good feeling and positive attention in donors. The Bhikkhunī Vibhaṅga tells of a nun who is a regular diner *(niccabhattikā)* at a certain family's house. It comes to the attention of the other nuns one day that this nun, upon leaving, never asks the family for permission to leave. A rule is then established that, except in certain cases, permission to leave from a donor family must be received by a renunciant before leaving, as well as before sitting or lying down on a seat.[119] While special circumstances prevail, the general focus on open communication between donor and renunciant and on the maintenance of certain social formalities are underscored as strategies for preserving householder sympathy towards the Saṅgha.

Finally, maintaining donor goodwill is especially critical in times of famine or scarcity of resources. While there's always concern that a renunciant or group of renunciants does not experience shortage of almsfood,[120] famines do occur[121] and their presence means a slightly altered relationship with those who give food. Times of famine are usually marked by a shortage of almsfood for renunciants, the issuing of food tickets *(salākāvuttā)* to them as a form of rationing, and their inability to find maintenance through gleaning or favor.[122] When this happens, canonical texts describe several kinds of things that can take place: a especially charitable group of donors[123] can get together and provide a meal for the renunciants; the renunciants can go to another town where there's no scarcity, often where there are relatives of one or more of the renunciants;[124] or renunciants can eat in special smaller groups by invitation of the donor, their selection being made known through the issuing of a ticket.[125]

There are, however, several things especially prohibited to renunciants during times of scarcity. Among them are disturbing the earth to find edibles beneath (as such action might cause harm to living creatures),[126] stealing food from householders,[127] and conniving to offer services to householders in return for food.[128] Two things, however, are especially reprehensible during such times. First, renunciants are prohibited from praising their fellow renunciants' spiritual achievements in order to get food for the group—especially if the donors' gifts of food mean their own families' going without.[129] And, second, renunciants are prohibited from excessive begging as it often makes potential donors run and hide in their houses.[130] Thus, no goodwill is fostered by deception and greediness when resources are hard to come by for everyone.

There is positive response, however, when renunciants demonstrate moderation and restraint. When there is scarcity of food once, for example, and only a little food can be offered, renunciants thoughtfully refuse.[131] As behavior during times of shortage becomes an ongoing issue, Gotama eventually has to highlight practices allowable during deprivation; while the Saṅgha's rules on gathering and cooking can be loosened in such times of need, maintaining a strictness in normal times is essential to harmony with donors.[132]

When the Donor's Goodwill is Lost

Equally important in engendering donor goodwill is recognizing practices that put donors off and making serious efforts to avoid them. In this way, for example, renunciants are encouraged not to stay too long in any one place. Not only will they amass too many properties and too many duties, but the continuous contact with householders will produce attachments and tensions.[133] One advantage of the life of wandering, in fact, is avoiding interpersonal stress with donors when, during lengthy renunciant presence, relations become too close for comfort.

No matter how long renunciants stay in one vicinity, however, donors watch their conduct closely even after a gift is given, and the Vinaya records significant donor affront, for example, when the people notice that the food they've given monks is then given over to nuns. While a subsequent rule forbids a renunciant from giving away what's been given to him for his own use and enjoyment, renunciants eventually can give away food given in times of abundance to the Saṅgha, and during even greater abundance to an individual in the Saṅgha.[134] Presumably, the donor goodwill that has been lost through perceived ungratefulness or rejection of the gift is recovered when donors see Saṅgha attempts at equal distribution and avoidance of waste.

Threats to the maintenance of donor goodwill are present in a number of the individual situations that grow up in the early *dāna* context, and many come from too great a familiarity by a renunciant in the affairs of a donor. The monk Sudhamma, for example, who becomes an advisor in the household of the great lay donor Citta, is insulted once when Citta doesn't ask his permission to invite other monks for a meal. When Sudhamma reproaches the householder for forgetting this, Gotama steps in and resolves the case ceremonially and is, fortunately, successful in not losing this pivotal donor's goodwill.[135]

The monk Upananda puts donor goodwill in jeopardy once when he is overanxious in getting robes from the son of a great merchant, and once again when he intervenes in a householder's directives to his wife about the proportion of robes to be given over to the Saṅgha. Although there's a ruling against Upananda's actions in both cases, it's clear that there's frequently too personal an involvement in a donor's gift-giving and that it's often carried out at great peril to the relationship.[136] Other examples of monastic threat to donor goodwill occur when a group of six monks try to appropriate robes already allocated to the Saṅgha, angering the guild that donates them,[137] and when the nun Thullanandā gives robes given to the Sangha by householders back to other householders.[138] Although Gotama is able to rule against both sets of transgressors, the development of rules against offending donors is no substitute for direct expression of authentic spirituality in social relations with householders.

Perhaps the most offensive behavior undermining donor goodwill is the obviousness and aggressiveness that sometimes accompanies petitions for requisites. Renunciants are urged not to cajole householders into giving them excessive requisites,[139] and not to engage in insistent begging and hinting for gifts, especially if the gifts are to be things like sheep's wool.[140] The most blatant and heinous example of pressing donors may be by the monks of Āḷavī who have no benefactor but who want to build huts on their own. Needing supplies, they tyrannize the people of the area with demands for building materials and tools—so much so that the people begin to run away from the renunciants whenever they see them coming. When Gotama is told of this, he rebukes the offending monks and says their behavior will make them hated: 'the beggar is not liked' *(yācako appiyo hoti),* he says,[141] for such action interferes with the natural and normal symbiosis that exists between donor and donee.

When affairs go awry between a donor and a renunciant, one of the options for rectifying the imbalance is the performance of a formal act of reconciliation. The *paṭisāraṇiya-kamma* is one of the five Saṅgha *kammas* that can be carried out concerning a specific renunciant.[142] *Paṭisāraṇiya,* specifically, can also be carried out with reference to a householder if a renunciant has alienated a non-renunciant from sympathy with the Buddhist movement.[143] The most well-known example is the monk Suddhamma who openly mocks and jeers at his benefactor, the householder Citta, and whose action requires a formal act of restitution for normal, harmonious relations between Saṅgha and donor. In this act (kamma), Sudhamma is reproved, is made to remember the details of his offense, and is formally accused under the leadership of an experienced, competent monk; Citta is then asked if he will pardon *(khamāpeti)* him. If the proceedings please the monks present, three times through, they respond in silence, thus effecting the formal act of reconciliation. This act can be carried out for any number of offenses against householders, and the Vinaya makes clear, in its wealth of details concerning offending acts, that negative householder sentiment toward renunciants is a state of affairs to be taken extremely seriously.[144]

The Quid Pro Quo Dilemma: Dhamma for Gifts?

Talk of the need to garner donor goodwill and to avoid donor offense suggests that all Buddhist action among householders is to ensure a steady flow of requisites into the Saṅgha. It also suggests that the particular way to guarantee such a flow is to continue preaching Dhamma to householders. It often appears, for example, especially in the case of an invited meal, that the Dhamma talk given at the end of the meal for the benefit of the householder is a gift in return, a *dhammadāna,* for that which has just been given as requisite to the Saṅgha.[145] Is it the case, then, that the most powerful strategy for encouraging *dāna* is the development of a structure that offers one thing in return for another? Is the promise of spiritual advancement to householders a direct payment for the giving of requisites to the Buddhist community—and is it thus an example of a straight exchange economy?

In answer to possible charges that he might be "singing for his supper," i.e., preaching Dhamma to encourage *dāna,* Gotama responds directly in the negative in the Kinti Sutta. No, he says, the teaching that is the spread of Dhamma is not done for the sake of any of the four requisites, but instead only out of compassion *(anukampā)* and for the welfare of others.[146] The requisites, he implies, appear for the use and enjoyment of the renunciants, much like the resources do and, while householders might find the early Buddhists to be spiritually worthy recipients of gifts and give hoping for their own meritorious reward, the Dhamma is taught to them not in exchange for gifts but out of empathy for the interdependence and transitoriness of sentient beings.

Another passage contrasts Gotama's lifestyle maintenance with that of the householder herdsman, Dhaniya. While Dhaniya is able to maintain himself and his family quite nicely supported by his own earnings, Gotama claims that he's no one's hireling, and that he wanders around the whole world by means of his earnings and therefore has no need for wages.[147] While what sustains Gotama in his worldly wanderings are certainly his spiritual earnings, perhaps the fruit of past kamma, it is a troublesome verse as the only other example of the word for 'wages' *nibbiṭṭha,* is recorded in the Bhikkhunī Vibhaṅga where it clearly refers to material wages earned.[148] Although the conversation attributed to Gotama seems to include a play on words, the point, nevertheless, is that the *quid pro quo* issue is indeed present for compilers and that it is an important one to be addressed.

To delineate the obvious linkage between Dhamma and *dāna* is in no way to demean Buddhist teachings on possession and donation, however, but rather to note that their appearance in Pali texts is no accident and to admire the care and empathy that go into their formulation. Just as Gotama can argue that he does not preach Dhamma in order to get food, robes, and lodgings but out of compassion for the whole world, so the householder of Pali texts can argue that he or she does not give for the purpose of gaining merit but to ensure the welfare of the monks. While the ritual relationships resulting from the teachings can be reduced to the simple interweaving of selfish aims, the integrity of the relationship and its meaning to the participants can only be appreciated as the intricacies work themselves out in detail, for each new case brings the participants back to the spiritual dynamics at play. That things are gained on either side is not the point; that a middle way is found that produces ease and serenity for all involved, however, is.

ENDNOTES

1. S. Dutt, *Monks and Monasteries,* pp. 25, 35.
2. Horner, *Discipline* l:ix; 4:xxiv.
3. S. Dutt, *Monks and Monasteries,* pp. 47, 74; Bhagvat, p. 47.
4. Horner, *Discipline* l:xi.
5. Horner, *Discipline* l:xiv; see Bhagvat, p. 47.
6. Misra, pp. 20-22.
7. Bhagvat, p. 47.
8. Bhagvat, pp. 54-55.
9. Bhagvat, pp. 56-57.
10. Horner, *Discipline* l:xxix.
11. S. Dutt, *Monks and Monasteries,* p. 25.
12. Vin 2.118-19.
13. Vin 1.305-306.
14. Vin 3.111, 120, 128, 132, 137, 175, 177, 191, 195, 209, 227, 239, 245, 254, 256; 2.1, 4, 12, 14, 15, 31, 32, 34, 38, 41, 42, 44, 46, 47, 55, 56, 58, 59, 61, 62, 64, 68, 70, 71, 81, 84, 85, 87, 89, 96, 97-98, 113, 114, 115, 121, 123, 124, 125, 126, 127, 131, 132, 137, 139, 141, 143, 144, 147, 149, 150, 151, 152, 154, 156, 161, 169, 170, 172, 177, 185, 193, 218, 220, 226, 229, 232, 234, 235,

238, 239, 243, 245, 248, 250-51, 255, 258, 260, 261, 263, 264, 265, 266, 267, 268, 269, 270, 272, 273, 274, 275, 276, 277, 280, 281, 283, 284, 285, 286, 288, 290, 291, 293, 295, 296, 298, 299, 300, 301, 303, 304, 305, 308, 310, 316, 317, 318, 320, 321, 322, 324, 325, 326, 328, 329, 332, 333, 334, 335, 336, 337, 338, 339, 340, 342, 345, 346, 349. Horner, *Discipline* 1:xv; 2:ix, xxvi; 3:xxi.

15. Vin 4.173.
16. Vin 4.134, 138.
17. Vin 4.249-250.
18. Horner, *Discipline* 2:ix.
19. Vin 4.248-49.
20. A 4.345-46.
21. Horner, *Discipline* 1:xxxii-xxxiii.
22. Horner, *Discipline* 3:xxi.
23. *Sant' amhākaṃ sikkhāpadāni gihigatāni, gihī pi no jānanti idaṃ vo samaṇānaṃ Sakyaputtiyānaṃ kappati idaṃ vo na kappatīti* (Vin 2.288).
24. Vin 4.75.
25. Vin 4.259-260.
26. Vin 1.153-55.
27. Wagle, p. 37; Horner, *Discipline* 2:xxvi.
28. *Manussā ujjhāyanti khīyanti vipācenti: katham hi nāma samaṇā Sakyaputtiyā* (Vin 3.44, 144, 155, 181; 2.185, 336, 337, 338, 339, 340, 341, 342, 346, 349; see Vin 1.44, 185, 203-204, 287; 2.105, 106, 107, 108, 112, 113, 114, 116-17, 123, 124, 132, 133, 134, 135, 136, 137, 138, 139, 149, 150, 151, 212, 260, 263-64, 266, 267, 271, 276).
29. Vin 3.233-34.
30. Horner, *Discipline* 2:ix.
31. D 2.106; S 2.107; 5.262.
32. S. Dutt, *Monks and Monasteries,* p. 23; Wagle, p. 34.
33. D 1.4.
34. S 3.18, 164; 4.201; 5.381-84.
35. Vin 2.88.
36. The four authentically grounded types of monastic law *(mahāpadesa)* are rules formulated only by recognized authorities: 1) a rule framed directly by Gotama himself (M 1.309-310; Horner, *Discipline* 1:xvi; 4:xxiii; Frauwallner, p. 64), 2) a rule framed at a particular monastery *(āvāsa)* by a Saṅgha made up of elder and learned monks, 3) a rule framed at an *āvāsa* by a group of elder monks who are widely learned *(bahussuta)* and versed in doctrine *(āgatāgama),* and who know the Dhamma, the Vinaya, and the Summaries *(mātikā),* and 4) a rule framed at an *āvāsa* by a single elder monk who is learned in the above same ways (A 2.167-170; Misra, p. 23; Bhagvat, pp. 83-91).

37. E.g., the renunciant has caused loss to householders, has brought misfortune on them, has abused and insulted them, has caused disharmony among them, has spoken reproachful things about the Buddha, the Dhamma, and the Saṅgha among them, or has been seen by them in unfit areas (A 4.345-46).
38. See Vin 3.181.
39. Vin 3.179, 182-84; Vin 2.9-13.
40. Vin 2.112-114.
41. Vin 1.44-45.
42. Vin 4.346-48.
43. Vin 4.248-49.
44. Vin 2.212.
45. Misra, p. 111.
46. *Gihī kāmabhogino* (Vin 2.108).
47. Vin 2.135-36; see Vin 2.185.
48. Vin 2.136-37.
49. Vin 2.266-67.
50. Vin 1.306; Vin 2.267.
51. Vin 2.115.
52. Vin 2.137.
53. Vin 4.339-340, 344-45.
54. Vin 3.227-29.
55. *Dunnivattha, duppāruta, anākappasampanna* (Vin 1.44; Vin 2.212-213).
56. Vin 3.181.
57. Vin 2.106-107; 133-34.
58. Vin 2.134-35.
59. Vin 4.259-260.
60. Vin 2.133.
61. Vin 2.134-35.
62. Vin 2.107.
63. Vin 2.106; Vin 4.340.
64. Vin 2.107; 266-67.
65. Vin 4.341-42.
66. Vin 1.185-87; Vin 2.129-131; Vin 4.337-38.
67. Vin 4.338.
68. Vin 2.105-106.
69. Vin 2.280-81.

70. Vin 2.266; Vin 4.342-43.
71. Vin 2.123-24.
72. Vin 2.276-77, 135.
73. Vin 2.137-38.
74. Vin 2.139-140.
75. Vin 1.151-53.
76. Vin 3.42-45.
77. Vin 3.89-90.
78. Vin 3.144-49.
79. Vin 3.155-57.
80. Misra, p. 129.
81. Bhagvat, p. 68.
82. Horner, *Discipline* 2:xxvii.
83. S 5.381. *Kacci te gahapati khammanīyaṃ kacci yāpanīyaṃ kacci dukkhā vedanā patikkamanti no abhikkamati paṭikkamo sānam paññāyati no abhikkamo ti.*
84. *Iṅgha tvaṃ gahapati saṅghe dānaṃ dehi* (A 3.392).
85. M 2.162-63.
86. *Saṃgho Vaḍḍhassa Licchavissa pattaṃ nikkujatu* and *asambhogaṃ saṃghena karotu,* respectively.
87. Vin 2.124-127; Thera no. 40; see nos. 1162, 1163.
88. Vin 2.125-26. These conditions focus on lay intrusions into renunciant life, abuse of renunciants or the creation of disharmony among them, or lay attacks on any of the three refuges.
89. Gombrich, p. 95.
90. Horner, *Discipline* 3:xxvii-xxviii; see 1:xvii.
91. M 3.10.
92. D 3.77-78.
93. *Na gilānapaccayabhesajjaparikkhārahetu agārasmā anagāriyaṃ pabbajito* (M 1.104-108; A 1.147-48; see A 2.248-49; 3.196-200; 4.228-235, 365-69; 5.98-102).
94. *Adinnādānaṃ pahāya adinnādānā paṭivirato...dinnādāyī dinnapāṭikaṅkhī* (D 1.4; A 4.388.)
95. M 1.379.
96. D 3.245.
97. The Aṅguttara Nikāya teaches that the effectiveness of a gift is due in three parts to the mental attitude of the giver and three parts to that of the receiver; the receiver or the renunciant makes the gift effective by his or her being free from passion *(rāga),* hatred *(dosa),* and delusion *(moha),*

and it is this freedom that is pursued in the development of mindfulness (A 3.336; see D. 3.228; A 3.93-94).

98. M 1.57.

99. M 3.293-297.

100. Vin 4.191.

101. E.g., it does not include greedy finagling for good food; eating with large mouthfuls, an open mouth, or while talking; tossing balls of food in the air; stuffing one's cheeks; sticking out the tongue; smacking the lips; or, finally, licking the fingers, the lips, or the bowl.

102. Vin 2.214-15.

103. M 2.116.

104. See A 3.391-92.

105. M 1.224.

106. A 2.39-40.

107. Vin 2.215-216; M 2.137.

108. M 1.24-32.

109. S 4.291.

110. Vin 3.145; 2.71.

111. Vin 3.148.

112. Vin 1.300-301.

113. Vin 3.148-49.

114. D 1.63; M 1.179; 3.33.

115. S 1.78; A 3.391.

116. M 3.33-37.

117. Vin 2.147. *Vihāradānaṃ saṃghassa aggaṃ buddhena vaṇṇitaṃ / tasmā hi paṇḍito poso sampassaṃ attham attano / vihāre kāraye ramme vāsayettha bahussute.*

118. Vin 3.184.

119. Vin 4.271-75.

120. M 3.155.

121. Misra, p. 248.

122. Vin 3.6, 15; 4.23.

123. Vin 3.6.

124. Vin 3.7, 15.

125. Vin 2.175.

126. Vin 3.7.

127. Vin 3.59, 64.

128. Vin 4.23.

129. Vin 4.23-30.
130. Vin 3.144-45.
131. But when the whole Saṅgha is then offered food, and again the renunciants refuse, Gotama urges them to accept it (Vin 1.214, 215).
132. Vin 1.238.
133. A 3.258.
134. Vin 2.269-270.
135. Vin 2.15-18.
136. Vin 3.210-11, 257-59.
137. Vin 3.265.
138. Vin 4.285.
139. Vin 3.90.
140. Vin 3.227-28.
141. Vin 3.144-49.
142. Viz., *tajjaniya* 'censure,' *nissaya* 'guidance,' *pabbājaniya* 'banishment,' *paṭisāraṇiya* 'reconciliation,' and *ukkhepaniya* 'suspension' (Vin 1.49, 143, 326).
143. Misra, pp. 129-133.
144. Vin 2.17-21.
145. E.g., Vin 1.247-29.
146. M 2.239. See Aronson, p. 9.
147. Sn nos. 24, 25.
148. Vin 4.265.

CHAPTER 9

The Renunciant as Facilitator: The Case of Ānanda

At the point of contact between the two worlds of householder and renunciant—at the human "ecotone" where the worldly ends and the otherworldly begins—a number of figures roost in order to keep this transition zone open and pliable, and eminently responsive. One of these is the monk Ānanda who serves as Gotama Buddha's attendant *(upaṭṭhāka)* and companion *(santikāvacara)*[1] for the last twenty-five years of the teacher's life, scouting out resting places and hospitable donors, mediating the flow of visitors and supplicants to the seat of the enlightened, and often giving Dhamma talks in the Buddha's stead. Chosen specifically by the Buddha after a number of others have already served,[2] Ānanda is loved dearly by his cousin who acts both as father and teacher to him, and who allows him considerable leeway in fulfilling the duties of his office. One of the most important things Ānanda is able to do is to develop the points of contact between householders and renunciants and facilitate, remarkably well, the dynamics of *dāna* practice. At this threshold of contact, the standard hagiography of Ānanda suggests some of the reasons why Ānanda, making strength out of weaknesses, is so good at doing what he does. This last chapter, then, will focus on those aspects of the figure Ānanda that most relate to his mediational work between the lay and monastic life.

For the Buddhist tradition, the most important thing about Ānanda is that he is *bahussuta* (Skt., *bahuśruta),*[3] the one who 'has heard much.' Drawing on the Vedic tradition of revelation *(śruti),* of what is divined by listening with insight, the 'heard much' characterization of Ānanda places him in a unique relation to the Buddha. Because the Buddha is the one to make arise what has not arisen before, a Tathāgata come to teach a teaching not yet spoken in this world age, the words of the Buddha *(buddhavacana)*[4] take on immense importance as they are the first and most foundational of all doctrine that might be formulated. Because of this, when Ānanda is attendant on the Buddha, he is said to hear what the Buddha preaches and, with his great memory, is called upon to recite the Dhamma at what is called the First Council.[5] Whether or not this council ever actually takes place, many Pali *suttas* begin with the phrase *evaṃ me sutaṃ* 'thus I have heard,' in this way directly designating the sermons so noted as the oral testimony of Ānanda.[6] Ānanda's role here is one of witnessing and authenticating important discourses of the Buddha and, thus, of providing the semblance of a historical basis for the delivery of the Buddha's teachings. After Gotama dies, moreover, no one is to replace him as master *(satthar)* and his words, as the origin of the Buddhist doctrine *(sāsana),* will come to an end. The face-to-face encounters that Ānanda has with the Buddha, and that the other first disciples of the Buddha have as well, put them in the unique position of being present during the lifetime of the giver of Dhamma. No one else will hear as these disciples have heard, and no one else will ever be *bahussuta* in the same way that they, and especially Ānanda, are *bahussuta.* Most important is that what Ānanda, and they, have 'heard much' of is religious knowledge, knowledge that is transformative and, ultimately, salvific.

As attendant to the Buddha, Ānanda is a monk of many duties. He goes with the Buddha on his alms rounds and on his walking tours, he stays with the Buddha during the rainy season, and he serves the Buddha in ways that reveal "his 'feminine' ability to perform household tasks."[7] Accompanying the Buddha as his companion, and attending to his material needs as a kind of valet, Ānanda's travels take him across the vast range of the Gaṅgā Valley, across fields and plains, through forest and jungle, over hills and through high passes, and amongst every manner of village, town, and city population that has grown up at the time. The Buddhist tradition is one of conversion in which proselytization and missionary work are the necessary means to growth and development. Although most monks are ordinarily on the move gathering alms and preaching the Dhamma, Ānanda's unique position as attendant to the Buddha allows him a geography of wandering that provides substantial access to the most diverse populations within north Indian rural and urban life.[8]

As a rule, monks and nuns live in a liminal state with regard to householding. Although the Buddhist world is divided between those who form ties with the village and those who do not,[9] the renunciant is not quite fully free from the householding world she or he has left behind. The need for material support, for ongoing converts, and for meeting a variety of responsibilities to the lay, necessitates continued contact and interaction of some sort. That there are several monks and nuns who are especially good at working with householders is, of course, very helpful to the early community. That there is one whom the canonical texts portray as uniquely suited to facilitate this interaction between renunciant and lay, between monastics and householders, is exceedingly provident. The ease with which Ānanda slips into the role of the great facilitator is as much a result of what is perceived as his affable and personable nature as it is of his role as attendant to the Buddha. In so many ways, Ānanda is facilitator not only of the personal needs of the Buddha himself, but of the institutional needs of the Saṅgha as it experiences growing pains in almost every arena. Without Ānanda as the grease that makes the larger community-as-machine run more smoothly, the shape of Buddhism would probably not be what it is today.

ĀNANDA'S CAREER IN THE ORDER

According to one tradition, Ānanda's father is Amitodana, member of the Sakyan clan and brother to Suddhodana.[10] This would make Ānanda brother or step-brother to Mahānāma and Anuruddha, as well as cousin to Siddhattha Gotama.[11] It is suggested that at the time of Ānanda's going forth, the final ordination *(upasampadā)* system is not yet in place, and that Ānanda's *upasampadā* is given at the same time as his admission *(pabbajjā)* to the community.[12] By tradition, Ānanda has a preceptor *(upajjhāya)*, a monk named Belaṭṭhasīsa,[13] as well as other teachers drawn from among the monks present in the Saṅgha. The most important of these is the venerable Sāriputta who shares with Ānanda a mutual respect and friendship. These two monks often travel, eat, and stay together, and they both have a love of studying and teaching the Dhamma.[14] Although Ānanda, like Sāriputta and Mahā Moggallāna, is entitled to settle disputes whenever they arise,[15] and although Ānanda and Sāriputta discuss many doctrinal issues as companionable confreres,[16] Sāriputta is not only the elder in rank and age[17] but the monk noted by all others, including and especially Ānanda, as being the 'one of great wisdom' *(mahāpañña)*.[18] Whenever it should happen that Ānanda and Sāriputta are set side by side, it is Sāriputta who is highlighted and who is acknowledged as the clear discerner of the teaching.[19] Although of brahmin background to Ānanda's *khattiya*,[20] Sāriputta's eminence is due less to caste and more to individual temperament and personal achievement.[21] In the Mahāgosiṅga Sutta, for example, Sāriputta's facility in the Dhamma is so evident that each of the other disciples gathered around him can only respond to Sāriputta's words *yathā sakaṃ paṭibhānaṃ* (each 'according to his own [lesser] capacity').[22] As Freedman points out, however, the structure of the *sutta*, even with its belittling of all the monks in comparison to Sāriputta, is yet especially unfavorable to Ānanda:

> *The list of* bhikkhus *which opens the* Sutta *starts with Sāriputta and ends with Ānanda, while the order in which Sāriputta's question is answered begins with Ānanda and ends with Sāriputta. Both lists support the view that Ānanda, while of notable stature as a* thera, *is below that of the other named* bhikkhus.[23]

The more usual portrayal of Sāriputta's seniority, however, is simply that he is Ānanda's regular teacher: from him Ānanda learns not only the fine points of doctrine but also how to give effective Dhamma talks. In fact, Sāriputta is often part of Ānanda's audience and often the one to tell him 'well done!' after an especially good presentation.[24]

But Belaṭṭhasīsa and Sāriputta are not the only teachers of Ānanda; others instruct him as well. The monk Puṇṇa, son of Mantānī, is said to have preached a sermon to Ānanda that makes him fully understand the Dhamma.[25] And later tradition identifies the monk Vajjiputta as the one who, after Gotama's death, admonishes Ānanda against spending too much time chatting with lay people and directs his attention to attaining his own *arahant*-hood.[26]

One of the great characterizations of the monk Ānanda, then, is his continued studenthood, his openly marked experiences of being a *sekha* 'student, learner.' A *sekha* is one who, though aware of the elements of Buddhist doctrine, is still in training, has still fully to learn, and is still imperfect.[27] Thus, while he or she may have experienced the fruits of the first three stages of training—stream-winner, once-returner, and non-returner[28]—he has not yet experienced the fruit of *arahant*-hood: 'Alas,' says Ānanda just before Gotama dies, 'I am still a learner, and still have things to do in order to reach perfection.'[29] The things a learner has to do to reach *arahant*-hood[30] include training in higher morality, higher thought, and higher insight.[31] The final experience of *nibbāna,* then, which brings an end to the period of *sekha*-hood and upon which one is eligible for the title *arahant,*[32] is the goal of monastic life, and Pali texts are replete with narratives of monks' spiritual trials ending in their full enlightenment.

The stages of Ānanda's quest are hinted at in the canon. Characterized as a *sekha* throughout,[33] Ānanda is nevertheless known as having great insight[34] and as someone who routinely preaches the learner's discourse *(sikkhāpada; sekkhapāṭipadā)* to lay audiences.[35] Although, as Freedman points out, Ānanda can make errors in his Dhamma talks because he is still a learner, in general he has tremendous "ability to expound the Buddha's doctrine,"[36] and many share one householder's view that Ānanda is himself so worthy a monk, and his teaching so clear and wise, that hearing him preach can easily bring the hearer to take refuge in the Buddha, the Dhamma, and the Saṅgha.[37] Ānanda is said to have himself become a stream-winner at the time when, with a group of other Sakyans, he is accepted by the Buddha into the homeless life.[38] There is little if any evidence, however, of his then becoming a once-returner or a non-returner. But the question of his experiencing the final goal, that of *nibbāna,* and thus becoming an *arhant* is much discussed, and the general narrative is that he is unable to reach *arahant*-hood because of his excessive attention and attachment to things of the householder world, and especially to the person of the Buddha. According to the story in the Vinaya, Ānanda, still not an *arahant,* is required to be present at the council called after the Buddha's death in order to chant the sermons he's heard while serving as the Buddha's attendant. Because only *arahants* can attend, special efforts are made on behalf of Ānanda's *nibbāna* and, because they are eventually successful, he is able to attend and recite the Dhamma.[39] Although Ānanda's final spiritual perfection is fully expected, and even prophecied,[40] the "putting off" of his *nibbāna,* purposeful or not—or even his never-attainment of *nibbāna*—is intimately tied to his mediational work between lay people and renunciants.

ĀNANDA'S SERVICE TO THE BUDDHA

At some point after Ānanda's 'going forth' into the homeless life, he is chosen by the Buddha to become his permanent attendant,[41] a position he holds for about twenty-five years until the Buddha's death.[42] Ānanda becomes the Buddha's attendant around the twentieth year of the latter's preaching career,[43] and so is intimately present as the Buddha's personal ministry flourishes and then winds down.[44] A clear account of the choice of Ānanda as attendant, however, is not found in early Pali texts but only in the Manorathapūraṇī, a commentary on the Aṅguttara Nikāya. Freedman remarks that the lateness of this account "should raise our suspicions about the *availability* of information on Ānanda's assuming the role of the Buddha's permanent attendant."[45] The concern here is not, however, as in Freedman's case, discerning the layers of the canon (and, therefore, the historical value of certain accounts), but rather the hagiographic portrayal of Ānanda and, therefore, the "tradition-value" of the material. In the latter, for example, lies the importance of Gotama choosing Ānanda and not vice versa, and Gotama choosing Ānanda and not someone else—issues whose major import are for Buddhist practice, not for knowledge about the past.

Many things endear Ānanda to the Buddha: he is clever and wise, he is sensitive to the needs of the Buddha, and his very presence and his preaching of the Dhamma fill both renunciants and lay with joy and ease.[46] Moreover, his memory is good, he retains all that he hears, he carefully follows established codes of behavior, and he is resolute about his spiritual practice.[47] These characteristics—knowledge about and propensity towards doing service—are fully consonant with the later story told of the Buddha's choice of Ānanda. It is said that, at the twenty years mark of his ministry, the Buddha decides on having a permanent attendant who will be fully respectful of his wishes. All the notable disciples speak up for the position, but the Buddha passes over them when he notices that only one, Ānanda, has remained silent. When the Buddha asks him about his silence, Ānanda replies that the choice of attendant is up to the Buddha—who then, of course, chooses him. Ānanda agrees, but only on the condition that the Buddha not favor him in any way in matters of food, robes, lodging, or invitations, for example—for fear that people will suspect material motive in Ānanda's taking the post.[48] Thus, Ānanda is "called" to the office of attendance on the Buddha, rather than having sought it out himself, but, once called, he becomes a significant, if not the most significant, player in early Buddhist interface with the public.[49]

As attendant, Ānanda's duties are clearly marked. Most importantly, Ānanda is a *bhikkhu,* one "gone forth from the home into the homeless life" and, as such, his baseline is that of an ordinary monk—following patterns of the Saṅgha in tending to donor gifts of food, robes, lodgings, and medicine, to monastic relationships and community governance, and to spiritual practice in his own, perhaps less than zealous, quest for perfection. Becoming the Buddha's attendant, however, lays over this baseline certain new dimensions—all of which draw on valuable resources in the traditional portrayal of Ānanda's own personality.

First, Ānanda's relationship with Gotama Buddha is one of strong friendship, respect, and intimacy.[50] On the one hand, the Buddha acts as both a concerned and loving father, intent on Ānanda's continuing the lineage now established between them,[51] and a stern yet compassionate teacher, intent on Ānanda's knowing the Dhamma well and being able to teach it effectively to others.[52] On the other, Ānanda is not only conscientious about his various duties to this senior, and very special, monk, but would, according to the Jātakas, be willing to give up his life for him.[53] Such a dynamics emphasizes two elements in the canonical portrayal of Ānanda: his charismatic appeal to others (i.e., his "lovableness") as clearly experienced by the Buddha, and his own deep affection for people, as in his emotional attachment to the Buddha.

Second, as noted earlier, Ānanda's auditory and mnemonic skills are extraordinary, and account for the traditionally significant results of his long-term attendance on the Buddha, that of hearing many sermons and being able to repeat them from memory. Although applied to others, the term *bahussuta* is most often an epithet of Ānanda and its application draws on traditional Vedic and Hindu notions of revelation. This is important in Ānanda's case because of the early Buddhist centrality of hearing the Dhamma directly from the historical Buddha. As in the Vedic tradition, where hearing sacred verses as they are spoken by priests is pivotal, immediate access to the *buddhavacana* or 'words of the Buddha' is a powerful tool in one's spiritual quest, especially when the words of the Buddha are spoken explicitly by the Buddha himself.[54] As both consistent hearer of the revelation and transmitter of it to posterity, Ānanda is endowed then with both a gift and a burden.

To have 'heard much' is Ānanda's gift, in that he 'bears the Dhamma' for the present and future community. In receiving the gift, the community takes it in trust that Ānanda has not, as a matter of course, paused to reflect on or rework the Dhamma, and has borne the Dhamma nobly and without intrusion.[55] This same, then, is Ānanda's traditional burden: that he bears, with the Dhamma (because he bears it solely), the responsibility to keep it as accurately and faithfully as possible so that it matches what he has heard. Because to stop and reflect on the Dhamma as he hears it (as a conscientious monk might ordinarily do) may contaminate what he's heard with his own bemusings, Ānanda's canonical restraint, though appropriate, exposes a tension: while he "succeeds" as an attendant by holding the Dhamma faithfully, he "fails" as a monk by not considering it seriously. Such an argument assumes that, should Ānanda consider the Dhamma he is hearing seriously, he would have experienced *arahant*-hood well before the Buddha's death and not caused such a ruckus prior to the First Council. What it doesn't take into account, however, are the many discussions in the Nikāyas on Dhamma that Ānanda initiates or the many Dhamma talks in the Nikāyas that Ānanda gives, both of which are consistent, regular, and plentiful. Such an accounting would lead to the conclusion that, in his life as recorded in Pali texts, Ānanda can do no other than what he does and, indeed, accomplishes just about everything he is able.

Ānanda's close attendance on the Buddha is undoubtedly guided by the *brahmacārin* template,[56] with the great difference that in the Vedic tradition attendance on the teacher is in clear exchange for teachings on the Veda given to the student while, in Ānanda's case, the attendance is a thing in itself with instruction on Dhamma and on Dhamma teaching an almost incidental sideline. An elaborate description of what it means for Ānanda to attend the Buddha is found in the Manorathapūraṇī:

> *He served the Buddha, following*
> *him everywhere like a shadow,*
> *bringing him tooth wood and water,*
> *washing his feet, rubbing his body,*
> *cleaning his cell and fulfilling all his*
> *duties with the greatest care. By day*
> *he was at hand forestalling the*
> *slightest wish of the Buddha. At*
> *night, staff and torch in hand, he*
> *went nine times round the Buddha's*

> *cell and never put them down lest he would fall asleep and fail to answer a call from the Buddha.*[57]

Like others close to the Buddha, notably Mahāpajāpatī, the Buddha's aunt and among the first women to 'go forth,' Ānanda is, canonically, a monk 'of many duties,' 'having much to do' *(bahukicca, bahukaraṇīya)*,[58] and it seems that most of these duties stem from the almost constant company Ānanda keeps with the Buddha. Although the Buddha does go out alone,[59] most often he is accompanied by Ānanda: when the Buddha says "let's go...," Ānanda says "so be it," and they go. Ānanda accompanies the Buddha on alms rounds,[60] on walking tours to preach the Dhamma,[61] and on special visits to householder's homes—to visit the sick, to inquire about a particular householder problem, or to eat an invited meal. Ānanda procures food and water for the Buddha[62] and watches over his eating habits; he takes care of the Buddha's robes,[63] helps him at bath time, and finds him places to stop, rest, and stay over night.[64] Finally, he acts as liaison between the Buddha and the other monks, between the Buddha and lay people, and the Buddha and any special highly ranked religious or political petitioners. In general, Ānanda's regular duties in service to the Buddha include being a conscientious and efficacious assistant to the Buddha in his daily affairs, a neutral intermediary between the Buddha and a variety of groups anxious for an interview with or talk from him, a mouthpiece of the Buddha in charge of announcing schedules, events, policies, and general concern, an accurate and trustworthy repository of the Dhamma, and, most often, an example of virtuous conduct.

For performing these tasks, Ānanda receives praise from the Buddha, other monastics, and the lay. There are times, however, when he's criticized for shortcomings, both in aptitude and in mindfulness. The Buddha praises Ānanda for his understanding of the Dhamma and for his ability to deliver clear, engaging, and insightful Dhamma talks: "that was good," "you answered as I would have," and "your talks are wonderfully received by all who hear them," are the kinds of words Gotama often has for Ānanda. The Buddha also has a high regard for

Ānanda's honesty, for his requests for clarity on doctrinal issues, for his need for confirmation in the Dhamma, and for his sensitivity to any breaches in right view and right conduct. Ānanda is not only a student of the Buddha, but a monk who serves as a model to all for his insight and character. 'That Ānanda,' says the Buddha, 'is a clever man and very wise;' he knows the right time for visitors of all backgrounds to be presented to the Buddha and has four wonderful and marvelous qualities. 'What are the four? that monks...nuns...laymen...and laywomen are filled with joy in his presence and, when he preaches the Dhamma, with joy at his discourse.'[65] Likewise, they are saddened when he falls silent.

There is also criticism of Ānanda, however, and it falls mostly around two issues: that he is weak and slow-witted and that he is unmindful and inattentive in his daily life. When the Buddha says, for example, that even the most backward *(pacchimaka)* of the five hundred monks has become a stream-winner and is assured of *arahant*-hood, the commentator Buddhaghosa notes that this reference is to Ānanda.[66] Moreover, in a number of instances, the Buddha corrects the instruction Ānanda gives to a pupil and urges his attendant to be more diligent.[67] Again, when Ānanda thinks the doctrine of causality is easy, the Buddha says 'this is not so.'[68] And when Ānanda explains the differences in future courses of people, the Buddha cautions him and says that only he, the Buddha, or someone like him can take the measure of a person.[69]

Likewise, in the case of Ānanda's inattentiveness, examples are numerous—either because he really behaves unmindfully *(asatiyā)* much of the time, or because, as the Buddha's attendant, his behavior is especially noticeable and even small aberrations become points of discussion. When Ānanda goes into town with only two of the three required robes for public wear, for example, he is rebuked by fellow monks and then by the Buddha.[70] Again, he once mistakenly wears the robe of another monk, but is not rebuked this time as he honestly thinks that it's his own.[71] (Thus, intention normally counts more than results in matters of judging action.) Again, at the instigation of the Buddha, he gives admission to the wanderer Susīma, who turns out to be foolish and wrong and who realizes that he has gained admission as a 'thief of the Dhamma;'[72] the suggestion here is that Ānanda should have known better than to admit an unready practitioner. Finally, Ānanda disturbs the Buddha repeatedly when he should have discerned, as all the other monks do, that the Buddha is in a state of concentration, and needs to be left alone.[73]

In matching Ānanda with the Buddha as steward and lord, there is an ideally didactic relationship. Ānanda is a highly motivated, diligent, and loyal aide who wants to do the right thing, to learn what he needs to learn, and to be as much help to the Buddha as possible. Portrayed with weaknesses of wit and will, however, the figure Ānanda is the perfect object for the Buddha's instruction and counsel. In that the Buddha's life is a paradigm for the Buddhist career, he can, with Ānanda, give lessons on how to express compassion, how to give Dhamma, how to guide behavior, and how to encourage attention—and thus how to develop skills central to Buddhist life with others. When the Buddha tells Ānanda not to be slothful, to abide carefully by the training, and to follow a teacher for his teaching not his person, the attentive reader of the texts can take heed of this advice, correcting as Ānanda corrected, and using the Buddha's own posture as a model. In stepping into the more humbling role of Ānanda as the receiver of instruction, one begins to learn the breadth of possibilities available in a life of compassion as exemplified by this disciple.

ĀNANDA'S SERVICE TO THE LAY

Ānanda's service to the lay is an extension not only of his attendance on the Buddha, but also of the duties he has and services he provides to other monks. Among his duties, of course, is that of teaching, and with Sāriputta and the Buddha as mentors, Ānanda learns how to preach the Dhamma effectively among his colleagues: he preaches not only in the Buddha's stead (due to sickness or absence) but often on his own as the community's first choice. Monks have great faith in his understanding of Dhamma and often approach him on questions of doctrine; moreover, Ānanda is instrumental in bringing about changes in the admission and preceptorial system with regard, for example, to lowering the age for young men at their entrance into the community and to providing greater flexibility in the length of time to be spent under a preceptor.[74]

Ānanda also has personal and pastoral duties towards other monks. He finds lodging for them,[75] for example, and provides them with robes.[76] He comforts and consoles them, as he does Cunda, who is filled with remorse at having given the Buddha his last and, thus, fatal meal,[77] and he frequently treats those monks who are ill with special medicines. Within the Saṅgha community, Ānanda is one of the few designated to settle disputes,[78] whether they be disagreements about Dhamma or discipline, or personal discord. He can discern that there are "weak" members of a Saṅgha group and is ever concerned about the possibility of a schism within the community *(saṅghabheda).* In the Saṅgha, then, Ānanda works to keep the bindings of the community effective and efficacious and for this he is praised and respected. If there is envy, it is of his closeness to the Buddha, and if there is hostility—as there, sometimes, seems to be on the part of Mahā Kassapa—it is due to favoritism that can be directed Ānanda's way, especially by nuns and the lay.

Attendance on the Buddha and specialized service to other monks are, then, fully in keeping with what seems to be Ānanda's "special mission" to minister beyond the walls of the Saṅgha. By virtue of being the Buddha's attendant, by virtue of the conversion posture of Buddhism—so important for all monks in their relations with non-monastics—and by virtue of his open and sympathetic personality, Ānanda has, as one of his main tasks, to advocate the well-being of all he meets in the outside community. The canon notes that often "the venerable Ānanda...[is] excessively busy imparting matters to the laity,"[79] and the most important of the matters he attends to is the preaching of Dhamma. Sometimes, lay people come to him, and at other times he goes to them; sometimes, he is the main teacher, and, sometimes, he preaches in the Buddha's stead. Ānanda acts as Buddha-stand-in for the lay when the Buddha is tired, sick, or in solitary meditation, when the Buddha is on alms-tour, or when for some other reason he is not around. He can expound in detail on the meaning of a sermon the Buddha has delivered in brief and, should another monk's sermon leave its lay audience unsatisfied, Ānanda can fill in. Ānanda discusses Buddhist doctrine amicably with most—e.g., Dasama, Pasenadi, Sandaka, Uṇṇābha, Subha, and a host of householder lay—but sometimes hostility arises when the hearer has false intentions, holds fast to premises of another religious view, or is arrogantly dismissive of anything different. Often Ānanda preaches on topics the outside community is most interested in, such as the self[80] and meditation.[81] It is evident, however, that, no matter what he preaches on, he is a clear and inspiring teacher and brings many converts into the Buddhist fold—some reach the state of stream-winner, while others reach that of non-returner; some become lay disciples, while others take vows of 'going forth' as monastics.

Ānanda does more with the lay community than preach the Dhamma, however. As he does among his fellow monks, Ānanda witnesses controversy and settles disputes, visits and attends to the sick, and performs certain rituals such as the "safeguarding ritual" that protects against, for example, an outbreak of plague.[82] He is often in the position of bringing bad news, as when he has to tell the Licchavi, Vaḍḍha, that he cannot eat with the Saṅgha,[83] or, tell laypeople something that may offend them, such as exactly how to approach the Buddha with a petition or what the Buddha's rulings actually mean. Ānanda, as some other monks do, develops special relationships with a number of prominent citizens-e.g., Anāthapiṇḍaka, King Pasenadi, Roja the Malla, and several wealthy and well-placed householders—and the canon is filled with testimonials to the power of the encounter lay ordinarily have with him. Ānanda is personally charismatic, open to the great variety of the human condition, and exceptionally compassionate and empathetic. Moreover, his great reputation among the lay depends as well on their seeing him as an authority on the Dhamma—or at least on the letter of the Dhamma, if not always its true meaning. In all, then, as the front man, agent, and facilitator for the Buddha's day-to-day activities and concern, Ānanda makes it possible not only for the Buddha to get his message out to as many as possible, but also for trust in and high regard for the Buddhist project to develop in all who hear the message—a message that will ultimately result in their material support. In thus making the Buddha and Buddhism more open to the world, Ānanda helps make the world more open to Buddhism.

ĀNANDA'S SPECIAL RELATIONSHIP TO BUDDHIST WOMEN

As is generally acknowledged, Pali texts reflect a somewhat contradictory assessment of women. On the one hand the Buddha is clear that women *as women*, like all human beings, are capable of full enlightenment. Gender patterns, like those of caste, class, or ethnic background, are seen as cultural constructs.[84] On the other hand, however, as a cultural construct itself, Buddhist Dhamma reflects the values and belief systems of the culture out of which it grows, which in this case is the Vedic and early Hindu tradition. Thus, there are often misogynistic views expressed, such as those that hold that women are more emotional and sexually seductive than men, that they are less intelligent and responsible than men, and that they are more polluting and less spiritually advanced than men. Furthermore, women are major distractions to men in spiritual practice and so must be attended to with great caution—'keep wide awake' around women, the Buddha tells Ānanda,[85] for they are foolish and unwise,[86] they are greedy and uncontrolled,[87] and they are unsuitable to the religious life.

This assessment has led to the disenfranchisement of women across the broad spectrum of Buddhist traditions, but is founded in practices already present in Pali texts. Such disenfranchisement appears in at least four areas. First, women renunciants have fewer religious forms and practices available to them than men renunciants do, as evident in the early curtailment of educational opportunities for women on the path.[88] Second, women renunciants are restrained by more, and stricter, disciplinary rules than men, such as the one that allows men to be ordained by only the male Saṅgha but that requires that women be ordained by both the male and female Saṅghas.[89] Third, although women are known to achieve high states of spiritual accomplishment, even to experience *nibbāna,* they are not always given the official recognition paid to men for the same achievement—note, for example, the lack of application of the term *arahant* in early Pali texts to women who without doubt, and with clear textual support, fully deserve it.[90] And, finally, donations to women renunciants are much fewer than to men renunciants—note the term *dullabha* or *kicchalabha* 'obtaining [material support] with difficulty' that is occasionally applied to nuns—a phenomenon some see as the cause of the decline of the *bhikkhunīsaṅgha* in India.

Although views of women in the canon can often be derogatory, and although the institutional plight of nuns can be seen as gloomy, there is one bright hope for lay and renunciant women as presented in the canon, and that is the monk Ānanda. Horner notes that Ānanda is "always showing a touching regard for women"[91] and Robert Chalmers states that "Ānanda held 'advanced views on the woman questions.'"[92] The textual anchor for this characterization of Ānanda is the Vinaya story of the first 'going forth' of women into the homeless life. Briefly, Mahāpajāpatī and a group of Sakyan women approach the Buddha three times about 'going forth' as nuns, and three times he refuses. Greatly distressed and having shaved their heads and donned ochre robes, they follow the Buddha to his next destination and meet Ānanda. Ānanda offers to ask the Buddha on their behalf but, three times he is also refused. He then changes his tactics and, instead of asking if women can be allowed to 'go forth' (a disciplinary and, therefore, sociological question), he asks, instead, if, having gone forth, women are able to experience full perfection (a Dhammic and, therefore, soteriological question).[93] Having been asked now the theoretical as opposed to the practical question by Ānanda, the Buddha is obliged to answer "yes" and to agree to the founding of the *bhikkhunīsaṅgha.*

Ānanda features prominently in a story with another nun, a woman named Thullatissā. It happens one morning that Ānanda decides to go to a residence of nuns and invites Mahā Kassapa to go, for whom Ānanda will serve as attendant if he agrees. Mahā Kassapa refuses at first, but then consents to go and, once among the nuns, gives a Dhamma talk. When Mahā Kassapa leaves, the nun Thullatissā expresses her great displeasure—not at the talk itself but at the fact that Mahā Kassapa gives it and not Ānanda, whom she considers so much more learned a monk than Mahā Kassapa. "It is as if the needle-pedlar were to deem he could sell a needle to the needlemaker!"[94] Mahā Kassapa is not pleased to hear a report of Thullatissā's preference for a talk by Ānanda and confronts the favored monk—cajoling him into agreeing that he, Mahā Kassapa, is indeed a monk of great spiritual attainment. As a result of her insubordination, however, Thullatissā abandons her Buddhist career.

Although other monks have special relations with the nuns and their communities—notably Nandaka[95] and Phagguna[96]—Ānanda's is one of consistent teaching and special advocacy. He converts women to becoming nuns, he preaches to nuns on things such as mindfulness and *samādhi,*[97] and, occasionally, he has to be nudged away from distraction by them. Beyond teaching, Ānanda tends fellow nuns when they are sick—as he does for a nun who feigns illness in order to be treated by him whom, reputedly, she holds in high regard.[98] And he goes out of his way to give added support to their causes, as he does for Mahāpajāpatī in the founding of the *bhikkunīsaṅgha.*

Ānanda provides advocacy for lay women as well. In the case of Migasālā, for example, Ānanda hears her query and appraises it in good faith, but is then rebuffed by the Buddha for taking her seriously. Migasālā's question is about how to understand the similar good rebirths of two people who have lived lives of very different moral quality—her father, who has lived virtuously, and her uncle, who has not. Ānanda cannot, in this case, give instruction beyond the unsatisfactory talk the Buddha has already given, and so he goes to the Buddha—only to be told that women are foolish and frail, and are of too low a mental capacity to understand the diversity of humans. The only one who can take the measure of a person, he says, is the Buddha himself or someone like him.[99] Just as the teaching of nuns has stricter guidelines than that of monks, so the teaching of laywomen is restricted as well,[100] and given the canon's theoretical position on enlightenment possibilities for women, it would seem that these restrictions, as well as the Buddha's words on Migasālā, represent cultural values at the time the materials are compiled.

Ānanda works with other women as well. The Buddha assigns him, for example, to teach Dhamma in the women's apartments of King Pasenadi and, although ordinarily he performs tasks with integrity, one incident is indicative of the canonical bias against Ānanda's innocence when in relationship with women. Once, then, Ānanda approaches Queen Mallikā's apartment; she is in bed with her husband Pasenadi and, when she quickly stands up, her garment slips down and Ānanda hastily turns around and returns to the monastery. The Buddha then lays down rules for approaching the kings' apartments.[101]

Ānanda gets into another predicament when there is surplus food at the residence and the Buddha asks him to pass it out to local scrap-eaters. This Ānanda does, but mistakenly gives two cakes, thinking they are one, to a woman wanderer. Her fellow woman wanderer notices the extra food and accuses her colleague of being Ānanda's lover. No matter how vociferously the two-cake-receiver defends Ānanda and his mistake, and rejects the notion that she is Ānanda's lover, the quarrel between the two women wanderers continues.[102]

A final example of the allocation of Ānanda to special place among and appeal to women is the request put forward by the concubines of King Udena. Once, they hear that "their teacher" Ānanda is nearby, and ask that he visit them. This he does and, because they are thoroughly inspired by his Dhamma talk to them, the concubines give Ānanda five hundred inner robes. Critical of Ānanda for accepting so many robes, King Udena mocks him with the suggestion that he plans to set up shop, but Ānanda carefully persuades Udena of the distribution process: that the new robes will replace old, thin robes now in use in the Saṅgha, that the old robes will be used for new bed covers, that the old bed covers will be used for new mattress covers, that the old mattress covers will be used for new ground cloths, that the old ground cloths will be used for new foot-wipers, that the old foot-wipers will be shredded into mud to be used for floor plaster.[103] Thus the donor's household is satisfied once an accounting is given of the proper use of its gifts.

It is not fully clear what the particular appeal of Ānanda is for Buddhist women. Certainly a part of it is an overt compassion and empathy that is directed to all human beings. Ānanda is tender-hearted and is touched by those in affliction and, while this may position such an innocent monk in some potentially explosive situations, it also positions Ānanda in contexts where he can develop important social views for the new religion as well. Although there is criticism of Ānanda for so often taking the side of women,[104] it may well be that the canon needs to explain the actual presence of women renunciants within the historical Buddhist tradition that itself exists in a larger context critical of women. The figure of Ānanda then allows Buddhism to be both theoretically gender-neutral (in terms of enlightenment), but practically misogynistic (in terms of specific disciplinary rules and particular sermons) at one and the same time.

ĀNANDA'S ROLE IN *DĀNA*

It is suggested that Ānanda's influence with householders puts him in a unique position to encourage donation and to help develop policy on *dāna.* This may be especially so because of his ease with women and the fact that women are so often the donors who, as housemistresses, meet alms-touring monks (and therefore Ānanda accompanying the Buddha) at the household door. As that monk who, perhaps more than any other, is positioned at the liminal area between worldly and otherworldly, Ānanda is particularly vulnerable to pulls from both householder's and renunciant's lives. This vulnerability, however, is also an advantage for not only can Ānanda's service go to both directions, but he can test the needs of each life-style and match it with responses from the other. Ānanda is especially well-placed, thus, to "bring in wealth." Whether he is specifically charged with doing so or self-selects to do so, Ānanda's unique position has him traversing liminal grounds to develop and maintain *dāna* structures.

As an important mediational link between donors and the Saṅgha, Ānanda facilitates *dāna* in a number of ways. As the Buddha's attendant, donors often contact him; but just as often he initiates contact with them—not for the purpose of donation, but as part of his general outreach duties, both didactic and pastoral. Contact with donors, no matter who initiates them, however, often results in donors giving things directly to Ānanda. Sometimes, these items are in such enormous amounts that suspicion of avarice or special dealing falls on Ānanda, but on the whole he is seen as a fair and judicious mediator of donations. Ānanda is not just a receiver and disposer of gifts coming in but, because of this activity, but is also a developer of policy on *dāna* itself. This is especially evident in both the setting and content of the Dakkhiṇavibhaṅga Sutta 'discussion on the analysis of donations.' The Buddha's aunt, Mahāpajāpatī, decides once that in the twenty-nine years the Buddha lived as a householder she, his aunt and foster-mother, did not personally give him anything. She wants to make up for this now by giving him two new robes, but three times the Buddha rejects her offer to him by saying that instead she should give the robes to the Saṅgha.

Ānanda now steps in and beseeches the Buddha on her behalf, reminding the Buddha of all Mahāpajāpatī has done for him while she brought him up, and all the Buddha has contributed to her own considerable spiritual development. The Buddha acknowledges both of these things, but reminds the apparently befuddled Ānanda that actions on the Buddhist path are not to be done *for the sake* of any one or other person (though they can be done *with regard* to an individual person) but for the sake of the action itself. He then goes on, per the discussion here, to discuss, as he rarely does elsewhere, the gradation of donations given to various individuals and to various categories of Saṅgha membership.[105]

That it is Ānanda who is given this very detailed description of *dāna* offerings and not, for example, Upāli, a Vinaya master, or Mahā Mogallāna, an *iddhi* master, is significant. To be sure, as attendant, Ānanda is the hearer of record for many sermons and, to be sure, Ānanda may need more Dhammic guidance than many of the monks. But the more specific reason why this sermon needs to be made clear to Ānanda is that it is Ānanda, more than any other monk, who is likely (by office and by temperament) to be approached by lay who are making donations and in turn to be accountable to other monks for their proper apportion.

From the very beginning, the Vinaya suggests, Ānanda is the man to talk to if you want to give to the Saṅgha. Three examples from the Mahāvagga are illustrative. In the first, a brahmin has been patiently waiting his turn to make and serve a meal for a large number of monks. After waiting for two months and still not getting his turn, the brahmin approaches Ānanda, states his case, adding that he has just looked into the monastery refrectory and found what's missing, and suggests that he now make the missing food and present it to the Saṅgha. Would the Buddha accept this food from me, he asks Ānanda, and, consulting the Buddha, Ānanda tells him yes.[106] In a second example, repeated several times in the Mahāvagga, country people, who have loaded their wagons with mounds of salt, oil, rice, and solid food, now await their turn, like the brahmin above, to prepare a meal for the Buddha and his fellow monks. When, in one narrative, a rainstorm looms on the horizon, they approach Ānanda and ask his advice about caring for their food-stuff while they await their meal-giving turn. Ānanda goes to the Buddha with this dilemma, thus allowing the Buddha to give a teaching on appropriate storage places. In time, as for the brahmin, the country people's promised meal opportunity comes to fruition.[107]

The third example involves Roja the Malla, said to be a friend or companion *(sahāya)* of Ānanda's. Roja is unimpressed with the aspects of Buddhism he's encountered so far, and goes out to meet the Buddha only because his kinsmen have a contract whereby anyone who does not go is fined five hundred pieces. Fearing the punishment *(daṇḍabhaya),* Roja travels to hear the Buddha and on the way meets Ānanda to whom he tells his story. Ānanda tells Roja's story to the Buddha, and the Buddha's subsequent Dhamma talk is then so efficacious for Roja that he follows the Buddha to his dwelling place where the Buddha, sensing the receptive and evolving state of Roja's mind, gives him progressively more advanced instruction in the Dhamma. Wanting now to give gifts in all four categories of requisites—robes, food, lodging, and medicine—and wanting to be the only one to be such a donor, Roja is told by the Buddha that everyone wants to be such a donor and that he must now wait his turn. Handed over now to the "donations master," i.e., Ānanda, Roja, like the brahmin before him, is impatient and, on his own, finding out what is lacking food-wise in the refrectory, negotiates with Ānanda to donate the items.[108] As with the brahmin before, however, Ānanda again can't make any *dāna* ruling without first consulting with the Buddha.

As is routinely the case with the Buddha, the Dhamma-*dāna* exchange is fully operative for Ānanda as well—that is, he delivers a discourse to lay people and in return they donate requisites to the Saṅgha. A good example is the story of the householder Dasama of Aṭṭhaka who has heard excellent things about Ānanda and who comes to him once with many Dhamma questions. Having had them answered fully and clearly, the householder Dasama gives food and robes to the monks, and robes and a dwelling place to Ānanda—which latter he explains as a teacher's fee *(ācariyadhana),* such as is given by all pupils to their teachers in the various religious sects of the time.[109]

Of all the donations accruing to Ānanda as charismatic front man for the Saṅgha, that of cloth for robes is the most prominent. There is the story, for example, of the foreign cloth that King Pasenadi tries to give Ānanda at the end of a Dhamma discussion. Pasenadi, with great respect and fanfare, invites Ānanda to a river-side instruction spot where the two engage in an intense question and answer session. Pleased with Ānanda's performance, Pasenadi wants to give the monk some beautiful foreign cloth that has been given to him by King Ajātasattu. Ānanda declines the offer of cloth as he is set for robes but, when Pasenadi argues that Ānanda can give away his old robes and take the new cloth, Ānanda agrees, eventually, however, handing the new cloth over to the Buddha.[110] Note again, the story of King Udena's concubines who give Ānanda five hundred inner robes after a especially inspiring Dhamma talk. Upon discovery of this, Udena criticizes Ānanda for accepting the robes for the purpose of gain but backs off when he hears of the complicated recycling process the new robes will engender within the Saṅgha. Udena is so impressed with Ānanda's plan for use of every scrap, in fact, that he gives him five hundred more.[111] This marks, then, the first time that a thousand robes *(cīvarasahassa)* have come to Ānanda as a robes donation *(cīvarabhikkhā)*.[112]

Ānanda's middle-ground activities don't remain untested, however. Roja the Malla, for example, tries to persuade Ānanda to leave monastic life and return to householding, where he can have half of Roja's assets for starting anew. Ānanda declines, naturally, as such a life of desire will only compound his experience of suffering.[113] Again, a local spirit of the forest sets out to agitate Ānanda for spending so much time on matters connected with the lay. The "babble-babble" of lay conversation will do him no good in matters of his own spiritual achievement, the spirit argues, and he'd best leave it be if he's concerned at all for his own inner welfare.[114]

IS THERE A COST TO ĀNANDA'S SOCIAL OUTREACH?

It is precisely this inner welfare that is of final concern, for the canon implies (as the story of the spirit's counsel suggests) that Ānanda suffers a severe personal consequence as a result of tending to others when he should be tending to himself. Of specific concern in this section is Ānanda's own spiritual life—testing the linkage between parts of his progress as cause and effect, and assessing the outcome of choices Ānanda makes, as well as the kind of model he presents to practising Buddhists.

In terms of Ānanda's own religious life, it is clear that he has a substantial practice. Not only does he hear Dhamma preached on many subjects, but he is one of the most highly regarded teachers of Dhamma as well—able to discourse on just about any Buddhist topic necessary. He is, moreover, an exemplar in Buddhist conduct, and has substantial hand in discussing and developing disciplinary rules as well. Ānanda also has a regular meditation practice, emerging as he often does around evening from having spent hours in solitude,[115] and is able to articulate clearly and with precision Buddhist teaching on meditation.[116]

There is some suggestion in Pali texts of weaknesses in Ānanda's practice, however, particularly in his knowledge and experience of the *jhānas,* the four mental states of meditation.

Although Ānanda receives instruction in breathing practice, in the *jhānas,* and in *samādhi* from teachers like the Buddha and Sāriputta, and although he himself preaches on the *jhānas*[117] and is, in fact, asked to preach on the *jhānas,*[118] he occasionally makes mistakes—such as thinking the Buddha is dead when he is only passing through rapturous mental states. Freedman concludes, in fact, that Ānanda though "great in wisdom *(paññā)* was inexperienced in *samādhi*" and adds that though Ānanda "had heard, retained, recited and meditated on all sorts of *suttas* [and] had, as a result, vast wisdom,...his concentration of thought *(cittasaṃgraha)* was mediocre."[119] Moreover, Freedman argues, the canon has gone to particular trouble "to ensure that Ānanda appears devoid of 'psychic powers.'"[120] Granted that most monks do not develop *iddhis* or psychic powers as a secondary result of their meditation, these powers do constitute evidence of high spiritual achievement. In fact, Ānanda's lack of *iddhi* powers is criticized implicitly when he cannot locate the specific weak spot in a company of monks and Mahā Moggallāna (a specialist *iddhi* powers) can.[121]

The most critical issue in Ānanda's development is his "failure" to experience *nibbāna* and, consequently, to be recognized as an *arahant.* This becomes a community issue when, following the Buddha's death, the Cullavagga notes, it is decided to hold a council during which the Dhamma and the discipline are to be chanted and held as the foundation of the tradition. Mahā Kassapa decides to convene five hundred *arahants* minus one, reserving the last spot for Ānanda who knows the Buddha's sermons by heart but is not yet an *arahant.* Other monks persuade Kassapa to choose Ānanda anyway and Kassapa agrees. The night before, however, according to the Cullavagga, Ānanda feels it is not appropriate for him (still a *sekha* 'learner') to speak as a Dhamma expert before 499 *asekhas* ('completed learners') without himself being an *arahant.* Working hard on his mindfulness practice, then, Ānanda experiences *nibbāna* and is an *arahant* by the time the council is convened.[122]

Whether Ānanda actually experiences *nibbāna* and how, if he does, it actually comes about are not at issue here. Nor at issue are textual questions pertaining to the compilation of the canon, and how canonical figures get characterized to make certain points and to reflect competing views within the tradition. What is at issue is that, hagiographically, Ānanda's *arahant*-hood is late or, for doubters, nonexistent. The traditional explanation for why it is late is that Ānanda holds off working on his own perfection so that he can better serve the Buddha. The linkage raises two possibilities: would Ānanda experience *nibbāna* late anyway, that is, by virtue of the qualities of his character, regardless of whether or not he's the Buddha's attendant? or, does he experience it late only because his focus is elsewhere—busy with service to the Buddha and, by consequence, to other monks and to the lay? Clearly, these two scripts are interdependent. Ānanda is chosen by the Buddha to be his attendant because he is a humble, self-effacing monk, not prone to putting himself forward but waiting to respond to the wishes of others. Ānanda then works well as an attendant because, first, he has a good memory—and a good memory perhaps because, or in spite, of his not being a especially intellectual type, i.e., not stopping and analyzing what he has heard but simply committing it to memory. He works well, second, because he does in fact put others before himself and is uniformly willing to serve them and to work on their behalf.

He is a good attendant, then, because of who he is—a humane, generous, and empathetic person—and, conversely, because he is the Buddha's attendant he can develop these special qualities that are already central to his personality even more. Characteristic of Ānanda's portrayal in the texts is a especially strong attachment, most often to the person of the Buddha, but to other persons as well. Ordinarily, a posture of *saddhā* or trust and confidence in the Buddha, the doctrine, and the discipline of the Saṅgha is encouraged. To have *saddhā* is to have confidence in the reality and relevance of the enlightenment of the historical Buddha, in the truth of the experience that he has and of the doctrine that he teaches, and in the rightness of the practice as embodied in the rules of his community. This confidence is an initial trust, carrying one along the Buddhist path until one experiences wisdom for her or himself. *Saddhā* is the proper posture toward the Dhamma—and growth in the Dhamma is impossible without it—but it must be given up as personal experience is realized. In the case of Ānanda, there is plenty of *saddhā*, especially *saddhā* in the Buddha, but it is clear that more often than not Ānanda is overly concerned with the person of the Buddha rather than with the discoveries that the Buddha makes about the human condition.[123] Granted that any attendant must attend to the personal needs of his master, but Ānanda is a especially attached attendant, as Mahāparinibbāna Sutta shows: Ānanda becomes weak, dizzy, and muddle-headed when he sees that the Buddha is sick; he weeps, leaning against a doorpost, when he realizes that the Buddha will die while he Ānanda is still a learner *(sekha)* with so much more to do before enlightenment; and along with those not yet freed from passions, he weeps uncontrollably when the Buddha himself actually dies. Such attachment might not be necessary in an attendant, but in the case of Ānanda, it probably enhances the quality and enthusiasm of his service.

Notable as well is that any attendant probably has a hard go of it in the quest for enlightenment. The Buddhist path of the Pali texts, and of the Theravāda tradition, emphasizes self-cultivation and solitary living, and stresses the quiet, restrained, ascetic tendencies present in the Buddha's teachings. As Freedman notes, many of the *suttas* in the canon "emphasize the fact that the Buddha regarded the solitary life of meditation as lying at the root of his praxis."[124] In this way, Ānanda is structurally constrained from cultivating his own perfection, because his monastic position requires that he spend much of his time with others. It could be, then, that no one in the liminal position of attendant has a real chance at enlightenment in this life, but in its stead must cultivate elements valuable to other dimensions of the practice.

In his discussion of a Saṃyutta Nikāya *sutta,*[125] Freedman details a "way of knowledge" *(mahāpañña)* and a "way of action" *(iddhimant)*, as ways of freedom exemplified by Sāriputta and Moggallāna respectively.[126] What he does not explicitly do, however, is note that, in Ānanda, the canon designates, and is beginning to develop, a third way that might be called the "way of compassion." It seems clear that the message of the canon vis-à-vis Ānanda is that one cannot be an attendant to another and also work on one's own quest for *nibbāna,* that is, for *arahant*-hood. Therefore, it seems that the office of attendant and the acquisition of *arahant*-hood are incompatible. As Freedman notes. developed as a fringe figure, the

> *picture of Ānanda reflects the 'ideals' of the Theravāda school, which, as we have seen, are particularly* vinaya*-centered and interested in the arahant, or that type of arahant who is an example* par excellence *of the* bhikkhu *who is entirely in control of his faculties and shows little if any concern with the world outside of himself.*[127]

While Ānanda is set, negatively, in contrast to the current *bhikkhu,* the norm described above, turning the emphasis around, shows that the figure of Ānanda is the canon's earliest critique of the *arahant* ideal. As a character in the Gotama narrative, Ānanda's role is to help make it easier for the Buddha to do his job — thus, he works to facilitate the work of the Buddha. As a character in his own right, Ānanda embodies elements that will become important only later on. The Ānanda character, for example, shows that it may be harder than is currently assumed to move quickly and efficaciously toward the experience of *nibbāna,* and that movement on this pathway probably takes a much longer time than just one lifetime. The Ānanda character reflects, moreover, the need to be attuned to social issues in a proselytizing tradition, to be tolerant of all others, to be universal and adaptable in appeal, and to see caste, class, gender, and ethnic background as, like all views of the self, elaborate cultural constructs.

Reaching out to all lay and to all non-Buddhists, moreover, Ānanda is truly "a person before his time" who, unlike the perfected *bhikkhu* performing admirably as if all situations call for composure, reveals at these times instead "the feelings and desires of an ordinary man."[128] Rather than responding with calm reserve, the Ānanda character responds with compassion: not the compassion *karuṇā* canonically used as the second of the four *brahmavihāras,*[129] however, but the more common canonical compassion, *anukampā.*

Ānanda has always been on the merciful side of the Buddha's compassion, and as a good student he now extends this compassion to others—thus, Ānanda's compassion for others is based on the Buddha's for him. More widely, *anukampā* infuses all lay-renunciant relations: lay people ask for Dhamma talks to be given to them out of compassion; out of their own compassion, lay people give donations to renunciants; and out of compassion for lay people, renunciants receive their donations. In fact, one might say that the Buddha's ideal for the whole of the religious life is that all relations be infused with righteous friendship, spiritual intimacy, and compassion. In passing by the possibility of his own enlightenment, in order to help others Ānanda, then, is a proto-*bodhisattva*: for whom the duration of the quest for enlightenment is longer, the effort harder, the focus more universal, and the business of practice more situational, socially engaged, and empathically moral than for those religious colleagues he currently works among.

As an important mediator in the liminal "ecotone" between donating householders and the renunciant community, Ānanda sets the pace for the complexity, centrality, and necessity of both the mediational position itself and its essential tie to *dāna.* Although every monk and nun is engaged in the process of winning donations—most basically through silent, humble behavior at the household door—not many are especially open and accessible channels for gifts to the Saṅgha. By temperament, inclination, or office most renunciants receive requisites, especially robes and lodgings, through channels most immediately within the Saṅgha. The canon portrays only a few monks and nuns as being "out there" in contact with the lay and in advantageous positions for extra or special donations. It is not clear whether Ānanda would have received any additional donations had he not been the Buddha's attendant, but chances are that, given the agreeableness of his personality, he would have.

That Ānanda is so bound up in the back and forth of the

donation process is significant in terms of the Mahāyāna tradition in two ways. First, perhaps the most notable locations of *anukampā* 'compassion' are around *dāna* issues: renunciants teach out of compassion, donors give out of compassion, and renunciants receive donations out of compassion. Second, as the goal of Buddhism is to give up attachment to impermanent things whose ordinary loss can only cause suffering, *dāna* begins the development of non-attachment with a clear and structured process. By giving over part of what has been appropriately gained, a person not only acts compassionately towards others but initiates the practice of loosening his or her possessive grip over things and eventually on aspects of the "self." It is no wonder, then, that *dāna* begins so many of the Buddhist lists of practice, not the least of which is the *pāramitā* list of the Mahāyāna *bodhisattva.*

ENDNOTES

1. D 2.52; M 1.212, 216; A 1.25.
2. For a discussion, see Freedman, pp. 71-74, 148-149, 151-155.
3. M 1.216; A 1.24; 3.201-202, 361-362; Thera nos. 1019, 1021, 1026, 1027, 1030, 1031, 1047, 1048. See also A 2.185-187; 3.380-383.
4. D 2.124; A 2.147-148. See D 2.144-146; S 4.93-97.
5. See discussions in Bareau, pp. 1-30; Franke, pp. 1-80; Prebish, "Buddhist Councils," pp. 240-246; and Przyluski.
6. See Brough, pp. 423-426.
7. Freedman, p. 85.
8. For the sake of making best use of this wide range of contact with peoples, the Buddha urges his disciples not to use metrical forms of language *(chando),* that is, traditional Vedic verse, in their preaching but to give teachings in the 'own dialect' *(saka nirutti)* (Vin 2.139) of the hearers. This, presumably, Ānanda is able to do, as he is not only the one who 'has heard much' of what the Buddha himself has preached in diverse locales along the Gaṅgā Valley, but is himself known as the *dhammadhara* (A 3.361-362), the one who learns the teaching by heart, the one who holds the teaching in store, the one who is its treasurer and its repository. Thus, he hears the Dhamma taught in the own language of each local group and himself—when he is to give Dhamma talks—possibly speaks in the own native dialect of his audiences. To be *dhammadhara,* a trustee and guardian of the teaching, then, is to be holder as well of an array of

linguistic and personal ties to those many local groups among whom the Buddha works.

9. *Gāme santhavajāto* and *gāme na santhavajāto,* respectively (S 3.12).

10. S 1.187-188; Kh 92; see also A 5.196 where Ānanda is called a Sakyaputtiya, 'son or follower of the Sakyan.'

11. According to the Cullavagga, Ānanda enters the order of monks at the same time as the Sakyan chief Bhaddiya, and the Sakyan clansmen Anuruddha, Bhagu, Kimbila, and Devadatta. Upāli, barber for the Sakyans, is initially reluctant to go forth because of the Sakyans' famous fierceness, but is eventually convinced, by the strength of the other six's commitment and by their humility, to enter the order along with them (Vin 2.180-184).

12. Freedman, pp. 55-56, 63.

13. Belaṭṭhasīsa is said to be afflicted with terrible thick scabs that cause his robes to stick to his skin (Vin 1.202, 295-296) and, again, is rebuked by the Buddha for eating a meal from food that has been laid aside and stored up (Vin 4.86-87).

14. Ānanda's high regard for Sāriputta is evidenced, for example, in his desire to give him an extra robe (Vin 3.195-196) and an extra bowl (Vin 3.243) that have come into his possession, and this generosity betokens a more general veneration that is clearly one of junior to senior.

15. A 2.239-240.

16. E.g., S 2.274-75; 5.346-47, 362-64; A 2.167; 3.201, 361-62.

17. E.g., A 3.192-96.

18. M 3.25-29; S 1.63-65; A 1.23.

19. E.g., S 5.385-87.

20. See Freedman, pp. 89-90.

21. Indeed he is so accomplished in the attainment of the *jhānas* (meditative states) that the color of his face has become translucent and clear (S 3.235-240).

22. M 1.212-219.

23. Freedman, p. 178.

24. S 2.34-41; 3.235-240; 5.346-347, 362-364, 380-385; A 2.167; 3.201, 361-362. Concerning the canonical presentation of the figures Ānanda and Sāriputta, Freedman develops an argument based on the observations of André Migot. A number of places cast the two monks in similar ways: in one example, neither Ānanda nor Sāriputta is able to exercise the power of *cetasā ceto paricca* ('mind compassing mind')—that is, the discernment of the hearts and minds of other people as well as of their future dispositions—as the Buddha does in the case of the schismatic monk Devadatta (A 3.402-409). In summing up his evidence, Freedman concludes: "Once again we see that Sāriputta and Ānanda have similarities

in their characterizations" (Freedman, p. 366). Developing Bareau's suggestion that "Ānanda...seems very much like another Sāriputta," and his own that Ānanda "often appears like a second Sāriputta," Freedman turns to the question of why Ānanda and Sāriputta are treated so differently in tradition (Ānanda negatively and Sāriputta positively) if in fact they are portrayed with so many similar characteristics. In his answer, Freedman makes the following points. First, Ānanda is "more ancient [a character] than Sāriputta" and, if he is "the more ancient" (Freedman, pp. 424, 493-94) "then his characterization, which later would be regarded in a negative light, had more time to solidify than did that of Sāriputta. Further, the fact that Ānanda is credited with having been the Buddha's personal attendant would also have contributed to the fossilization of his characterization during the lifetime of the Buddha" (Freedman, p. 494). Second, Migot submits that the real Sāriputta is "plus près du coeur du peuple que le Śāriputra canonique" (Freedman, p. 493) but, because he died before the Buddha (S 5.161-163), later compilers, in the fluidity of the canonical process, can locate humaneness (that is, wayward vulnerability) fully with Ānanda, and wisdom or attentive clear sight with Sāriputta. Thus, this theory addresses the problems of canonical compilation, especially with regard to negative attitudes towards Ānanda, at the same time as it highlights the traditional hagiographic view of Sāriputta as Dhammic model and mentor to Ānanda.

25. S 3.105-106; see also S 2.155-57; A 1.23.
26. S 1.199-200; Thera no. 119. See also the discussion in Freedman, pp. 265-272 on the role of Vajjiputta/Vṛjiputra in Ānanda's attaining *arahant*-hood.
27. Vin 1.17, 248; 3.24; S 5.229-230.
28. Vin 2.240.
29. D 2.143; see M 1.4, 144; A 1.63.
30. Vin 1.62-63; 3.24; D 3.218-219; S 1.99; 5.174-175.
31. *Adhisīla, adhicitta,* and *adhipañña* (A 1.231; see S 5.14, 145, 327).
32. Findly, "Women and the *arahant* Issue."
33. Thera no. 1045.
34. A 1.225.
35. Vin 3.91; M 1.353-359.
36. Freedman, pp. 302-304.
37. A 1.217-219.
38. Vin 2.182-183.
39. Vin 2.286.
40. A 1.228.
41. Terms include *aggupaṭṭhāka* 'chief personal attendant,' *upaṭṭhāka* 'personal attendant,' *pacchāsamaṇa* 'junior wandering companion,' and

santikāvacara 'close attendant' (Vin 3.10; 4.78; D 2.6, 52; M 1.212; A 1.25).

42. Ānanda is not Gotama's first or only attendant for others, such as Cunda Samaṇuddesa (see discussion in Malalasekera 1.878 of commentarial and Jātaka sources on his position of attendance), Meghiya (A 4.354), Nāgasamāla (M 1.83), Nāgita (D 1.151), Sāgata (Vin 1.179-180), Sunakkhatta (M 1.68-69), and Upavāṇa (D 2.138-139; 3.141; S 1.174; A 3.195-196) also perform these duties either prior to Ānanda taking them up or for short periods during Ānanda's own long tenure.

43. The tradition of the appointment of Ānanda as attendant around the twentieth year of the Buddha's ministry—when the Buddha is settled at Sāvatthi—is at odds with the story of Ānanda's role in the 'going forth' of Mahāpajāpatī, the Buddha's aunt, along with several hundred other Sakyan women, that is said to take place in the second year of the Buddha's ministry. See Findly, "Ānanda's Case for Women."

44. Note Ānanda's surprise at the Buddha's dulling and wrinkled skin, the slackness of his limbs, and the bending forward of his body (S 5.216-217).

45. Freedman, pp. 104-105 (author's italics).

46. D 2.144-146; A 2.132.

47. A 1.24-25; KP 100-101. At least two experiences shape Ānanda's attendance on the Buddha. In the first, Ānanda is aware of the ways in which another attendant, e.g., Upavāṇa, has fallen down on the job—in this case by standing up in front of the Buddha and preventing access to him from others, thus causing the Buddha great displeasure (D 2.138-140). And, in the second, Ānanda has acted as de facto attendant to at least one other monk, e.g., Sāriputta—following behind him while walking, showing concern about the elder's food and robes, and learning the Dhamma from him on a regular basis (S 5.380-385).

48. Malalasekera 1.250.

49. A general comparison regarding Ānanda is often made: just as Christianity may be seen as a religion rooted in Jesus, but founded by Paul, so Buddhism may be see as a religion rooted in Gotama, but founded by Ānanda.

50. E.g., D 2.143-146.

51. E.g., M 2.82-83.

52. E.g., M 2.264-266; 3.109-118.

53. Jātakas nos. 389, 501, 502, 533.

54. Drawing on their Vedic heritage, Pali texts make clear that disciplined and attentive hearing will ensure that texts are not wrongly interpreted, and that words and sense are not wrongly arranged so as to mislead the listener in meaning (A 2.147-149). Thus, not only is the *buddhavacana* insufficient unless preached, but it must be given and received with skill,

care, and insight. Ānanda is, of course, the recognized master in *buddhavacana* (D 2.145-146), partly because he is an accurate listener with a powerful and retentive memory but also because, like the earliest disciples, and none other, he is actually physically present when the historical Buddha preaches his sermons. And, like no others even of those alive and to hand at the time of the historical Buddha, Ānanda is said to have been in attendance for most of the Buddha's sermons during the last twenty-five years of the latter's life.

Thus, no one is immediately in the Buddha's vicinity as much as Ānanda and no one hears as much Dhamma springing directly from its original source as Ānanda. While many Vedic *ṛṣis* had access to divine truth through ritualized tools of inspiration, only Ānanda in the early Buddhist tradition has almost unlimited access to those early utterances, words from the mouth of the Buddha himself that are the first, and most authoritative, of the four great sources of Dhamma (D 2.123-124). As Freedman points out, it's not clear how unique and singular the words of the Buddha are actually thought to be by those who hear them during the Buddha's lifetime, but after his death they become almost "magical" (Freedman, p. 234)—there will never be any more authentic sermons, and those that have been uttered may be lost unless efforts are made to preserve them.

55. A 3.361-362.

56. Ānanda's specific duties as attendant draw on those prescribed for the Vedic student. Following *gṛhya* and *dharma* texts, Kane (2.1:304-352) notes that during the *brahmacārin's* time of studying the Veda when he also learns the ritual system, yogic breathing, and how to live a morally and respectfully restrained life, he has certain obligations with regard to his teacher with whom he lives and to whom he eventually pays a fee. The student, for example, obeys his teacher without question in all matters of ritual, behavior, and study, and shows him the greatest respect at all times in matters of thought, word, and action. He gathers fuel for his teacher's daily fire, helps keep the fire area clean, attends the teacher during oblation time when the latter is present and performs the oblation when he is absent. The student follows after the teacher wherever he goes, helps him with his toilet and bath, and takes food that is left by him. Moreover, whenever the teacher needs such things the student brings him water, soil, cow dung, flowers and ritual grass.

57. As quoted by Freedman, pp. 23-24.

58. S 2.215.

59. E.g., M 1.160; S 3.94-95; 5.258-259.

60. E.g., Vin 3.10-11; 4.77-78.

61. E.g., D 2.13.

62. Vin 1.248-249; 3.6-7; Ud 78-79, 83.

63. Vin 1.287; D 2.133-134; Ud 83.

64. Vin 1.196-197; Ud 83.
65. D 2.145-146; A 2.132.
66. D 2.155; T.W. and C.A.F. Rhys Davids, *Dialogues* 2.173n.
67. M 3.298-302.
68. D 2.55-71; S 2.92-93.
69. A 3.347-351.
70. Vin 1.298.
71. Vin 3.58.
72. S 2.119-128.
73. Ud 24-27.
74. Vin 1.78-81.
75. Vin 1.196.
76. Vin 1.287.
77. D 2.135-136.
78. A 2.239-240.
79. C.A.F. Rhys Davids, *Kindred Sayings* 1.254; S 1.199-200.
80. S 4.400-401.
81. M 3.13-15.
82. KP 164-165.
83. Vin 2.126.
84. See Findly, "Women and the *arahant* Issue," and *Women's Buddhism*, pp. 3-5.
85. D 2.141.
86. A 5.137-144.
87. A 2.82-83.
88. Findly, *Women's Buddhism*, pp. 133-155.
89. Vin 2.255.
90. Findly, "Women and the *arahant* Issue."
91. Horner, *Discipline* 2.xliii.
92. Chalmers, *Jātaka* 1.223n.
93. Vin 2.253-255.
94. C.A.F. Rhys Davids, *Kindred Sayings* 2.145; S 2.214-217.
95. M 3.270-277.
96. M 1.122-126.
97. S 5.154-158; A 4.426-428.
98. A 2.144-146.
99. A 3.347-351; 5.137-144.

100. Vin 4.20-23.
101. Vin 4.158-159.
102. Vin 4.91.
103. Vin 2.290-293.
104. Vin 2.288-289.
105. M 3.253-257. Note here the BĀU passage (2.4.1-14) in which the Upaniṣadic sage Yājñavalkya instructs one of his wives, Maitreyī, as his gift to her upon his entrance into the wandering life, that "the husband is not dear for the sake of the husband but for the sake of the Self."
106. Vin 1.220-221.
107. Vin 1.220; 238-239.
108. Vin 1.247-249.
109. M 1.349-353; A 5.342-347.
110. M 2.112-117.
111. Vin 2.290-292.
112. Versions of these stories can then be found associated with the Jātakas: e.g., one thousand (or five hundred) expensive robes given to Ānanda by the women of the Kosalan King's palaces (nos. 157 and 259) and three fancy robes given to Ānanda by a wealthy landowner (no. 496).
113. Jātaka no. 235.
114. S 1.199-200.
115. E.g., M 1.513.
116. M 3.13-15.
117. A 2.194-196.
118. M 3.13-15.
119. D 2.156; Freedman, pp. 454, 453.
120. Freedman, p. 315.
121. Ud 51-53.
122. Vin 2.284-293.
123. D. 2.99-100, 143-144. 157-158.
124. Freedman, p. 220.
125. S 1.190-192.
126. Freedman, p. 281.
127. Freedman, pp. 497-498.
128. Freedman, p. 140.
129. E.g., *mettā* 'empathy,' *karuṇā*, 'compassion,' *muditā* 'sympathetic joy,' and *upekkhā* 'equanimity.'

Final Thoughts

The *dāna* process is a complex system of interwoven relationships that draws on past religious traditions, contemporary economic and social developments, and a range of religious goals increasingly suited to new demands. Buddhist material, first, for both householders and renunciants, often develops out of older tensions and tendencies present in Vedic ritual traditions and reworks them to suit more immediate needs. In the case of *dāna,* Pali texts integrate older vocabulary and traditional views on personal development and ritual efficacy into newer understanding of how *dāna* practices can respond to the suffering inherent in human existence.

Second, as parallels emerge between aspects of the Buddhist merit system and the merchant/householder life-style, the young Saṅgha discovers, and then develops, what might be called a "marketing niche." Newly emphasizing earned rather than assigned value, initial investments fueling later growth, individual efforts leading to individual rewards, just and fair notions of social contract, soteriological parity for all, regardless of caste or gender, religious practice without monumental expense, and affirmation of local languages and customs as media for the transmission of the tradition, Buddhism not only finds venues where its message can be most effective, but happily matches itself with people, groups, and locations where the "fit" is most advantageous. A version of the middle way, this posture is opportunistic only in that the Buddha's message is meant for the great benefit of all sentient beings, and finding marketing niches where more will encounter the message rather than less, and in as effective a form as possible, is an excellent example of a notion more prominent in later Buddhism known as *upāya,* 'skillful or expedient means.'

Finally, early Buddhism works to expand the range of spiritual pathways available to its constituency. These pathways differ one from the other in part because of their short and long term goals, e.g., monks and nuns move toward *nibbāna* and *parinibbāna,* while laymen and women may immediately have heaven or a good rebirth in mind. But Buddhism does something in addition, however. As it institutionalizes around a middle class ethic, a new focus emerges: not only might one reap heaven or an advantageous rebirth as a result of meritorious action, but a happy and tranquil state of mind here and now as well. The quality of action in the present, not just the future reward, becomes valuable and, in the case of *dāna,* giving itself comes to be understood as perfected action. Because teachings on charitable donation serve to give boundaries and curb excesses as each of the two groups, worldly and other-worldly, work within a context of reciprocity means that the actions of each have an affect on the other. In that these actions have mutual and symbiotic effect, what appears to be the future-orientedness of Buddhist practice becomes, in fact, increasingly present-centered as details of the process here and now draw much of the attentive focus.

Bibliography

Primary Texts in Pali

Andersen, Dines and Helmer Smith, eds. *Sutta-Nipāta*. London, 1913. Rpt. London: The Pali Text Society, 1984.

Carpenter, J. Estlin, ed., *The Dīgha Nikāya*, vol. 3. London, 1911. Rpt. London: The Pali Text Society, 1976.

Chalmers, Robert, ed. *The Majjhima Nikāya*, vols. 2 and 3. London, 1896, 1899. Rpt. London: The Pali Text Society, 1977.

De La Vallée Poussin, L. and E.J. Thomas, eds. *Mahāniddesa*, vols. 1 and 2 London, 1916, 1917. Rpt. London: The Pali Text Society, 1978.

Fausboll, V., ed. *The Jātaka*, vols. 1-7. London, 1877, 1879, 1883, 1887, 1891, 1896, 1897. Rpt. London: The Pali Text Society, 1990, 1963, 1964.

Feer, M. Leon, ed. *The Saṃyutta Nikāya*, vols. 1-5. London, 1884, 1888, 1890, 1894, 1898. Rpt. London: The Pali Text Society, 1973, 1989, 1975, 1990, 1976.

Geiger, Wilhelm, ed. *Cūlavaṃsa*, vols. 1 and 2. London, 1925, 1927. Rpt. London: The Pali Text Society, 1980.

Hardy, E., ed. *The Aṅguttara Nikāya*, vols. 3, 4, and 5. London, 1897, 1899, 1900. Rpt. London: The Pali Text Society, 1976, 1979.

Hunt, Mabel, ed. *The Aṅguttara Nikāya*, vol. 6. Rev. and ed. by C.A.F. Rhys Davids. London, 1919. Rpt. London: The Pali Text Society, 1981.

Jayawickrama, N.A., ed. *Buddhavaṃsa and Cariyāpiṭaka*. London: The Pali Text Society, 1974.

Jayawickrama, N.A., ed. *Vimānavatthu and Petavatthu*. London: The Pali Text Society, 1977.

Morris, Richard, ed. *The Aṅguttara Nikāya*, vol. 1., 2nd ed. rev. by A.K. Warder. London, 1885. Rpt. Oxford: The Pali Text Society, 1989.

Morris, Richard. ed., *The Aṅguttara Nikāya*, vol. 2. London, 1888. Rpt. London: The Pali Text Society, 1976.

Oldenberg, Hermann, ed. *Vinaya Piṭakam*, vols. 1-5. London, 1879, 1880, 1881, 1882, 1883. Rpt. London: The Pali Text Society, 1969, 1977, 1984, 1984, 1982.

Oldenberg, Hermann and Richard Pischel, eds. *The Thera- and Therīgāthā*. London, 1883. Rpt. Oxford: The Pali Text Society, 1990.

Rhys Davids, C.A.F., ed. *The Majjhima Nikāya*, vol. 4. London, 1925. Rpt. London: The Pali Text Society, 1974.

Rhys Davids, C.A.F., ed. *The Saṃyutta Nikāya*, vol. 6. London, 1904. Rpt. London: The Pali Text Society, 1980.

Rhys Davids, T.W. and J. Estlin Carpenter, eds. *The Dīgha Nikāya*, vols. 1, 2 London, 1890, 1903. Rpt. London: The Pali Text Society, 1975, 1982.

Smith, Helmer, ed. *The Khuddaka-Pāṭha*, From a collation by Mabel Hunt. London, 1915. Rpt. London: The Pali Text Society, 1978.

Stede, W., ed. *Cullaniddesa*. London, 1918. Rpt. Oxford: The Pali Text Society, 1988.

Steinthal, Paul, ed. *Udāna*. London, 1885. Rpt. London: The Pali Text Society, 1982.

Taylor, Arnold C., ed. *Kathāvatthu*, vols. 1, 2. London, 1894. Rpt. London: The Pali Text Society, 1979.

Taylor, Arnold C., ed. *Paṭisambhidāmagga*, vols. 1, 2. London, 1905, 1907. Rpt. London: The Pali Text Society, 1979.

Trenckner, V., ed. *The Majjhima Nikāya*, vol. 1. London, 1888. Rpt. London: The Pali Text Society, 1979.

Trenckner, V., ed. *The Milindapañho*, London, 1880. Rpt. London: The Pali Text Society, 1986.

Windisch, Ernst, ed. *Iti-Vuttaka*, London, 1889. Rpt. London: The Pali Text Society, 1975.

Primary Texts in Sanskrit

Aufrecht, Theodor, ed. *Ṛg Veda*. 2 vols. Bonn: Adolph Marcus, 1877.

Bühler, Georg, ed. *Āpastamba Dharma Sūtra*. Bombay: Education Society's Press, 1868-1871.

Führer, Alois Anton, ed. *Vāsiṣṭha Dharma Sūtra*. Bombay: Government Central Book Depot, 1883.

Gangānātha, Mahāmahopādhyāya, ed. *Manusmṛti*. Calcutta: Royal Asiatic Society of Bengal, 1939.

Garbe, Richard, ed. *Āpastamba Śrauta Sūtra*. Calcutta: Baptist Mission Press, 1882-1902.

Hultzsch, E., ed. *Baudhāyana Dharma Sūtra*. Nendeln. Liechtenstein: Kraus Reprint, 1966.

Kirste, J., ed. *Hiraṇyakeśi Gṛhya Sūtra*. Vienna: A. Holder, 1889.

Lindner, B., ed. *Kauṣītaki Brāhmaṇa*. Jena: H. Costenoble, 1887.

Müller, F. Max, ed. *Hymns of the Rig-Veda in the Saṁhita and Pada Texts*, vols. 1, 2. 1877. Rpt. Varanasi: Chowkhamba Sanskrit Series Office, 1965.

Oldenberg, H., ed. *Śāṅkhāyana Gṛhya Sūtra*. Leipzig: F.A. Brockhaus, 1876.

Roer, E. and E.B. Cowell, eds. *Taittirīya Saṃhitā*. Calcutta: Baptist Mission Press, 1860-1899.

Sāmaśramī, Ācārya Satyavrata, ed. *Śatapatha Brāhmaṇa*. Calcutta: Baptist Mission Press, 1903-1912.

Sāmaśramī, Satyavrata, ed. *Aitareya Brāhmaṇa*. Calcutta: Satya Press, 1895-1906.

Sastri, A. Mahadeva and L. Srinivasacharya, eds. *Khādira Gṛhya Sūtra*. Mysore: Government Branch Press, 1913.

Srinivasacharya, L., ed. *Gautama Dharma Sūtra*. Mysore: Government Branch Press, 1917.

Stenzler, Adolf Friedrich, ed. *Pāraskara Gṛhya Sūtra.* Leipzig: F.A.Brockhaus, 1876-1878.

Tarkalaṅkara, Chandrakanta, ed. *Gobhila Gṛhya Sūtra.* Calcutta: Baptist Mission Press, 1880.

Vidyāratna, Rāmanārāyana, ed. *Āśvalāyana Śrauta Sūtra.* Calcutta: Baptist Mission and Vālmiki Presses, 1868-1871.

Vidyāratna, Rāmanārāyana and Ānandachandra Vedāntavāgīsa, eds. *Āśvalāyana Gṛhya Sūtra.* Calcutta: Baptist Mission Press, 1869.

Von Schroeder, Leopold, ed. *Maitrāyaṇī Saṃhitā.* Leipzig: F.A. Brockhaus, 1881-1886.

Winternitz, M., ed. *Āpastamba Gṛhya Sūtra.* Vienna: A. Holder, 1887.

Primary Texts in Translation

Aung, Shwe Zan and C.A.F. Rhys Davids, trans. *Points of Controversy or Subjects of Discourse (Kathā-Vatthu),* London, 1915. Rpt. London: The Pali Text Society, 1979.

Bühler, Georg, trans. *The Laws of Manu.* Oxford, 1886. Rpt. New York: Dover, 1969.

Cowell, E.G., ed. *The Jātaka or Stories of the Buddha's Former Births,* vol. 1 (trans., Robert Chalmers), vol. 2, 4 (trans., W.H.D. Rouse), vol. 3 (trans., H.T. Francis, R.A. Neil), vol. 5 (trans., H.T. Francis), vol. 6 (trans., E.B. Cowell, W.H.D. Rouse). London, 1895. Rpt. London: The Pali Text Soci ety, 1981.

Eggeling, Julius, trans. *The Śatapatha Brāhmaṇa,* vols. 1-5. Oxford: Clarendon Press, 1882, 1885, 1894, 1897, 1900. Rpt. Delhi: Motilal Banarsidass, 1972.

Geldner, Karl Friedrich, trans. *Der Rig-Veda,* vols. 1-4. Harvard University Press, 1951, 1957.

Hare, E.M. trans. *The Book of the Gradual Sayings (Aṅguttara Nikāya),* vol. 4. Introduction by C.A.F. Rhys Davids. London, 1935. Rpt. Oxford: The Pali Text Society, 1989.

Horner, I.B. trans. *The Book of the Discipline (Vinaya-Piṭaka*), vol. 1, 2, 3 *(Suttavibhaṅga),* vol. 4 (*Mahāvagga),* vol. 5. (*Cullavagga),* vol. 6 *(Parivāra),* 1938, 1940, 1942, 1951, 1952, 1966. Rpt. London: The Pali Text Society, 1982, 1983, 1988, 1986.

Horner, I.B., trans. *The Collection of the Middle Length Sayings (Majjima Nikāya),* vols. 1, 2, 3. London,1954, 1957, 1959. Rpt. London: The Pali Text Society, 1987, 1989, 1977.

Horner, I.B. trans. *Milinda's Questions,* vols. 1, 2. London, 1963, 1964. Rpt. Oxford: The Pali Text Society, 1990, 1991.

Horner, I.B., trans. *The Minor Anthologies of the Pali Canon,* Pt. 3. *Buddhavaṃsa, Cariyāpiṭaka.* London: The Pali Text Society, 1975.

Horner, I.B. and H.S. Gehman, trans. *The Minor Anthologies of the Pali Canon,* Pt.4 *Vimānavatthu* (Horner), *Petavatthu* (Gehman). London, 1942 Rpt. London: The Pali Text Society, 1974.

Jacobi, Hermann, trans. *Jaina Sūtras*, 2 vols. Oxford University Press, 1884, 1895. Rpt. Delhi: Motilal Banarsidass, 1973.

Keith, Arthur Berriedale, trans. *Rigveda Brahmanas (Aitareya and Kauṣītaki Brāhmaṇas)*. Harvard University Press, 1920. Rpt. Delhi: Motilal Banarsidass, 1971.

Keith, Arthur Berriedale, trans. *The Veda of the Black Yajus School (Taittriya Samhita)*, vols. 1, 2. Harvard University Press, 1914. Rpt. Delhi: Motilal Banarsidass, 1967.

Ñāṇamoli, Bhikkhu, trans. *The Minor Readings (Khuddakapāṭha). The First Book of the Minor Collection (Khuddakanikāya)*. London, 1960. Rpt. London: The Pali Text Society, 1978.

Ñāṇamoli, Bhikkhu, trans. *The Path of Discrimination (Paṭisambhidāmagga)*. London: The Pali Text Society, 1982.

Ñāṇamoli and Bodhi, Bhikkhus, trans. *The Middle Length Discourses of the Buddha, A New Translation of the Majjhima Nikāya*. Boston: Wisdom Publications, 1995.

Norman, K.R., trans. *The Elders' Verses, 1. Theragāthā*. London: The Pali Text Society, 1969.

Norman, K.R., trans. *The Elders' Verses, 2. Therīgāthā*. London: The Pali Text Society, 1971.

Norman, K.R. trans. *The Group of Discourses (Sutta-Nipāta)*, vol.1. With alternative translations by I.B.Horner and Walpola Rahula. London: The Pali Text Society, 1984.

O'Flaherty, Wendy Doniger, trans. *The Rig Veda, An Anthology*. New York: Penguin Books, 1981.

Oldenberg, Hermann, trans. *The Gṛhya Sūtras, Rules of Vedic Domestic Ceremonies*, vols. 1, 2. Oxford University Press, 1886, 1892. Delhi: Motilal Banarsidass, 1967.

Olivelle, Patrick, trans. *Dharmasūtras, The Law Codes of Ancient India*. Oxford: Oxford University Press, 1999.

Olivelle, Patrick, trans. *The Early Upaniṣads*. New York: Oxford University Press, 1998.

Olivelle, Patrick, trans. *Saṃnyāsa Upaniṣads, Hindu Scriptures on Asceticism and Renunciation*. New York: Oxford Unviversity Press, 1992.

Radhakrishnan, S., trans. *The Principal Upaniṣads*. London, 1953. Rpt. New York: Humanities Press, 1969.

Rhys Davids, C.A.F., trans. *The Book of the Kindred Sayings (Saṃyutta Nikāya)*, vol. 1. Assisted by Sūriyagoḍa Sumangala Thera. London, 1917. Rpt. Oxford: The Pali Text Society, 1989.

Rhys Davids, C.A.F., trans. *The Book of the Kindred Sayings (Saṃyutta Nikāya)*, vol. 2. Assisted by F.H. Woodward. London, 1922. Rpt. London: The Pali Text Society, 1982.

Rhys Davids, T.W., trans. *Dialogues of the Buddha*, vols. 1, 2, 3. London, 1899, 1910, 1921. Rpt. London: The Pali Text Society, 1977, 1989, 1977.

Walshe, Maurice, trans. *The Long Discourses of the Buddha, A Translation of the Dīgha Nikāya.* Boston, 1987. Rpt. Boston: Wisdom Publications, 1995.

Whitney, William Dwight, trans. *Atharva-Veda-Saṃhitā,* vols. 1, 2. Harvard University Press, 1905. Rpt. Delhi: Motilal Banarsidass, 1971.

Woodward, F.L., trans. *The Book of the Gradual Sayings (Aṅguttara Nikāya),* vols. 1, 3. Introduction by C.A.F. Rhys Davids. London, 1932, 1934. Rpt. Oxford: The Pali Text Society, 1989, 1988.

Woodward, F.L. trans. *The Book of the Gradual Sayings (Aṅguttara Nikāya),* vol. 2. London, 1933. Rpt. London: The Pali Text Society, 1982.

Woodward, F.L., trans. *The Book of the Gradual Sayings (Aṅguttara Nikāya),* vol. 5. Introduction by C.A.F. Rhys Davids. London, 1935. Rpt. Oxford: The Pali Text Society, 1986.

Woodward, F.L. trans. *The Book of the Kindred Sayings (Saṃyutta Nikāya),* vol. 3. Edited by C.A.F. Rhys Davids. London, 1925. Rpt. London: The Pali Text Society, 1975.

Woodward, F.L. trans. *The Book of the Kindred Sayings (Saṃyutta Nikāya),* vols. 4, 5. Introduction by C.A.F. Rhys Davids. London, 1927, 1930. Rpt. London: The Pali Text Society, 1980, 1990.

Woodward, F.L., trans. *The Minor Anthologies of the Pali Canon* Pt. 2 *Udāna, Itivuttaka.* Introduction by C.A.F. Rhys Davids. London, 1935. Rpt. London: The Pali Text Society, 1987.

Secondary Sources

Acharya, Kala. *Purāṇic Concept of Dāna.* Delhi: Nag Publishers, 1993.

Altekar, A.S. *The Position of Women in Hindu Civilization, From Prehistoric Times to the Present Day.* 1938. Rpt. Delhi: Motilal Banarsidass, 1973.

Amore, Roy Clayton. *The Concept and Practice of Doing Merit in Early Theravāda Buddhism.* Ph.D.Diss., Columbia University, 1971.

Ansari, A.Q. *Archaeological Remains of Bodhgaya.* Delhi: Ramanand Vidya Bhawan, 1990.

Aronson, Harvey B. *Love and Sympathy in Theravāda Buddhism.* Delhi : Motilal Banarsidass, 1980.

Aronson, Harvey B. "Motivations to Social Action in Theravāda Buddhism: Uses and Misuses of Traditional Doctrines." In A.K. Narain, ed., *Studies in History of Buddhism.* Delhi: B.R. Publishing Corp., 1980, pp. 1-12.

Bareau, André. *Les Premiers Conciles Bouddhiques.* Paris: Presses Universitaires de France, 1955.

Basham, A.L. *History and Doctrine of the Ājīvikas: A Vanished Indian Religion.* London: Luzac and Company, Ltd., 1951.

Bechert, Heinz. *Buddhismus, Staat und Gesellschaft in den Landern des Theravāda-Buddhismus,* 3 vols. Frankfurt am Main, Berlin: Alfred Metzner Verlag, 1966-73.

Bechert, Heinz. "The Date of the Buddha Reconsidered." *Indological Taurinensia.* Torino: Istituto di Indologial 10(1981):29-36.

Bechert, Heinz, ed. *The Dating of the Historical Buddha/Die Datiering des historischen Buddha.* 2 vols. Göttingen: Van den Hoeck & Ruprecht, 1991.

Bechert, Heinz and Richard Gombrich, eds. *The World of Buddhism: Buddhist Monks and Nuns in Society and Culture.* London: Thames and Hudson, 1984.

Beck, Brenda. "Color and Heat in South Indian Ritual." *Man* n.s. 4(1969):553-572.

Bhagvat, Durga N. *Early Buddhist Jurisprudence (Theravada Vinaya-Laws).* New Delhi: Cosmo Publications, 1939.

Biardeau, Madeleine, and Charles Malamoud. *Le Sacrifice dans l'Inde ancienne.* Paris: Presses Universitaires de France, 1976.

Bloomfield, Maurice. *A Vedic Concordance.* Harvard University Press, 1906. Rpt. Delhi: Motilal Banarsidass, 1964.

Bodhi, Bhikkhu, ed. *Dāna: The Practice of Giving.* Wheel Publication No. 367/369. Kandy, Sri Lanka: Buddhist Publication Society, 1990.

Bond, George D. *The Buddhist Revival in Sri Lanka: Religious Tradition, Reinterpretation and Response.* Columbia: University of South Carolina Press, 1988.

Bond, George D. *"The Word of the Buddha:" The Tipiṭika and its Interpreta tion in Theravāda Buddhism.* Colombo: Sri Lanka: M.D. Gunasena, 1982.

Boulding, Kenneth E. *The Economy of Love and Fear: A Preface to Grants Economics.* Belmont, California: Wadsworth Publishing Company, Inc.1973.

Boulding, Kenneth E. "Notes on a Theory of Philanthropy." In Frank G. Dickinson, ed., *Philanthropy and Public Policy.* New York: National Bureau of Economic Research, Inc., 1962.

Bremner, Robert H. *Giving: Charity and Philanthropy in History.* New Brunswick and London: Transaction Publishers, 1994.

Brereton, Joel. "The Upanishads." In *Approaches to the Asian Classics.* Ed. by Wm. Theodore de Bary and Irene Bloom. New York: Columbia University Press, 1990, pp. 115-135.

Brough, John. "'Thus Have I Heard...'" *Bulletin, School of Oriental and African Studies* 13(1950):416-426.

Cabezón, José Ignacio, ed. *Buddhism, Sexuality and Gender.* Albany: State University of New York Press, 1992.

Carrithers, Michael. *The Buddha.* New York: Oxford University Press, 1983.

Chakravarti, Uma. *The Social Dimensions of Early Buddhism.* Delhi: Oxford University Press, 1987.

Chaudhury, Binayendra Nath. *Buddhist Centres in Ancient India.* Calcutta: Sanskrit College, 1969.

Church, Cornelia Dimmitt. "Temptress, Housewife, Nun: Women's Role in Early Buddhism." *Anima* 1.2(Spring 1975):53-58.

Collins, Steven. *Selfless Persons.* Cambridge: University Press, 1982.

Darian, Jean C. "Social and Economic Factors in the Rise of Buddhism." *Sociological Analysis* 38.3(1977):226-238.

Dumont, Louis. "World Renunciation in Indian Religions." *Contributions to Indian Sociology* 4(1960):33-62.

Dutt, Nalinaksha. *Aspects of Mahāyāna Buddhism and its Relation to Hīnayāna.* London: Luzac & Co., 1930.

Dutt, Nalinaksha. *Buddhist Sects in India.* 2nd ed. Delhi: Motilal Banarsidass, 1978.

Dutt, Nalinaksha. *Early Monastic Buddhism.* Calcutta, 1960. 2nd ed., Calcutta: 1971. Rpt. Calcutta: S.P. Ghosh, Firme KLM Private, Ltd., 1981.

Dutt, Nalinaksha. "Place of Faith in Buddhism." *Indian Historical Quarterly* 16:639-646.

Dutt, Sukumar. *Buddhist Monks and Monasteries of India: Their History and Their Contribution to Indian Culture.* London: George Allen and Unwin, Ltd., 1962.

Dutt, Sukumar. *Early Buddhist Monachism, 600 B.C.-100 B.C.* London: Kegan Paul, Trench, Trubner & Co., Ltd., 1924.

Erdosy, George. "City States of North India and Pakistan at the Time of the Buddha" in F.R. Allchin, ed., *The Archaeology of Early Historic South Asia: The Emergence of Cities and States.* Cambridge: University Press, 1995.

Erdosy, George. "Ethnicity in the Rigveda and its Bearing on the Question of Indo-European Origins." *South Asian Studies* 5:35-47.

Erdosy, George. "Language, material culture and ethnicity: Theoretical per spectives," in George Erdosy, ed., *The Indo-Aryans of Ancient South Asia: Language, Material Culture and Ethnicity.* Berlin, New York: Walter de Gruyter, 1995.

Erdosy, George. "The Prelude to Urbanization: Ethnicity and the Rise of Late Vedic Chiefdoms," in F.R. Alchin, ed., *The Archaeology of Early Historic South Asia: The Emergence of Cities and States.* Cambridge: University Press, 1995.

Erdosy, George. *Urbanisation in Early Historic India.* Oxford: B.A.R. Inter national Series 430, 1988.

Ergardt, Jan. T. *Faith and Knowledge in Early Buddhism.* Leiden: E.J. Brill, 1977.

Falk, Nancy Auer. "The Case of the Vanishing Nuns: The Fruits of Ambiva lence in Ancient Indian Buddhism," in Nancy Auer Falk and Rita M. Gross, eds. *Unspoken Worlds: Women's Religious Lives in Non-Western Cultures.* San Francisco: Harper & Row, 1980.

Falk, Nancy Auer. "Exemplary Donors of the Pāli Tradition." In Russell F. Sizemore and Donald K. Swearer, eds., *Ethics, Wealth, and Salvation: A Study in Buddhist Social Ethic.* Columbia: University of South Carolina Press, 1990, pp. 124-143.

Falk, Nancy Auer. "An Image of Woman in Old Buddhist Literature: The Daughters of Māra." In Judith Plaskow and Joan Arnolds, eds. *Women and Religion.* Rev. ed. Missoula, Montana: University of Montana, for Scholars Press, the American Academy of Religion, 1974, pp. 105-112.

Fenn, Mavis. "Two Notions of Poverty in the Pāli Canon." *Journal of Buddhist Ethics* 3(1996):98-125.

Fick, Richard. *The Social Organisation in North-East India in Buddha's Time.* Varanasi, Delhi: Indological Book House, 1972.

Findly, Ellison Banks. "Ānanda's Case for Women." *International Journal of Indian Studies* 3.2(July 1993):1- 31.

Findly, Ellison Banks. "Ānanda's Hindrance: Faith (*saddhā*) in Early Buddhism." *Journal of Indian Philosophy* 20(1992):253-273.

Findly, Ellison Banks. "Women and the *arahant* Issue in Early Pāli Literature." *Journal of Feminist Studies In Religion* 15.1(Spring 1999):57-76.

Findly, Ellison Banks, ed. *Women's Buddhism, Buddhism's Women: Tradition, Revision, Renewal.* Boston: Wisdom Publications, 2000.

Findly, Ellison Banks. "The Housemistress at the Door: Vedic and Buddhist Perspectives on the Mendicant Encounter." In Laurie Patton, ed., *Jewels of Authority: Women, Text, and the Hindu Tradition.* New York: Oxford University Press, 2001, pp. 13-31.

Frank, R. Otto. "The Buddhist Councils at Rājagaha and Vesālī, as Alleged in Cullavagga XI., XII." *Journal of the Pali Text Society* 6(1908):1-80.

Frauwallner, E. *The Earliest Vinaya and the Beginnings of Buddhist Literature.* Serie Orientale Roma, VIII.Roma: Istituto Italiano Per Il Medio Ed Estremo Oriente, 1956.

Freedman, Michael. *The Characterization of Ānanda in the Pāli Canon of the Theravāda: AHagiographic Study.* Ph.D. Diss., McMaster University, 1978.

Gellner, David. "Max Weber, Capitalism and the Religion of India." *Sociology* 16.4(November 1982):526-543.

Ghosh, A. *The City in Early Historical India.* Indian Institute of Advanced Study, Simla. 1973. Rpt. New Delhi: Munshiram Manoharlal, 1990.

Gokhale, B.G. "The Early Buddhist Elite." *Journal of Indian History* 42.2(1965):391-402.

Gombrich, Richard F. *Buddhist Precept and Practice: Traditional Buddhism in the Rural Highlands of Ceylon.* Oxford: Clarendon Press, 1971.

Gombrich, Richard F. "The Ethnic of Intention," in Charles S. Prebish. *Buddhist Ethics: A Cross-Cultural Approach.* Dubuque, Iowa: Kendall/Hunt Publishing Company, 1992.

Gombrich, Richard. "'Merit Transference' in Sinhalese Buddhism: A Case Study of the Interaction Between Doctrine and Practice." *History of Religions* 11.2(November 1971):203-219.

Gombrich, Richard F. *Theravada Buddhism: A Social History from Ancient Benares to Modern Colombo.* London, 1988. Rpt. London: Routledge, 1991.

Grassman, Hermann. *Wörterbuch zum Rig-Veda.* Wiesbaden: Otto Harrassowitz, 1964.

Green, Ronald M. "Buddhist Economic Ethics: A Theoretical Approach." In Russell M. Sizemore and Donald K. Swearer, eds. *Ethics, Wealth, and Salvation: A Study in Buddhist Social Ethics.* Columbia: University of South Carolina Press, 1990, pp. 215-234.

Gross, Rita M. "'The Dharma...Is Neither Male Nor Female': Buddhism on Gender and Liberation." In *Women's and Men's Liberation: Testimonies of the Spirit.* Ed. by Leonard Grob, Riffat Hassan, and Haim Gordon. New York: Greenwood Press, 1991.

Gupta, Mrinal Das. "Śraddhā and Bhakti in Vedic Literature." *Indian Historical Quarterly* 6(June and September 1930):315-333, 487-513.

Harrison, Paul M. "Buddhānusmṛti in the Pratyutpanna-Buddha-Saṃmukhāvasthita- Samādhi- Sūtra." *Journal of Indian Philosophy* 6(1978):35-57.

Harvey, Peter. "Criteria for Judging the Unwholesomeness of Actions in the Texts of Theravāda Buddhism." *Journal of Buddhist Ethics* 2(1995):140-151.

Heesterman, J.C. *The Broken World of Sacrifice: An Essay in Ancient Indian Ritual.* Chicago: The University of Chicago Press, 1993.

Heesterman, J.C. *The Inner Conflict of Tradition; Essays in Indian Ritual, Kingship, and Society.* Chicago: The University of Chicago Press, 1985.

Heesterman, J.C. "Reflections on the Significance of the *Dákṣiṇā.*" *Indo-Iranian Journal* 4(1959):241-258.

Hirakawa, Akira. "The Rise of Mahāyāna Buddhism And Its Relationship to the Worship of Stupas." *Memoirs of the Research Department, Toyo Bunko* 22(1963):57-106.

Hoffman, Frank J. "The Pragmatic Efficacy of *Saddhā.*" *Journal of Indian Philosophy* 15.4(December 1987):399-412.

Hoffman, Frank. J. *Rationality and Mind in Early Buddhism.* Delhi: Motilal Banarsidass, 1987.

Holt, John. C. *Discipline: The Canonical Buddhism of the Vinayapiṭaka.* Delhi: 1981. Rpt. Delhi: Motilal Banarsidass, 1995.

Hopkins, E. Washburn. *Ethics of India.* Port Washington, New York: Kennikat Press, facsimile reprint of 1924 edition.

Horner, I.B. *The Early Buddhist Theory of Man Perfected: A Study of the Arahan.* London: Williams & Northgate, Ltd., 1936.

Horner, I.B. *Women Under Primitive Buddhism: Laywomen and Almswomen.* London, 1930. Rpt. Delhi: Motilal Banarsidass, 1989.

Hubert, Henri and Marcel Mauss. *Sacrifice: Its Nature and Function.* Trans. by W.D. Halls. Orig. pub. in French 1898. Chicago: University of Chicago Press, 1964.

Jaini, Padmanabh S. *Gender and Salvation: Jaina Debates on the Spiritual Liberation of Women,* Berkeley: University of California Press, 1991.

Jamison, Stephanie W. *Sacrificed Wife/Sacrificer's Wife: Women, Ritual, and Hospitality in Ancient India.* New York: Oxford University Press, 1996.

Jayatilleke, K.N. "The Buddhist Doctrine of Karma." *Maha Bodhi* 76(1968):314-320.

Jayatilleke, K.N. "The Case for the Buddhist Theory of Survival and Kamma V." *Maha Bodhi* 78(1970):350-355.

Jayatilleke, K.N. *Early Buddhist Theory of Knowledge.* Delhi: Motilal Banarsidass, 1963.

Jones, Richard H. "Theravāda Buddhism and Morality." *Journal of the American Academy of Religion* 47.3:371-387.

Kaelber, Walter O. *Tapta Mārga: Asceticism and Initiation in Vedic India.* Albany: State University of New York Press, 1989.

Kalupahana, David J. *Causality: The Central Philosophy of Buddhism.* Honolulu: The University Press of Hawaii, 1975.

Kalupahana, David J. *Ethics in Early Buddhism.* Honolulu: University of Hawaii Press, 1995.

Kane, Pandurang Vaman. *History of Dharmaśāstra,* vols. 2.1, 2.2, 3. Poona: Bhandarkar Oriental Research Institute, 1941, 1946.

Katz, Nathan. *Buddhist Images of Human Perfection: The Arahant of the Sutta Piṭaka Compared with the Bodhisattva and the Mahāsiddha.* Delhi: Motilal Banarsidass, 1982.

Keay, John. *India: A History.* New York: Atlantic Monthly Press, 2000.

Keyes, Charles F. "Merit-Transference in the Kammic Theory of Popular Theravāda Buddhism." In Charles F. Keyes and E. Valentine Daniel, eds. *Karma: An Anthropological Inquiry.* Berkeley: University of California Press, 1983, pp. 261-286.

Keith, Arthur Berriedale. *The Religion and Philosophy of the Veda and Upanishads.* Harvard University Press, 1925. Rpt. Delhi: Motilal Banarsidass, 1970.

Khenchen Thrangu Rinpoche, Venerable. *The Tibetan Vinaya: Guide to Buddhist Conduct.* Trans. by Sonam Palden and Chojor Radha. 1990. Rpt. Delhi: Sri Satguru Publications, 1998.

Knipe, David M. *In the Image of Fire: The Vedic Experiences of Heat.* Delhi: Motilal Banarsidass, 1975.

Knipe, David M. "Sapiṇḍīkaraṇa: The Hindu Rite of Entry into Heaven." In Frank E. Reynolds and Earle H.Waugh, eds., *Religious Encounters With Death.* University Park: The Pennsylvania State University Press, 1977, pp. 111-124.

Köhler, Hans-Werben. *Śrad-dhā — in der Vedischen und Altbuddhistischen Literatur.* Herausgegeben von Klaus L. Janert. Wiesbaden: Franz Steiner Verlag, 1973.

Kuiper. F.B.J. "The Ancient Aryan Verbel Context." *Indo-Iranian Journal IV.* 4(1960):217-281.

Lamotte, Etienne. "Le Bouddhisme des Laics." *Studies in Indology and Buddhology.* Presented in Honor of Prof. Susumu Yamaguchi. Hozokan, Kyoto: Indogaku Bukkyogaku Ronso, 1955, pp. 73-89.

Lamotte, Etienne. "Sur la Formation Du Mahāyāna." *Asiatica: Festschrift Friedrich Weller.* Leipzig: Otto Harrassowitz, 1954, pp. 377-396.

Lang, Karen Christina. "Lord Death's Snare: Gender-Related Imagery in the Theragāthā and the Therīgāthā." *Journal of Feminist Studies in Religion* 2.2(Fall 1986):63-79.

Law, Bimala Churn. *The Buddhist Conception of Spirits.* London: Luzac, 1936.

Law, Bimala Churn. "Data from the Sumaṅgalavilāsinī, Buddhaghosa's Commentary on the Dīgha Nikāya of the Sutta Piṭaka." *Journal, Asiatic Society of Bengal* n.s. 21(1925):107-121.

Law, Bimala Churn. *Geography of Early Buddhism.* 1932. Rpt., Varanasi: Shrī V.S. Singh, Bhartiya Publishing House, 1973.

Little, David and Sumner B. Twiss. "Religion and Morality in Theravada Buddhism." In Charles S. Prebish, ed., *Buddhist Ethics: A Cross-Cultural Approach.* Dubuque, Iowa: Kendall/Hunt Publishing Company, 1992.

Locke, John. *The Second Treatise of Government.* Indianapolis, New York: Bobbs-Merril, 1952.

Malalasekera, G.P. *Dictionary of Pāli Proper Names.* 2 vols. Indian Text Series. London: 1937, 1938. Rpt. London: The Pali Text Society, 1974.

Malalasekera, G.P. "'Transference of Merit' in Ceylonese Buddhism." *Philosophy East and West* 17.1-4 (January-October 1967):85-90.

Marriott, McKim. "Hindu Transactions: Diversity Without Dualism." In *Transaction and Meaning.* Ed. Bruce Kapferer. Philadelphia: Institute for the Study of Human Issues, 1976, pp. 109-111.

McDermott, James Paul. *Development in the Early Buddhist Concept of Kamma/Karma.* New Delhi:Munshiram Manoharlal, 1984.

McDermott, James Paul. "Is There Group Karma in Theravāda Buddhism?" *Numen* 23.1 (1976): 67-80.

McDermott, James Paul. "Karma and Rebirth in Early Buddhism." In Wendy Doniger O'Flaherty, ed., *Karma and Rebirth in Classical Indian Traditions.* Berkeley: University of California Press, 1980, pp. 165-192.

McDermott, James Paul. "Nibbāna as a Reward for Kamma." *Journal of the American Oriental Society* 93.3(1973):344-347.

McDermott, James Paul. "Sādhāna Jātaka: A Case Against the Transfer of Merit." *Journal of the American Oriental Society* 94(1974):385-87.

Miller, Barbara Stoler. "On Cultivating the Immeasurable Change of Heart: The Buddhist Brahma-Vihāra Formula." *Journal of Indian Philosophy* 7(1979):209-221.

Misra, G.S.P. *The Age of the Vinaya.* New Delhi: Munshiram Manoharlal, 1972.

Misra, S.C. "Urban History in India: Possibilities and Perspectives." In Indu Banga, ed., *The City in Indian History: Urban Demography, Society, and Politics.* Columbia, MO: South Asia Publications, 1991.

Mitra, Debala. *Buddhist Monuments.* Calcutta: Sahitya Samsad, 1971.

Monier-Williams, Monier. *A Sanskrit-English Dictionary.* Oxford, 1899. Rev. ed., Oxford: Clarendon Press, 1970.

Mumford, Lewis. *The City in History.* New York: Harcourt, Brace & World, Inc., 1961.

Munzer, Stephen R. *A Theory of Property.* Cambridge: Cambridge University Press, 1990.

Murcott, Susan. *The First Buddhist Women: Translations and Commentary on the* Therigatha. Berkeley: Paralax Press, 1991.

Nath, Vijay Nath. *Dāna: Gift-System in Ancient India (c. 600 B.C-c.AD 300): A Socio-Economic Perspective.* New Delhi: Munshiram Manoharlal, 1987.

Nattier, Janice J. and Charles S. Prebish. "Mahāsāṃghika Origins: The Beginnings of Buddhist Sectarianism." *History of Religions* 16.3 (February 1977):237-272.

Neufeldt, Ronald W., ed. *Karma and Rebirth: Post Classical Developments.* Albany: State University of New York Press, 1986.

Norman, K.R. "Dhammapada 97: A Misunderstood Paradox." *Indological Taurinensia* 7(1979)325-331.

Nyanaponika Thera and Hellmuth Hecker. *Great Disciples of the Buddha: Their Lives, Their Works, Their Legacy.* Edited with an introduction by Bhikkhu Bodhi. Boston: Wisdom Publications, 1997.

Obeyesekere, Gannanath. "Religious Symbolism and Political Change in Ceylon." *Modern Ceylon Studies* 1.1(1970):43-63.

Obeyesekere, Gannanath. "Theodicy, Sin and Salvation in a Sociology of Buddhism." In E.R. Leach, ed., *Dialectic in Practical Religion.* Cambridge: University Press, 1968, pp. 7-40.

O'Flaherty, Wendy Doniger, ed. *Karma and Rebirth in Classical Indian Traditions.* Berkeley: University of California Press, 1980.

Olivelle, Patrick. *The Origin and the Early Development of Buddhist Monachism.* Colombo, Sri Lanka: M.D.Gunasena, 1974.

Ornatowski, Gregory K. "Continuity and Change in the Economic Ethics of Buddhism: Evidence From the History of Buddhism in India, China and Japan." *Journal of Buddhist Ethics* 3(1996):198-240.

Orr, Leslie C. *Donors, Devotees, and Daughters of God.* New York: Oxford University Press, 2000.

Parry, Jonathan. "Death and Digestion: The Symbolism of Food and Eating in North Indian Mortuary Rites." *Man* n.s., 20.4:612-630.

Patel, Manilal. *The Dānastutis of the Ṛg-Veda.* Trans. by B.H. Kapadia. Delhi: Munshiram Manoharlal, 1961.

Patton, Laurie L., ed. *Authority, Anxiety, and Canon.* Albany: State University of New York Press, 1994.

Possehl, Gregory L., ed. *Ancient Cities of the Indus.* Durham, North Carolina: Carolina Academic Press, 1979.

Prebish, Charles S. *Buddhist Ethics, A Cross-Cultural Approach.* Dubuque, Iowa: Kendall/Hunt Publishing Company, 1992.

Prebish, Charles S. *Buddhist Monastic Discipline: The Sanskrit Prātimokṣa Sūtras of the Mahāsāṃghikas and Mūlasarvāstivādins.* University Park, London: The Pennsylvania State University Press, 1975.

Prebish, Charles S. "The Prātimokṣa Puzzle: Fact Versus Fantasy." *Journal of the American Oriental Society* 94.2(April 1974):168-176.

Prebish, Charles S. "A Review of Scholarship on the Buddhist Councils." *Journal of Asian Studies* 33.2(February 1974):239-254.

Przyluski, Jean. "Bouddhisme et Upaniṣad." *Bulletin de l'Ecole Francaise d'Extreme-Orient* 32(1932):141-169.

Przyluski, Jean. *Le Concile de Rājagṛha: Introduction a l'Histoire des Canons et des Sectes Bouddhiques.* Paris: Librairie Orientaliste Paul Geuthner, 1926.

Przyluski, Jean. *The Legend of Emperor Aśoka in Indian and Chinese Texts.* Trans. by Dilip Kumar Biswas.Calcutta: Firma K.L. Mukhopadhyay, 1967.

Puri, B.N. *Cities of Ancient India.* Meerut: Meenakshi Prakashan, 1966.

Radin, Margaret Jane. "Property and Personhood." *Stanford Law Review* 34(1982):957-1015.

Rājavaramuni, Phra. "Foundations of Buddhist Social Ethics." In Charles S. Prebish, ed., *Buddhist Ethics: A Cross-Cultural Approach.* Dubuque, Iowa: Kendall/Hunt Publishing Company, 1992, pp. 30-55.

Rao, S.K. Ramachandra, ed. *Encyclopedia of Indian Medicine.* 3 vols. Bombay: Popular Prakashan, 1985 (vol I), 1987 (vols. II, III).

Ray, Himanshu P. *The Winds of Change: Buddhism and the Maritime Links of Early South Asia.* Delhi: Oxford University Press, 1994.

Reichenbach, Bruce R. *The Law of Karma: A Philosophical Study.* Honolulu: University of Hawaii Press, 1990.

Reynolds, Frank E. "Ethics and Wealth in Theravāda Buddhism: A Study in Comparative Religious Ethics." In Russell F. Sizemore and Donald K. Swearer, eds. *Ethics, Wealth, and Salvation: A Study In Buddhist Social Ethics.* Columbia: University of South Carolina Press, 1990, pp. 59-76.

Rhys Davids, C.A.F. "The Relations between Early Buddhism and Brahman ism." *Indian Historical Quarterly* 10(1934):274-287.

Rhys Davids, C.A.F. "The Unknown Co-Founders of Buddhism." *Journal of the Royal Asiatic Society* 1927:193-208; "A Sequel." 1927:271-286.

Rhys Davids, T.W. *Buddhist India.* New York: G.P. Putnam's Sons, 1903.

Rhys Davids, T.W. and William Stede, eds. *The Pali Text Society's Pali-English Dictionary.* London: The Pali Text Society, 1921-1925.

Rose, Carol M. *Property and Persuasion: Essays on the History, Theory, and Rhetoric of Ownership.* Boulder: Westview Press, 1994.

Saddhātissa, H. "The Process of Rebirth in Buddhism." *Maha Bodhi* 79(1971):334-338.

Sangharakshita, Bhikshu. *A Survey of Buddhism.* Boulder: Shambala, 1980.

Schopen, Gregory. "On Avoiding Ghosts and Social Censure: Monastic Funerals in the Mūlasarvāstivāda-Vinaya." *Journal of Indian Philosophy* 20 (1992):1-39.

Schopen, Gregory. "The Buddha as an Owner of Property and Permanent Resident in Medieval Indian Monasteries." *Journal of Indian Philosophy* 18(1990):181-217.

Schopen, Gregory. "Burial 'Ad Santos' and the Physical Presence of the Buddha in Early Indian Buddhism: A Study in the Archeology of Religions." *Religion* 17(1987):193-225.

Schopen, Gregory. "Deaths, Funerals, and the Division of Property in a Monastic Code." In Donald S. Lopez, Jr., ed. *Buddhism in Practice.* Princeton: University Press, 1995.

Schopen, Gregory. "Doing Business for the Lord: Lending on Interest and Written Loan Contracts in the *Mūlasarvāstivāda-vinaya.*" *Journal of the American Oriental Society* 114.4 (October-December 1994):527-554.

Schopen, Gregory. "The Inscription on the Kuṣān Image of Amitābha and the Character of the Early Mahāyāna in India." *The Journal of the International Association of Buddhist Studies* 10.2(1987):99-137.

Schopen, Gregory. "Mahāyāna in Indian Inscriptions." *Indo-Iranian Journal* 21(1978):1-9.

Schopen, Gregory. "Monastic Law Meets the Real World: A Monk's Continuing Right to Inherit Family Property in Classical India." *History of Religions* 35.2(1995):101-123.

Schopen, Gregory. "The Monastic Ownership of Servants or Slaves: Local and Legal Factors in the Redactional History of Two *Vinayas.*" *Journal of the International Association of Buddhist Studies* 17.2(Winter 1994):145-173.

Schopen, Gregory. "On Monks, Nuns and 'Vulgar' Practices: The Introduction of the Image Cult into Indian Buddhism." *Artibus Asiae* 49.1-2 (1988-89):153-168.

Schopen, Gregory. "Ritual Rights and Bones of Contention: More on Monas tic Funerals and Relics in the *Mūlasarvāstivāda-Vinaya.*" *Journal of Indian Philosophy* 22(1994):31-80.

Schopen, Gregory. "Two Problems in the History of Indian Buddhism: The Layman/Monk Distinction and the Doctrines of the Transference of Merit." *Studien Zur Indologie und Iranistik* 10(1985):9-47.

Schumacher, E.F. *Small is Beautiful: Economics as if People Mattered.* New York: Harper & Row, 1973.

Singh, Upinder. "Sanchi: The History of the Patronage of an Ancient Buddhist Establishment." *The Indian Economic and Social History Review* 33(January-March 1996):1-35.

Sizemore, Russell F. and Donald K. Swearer, eds. *Ethics, Wealth, and Salvation: A Study in Buddhist Social Ethics.* Columbia: University of South Carolina Press, 1990.

Smart, Ninian. "Problems of the Application of Western Terminology to Theravada Buddhism, with Special Reference to the Relationship Between the Buddha and the Gods." *Religion:Journal of Religion and Religions* 2(Spring 1972):37-41.

Smith, Brian K. *Classifying the Universe: The Ancient Indian Varṇa System and the Origins of Caste.* New York: Oxford University Press, 1994.

Snellgrove, David L. "Śākyamuni's Final *Nirvāṇa.*" *Bulletin, School of Oriental and African Studies* 36(1973):399-411.

Spiro, M.E. *Buddhism and Society.* New York: Harper & Rowe, 1970.

Sponberg, Alan. "Attitudes Toward Women and the Feminine in Early Buddhism." In José Ignacio Cabezón ed. *Buddhism, Sexuality, and Gender.* Albany: State University of New York Press, 1992.

Śrautakośa. Vol. 1, pts. 1, 2. Poona: Vaidika Saṃśodhana Maṇḍala, 1958, 1963.

Strenski, Ivan. "On generalized exchange and the domestication of the *sangha.*" *Man* n.s. 18.3 (September 1983):463-477.

Tambiah, Stanley Jeyaraja. *Buddhism Betrayed? Religion, Politics, and Violence in Sri Lanka.* Chicago: University of Chicago Press, 1992.

Tambiah, Stanley Jeyaraja. "Dowry and Bridewealth, and The Property Rights of Women in South Asia." In Jack Goody and S.J. Tambiah, eds., *Bridewealth and Dowry.* Cambridge: University Press, 1973.

Tambiah, S.J. "The Ideology of Merit and the Social Correlates of Buddhism in a Thai Village." In E.R. Leach, ed., *Dialectic in Practical Religion.* Cambridge: University Press, 1968, pp. 41-121.

Thanissaro, Bhikkhu, trans. *The Buddhist Monastic Code.* Valley Center, California: Metta Forest Monastery, 1994.

Thapar, Romila. *A History of India,* vol. 1. Baltimore: Penguin, 1966.

Thapar, Romila. *From Lineage to State: Social Formations in the Mid-First Millennium B.C. in the Ganga Valley.* Bombay: Oxford University Press, 1984.

Tull, Herman W. *The Vedic Origins of Karma: Cosmos as Man in Ancient Indian Myth and Ritual.* Albany: State University of New York Press, 1989.

Tully, James. "Aboriginal Property and Western Theory: Recovering a Middle Ground." *Social Philosophy and Policy* 11.2(Summer 1994):153-180.

Varma, V.P. "The Origins and Sociology of the Early Buddhist Philosophy of Moral Determinism." *Philosophy East and West* 13.1(April 1960):25-47.

Wagle, Narendra. *Society at the Time of the Buddha.* Bombay: Popular Prakashan, 1966.

Walters, Jonathan. S. "A Voice from the Silence: The Buddha's Mother's Story." *History of Religions* 33.4(May 1994):358-379.

Warder, A.K. *Indian Buddhism.* Delhi: Motilal Banarsidass, 1970.

Warder, A.K. "On the Relationships Between Early Buddhism and Other Contemporary Systems." *Bulletin, London School of Oriental and African Studies* 18(1956):43-63.

Weiler, Royal W. "The Buddhist Act of Compassion." In Ernest Bender, ed., *Indological Studies in Honor of W. Norman Brown.* New Haven, Connecticut: American Oriental Society, 1962. pp. 238-249.

Wheeler, Samuel III. "Natural Property Rights as Body Rights." *Nous* 14.2 (May 1980): 171-202.

Wijayaratna, Mohan. *Buddhist Monastic Life, According to the Texts of the Theravāda Tradition.* Trans. by Claude Grangier and Steven Collins. Cambridge: Cambridge University Press, 1990.

Willis, Janice D. "Female Patronage in Indian Buddhism." In Barbara Stoler Miller, ed., *The Powers of Art: Patronage in Indian Culture.* Delhi: Oxford University Press, 1992, pp. 46-53.

Willis, Janice. D. "Nuns and Benefactresses: The Role of Women in the Development of Buddhism." In Yvonne Yazbeck Haddad and Ellison Banks Findly, eds., *Women, Religion and Social Change.* Albany: State University of New York Press, 1985, pp. 59-85.

Wilson, Liz. *Charming Cadavers: Horrific Figurations of the Feminine in Indian Buddhist Hagiographic Literature.* Chicago and London: The University of Chicago Press, 1996.

Woodward, F.L. "The Buddhist Doctrine of Reversible Merit." *The Buddhist Review* 6(1914):38-50.

Zysk, Kenneth. *Asceticism and Healing in Ancient India: Medicine in the Buddhist Monastery.* New York: Oxford University Press, 1991.

Index

A

E

F

G

R

T

(Some words such as *Buddha*, *Dhamma*, *donor*, *Nikāya*, *re-nunciant*, *Saṅgha*, *Theravāda*, *Vedic*, and *Vinaya* are simply too frequently mentioned to include in the index.)